Edward S. Rand

Garden Flowers

how to cultivate them - A treatise on the culture of hardy ornamental trees, shrubs,

annuals, herbaceous and bedding plants

Edward S. Rand

Garden Flowers

how to cultivate them - A treatise on the culture of hardy ornamental trees, shrubs, annuals, herbaceous and bedding plants

ISBN/EAN: 9783337224943

Printed in Europe, USA, Canada, Australia, Japan

Cover: Foto ©Lupo / pixelio.de

More available books at **www.hansebooks.com**

Garden Flowers:

How to Cultivate Them.

A TREATISE ON THE CULTURE OF HARDY ORNAMENTAL
TREES, SHRUBS, ANNUALS, HERBACEOUS
AND BEDDING PLANTS.

BY

EDWARD SPRAGUE RAND, JR.,

AUTHOR OF "FLOWERS FOR THE PARLOR AND GARDEN."

BOSTON:
J. E. TILTON AND COMPANY.
1866.

TO

DR. J. P. KIRTLAND,

OF CLEVELAND, OHIO,

THE PIONEER OF HORTICULTURE IN THE GREAT WEST.

INTRODUCTION.

In presenting the present volume, the author can lay but little claim to originality. The work was undertaken to supply the want, which has long been felt, of a trustworthy handbook of garden-flowers; one which should comprise a short treatise on the culture of hardy perennials, biennials, and annuals, as well as the more showy family of bedding-plants. In a work of a few hundred pages, it is manifestly impossible to give minute directions for the successful cultivation of every plant. The volume is not intended to teach gardening; but, a knowledge of the several principles of gardening — the preparation of the soil, the application of manures, the sowing of seed, the formation of hot-beds — being presupposed, it is proposed to teach the peculiar culture each plant may require, to give the soil in which it best succeeds, and to furnish a condensed list of species and varieties best adapted to garden culture, with the height, color of flowers, season of bloom, native country, and date of introduction of each. This first plan has been somewhat amplified; and all hardy plants, comprising trees and shrubs, have been included, until the present volume comprises short and concise directions for the culture of every plant usually met with in the garden, including trees, shrubs, and climbers.

The labor of compilation has been greatly lessened by adaptations from two English works of somewhat similar character, Glenny's "Handbook of the Garden," and Johnson's "Cottage Gardener's Dictionary," books of great value, but almost useless to the American florist on account of the great difference in climate between our own country and England, which renders, in many cases, entirely different treatment necessary in the culture of the same plant.

Many plants which are hardy in England are not hardy with us, while, strange as it may seem, some plants which survive our severest winters uninjured require frame protection in England.

While the heat of our summer's sun will forever prevent our raising such florists' flowers as Pansies, Auriculas, and Pinks, in perfection, the same warm summers enable us to bring many plants to a perfection of bloom unknown in England. The directions for the culture of these florists' flowers are ample, and the list of species of trees will be found very complete.

The author has experienced great difficulty in the application of the word "hardy" to the various plants. The extent of our country is so great, and the range of temperature so varied, that it is impossible to fix with certainty the exact locality where a plant ceases to be hardy. Much also depends on situation and exposure.

Philadelphia, New York, and Boston, respectively, each have many hardy plants which are winter-killed farther north. The Liquidamber is hardy five miles south of Boston, but is killed to the ground each winter twenty-five miles north of the same city. Pyrus Japonica stands well as a hedge-plant in Massachusetts, yet is winter-killed in western New York. These instances might be multiplied a hundred-fold.

Again: neighborhood to the sea has much to do with the hardiness of plants, usually operating unfavorably; as also has the protection afforded by snow in each winter. Thus it will be seen no rule of general application can be laid down. Where a plant is called "hardy," it may be taken as hardy in Massachusetts, and, of course, southward; though often some species of such a plant may require frame protection. In this the author has given the results of his own experience and observation; and, while he cannot hope to have made no mistake, he trusts the experience of others may confirm his near approximation to accuracy.

The present volume omits entirely the hardy ferns, which it is proposed to embrace in a forthcoming volume devoted entirely to cryptogamous plants. A companion volume to the present, classifying and describing "Greenhouse Plants" in the same manner, is already in press, which, with his previous work on "Parlor Gardening," and his forthcoming work on "Orchids," now far advanced towards completion, the author hopes will form indispensable companions both to the florist and amateur, and indeed to all, both old and young, who love the culture of flowers, the bright and beautiful gifts which the Author of all good has so lavishly strewn around our earthly pathway, and which, if we rightly read their silent teachings, cannot but ennoble and elevate the soul.

GLEN RIDGE, January, 1866.

GARDEN FLOWERS,

AND

HOW TO CULTIVATE THEM.

ABIES. *Spruce Fir.* [Pinaceæ.] Hardy evergreen ornamental trees and shrubs, growing in common soil, and increased by seeds and by grafting. A numerous family.

A. Ajonesis (Ajona); large tree; Siberia. *A. alba* (white spruce); 50 feet; May; North America; 1700. *A. alba nana* (dwarf); May. *A. amabilis* (lovely); 180 feet; April; New California; 1831. *A. aromatica* (aromatic); 100 feet; Oregon. *A. balsamea* (balsam-fir); 45 feet; May; North America. *A. bracteata* (bracted); 120 feet; California. *A. Brunoniana* (Brown's); 75 feet; Nepaul. *A. Canadensis* (Canadian; hemlock-spruce); 85 feet; May; North America; 1736. *A. Cephalonica* (Cephalonian); 60 feet; May; Cephalonia; 1824. *A. concolor* (one-colored); mountains of Mexico. *A. Douglasii* (Douglas's); 170 feet; May; North America; 1826. *A. excelsa* (lofty); 150 feet; May; north of Europe. *Carpatica, Clanbrasiliana, gigantea, monstrosa, mucronata, nana, tenuifolia, variegata,* and *viminalis* are all varieties of *excelsa*. *A. falcata* (sickle-leaved); 35 feet; Oregon. *A. firma* (solid); mountains of Japan. *A. Fraseri* (Fraser's); 30 feet; May; 1811. *A. Fraseri nana* (dwarf). *A.*

grandis (great); 170 feet; May; New California; 1831. *A. heterophylla* (various-leaved); 180 feet; Oregon. *A. homolepis* (equal-scaled); 25 feet; mountains of Japan. *A. Jezoensis* (Jezo; spruce-fir); 55 feet; Japan. *A. Khutrow* (Khutrow); 50 feet; Himalayas. *A. lasiocarpa* (woolly-coned); North-west America; *A. Menziesii* (Menzies'); 60 feet; May; North-west America; 1831. *A. Mertensiana* (Merten's); Island of Sitcha. *A. microphylla* (small-leaved); 180 feet; Oregon. *A. Morinda* (Morinda); 40 feet; North India. *A. mucronata* (sharp-pointed); 180 feet; Oregon. *A. nigra* (black-spruce); 60 feet; May; North America; 1700. *A. nobilis* (noble); 65 feet; North America; 1831. *A. Nordmanniana* (Nordmann's); 80 feet; Crimea. *A. obovata* (reversed-egg-coned); Siberia. *A. orientalis* (eastern); 30 feet; May; Levant; 1825. *A. picea* (pitchy); 160 feet; May; Germany; 1603. *A. picea Apollinis* (Apollini); Greece. *A. picea leioclada* (smooth-branched); Levant. *A. pichta* (pitch); 50 feet; May; Siberia; 1820. *A. Pindrow* (Pindrow); 100 feet; May; Himalayas; 1837. *A. Pinsapo* (Pinsapo); 65 feet; Spain; 1838. *A. polita* (neat); 50 feet; mountains of Japan. *A. religiosa* (sacred); 150 feet; Mexico. *A. rubra* (red-spruce); 50 feet; May; North America; 1755. *A. rubra violacea* (violet). *A. rubra arctica* (arctic). *A. Schrenkiana* (Schrenk's); Siberia. *A. Sitchensis* (Sitchan); Island of Sitcha. *A. trigona* (three-angled); 300 feet; Oregon. *A. Tsuga* (Tsugan); North of Japan. *A. Tsuga nana* (dwarf). *A. Webbiana* (Webb's); 90 feet; Himalayas; 1822.

These are all now classed under PINUS.

ADOBRA. [Cucurbitaceæ.] A very ornamental climber, nearly allied to the ornamental gourds which have of late become so popular. The flowers are greenish and inconspicuous; the foliage finely cut, dark-green, and very ornamental; the fruit, which is the chief beauty, small, glossy scarlet, freely produced. The plant is diœcious.

Raised from seeds, in hot-bed, in pots, and turned out in a rich sunny border, the plants grow rapidly, and before autumn are very showy. It also strikes freely from cuttings.

We know of but one species. The plant is perennial, but succeeds best as an annual.

A. viridiflora (green-flowered); tender perennial; 15 feet; flowers green, fruit scarlet, all summer; South America; 1860.

ABRONIA. [Nyctaginaceæ.] A very pretty genus of trailing plants, which, though properly frame perennials, succeed better with us treated as annuals. The flowers are in heads like a verbena, and cover the plant.

Soil, a sandy peat and leaf-mould, though the plants succeed in any good garden soil. Propagated by cuttings rooted in sand in spring, from plants wintered in the greenhouse; or, better, by seeds sown in frame in May, and transplanted to the garden after the weather has become warm. *A. umbellata*, with rosy-lilac flowers, is the best variety.

A. mellifera (honey-bearing); flowers orange, from June to August; California; 1826. *A. pulchella* (neat); flowers pink, from July to September; California; 1848. *A. rosea* (rose-colored); flowers rosy-red, July to September; California; 1847. *A. umbellata* (umbel-flowered); flowers rosy-lilac, all summer; California; 1825. All the varieties grow about six inches high.

ACACIA. [Mimoseæ.] The only hardy species of this very extensive genus is *A. Julibrissin*, which succeeds well south of New York, as a hardy shrub or small tree, in any garden soil. Propagated by cuttings of year-old shoots, or by seeds.

A. Julibrissin (silk-tree); hardy tree; 10 to 12 feet; flowers pinkish-white, in August; Levant; 1745.

ACACIA PSEUDO. See ROBINIA.
ACACIA ROSE. See ROBINIA.
ACACIA THREE-THORNED. See GLEDITSCHIA.

ACAENA. [Sanguisorbeæ.] A family of not very showy perennials, growing in common garden soil, and propagated by seeds or division; generally tender.

A. millefolium (thousand-leaved); hardy perennial; 6 inches; flowers greenish, in September; south of Europe. *A. latebrosa pinnatifida* and *sericea* are other species.

ACANTHOLIMON. *Prickly Thrift.* [Plumbaginaceæ.] Dwarf hardy perennials, very pretty ornaments for rock-work. Soil, sandy loam and peat. Propagated by cuttings of the half-ripened shoots in a gentle heat, by division, or by seed.

A. glumaceum (glumaceous). Hardy evergreen perennial; 6 inches; flowers rose-color, in June; Armenia; 1845.

ACANTHUS. *Bear's-Breech.* [Acanthaceæ.] Hardy herbaceous perennials, somewhat coarse, but of stately appearance, the blooms being borne in a tall spike, white and purplish, protected by spiny bracts. They grow in any kind of soil, and propagate most readily by division of the root; also by seeds. *A. spinosissimus* has beautifully divided leaves.

A. Hispanicus (Spanish); hardy perennial; 2 feet; flowers white, in August; Spain; 1700. *A. mollis* (soft); hardy perennial; 3 feet; flowers white and purple, in summer; Italy; 1548. The leaves of this species, growing through an old basket, are said to have given the idea of the Corinthian style of architecture. *A. niger* (black); hardy perennial; 3 feet; flowers white, in August; Portugal; 1759. *A. spinosissimus* (most spiny); hardy perennial; 3 feet; flowers purple and white, in summer; south of Europe; 1629. *A. spinosus* (spiny); hardy perennial; 3 feet; flowers white, in August; Italy; 1629.

These plants, in the most northern States, need slight protection in winter.

ACER. *Maple.* [Aceraceæ.] Hardy trees and shrubs. Common soil. Propagated by seeds and layers. Cuttings will strike in the open ground, if inserted in spring and kept moderately moist. The usual method is by seeds, or, in variegated or dark-foliaged varieties, by budding, inarching, or grafting on the common maple.

A. Austriacum (Austrian maple); 40 feet; flowers green, in

May; Austria. *A. barbatum* (bearded-calyxed); 15 feet; flowers green and yellow, in April; North America; 1812. *A. campestre* (common); 25 feet; flowers green and yellow, in May; Britain. *A. campestre Austriacum;* 30 feet; flowers green and yellow, in June; Austria; 1812. *A. campestre collinum* (hill-dwelling); 25 feet; flowers green and yellow, in April; France. *A. campestre hebecarpum* (downy-fruited); 25 feet; flowers green and yellow, in June; Britain. *A. campestre lævigatum* (smooth-leaved); 30 feet; flowers green and yellow, in June. *A. campestre nanum* (dwarf); 6 feet; flowers green and yellow, in June. *A. campestre variegatum* (variegated); 25 feet; flowers green and yellow, in May; Britain. Must be grafted or budded. *A. circinatum* (round-leaved); 30 feet; flowers green and yellow, in April; Columbia; 1827. *A. Creticum* (Cretan); 6 feet; flowers in May; Levant; 1752. *A. dasycarpum* (hairy-fruited); flowers green and yellow, in April; North America; 1725. *A. heterophyllum* (various-leaved); flowers green and yellow, in May; Levant; 1759; evergreen. *A. Ibericum* (Georgian); 40 feet; flowers green; Asiatic; Georgia; flowers yellow; 1826. *A. lobatum* (lobed-leaved); 20 feet; flowers green; Siberia; 1820. *A. macrophyllum* (long-leaved); 25 feet; flowers green, in May; North America; 1812. *A. montanum* (mountain); 25 feet; flowers green and yellow; North America; 1750. *A. Monspessulanum* (Montpelier); 8 feet; flowers green and yellow, in May; France; 1739. *A. nigrum* (black); 40 feet; flowers green and yellow, in April; North America; 1812. *A. oblongum* (oblong-leaved); 20 feet; flowers green and white; Nepaul; 1824. *A. obtusatum* (blunt-lobed-leaved); 40 feet; flowers green and yellow, in May; Hungary; 1825. This is the *Neapolitanum* of the Italians, and the *hybridum* of London nurseries. *A. obtusifolium* (blunt-leaved); 4 feet; flowers green and yellow, in May; Crete. *A. opulifolium* (Guelder-rose-leaved); 20 feet; flowers green and yellow, in May; France; 1823. *A. opalus* (opal); 50 feet; flowers green and yellow, in May; Italy; 1752. *A. palamatum* (palmate-leaved); 10 feet; flowers green; Japan; 1820. *A. Pennsylvanicum* (Pennsylvanian or striped bark); 20 feet; flowers green and yellow, in May; North

America; 1755. A variety of this, *striatum*, must be increased by grafting or budding. *A. platanoides* (plane-like); 50 feet; flowers green and yellow, in June; Europe; 1683. *A. platanoides laciniatum* (cut-leaved); 30 feet; flowers green and yellow, in June; Europe; 1683. Must be grafted or budded. *A. platanoides Lobelli* (Lobels); 50 feet; flowers green and yellow, in May; Naples. *A. platanoides variegatum* (variegated); 30 feet; flowers green and yellow, in June; Europe; 1683. Must be grafted or budded. *A. pseudoplatanus* (the sycamore); 50 feet; flowers green and yellow, in April; Britain. *A. pseudoplatanus purpureum* (purple-leaved); flowers purple, in May; 1828. *A. pseudoplatanus subobtusum* (slightly blunt-leaved); 50 feet; flowers green and yellow, in May. *A. pseudoplatanus variegatum* (variegated); 50 feet; flowers green and yellow, in April; Britain. Must be grafted or budded. *A. rubrum* (red-flowered or swamp-maple). There are two varieties, one with leaves variegated with white, and the other with yellow; 20 feet; flowers red, in April; North America; 1656. *A. saccharinum* (sugar-maple); 40 feet; flowers yellow, in April; North America; 1735. *A. Tartaricum* (Tartarian); 20 feet; flowers green and yellow, in May; Tartary; 1759.

ACHILLEA. *Milfoil.* [Compositæ.] Hardy herbaceous perennials; many of the kinds weedy, but some very pretty. They are free-flowering, easily grown in common soil, and propagated by division of the plant, by cuttings, and by seed.

A. Clavennæ (Clavenna's); hardy perennial; 6 inches; flowers white, in June and July; Austria; 1656. *A. ptarmica flore pleno* (double Sneezewort); hardy perennial; 18 inches; flowers white, in July; gardens. *A. tomentosa* (woolly); hardy perennial; 9 inches; flowers yellow, in May; England.

There are some thirty other species; all, except one (*A. Ægyptiacæ*) hardy perennials. The flowers of all are white or yellow.

ACHYRANTHES. See IRESINE.

ACIS. [Amaryllidaceæ.] Hardy bulbs; small, but very

pretty. Soil, light sandy loam. Propagated by offsets from the bulbs, which should be carefully separated, and planted where they may not be disturbed. In the Northern States, a slight winter protection will be found necessary.

A. autumnalis (autumnal); hardy bulb; 6 inches; flowers white and pink, in September; Portugal; 1629. *A. grandiflorus* (large-flowered); hardy bulb; 6 inches; flowers white, in August; Numidia; 1820. *A. rosea* (rosy); hardy bulb; 6 inches; flowers rose-colored, in August and September; Corsica; 1820. *A. trichophyllus* (hair-leaved); 6 inches; flowers white, in early spring; Spain; 1820.

ACONITUM. *Monkshood.* [Ranunculaceæ.] Hardy perennials, with showy, curious hood-shaped flowers. Soil, any common loam. Propagated by parting the roots, which is best done after the bloom declines in the autumn. Divide the root into as many pieces as there are hearts to the plant, with a portion of root to each, and plant them in nursery-beds about a foot apart: the plants, however, need not be parted for several years; for, the larger they spread, the more showy they are. Once in three or four years is often enough to disturb the plant; and even then, if it be too large, you may cut away some all round to lessen it, without digging the main plant up. Propagated also by seeds.

Many of the species do well in partially shaded places. All species are poisonous, and possess powerful medical properties.

There are about one hundred and thirty species, of which about ninety are tuberous-rooted, and the remainder fibrous-rooted. The following are good species: —

A. autumnale (autumnal); hardy perennial; 2 feet; flowers deep-blue, in autumn; China; 1846. *A. Chinense* (Chinese); hardy perennial; 2 feet; flowers purple, in September; China; 1833. *A. Japonicum* (Japanese); hardy perennial; 5 feet; flowers purple, in August; Japan. *A. Napellus* (Monkshood);

hardy perennial; 4 feet; flowers blue, in June and July; Europe; 1596. *A. ochroleucum* (yellowish-white); hardy perennial; 3 feet; flowers yellowish-white, in June and July; Caucasus; 1794. *A. speciosum* (showy); hardy perennial; 3 feet; flowers blue, in July; 1804. *A. variegatum* (variegated); hardy perennial; 5 feet; flowers blue and white, in July; south of Europe.

ACORUS. [Orontiaceæ.] A small genus of hardy perennials with gladiate leaves, which succeed well in moist garden soil. Easily propagated by division.

A. calamus is the sweet-flag of druggists.

A. calamus (sweet-flag); 2 feet; flowers green, in June; England. *A. gramineus* (grassy); hardy perennial; 6 inches; flowers green, leaves very flagrant; China; 1796. *A. terrestris* (land); 1 foot; flowers green, in June; China; 1822.

ACROLINIUM. [Compositæ.] A beautiful half-hardy annual. Soil, sandy peat and loam. Propagated by seeds.

A. roseum (rosy); half-hardy annual; 18 inches; flowers rose-pink, in June; Swan River; 1853.

ACTÆA. [Ranunculaceæ.] A family of hardy perennials, conspicuous for their white flowers and red or white berries, succeeding in any garden soil, but preferring a moist, half-shaded position. Propagated by division of the root in early spring and by seeds.

A. alba (white); hardy perennial; 2 feet; flowers and berries white, in May and August; North America. *A. rubra* (red); hardy perennial; 2 feet; flowers white, in May; berries bright-red, in August; North America. These two have been considered varieties of *A. spicata*, but seem sufficiently distinct to constitute species. *A. spicata* (spiked); herb Christopher; hardy perennial; 3 feet; flowers white, in May; England.

ACTINOMERIS. [Compositæ.] Half-hardy ornamental perennials, nearly allied to Coreopsis, and of easy culture in any good garden soil. Propagated by division of the root and by seed.

A. alata (winged); hardy perennial; 3 feet; flowers yellow, in July; Mexico; 1803. *A. helianthoides* (sunflower-like); hardy perennial; 3 feet; flowers yellow, in July; Louisiana; 1825. *A. procera* (tall); hardy perennial; 8 feet; flowers yellow, in September; North America; 1766. *A. squarrosa* (spreading); hardy perennial; 3 feet; flowers yellow, in July; North America; 1640.

ADAM'S NEEDLE. See YUCCA.

ADENOPHORA. [Campanulaceæ.] Hardy herbaceous plants related to and resembling Campanula, thriving in common garden soil, and easily propagated by division.

A. denticulata (denticulated); hardy perennial; 1 foot; flowers blue, in June and July; Siberia; 1817. *A. intermedia* (intermediate); hardy perennial; 18 inches; flowers pale-blue, from July to September; Siberia; 1819. *A. verticillata* (whorled); hardy perennial; 2 feet; flowers pale-blue, in June; Siberia; 1783.

ADENOSTOMA. [Sanguisorbaceæ.] A hardy shrub nearly allied to Alchimilla. Propagated by cuttings of the young shoots, rooted in sand under a bell-glass in spring. Soil, rich peaty loam. Requires protection in winter in more Northern States.

A. fasciculata (fascicled); hardy shrub; 3 feet; flowers white, in June; California; 1848.

ADLUMIA. [Fumariaceæ.] A very pretty hardy biennial climber; flowers white, tipped with pink; foliage finely cut and very ornamental. Seeds sown in May produce plants which climb and flower the following year. Propagated by seeds. As with all biennials, to insure bloom every year, seed must be sown each spring: in rich soil, however, the seed sows itself, and the plants come up without further trouble. The genus is nearly allied to Corydalis.

A. cirrhosa (tendril bearing); hardy biennial; 8 to 15 feet; flowers white, rose tipped, all summer; North America; 1778.

ADONIS. *Pheasant's Eye.* [Ranunculaceæ.] Hardy annuals and perennials, with pretty poppy-like blooms. Common garden soil. The annuals may be sown in pots in February, a few in a three-inch pot, and kept under glass until May, when, if planted out with their ball of earth entire in the borders, they will flower directly; or they may be sown in patches in the open border or in beds, about May. The fault of the Flos Adonis as a garden plant is, that the bloom is scanty. The perennials like a cool situation, but require no peculiar culture : they are propagated by dividing the roots. There are several species.

ANNUALS. *A. aestivalis* (summer); 2 feet; flowers scarlet, in June; south of Europe; 1629. *A. autumnalis* (autumnal; Flos Adonis, Pheasant's Eye); 18 inches; flowers crimson, in July; England. *A. citrina* (citron-colored); 1 foot; flowers orange, in June; south of Europe; 1819.

PERENNIALS. *A. Appenina* (Appenine); 1 foot; flowers yellow, in May; Europe. *A. Daurica* (Dahurican); 1 foot; flowers yellow, in May; Siberia; 1827. *A. distorta* (distorted); 1 foot; flowers yellow, in spring; Naples; 1827. *A. Pyrenaica* (Pyrenean); 18 inches; flowers yellow, in July; Pyrenees; 1817. *A. Siberica* (Siberian); 2 feet; flowers yellow, in May; Siberia; 1827. *A. vernalis* (spring); 1 foot; flowers yellow, in April; Europe; 1629. *A. Volgensis* (Volga); 1 foot; flowers yellow, in May; Russia; 1818.

ÆGOCHLOA. [Polemoniaceæ.] Dwarf hardy annuals, nearly allied to Gilia, and requiring the same management. They grow in ordinary light garden soil; and seeds require to be sown about the middle of May in patches in the flower-borders, the young plants being thinned out while young, so that they may not grow up crowded. The genus is now called Navarrettia.

Æ. cotulæfolia (cotula-leaved); hardy annual; 3 inches; flowers white, in June; California; 1833. *Æ. intertexta* (interwoven); hardy annual; 1 foot; flowers blue, in June; California; 1833. *Æ. pubescens* (downy); hardy annual; 1 foot; flowers blue, in June; California; 1833. *Æ. squarrosa* (spreading); hardy annual; 1 foot; flowers blue, in August; Santa Cruz; 1847.

ÆSCULUS. [Sapindaceæ.] The Horse-chestnut is too well known to need description. All the species are hardy ornamental trees, flourishing in rich loam, of stately growth, alike desirable both for foliage and flower. Propagated by seed, layers, or by grafting.

Æ. glabra (smooth-leaved); 12 feet; flowers greenish-yellow, in May; North America; 1812. *Æ. hippocastanum* (common Horse-chestnut); 40 feet; flowers white, in May; Asia; 1629. *Æ. hippocastanum flore-pleno* (double-flowered); 40 feet; flowers white, in May; gardens. *Æ. hippocastanum foliis argenteis* (silver-leaved); 40 feet; flowers white, in May; gardens. *Æ. hippocastanum variegatum* (commmon striped-leaved); 16 feet; flowers white, in May; Asia; 1629; layers. *Æ. Ohiotensis* (Ohio); 30 feet; flowers white, in May; North America. *Æ. pallida* (pale-flowered); 12 feet; flowers greenish-yellow, in June; North America; 1812; grafts or buds. *Æ. rubicunda* (red-flowered); 12 feet; flowers red, in June; North America; grafts or buds; 1820.

The double-flowered variety is very desirable.

ÆTHIONÆMA. [Cruciferæ.] Annuals and perennials of low growth succeeding in light soil. Propagated by summer cuttings, or by seed sown in spring.

ANNUALS. *Æ. Buxbaumii* (Buxbaum's); 6 inches; flowers pale-red, in June; Levant; 1823. *Æ. gracile* (slender); 3 inches; flowers pale-red, in June; Carniola; 1823. *Æ. saxatile* (rock); 6 inches; flowers flesh-color, in June; south of Europe; 1759.

PERENNIALS. *Æ. heterocarpum* (various-podded); 6 inches; flowers purple, in July; Armenia; 1837. *Æ. membranaceum* (membranous); 1 foot; flowers lilac, in June; Persia; 1829. *Æ. monospermum* (one-seeded); 6 inches; flowers pale-purple, in July; Spain; 1778. *Æ. parviflorum* (small-flowered); 6 inches; flowers lilac, in July; Persia; 1830.

AFRICAN MARIGOLD. See TAGETES.

AGATHÆA. [Compositæ.] Greenhouse sub-shrubby plants, useful for the summer decoration of the flower-garden. Good garden soil, or loam and leaf-mould. Propagated freely by cuttings in August or February, the young plants being kept in a frame or greenhouse, and planted out in May.

A. cælestis (heavenly); frame sub-shrub; 18 inches; flowers pale-blue, from May onwards; Cape of Good Hope; 1753. *A. linifolia* (flax-leaved); frame sub-shrub; 18 inches; flowers blue, all summer; Cape of Good Hope; 1800.

AGERATUM. [Compositæ.] Hardy or half-hardy annuals, which may, however, be kept as perennials, by cuttings or in pots, if not allowed to ripen seed. Light rich soil. Propagated by seeds, which should be sown in April, in a frame, and the plants pricked out in the open border in May, not less than six inches apart. The best is *A. Mexicanum*.

A. Mexicanum vel odoratum (Mexican or fragrant); half-hardy annual; 18 inches; flowers blue, all summer; Mexico; 1822. *A. angustifolium*; from Monte Video; has white flowers, in July. *A. strictum*; from Nepaul; has white flowers, in June. *A. cæruleum*; from the West Indies; has sky-blue flowers, in July.

AGRIMONIA. [Rosaceæ.] Hardy herbaceous perennials, easily propagated by division of the root, and growing in common garden soil. The genus is allied to Potentilla.

A. Eupatoria (Eupatoria); hardy perennial; 3 feet; flowers yellow, in June; Great Britain. *A. odorata* (scented); hardy perennial; 3 feet; flowers yellow, in July and August; Italy; 1640. *A. suaveolens* (sweet-smelling); hardy perennial; 3 feet; flowers yellow, in July; Virginia; 1820.

AGROSTEMMA. [Caryophyllaceæ.] Hardy perennials,

with Lychnis-like flowers. They should be planted in a prepared rich loamy soil, and are increased by division.

The species commonly known as Rose Campion (*A. coronaria*) is now referred to Lychnis.

A. Bungeana (Bunge's); hardy perennial; 18 inches; flowers scarlet, in July; Asiatic Russia; 1834. *A. Pyrenaica* (Pyrenean); hardy perennial; 1 foot; flowers pale-rose, in June; Pyrenees; 1819. *A. Suecica* (Swedish); 1 foot; flowers pink, in August; Sweden; 1834.

AGROSTIS. [Graminaceæ.] A very beautiful annual ornamental grass. Easily grown from seed sown in light loamy soil. If grown in a frame, in pots, the plants develop well and are very ornamental.

A. pulchella (neat); hardy annual; 1 foot; apetalous, flower panicle slender, much branched; Italy; 1831. *A. dulcis, elegans, laxiflora, nebulosa, plumosa,* and *retrofracta* are fine new varieties, all succeeding with similar treatment.

AJUGA. *Bugle.* [Labiatæ.] Hardy perennials or annuals, the latter of little interest in gardens; some of the former are neat plants for damp rock-work, or for flower-borders in a cool situation. Common damp garden soil. Propagated by division.

A. alpina (alpine); hardy perennial; 6 inches; flowers blue, in May; England. *A. Genevensis* (Geneva); hardy perennial; 6 inches; flowers blue, from May to July; Switzerland; 1656. *A. pyramidalis* (pyramidal); hardy perennial; 6 inches; flowers blue, in May and June; Britain. *A. reptans* (common); hardy perennial; 6 inches; flowers blue, in May and June; England. There are white-flowered and red-flowered varieties of this.

AILANTHUS. [Xanthoxylaceæ.] Tree of Heaven. Deciduous trees formerly extensively planted on account of their rapid growth and graceful foliage, but now generally discarded on account of the vile smell of the blossoms. Cuttings and seed. Dry soil.

A. glandulosa (glanded); hardy tree; 20 feet; flowers green; China; 1751.

ALCHEMILLA. *Lady's Mantle.* [Sanguisorbaceæ.] Hardy perennials. Common soil. Propagated by division. The species have all insignificant flowers, but a pretty foliage. *A. alpina, conjuncta,* and *sericea* are the most interesting. *A. Capensis* and *sibbaldiæfolia* are greenhouse plants. Some other hardy species are *A. fissa* and *pentaphylla.*

ALDER. See ALNUS.

ALETRIS. *Colic Root.* [Liliaceæ.] Curious hardy perennials, requiring a cool, moist situation and peaty soil, and to be in a shady place. Propagated by offsets.

A. aurea (golden-tipped); hardy perennial; 6 inches; flowers yellow, in July; North America; 1811. *A. farinosa* (mealy); hardy perennial; 6 inches; flowers white, in June; North America; 1768.

ALISMA. *Water Plantain.* [Alismaceæ.] Hardy water plants. The plants may be planted in the muddy soil of the margins of ponds or lakes; or potted into large pots, and the pots set into water deep enough to cover them. Propagated by seeds, or division of the roots.

A. lanceolata (spear-leaved); hardy aquatic perennial; 18 inches; flowers pinkish-white, in July; England. *A. plantago* (plantain); hardy aquatic perennial; 2 feet; flowers blush, in July; England. *A. ranunculoides* (ranunculus-like); hardy aquatic perennial; 1 foot; flowers purplish, in August; Britain. *A. trivialis*; 2 feet; flowers white, in July; North America; 1816.

ALLIUM. *Garlic.* [Liliaceæ.] Hardy bulbs. Good loamy soil. Propagated by offsets.

A. acuminatum (sharp-pointed); half-hardy-bulb; 1 foot; flowers white and crimson, in March; California; 1847. *A.*

azureum (azure); hardy bulb; 1 foot; flowers blue, in September; Siberia; 1830. *A. bisulcum* (jonquil-leaved); hardy bulb; 1 foot; flowers purple, in June; south of Europe. *A. Cowani* (Cowan's); hardy bulb; 9 inches; flowers white, in June; Chili; 1823. *A. flavum* (yellow); hardy bulb; 2 feet; flowers yellow, in June; Austria; 1759. *A. longifolium* (long-leaved); hardy bulb; 1 foot; flowers dark purplish-red, in September; Mexico; 1826. *A. Moly* (Moly); hardy bulb; 1 foot; flowers yellow, in June; south of Europe; 1604. *A. Neapolitanum* (Neapolitan); hardy bulb; 1 foot; flowers white, in June; Italy; 1824.

There are about one hundred and twenty other species, some of which are ornamental; but the above list comprises the best.

ALMOND. See AMYGDALUS.

ALNUS. [Betulaceæ.] Hardy deciduous trees, with apetalous flowers, growing freely in moist situations. The tree is short-lived, but very useful where a temporary shade is needed. Propagated by layers or seeds.

A. barbata (bearded); flowers in March; Russia; 1838. *A. Canadensis* (Canadian); flowers in June; Canada. *A. cordifolia* (heart-leaved); flowers in June; Naples; 1818. *A. glauca* (milky-green); flowers in June; North America; 1820. *A. glutinosa* (sticky); flowers in April; Britain. *A. glutinosa emarginata* (five-notched-leaved); flowers in April; Britain. *A. glutinosa foliis variegatis* (variegated-leaved); flowers in April; Britain. *A. glutinosa incisa* (cut-leaved); flowers in April; Britain. *A. glutinosa laciniata* (jagged-leaved); flowers in April; Britain. *A. glutinosa quercifolia* (oak-leaved); flowers in April; Britain; 1838. *A. incana* (hoary-leaved); 20 feet; flowers in June; Europe; 1780. *A. incana angulata* (angular-leaved); 20 feet. *A. incana pinnata* (pinnate); 26 feet; flowers in June; Europe. *A. Jorullensis* (Jorulla); Mexico. *A. macrocarpa* (long-fruited); 20 feet; flowers in June. *A. macrophylla* (long-leaved); 20 feet; flowers in June; Naples. *A. obcordata* (two-lobed); flowers in March; Russia. *A. oblongata* (oblong-leaved);

20 feet; flowers in June; south of Europe; 1730. *A. oblongata elliptica* (elliptic-lobed); 20 feet; flowers in June. *A. oxyacanthifolia* (oxycanth-leaved); 20 feet; flowers in June. *A. pumila* (dwarf); 10 feet; flowers in June. *A. rubra* (red); 20 feet; flowers in June. *A. rugosa* (wrinkled); flowers in March; North America. *A. serrulata* (saw-leaved); 20 feet; flowers in June; North America; 1769. *A. Siberica* (Siberian); Siberia; 1820. *A. subrotunda* (roundish-leaved); 23 feet; flowers in April. *A. undulata* (wave-leaved); 20 feet; flowers in June; North America; 1782.

ALONSOA. [Scrophulariaceæ.] Greenhouse or half-hardy evergreen sub-shrubs, with pretty scarlet flowers. Soil, sandy loam and leaf-mould, equal parts. Propagated by seeds sown in March in a hot-bed; the seedlings pricked out when large enough, and by the end of April potted separately into small pots, and then hardened off in cold frames for planting out. Cuttings planted in sandy soil, and put in a hot-bed in spring, should be treated in the same way as soon as they are rooted: during summer they will root freely under a hand-glass, on a shady border. For pot blooming, strong young plants should be selected in March, and shifted into larger pots as they grow, the stronger branches being stopped to make the plants bushy; they should be grown in a greenhouse, or a well-glazed frame. The plants require plenty of air, and to be kept from frost in winter.

A. acutifolia (acute); greenhouse sub-shrub; 3 feet; flowers scarlet, from May to October; Peru; 1790. *A. incisifolia* (cut-leaved); greenhouse sub-shrub; 2 feet; flowers scarlet, from May to October; Chili; 1795. *A. linearis* (linear); greenhouse sub-shrub; 2 feet; flowers scarlet, from May to October; Peru; 1790. *A. Warczewiczii;* greenhouse perennial; 18 inches; flowers crimson scarlet, all summer; Peruvian Andes; 1854.

ALOYSIA. [Verbenaceæ.] A greenhouse shrub, which, kept in a cellar in winter, succeeds well in the border in summer. It is chiefly cultivated for the leaves, which possess a pleasant lemon-like fragrance, whence the common name "Lemon verbena." The flowers are in spikes purplish-white and inconspicuous. Soil, sandy loam and leaf-mould. Propagated by cuttings, which root freely in sand in March from the old wood, in August from the new.

A. citriodora (lemon-scented); greenhouse shrub; 1 to 5 feet; flowers purplish-white, in summer; Chili; 1784.

ALSINE. [Caryophyllaceæ.] Hardy annuals, some of which are rather pretty. *A. laricifolia*, introduced from Siberia in 1834, is a perennial; propagated by division. *A. mucronata*, *molluginea*, *pubescens*, and *segetalis*, are pretty annual species with white flowers. Propagated by seeds.

ALTHÆA. *Marsh Mallow*. [Malvaceæ.] Hardy annuals, biennials, and perennials, but, excepting the Hollyhocks *(A. rosea* and *ficifolia)*, of little horticultural importance. Common garden soil. Propagated, the annuals and biennials, by seeds; the perennials, by division of the root.

The Hollyhock (*Althæa rosea*) is a noble flower; and the varieties are becoming so numerous, and so much improved, that it is an established favorite. It is raised from seed, and multiplied by parting the roots; the former to produce new varieties, the latter to propagate old ones. In autumn the old plants must be dug up and parted, each heart being separated with a portion of root to it. These are to be planted out in a nursery-bed one foot apart, or they may be planted at once where they are to bloom. They will stand three years, or even more, if a large plant and a number of spikes of flower be the object. Even in parting them, they need not be divided into single hearts, unless increase is desired. Choice varieties may be increased by cuttings of the flowering stems; every leaf, with a portion of the old stem containing a bud, being capable of forming a plant if treated as a cutting. They are best planted at the back of borders, or in the midst of shrubs, the plants being in no way interesting; but the flower-spikes, which are produced at the upper part of the stem, are very noble objects. The variety of color afforded by this plant is now considerable, and some varieties are very rich and distinct. They bloom from the latter part of July to September.

A. ficifolia (Antwerp Hollyhock); hardy biennial; 6 feet; flowers various, in July; Levant; 1597. *A. rosea* (common hollyhock); hardy biennial, or perennial by culture; 8 to 10 feet; flowers various, in July; Levant; 1573.

For the newest varieties of double Hollyhocks consult the florists' catalogues, where a large list may be found, with colors and habit described.

ALYSSUM. *Madwort.* [Cruciferæ.] Dwarf hardy perennials, or sub-shrubby plants, with cruciferous flowers. *A. saxatile* is very suitable for rock-work, or the front part of a flower-border, and forms a beautiful spring-blooming bed in the flower-garden. It is increased by cuttings. Good garden soil. The herbaceous species are propagated by division, the sub-shrubby ones by cuttings. Vigorous two-year-old plants are the best for blooming: the others are unimportant. The plant commonly called Sweet Alyssum is not of this genus: it is *Koniga maritima*.

A. saxatile (rock); hardy sub-shrubby perennial; 1 foot; flowers yellow, in April; Candia; 1710.

There are some twenty other species, all with white or yellow flowers.

AMARANTHUS. *Amaranth.* [Amaranthaceæ.] Hardy and half-hardy annuals, sometimes showy from the large masses of rich-colored flowers, as in *A. caudatus*, in which they droop, and *A. hypochondriacus*, in which they grow erect; sometimes grown for the curiously-colored foliage, as in *A. tricolor*. Soil for the hardy sorts, rich garden mould. These are propagated by seeds sown in the open borders in April, the young plants thinned out to six inches apart. The tender sorts require a light and highly manured soil (equal parts light loam, leaf-mould, and decayed manure), and must be sown in a hot-bed in April, and carefully tended till the weather becomes settled, and then planted out. *A. melancholicus* is a very dark-foliaged species, which is now very popular for massing.

A. atropurpureus (dark-purple); hardy annual; 3 feet; leaves and flowers purple, in September; East Indies; 1820. *A. bicolor* (two-colored); hardy annual; 2 feet; leaves red and green, in August; East Indies; 1802. *A. caudatus* (Love-lies-bleeding); hardy annual; 4 feet; flowers red, in August; East Indies; 1596. *A. hypochondriacus* (Prince's feather); hardy annual; 3 to 4 feet; flowers crimson, in August; Virginia; 1684. *A. speciosus* (showy); hardy annual; 6 feet; flowers red, in July; Nepaul; 1819. *A. tricolor* (three-colored); tender annual; 2 feet; foliage variegated, — red, green, and yellow; East Indies; 1548.

AMBERBOA. [Compositæ.] Hardy annuals. Plant in rich garden soil. Propagated by seeds sown in the open border in May.

A. moschata (Sweet-Sultan); hardy annual; 2 feet; flowers lilac-purple, in July; Persia; 1629. *A. suavolens* (Yellow-Sultan); hardy annual; 18 inches; flowers yellow, in July; Levant; 1683.

AMELANCHIER. [Rosaceæ.] Hardy deciduous shrubs, sometimes attaining to the height of trees, bearing snowy-white flowers early in the season, followed by dark-purple edible berries. Propagated by seeds, layers, and grafting on thorn or quince. Called also June-berry and shad-bush.

A. Botryapium (snowy Mespilus); hardy tree; 12 feet; flowers white, in May; North America; 1746. This and *A. florida*, and variety *parviflora; ovalis*, and varieties *semi-integrifolia, subcordata, oblongifolia, rotundifolia, alnifolia, sanguinea*, and *oligocarpa*, — all seem varieties of one species, *A. Canadensis*, to which all can readily be referred. All are natives of North America. *A. vulgaris* (common); 6 feet; south of Europe; 1596.

AMERICAN COWSLIP. See DODOCATHEON.

AMBLYOLEPIS. [Compositæ.] A pretty and fragrant hardy annual. Common garden soil. Propagated by seeds sown in May.

A. setigera (bristly); hardy annual; 2 feet; flowers yellow, in August; East Indies.

AMETHYSTEA. [Lamiaceæ.] A pretty hardy annual. Sow the seeds in May in a light peaty soil, cover slightly, and thin out as they grow. Propagated by seeds.

A. cærulea (blue); hardy annual; 2 feet; flowers blue, in July; Siberia; 1759.

AMMOBIUM. [Compositæ.] Half-hardy herbaceous plants, flourishing in common garden soil. Propagated by cuttings and seed.

A. alatum (winged); half-hardy perennial; 2 feet; flowers white, in June; New Holland; 1822. *A. plantagyneum* (plantain-leaved); half-hardy perennial; 1 foot; flowers white, in August; New Holland; 1827.

AMMYRSINE. [Ericaceæ.] Dwarf hardy evergreen shrubs, separated from Ledum; conspicuous for masses of white flowers in June, and for neat evergreen foliage. They succeed well in a Rhododendron bed. A damp peaty soil will grow them in perfection, if well sheltered from the direct sunlight. Propagated by layers.

A. buxifolium (box-leaved); hardy evergreen shrub; 6 inches; flowers white, in May and June; North America; 1736. *A.*

prostrata (flat-lying); hardy evergreen shrub; 6 inches; flowers white, in May and June; North America.

AMMOGETON. [Compositæ.] A hardy herbaceous perennial, thriving in sandy loam. Propagated by division of the root.

A. scorzonerifolium (scorzonera-leaved); hardy herbaceous perennial; 1 foot; flowers yellow, in May; North America; 1834.

AMORPHA. [Leguminosæ.] Deciduous hardy shrubs, called also Bastard Indigo, natives of North America, thriving in common garden soil. Propagated by seed or layers. The tips of the shoots are very liable to be winter-killed. *A. herbacea*, *Lewisii*, *nana*, and *microphylla*, require winter protection in the Northern States.

A. fragrans (fragrant); hardy shrub; 3 feet; flowers purple, in July; North America; 1800. *A. fruticosa* (shrubby); hardy shrub; 6 feet; flowers purple, in July; Carolina; 1724. *A. microphylla* (small-leaved); half-hardy shrub; 2 feet; flowers purple, in August; Missouri; 1811. *A. nana* (dwarf); half-hardy shrub; 2 feet; flowers blue, in August; Missouri; 1811.

AMPELOPSIS. [Vitaceæ.] Hardy deciduous climbing shrubs. The Virginian Creeper (*A. hederacea*) is one of the best of all plants, not evergreen, for covering a large space of bare wall or fence, thriving in the most confined situations: in autumn the leaves assume a rich crimson tint. Common garden soil. Propagated by layers, cuttings, and seeds.

This plant is commonly known as Woodbine in the Northern States.

A. bipinnata (double-winged); half-hardy climber; 15 feet; flowers greenish, in August; North America; 1700. *A. cordata* (heart-leaved); half-hardy climber; 20 feet; flowers greenish, in May; North America; 1803. These two require winter protection in the Northern States. *A. hederacea* (Virginian creeper); hardy climbing shrub; 60 feet; flowers greenish, in June; North America; 1629. *A. hirsuta* (hairy); hardy climbing shrub; 60 feet; flowers greenish, in May; North America; 1806.

AMPHEREPHIS. [Compositæ.] A very pretty floriferous plant, of easy culture in good garden soil. Sow the seeds in May, in the open border, and thin out the plants.

A. aristata (awned); hardy annual; 1 foot; flowers purple, in July; Caraccas; 1824. *A. intermedia* (intermediate); hardy annual; 18 inches; flowers purple or lavender, in August; Brazil; 1821. *A. mutica* (awnless); hardy annual; 1 foot; flowers purple, in July; South America; 1803.

AMSONIA. [Apocynaceæ.] Very neat pretty hardy perennials, thriving in common garden soil, propagated by division of the root, or by cuttings, in summer.

A. angustifolia (narrow-leaved); hardy perennial; 2 feet; flowers blue, in June; North America; 1774. *A. latifolia* (broad-leaved); hardy perennial; 2 feet; flowers blue, in June; North America; 1759. *A. salicifolia* (willow-leaved); hardy perennial; 2 feet; flowers blue, in June; North America; 1812.

AMYGDALUS. *Almond.* [Rosaceæ.] Small deciduous flowering trees and shrubs. The double-flowered varieties are particularly beautiful. All grow freely in good loamy well-drained garden soil. Propagated by budding on plum-stocks; the shrubs by transplanting the suckers, or by layering.

A. communis (common); hardy tree, 15 feet; flowers pink, in April; Barbary; 1548. *A. incana* (hoary); hardy shrub; 2 feet; flowers red, in April; Caucasus. *A. nana* (common dwarf); hardy shrub; 3 feet; flowers pink, in April; Russia; 1683. *A. pumila* (double dwarf); hardy shrub; 4 feet; flowers red, in April; China; 1683.

There are about a dozen or more varieties of the common

almond. Most of these will survive the winter as far north as the peach-tree can live. They flower, but seldom fruit. The sweet almonds are more tender than the bitter varieties. To make the dwarf flowering-almond flower to greatest advantage, cut the plant off close to the ground as soon as the bloom has faded.

ANACYCLUS. [Compositæ.] A genus of hardy annuals, with rayed flowers of no special beauty. Easily grown in common garden soil. Propagated by seeds.

A. Alexandrinus (Alexandrian); 1 foot; flowers yellow, in July; Egypt; 1828. *A. aureus* (golden); 1 foot; flowers yellow, in August; Levant; 1570. *A. clavatus* (clavate); 2 feet; flowers white, in August; Barbary; 1810. *A. pyrethrum* (like pyrethrum); 2 feet; flowers white, in August; Barbary; 1837. *A. radiatus* (rayed); 2 feet; flowers yellow, in August; south of Europe; 1596.

ANAGALLIS. *Pimpernel.* [Primulaceæ.] Hardy and half-hardy slender annuals and herbaceous perennials, of prostrate habit. The hardy annuals are sown in May in the open border, and are propagated by seeds. The half-hardy sorts are increased by cuttings, planted in March in hot-beds, or in July or August under a hand-glass, and when potted off, should be grown in three parts loam and one part peat, and preserved during winter in a greenhouse. They all do well in beds and borders in the flower-garden.

A. alternifolia (alternate-leaved); perennial; 1 foot; flowers yellow and pink, in May; Rio Janeiro; 1839. *A. carnea* (flesh-colored); hardy annual; 1 foot; flowers flesh-colored, in August; Switzerland; 1819. *A. Indica* (Indian); hardy annual; 1 foot; flowers blue, in June; Nepaul; 1824. *A. Marryattæ* (Mrs. Maryatt's); half-hardy perennial; 1 foot; flowers copper-colored, in June; garden hybrid. *A. Monelli* (Monelli's); half-hardy herbaceous trailer; 1 foot; flowers blue, in June; Italy; 1648. *A. var. Brewerii* has red flowers. *A lilacina* has pale-lilac flowers. *A. Phœnecia* has scarlet flowers; introduced from Morocco in 1803. *A. Phillipsii* has blüe flowers. *A. Wilmoreana* has purple flowers; introduced from Madeira in 1834. *A. Webbiana* (Webb's); half-hardy perennial; 1 foot; flowers blue, in July; Portugal; 1828. *A. Wellsiana* (Wells's); half-hardy perennial; 1 foot; flowers copper-color, in July; hybrid. There are numerous seeding varieties.

ANANTHERIX. [Asclepiadaceæ.] A hardy herbaceous plant of no special beauty, growing in any garden soil, and readily increased by division.

A viridis (green); hardy perennial; 6 inches; flowers green and yellow, in September; North America; 1812.

ANARRHINUM. Very pretty half-hardy biennials, allied to Antirrhinum. Seed sown in summer will give bloom the following year. Common garden soil. May also be increased by cuttings. Winter in cold frame.

A. bellidifolium (daisy-leaved); 18 inches; flowers blue, in July; France; 1629. *A. fruticosum* (shrubby); 2 feet; flowers white, in July; south of Europe; 1826. *A. pubescens* (downy); 18 inches; flowers white, in July; south of Europe; 1818.

ANASTATICA. [Cruciferæ.] An annual plant of the Egyptian deserts, called Rose of Jericho. When full grown, it contracts its rigid branches into a ball, and is blown about by the wind; when it alights upon a damp place the branches relax as if it came to life; hence the name of Resurrection Flower. Aside from this, it is a plant of no interest, the flowers being small and white. It grows readily from seed, but needs a warm exposure.

A. Hierochuntina (Rose of Jericho); hardy annual; 18 inches; flowers white, in July; Levant; 1597.

ANCHUSA. *Bugloss.* [Boraginaceæ.] A genus of ornamental herbaceous plants, comprising perennials, biennials, and annuals. They all grow freely in common garden soil.

The perennials are increased by division and seeds; the biennials and annuals by seed. As they transplant badly, they should be sown where they are to bloom.

The flowers of most of the species — of which there are more than thirty — are blue; but *A. angustifolia, leptophylla, petiolata,* and *undulata,* have purple flowers; *A. incarnata* has flesh-colored, and *A. ochroleuca* and its varieties, have yellowish-white; *A. myosotiflora* has pink flowers. *A. Capensis* and *pulchella* require greenhouse protection. The following are good species:—

A. aggregata (cluster-flowered); hardy annual; flowers blue, in June; Levant; 1827. *A. amœna* (pleasing); hardy annual; flowers blue, in June; south of Europe; 1817. *A. Barrelieri* (Barrelier's); hardy perennial; 2 feet; flowers blue, in May; south of Europe; 1820. *A. Capensis* (Cape); greenhouse biennial; 6 inches; flowers blue, in July; Cape of Good Hope; 1800. *A. Milleri* (Miller's); hardy annual; 18 inches; flowers pink, in June; Levant; 1713. *A. ochroleuca* (yellowish); hardy perennial; 2 feet; flowers pale-yellow, in July; Mount Caucasus; 1810. *A. paniculata* (panicled); hardy perennial; 3 feet; flowers blue, in June; Madeira; 1777. *A. tinctoria* (alkanet); hardy biennial, or perennial; 18 inches; flowers purple, in June; Montpelier; 1596.

ANDROMEDA. [Ericaceæ.] Beautiful evergreen shrubs, principally hardy, but a few requiring a greenhouse or stove. Soil, good rich moist peat, or peat with a third part loam. They are best propagated from layers, put down in September, and taken off the following autumn. The seeds are very small, and require to be sown as soon as ripe, very lightly covered, and set in a cool close frame; but this is too tedious a process, except with very rare kinds. Perhaps *A. floribunda* may be set down as one of the most useful of all dwarf shrubs; for it looks well from the time the bloom-buds first appear till they are dead, and that comprises one-half the entire year.

There are some forty species, most of which are hardy; the genus has, however, by later botanists been separated into Leucothœ, Cassandra, Oxydendrum, and Cassiope : of *A. polifolia* there are many garden varieties. The following are most ornamental :—

A. (Leucothœ) *axillaris* (axil-flowering); hardy evergreen shrub ; 2 feet ; flowers white, in June ; North America ; 1765. *A.* (Cassandra) *calyculata* (small-calyxed); hardy shrub ; 2 feet ; flowers white, in March ; North America ; 1748. *A.* (Leucothœ) *Catesbœi* (Catesby's); hardy evergreen shrub ; 2 feet ; flowers white, in June ; North America ; 1793. *A. floribunda* (free-flowering); hardy evergreen shrub ; 3 feet ; flowers white, in May ; North America ; 1812. *A. polifolia* (poly-leaved); hardy evergreen shrub ; 1 foot ; flowers pink, in July; North America ; 1790. *A. Mariana* (stagger-bush); hardy deciduous shrub ; 3 feet ; flowers large white, in June; North America ; 1763. *Oxydendrum arboreum* (sorrel-tree) is a very ornamental tree of the second class, bearing in August large racemes of white flowers. Hardy south of Massachusetts.

ANDROSACE. [Primulaceæ.] Elegant alpine plants, related to the primroses ; the hardiest of them well adapted for sheltered rock-work, and all very interesting ; grown in pots. Soil, sandy peat and light turfy loam in about equal proportions. Their greatest risk is from excess of moisture about the crowns or roots ; and from dampness in winter they are much more liable to suffer injury than from the degree of cold. They ought to be kept in small pots, very well drained ; and, in the application of water, great care is necessary at all seasons, but especially in winter. In our summers, they require a cool situation. The perennial, biennial, and annual species require the same kind of treatment, differing only in the mode of propagation, which in the perennials is by division, and in the others by seeds.

A. carinata (keeled); hardy perennial; 3 inches; flowers yellow, in May; North America; 1826. *A. carnea* (flesh-colored); hardy perennial; 3 inches; flowers flesh-color, in July; Switzerland; 1768. *A. Chamæjasme* (bastard-jasmine); hardy perennial; 3 inches; flowers pink, in June; Austria; 1768. *A. lactea* (milk-white); hardy perennial; 6 inches; flowers white, in June; Austria; 1752. *A. lactiflora* (milk-flowered); hardy biennial; 6 inches; flowers white, in June; Siberia; 1806. *A. lanuginosa* (woolly); frame perennial; 6 inches; flowers rosy-lilac, in August; Himalaya; 1841. *A linearis* (linear); hardy perennial; 3 inches; flowers white, in May; North America; 1826. *A. maxima* (greatest); hardy annual; 6 inches; flowers white, in May; Austria; 1797. *A. septentrionalis* (northern); hardy annual; 6 inches; flowers white, in May; Russia; 1755. *A. villosa* (villous); hardy perennial; 3 inches; flowers pink, in June; Pyrenees; 1790.

ANDROSÆMUM. [Hypericaceæ.] A woody-stemmed herbaceous perennial, growing in the shade in common soil, and increased by division.

A. officinale (officinal); 1 foot; flowers yellow, in August; England.

ANDRYALA. [Compositæ.] A genus of composite plants of little beauty, comprising annuals, biennials, perennials, and greenhouse plants. Soil, garden loam. Increased by seed or division.

ANEMONE. [Ranunculaceæ.] A fine genus of hardy and half-hardy herbaceous perennials, many having tuberous roots, flourishing in rich light loam. Propagated by offsets, division, or seed sown in July, from which plants will bloom the next year. *A. japonica*, a fine autumnal blooming kind, makes a fine bed, and is propagated by every little fragment of its roots, these being thickly set with little buds or bulblets. Some of the smaller-growing spring kinds are very pretty if grown in large patches, or planted about in shrubberies: these propagate by separating their tubers when in a dormant state. *A. narcissiflora* is a very fine hardy species, blooming early in June.

There are about twenty tuberous-rooted species and varieties, and about forty with herbaceous roots.

The Anemone, the florist's flower of our gardens, is the offspring of *A. coronaria* (poppy anemone), and *A. hortensis*. Sprung from these are annually increased varieties. A variety lasts about twelve years.

Characteristics of a good single Anemone. — The stem strong, elastic, and erect, not less than nine inches high; the flower at least two inches and a half in diameter, consisting of large, substantial, well-rounded petals, at first horizontally extended, and then turning a little upwards, so as to form a broad, shallow cup; the color clear and distinct when diversified in the same flower, or brilliant and striking if it consists only of one color, as blue, crimson, or scarlet.

A double Anemone should have the outer petals quite flat; the second series a little shorter, the third shorter still, and so on till the centre is quite full, when the whole should form a rather flat hemisphere. Every double flower should be of one full color.

Propagation. — Offsets from the root, and new varieties from seed. In propagating by offsets, all the best kinds should be taken up annually at the decay of the leaf, and the root divided at the time of taking up, to allow the wound to heal, into as many pieces or knobs as are furnished with an eye or bud; observing, however, that, if they are divided very small, they flower very weak the first year.

The time for taking up the roots is June, when the leaf and stalk are withered; for then the roots cease to grow for a month or six weeks. Take them up in dry weather, spread in an airy place out of the sun for about a week, then clear from earth, and store in bags or boxes.

In propagating by seed, sow from the best single or semi-double flowers. Double flowers produce none.

The time for planting is October, or early in November, and the plants will come into flower in May or June.

Make the beds in a sheltered part of your garden, facing the south; remove the old soil from the beds to the depth of sixteen or eighteen inches. If it is low and swampy, with a wet, clay bottom, drain well, and do not dig so deep; if high and dry, or with a sandy or gravelly subsoil, you may go a little deeper. Then put in from four to six inches of unmixed cowdung, such as might be gathered up where cows feed. Upon this layer of dung, place as much good fresh loam as will raise the beds to their former level, or a little higher. During winter, cover the beds with an old frame, or with leaves and boughs.

Any common, moderately light earth suits the Anemone; overmoist and stiff soils rot the roots in winter. If necessary to make a soil, take maiden loam from the surface of a pasture, the top spit, turf and all; to every load of this add one of cowdung, and half a load of sea or sharp sand: blend the whole together, and form it into a ridge, in which let it remain a year, at least, turning it over once in two or three months. But, in default of pasture-earth, a good compost may be formed of common light garden soil and rotted cow-dung, adding to every load of the former half a load of the latter, and about a quarter of a load of sharp sand; and of either of the above composts the bed is to be formed. Make it about twelve or fifteen inches in depth, and three feet and a half broad.

A. Apennina (Apennine); hardy tuber; 6 inches; flowers blue, in May; England. *A. Caroliniana* (Carolina); hardy tuber; 1 foot; flowers white, in May; North America; 1824. *A. coronaria* (poppy); hardy tuber; 6 inches; flowers various, in May; Levant; 1596. *A. Halleri* (Haller's); hardy perennial; 6 inches; flowers purple, in May; Switzerland; 1816. *A. hortensis* (garden); hardy tuber; 6 inches; flowers rose, in May; Italy; 1597. *A. Hudsoniana* (Hudson's); hardy perennial; 6 inches; flowers white, in June; North America; 1827. *A. Japonica* (Japanese); hardy perennial; 3 feet; flowers rose, in September; Japan; 1844. *A. nemorosa* (grove); hardy tuber; 6 inches; flowers white, in April and May; England. *A. palmata* (palmate); hardy tuber; 6 inches; flowers yellow, in May; Portugal; 1597. *A. pavonia* (peacock); hardy tuber; 1 foot; flowers red, in May; France. *A. Pennsylvanica* (Pennsylvania); hardy perennial; 1 foot; flowers white, in May; North America; 1766. *A. pulsatilla* (pasque-flower); hardy perennial; 9 inches; flowers purple, in April; England. *A. ranunculoides* (ranunculus-like); hardy tuber; 6 inches; flowers yellow, in May; England. *A. vernalis* (spring); hardy perennial; 6 inches; flowers white, in May; Switzerland; 1752. *A. vitifolia* (vine-leaved); hardy perennial; 3 feet; flowers white, in September; Nepaul; 1829.

There are many other species, all more or less desirable.

ANISEED-TREE. See ILLICIUM.

ANISODUS. [Solanaceæ.] Coarse-growing perennials of little beauty, growing in common garden soil, and increased by division.

A. luridus (lurid); hardy perennial; 3 feet; flowers yellowish-green, in July; Nepaul; 1823.

Requires protection in the Northern States.

ANODONTEA. [Cruciferæ.] A genus of hardy plants allied to Alyssum, and requiring the same treatment. There are seven species, of no special interest.

ANODA. [Malvaceæ.] Hardy annuals, commonly called

Blue Hibiscus. Easily grown in common soil, and very pretty. Propagated by seed sown in open borders in May.

A. Dillenia; hardy annual; 18 inches; flowers blue, in August; Mexico; 1858.

ANOMATHECA. [Iridaceæ.] Pretty half-hardy bulbous perennials. Soil, light rich loam. Propagated readily by seeds or by offsets. *A. cruenta,* planted out in a bed, makes a pretty show, the bloom lasting till September. The seed should be sown in wide-mouthed pots or seed-pans, very thinly; and if the plants come up too thick, they must be thinned. The next season, they may be planted four or five in a pot, and the following year they may be bedded out in spring and the bulbs taken up in autumn. The flower is very bright, sparkling, and effective. The plants also do well in pot-culture, although very subject to red spider; and bloom all summer contrasting prettily in the greenhouse with Gloxineas and Achimenes.

A. cruenta (blood-colored); half-hardy bulb; 1 foot; flowers scarlet, in June; Cape of Good Hope; 1830. *A. juncea* (rush-leaved); half-hardy bulb; 1 foot; flowers lilac, in May; Cape of Good Hope; 1791.

ANTENNARIA. [Compositæ.] Small hardy and half-hardy herbaceous perennials. The smaller kinds are suitable for pot-culture. Soil, sandy loam. Propagated by division.

A. Alpina (Alpine); hardy perennial; 6 inches; flowers pink, in June; Europe; 1775. *A. Carpatica* (Carpathian); hardy perennial; 6 inches; flowers pink, in June; Carpathian Mountains; 1775. *A. dioica* (diœcious); hardy perennial; 6 inches; flowers pink, in June; England. *A. margariticia* (pearly); hardy perennial; 1 foot; flowers white, in July; England. *A. plantaginea* (plantain-leaved); hardy perennial; 1 foot; flowers white, in June; Virginia, 1759. *A. triplinervis* (triple-nerved); hardy perennial; 6 inches; flowers white, in August; Nepaul; 1823.

ANTHEMIS. [Compositæ.] A genus of mostly hardy plants, of which about twenty-three are herbaceous perennials, twelve annuals, and three evergreens. The common Chamomile is a familiar example. None of the species are particularly interesting. All are of easy culture in common garden soil.

ANTHERICUM. [Liliaceæ.] Greenhouse or hardy herbaceous perennials, with fleshy bundled roots. They are rather pretty, and desirable in a large collection. Soil, sandy loam, with plenty of drainage. Propagated by suckers, offsets, and seeds.

A. liliastrum (St. Bruno's Lily) is a fine hardy plant, with white flowers in May; Switzerland; 1629. *A. albucoides* (albuca-like); greenhouse perennial; 1 foot; flowers white, in July; Cape of Good Hope; 1788. *A. filifolium* (thread-leaved); greenhouse perennial; 1 foot; flowers white, in May; Cape of Good Hope; 1820. *A. floribundum* (free-flowering); greenhouse perennial; 1 foot; flowers white, in March; Cape of Good Hope; 1774. *A. fragrans* (sweet); greenhouse perennial; 1 foot; flowers white, in April; Cape of Good Hope; 1795. *A. sulphureum* (sulphur); hardy perennial; 1 foot; flowers pale-yellow, in May; Hungary; 1823. *A. vespertinum* (evening); greenhouse perennial; 2 feet; flowers white, in May; Cape of Good Hope; 1803.

There are some twenty other species.

ANTIRRHINUM. *Snapdragon.* [Scrophulariaceæ.] Hardy herbaceous plants, mostly perennials. The common Snapdragon *(A. majus)*, with its varieties, is the most important. It grows well in a common border, and seeds freely. The seeds may be sown in July or August in a pan or wide-mouthed pot, to be planted out, when large enough, in a bed, which, in the Northern States, should be protected by a frame during winter. Striking varieties, such as the double-flowered and the striped-flowered, may be propagated by cuttings of the small unblooming shoots, inserted in sandy soil under a hand-glass. When rooted, they may be potted singly into pots and preserved in frames during winter, ready to plant out in the following April. They bloom very well in six-inch pots. The annuals may be sown in pots in a frame in March, and planted out in May.

A. asarina (asarina); half-hardy trailing herb; flowers white, in July; Italy; 1699. *A. glandulosum* (glandulous); hardy annual; 2 feet; flowers red and yellow, in August; California; 1834. *A. majus* (common); hardy perennial; 2 feet; flowers various, in July; England. *A. molle* (soft); half-hardy trailing herb; flowers white, in July; Spain; 1752. *A. Montevidense* (Monte Videan); hardy annual; 1 foot; flowers red, in July; Monte Video; 1829. *A. sempervirens* (evergreen); hardy perennial; 2 feet; flowers pink, in June; Pyrenees; 1821.

Most of the species require frame protection during winter in the Northern States.

ANTWERP HOLLYHOCK. See ALTHÆA FICIFOLIA.

APARGIA. [Compositæ.] The only species worth cultivating is *A. aurantiaca*, a hardy herbaceous perennial, growing one foot high, with orange-colored flowers in June; introduced from Hungary in 1816.

APIOS. [Leguminosæ.] A tuberous-rooted hardy climbing perennial. The tubers have been recommended as a substitute for potatoes. Rich loamy soil. The plants flower better if left undisturbed. Propagated by division of the tubers.

A. tuberosa (tuberous); hardy climbing perennial; 6 feet; flowers purple, in August; very fragrant and pretty; North America; 1640.

APOCYNUM. *Dog's-bane.* [Apocynaceæ.] Acrid hardy herbaceous perennials, of rambling growth, with small cup-shaped flowers, not very showy. Common soil. Increased by division.

A. androsæmifolium (tutsan-leaved); hardy perennial; 3 feet; flowers pink, in July; North America; 1688. *A. cannabinum* (hemp-like); hardy perennial; 3 feet; flowers yellowish, in July; North America; 1699. *A. hypericifolium* (hypericum-leaved); hardy perennial; 3 feet; flowers white, in June; North America; 1758. *A. Venetum* (Venetian); hardy perennial; 2 feet; flowers white, in July; Adriatic Islands; 1690.

APONOGETON. [Fluviales.] Curious and elegant perennial water-plants; one or two require a stove temperature, others a greenhouse. *A. distachyon* is easily grown and flowered in the open air in summer, and may be preserved in a cellar during winter; the tender kinds in pots set into a tank or tub. Soil, peat and loam. Propagated by seeds, which should be sown in spring in the same kind of soil, and the pots set under water: they also increase by offsets.

A. distachyon (two-spiked); 1 foot; flowers white, in June; Cape of Good Hope; 1788. *A. angustifolium* (narrow-leaved); greenhouse aquatic; 1 foot; flowers white, in June; Cape of Good Hope; 1788. *A. juncifolium* (rush-leaved); greenhouse aquatic; 1 foot; flowers white, in July; 1847.

AQUILEGIA. *Columbine.* [Ranunculaceæ.] Handsome hardy perennials. Common garden soil; good turfy loam for the choicer sorts. Propagated by seeds, or by division. The seed of the common kinds may be sown in beds thinly in May; the young plants, when strong enough, planted out six inches apart every way. If they are to bloom in beds, they should be nine inches apart and eighteen inches from row to row. When they bloom, pull out and destroy all the single and ugly ones, and, if desirable, propagate the better ones. The common Columbine has sported into a variety of colors; and some of its double varieties are very beautiful.

A. Alpina (Alpine); hardy perennial; 1 foot; flowers blue, in May; Switzerland; 1731. *A. atropurpurea* (dark purple); hardy perennial; 1 foot; flowers purple, in May; Siberia; 1827.

A. Canadensis (Canadian); hardy perennial; 1 foot; flowers orange-red, in May; North America; 1640. *A. formosa* (beautiful); hardy perennial; 18 inches; flowers reddish-orange, in June; Kamtschatka; 1822. *A. fragrans* (fragrant); hardy perennial; 6 inches; flowers pale-yellow, in May; Himalayas; 1839. *A. glandulosa* (glandular); hardy perennial; 18 inches; flowers white and blue, in June; Siberia; 1822. *A. glauca* (glaucous); hardy perennial; 2 feet; flowers pale-yellow, in May; Himalaya; 1839. *A. jucunda* (joyous); hardy perennial; 1 foot; flowers blue and white, in June; Siberia; 1844. *A. Kanaoriensis* (Kanaor); hardy perennial; 1 foot; flowers violet with blue spurs, in May; Himalaya. *A. leptocæras* (slender-horned); hardy perennial; 1 foot; flowers blue and cream-color, in July; Siberia; 1846. *A. macrantha* (large-flowered); hardy perennial; 18 inches; flowers cream-colored tinged with pink; North America; 1847. *A. Siberica* (Siberian); hardy perennial; 18 inches; flowers blue and white, in June; Siberia; 1806. *A. Skinneri* (Skinner's); hardy perennial; 18 inches; flowers red and green, in May; Guatimala; 1841. *A. vulgaris* (common); hardy perennial; 2 feet; flowers various, in June; Britain. *A. blanda* is a fine hybrid with white and blue flowers. *A. cærulea* is a Rocky-Mountain species erect flowered with long spurs. *A. spectabilis* is a Siberian species with dark-purple flowers with yellow centre. A variety of *vulgaris*, *A. caryphylloides*, has double variegated flowers: the seeds are dark-green instead of black.

ARABIS. *Wall-cress.* [Cruciferæ.] Dwarf evergreen hardy perennials, with cruciferous flowers, particularly adapted for rock-work. Common soil. Propagated by cuttings, planted in a shady border, under hand-glasses, any time during summer. The annuals, which are insignificant, are raised from seeds sown in May.

A. albida (whitish); hardy perennial; 9 inches; flowers white, in April; Caucasus; 1798. *A. Alpestris* (Alpine); hardy biennial; 6 inches; flowers white, in May; Switzerland; 1819. *A. Alpina* (Alpine); hardy perennial; 9 inches; flowers white, in

May; Switzerland; 1596. *A. cærulea* (blue); hardy perennial; 6 inches; flowers pale-blue, in June; Switzerland; 1793. *A. lucida* (shining); hardy perennial; 6 inches; flowers white, in June; Hungary; 1790. *A. petræa* (rock); hardy perennial; 6 inches; flowers white, in May; Austria; 1800. *A. rosea* (rosy); hardy biennial; 6 inches; flowers rose, in April; Calabria; 1832. *A. undulata* (wavy); hardy perennial; 9 inches; flowers white, in May; south of Europe; 1810. *A. verna* (spring); hardy annual; 1 foot; flowers purple, in May; France; 1710.

There are pretty variegated varieties of *A. albida, præcox,* and *lucida.* There are some twenty other species.

ARALIA. [Araliaceæ.] Hardy deciduous shrubs, and tall-growing herbaceous perennials. They grow with erect stems, and leaves comparatively large and very compound; the herbaceous kinds being smaller. All desirable as specimen plants for the lawn or shrubbery. Common soil. Propagated by cuttings of the matured stems, planted in sandy soil under hand-glasses. There are some stove and greenhouse kinds. Soil, loam and peat. Propagated by cuttings.

A. hispida (bristly); hardy deciduous shrub; 8 feet; flowers white, in July; North America; 1799. *A. nudicaulis* (naked stemmed); hardy perennial; 3 feet; flowers white, in June; North America; 1731. *A. Muhlenbergii* (Muhlenberg's); hardy perennial; 2 feet; flowers white, in July; North America. *A. racemosa* (raceme-flowered); hardy perennial; 4 feet; flowers white, in June; North America; 1658. *A. spinosa* (thorny); hardy shrub; 8 feet; flowers white, in September; Virginia; 1688.

There are fifteen other species, mostly greenhouse plants.

ARAUCARIA. [Pinaceæ.] A genus of magnificent evergreen trees, hardy south of Philadelphia. The best-known species is *A. imbricata,* the Chili Pine. *A. excelsa,* the Norfolk-Island Pine, requires greenhouse protection.

GARDEN FLOWERS. 45

ARBOR-VITÆ. See THUJA.

ARBUTUS. [Ericaceæ.] A beautiful genus of evergreen shrubs, flourishing in loamy garden soil or peat. Flowers bell-shaped, white or pink. Increased by seeds or layers, the rarer species by inarching on the more common. The fruit resembles a strawberry, and is very ornamental. They are not hardy north of Philadelphia. Of the eighteen species seven are greenhouse evergreens.

A. andrachne (andrachne); 10 feet; flowers white, in April; Levant; 1724. *A. andrachnioides* (andrachne-like); 8 feet; flowers whitish-green, in April. *A. Canariensis* (Canary); greenhouse evergreen; 8 feet; flowers whitish-green, in June; Canaries; 1796. *A. densiflora* (thickly-flowered); greenhouse evergreen; 20 feet; flowers white; Mexico; 1826. *A. hybrida* (hybrid). *A. laurifolia* (laurel-leaved); greenhouse evergreen; 20 feet; flowers white; Mexico; 1825. *A. Menziesii* (Menzie's); flowers white; North America; 1827. *A. Milleri* (Miller's); hybrid; 10 feet; flowers white, in September; 1825. *A. mucronata* (sharp-pointed-leaved); greenhouse evergreen trailer; 1 foot; flowers white; Magellan; 1828. *A. pilosa* (hairy-branched); 1 foot; flowers white, in May; Mexico; 1829. *A. phillyreæfolia* (phillyrea-leaved); greenhouse evergreen; 1 foot; flowers white; Peru; 1812. *A. procera* (tall); 15 feet; flowers white; North America; 1825. *A. pumila* (dwarf); greenhouse evergreen; 4 feet; flowers white; Magellan; 1825. *A. serratifolia* (saw-edged-leaved); greenhouse evergreen; 6 feet; flowers whitish-green. *A. speciosa* (showy); Mexico; 1837. *A. tomentosa* (woolly-branched); 4 feet; flowers white; California; 1826. *A. tomentosa nuda* (smooth-branched.) *A. unedo* (unedo); 10 feet; flowers white, in October; Ireland. *A. unedo crispa* (curled); 8 feet; flowers white, in October. *A. unedo integrifolia* (entire-leaved); 6 feet; flowers pink, in October. *A. unedo plena* (double-flowered); 5 feet; flowers white, in October. *A. unedo salicifolia* (willow-leaved); 6 feet; flowers white, in October. *A. schizopetala* (cut-petalled); 7 feet; flowers white, in October. *A. schizopetala rubra* (red-flowered); 10 feet; flowers pink, in October.

The shrub called Strawberry-tree in the Northern United States is EUONYMUS.

ARCTOSTAPHYLOS. [Ericaceæ.] Dwarf evergreen shrubs, ornamental in foliage, flowers, and berry, succeeding in sandy peat. Increased by layers and seed. *A. Alpina* is deciduous.

A. Alpina (Alpine); deciduous trailer; 1 foot; flowers flesh-colored, in May; Scotland. *A. longifolia* (long-leaved); half-hardy evergreen under-shrub; Mexico; 1847. *A. nitida* (shining); half-hardy evergreen shrub; 4 feet; flowers white, in May; Mexico; 1836. *A. pungens* (stinging); half-hardy evergreen shrub; 1 foot; flowers white, in February; Mexico; 1839. *A. tomentosa* (downy); evergreen shrub; flowers white; North America; 1826. *A. uva ursi* (bear's-grape); evergreen trailer; 1 foot; flowers white, in April; Britain.

ARCTOTIS. *Bear's-ear.* [Compositæ.] Greenhouse perennial herbs, with showy composite flowers. Soil, sandy loam and leaf-mould. Propagated by division. Many of the species are remarkable for having the under surface of their leaves covered with a close white wool; and this, together with the form of the leaves, gives them a distinct appearance among other plants. Many of the species form good bedding plants, and give a mass of bloom all summer. Treated as annuals, they bloom the first year.

A. acaulis (stemless); greenhouse perennial; 6 inches; flowers yellow, in May; Cape of Good Hope; 1759. *A. arborescens* (arborescent); greenhouse perennial; 18 inches; flowers white and pink, in June; Cape of Good Hope; 1818. *A. aspera* (rough); greenhouse perennial; 2 feet; flowers pale-yellow, in June; Cape of Good Hope; 1710. *A. aureola* (golden); greenhouse perennial; 18 inches; flowers orange, in April; Cape of Good Hope; 1710. *A. breviscarpa* (short-podded); hardy annual; 1 foot; flowers orange with dark centre, in July; Cape of Good Hope. *A. grandiflora* (large-flowered); greenhouse perennial; 18 inches; flowers yellow, in April; Cape of Good

Hope; 1774. *A. speciosa* (showy); greenhouse perennial; 18 inches; flowers yellow, in June; Cape of Good Hope; 1812.

ARENARIA. [Caryophyllaceæ.] Small herbaceous perennials and annuals, suitable for rock-work. The perennials increased by division, the annuals by seed. All grow in good garden soil.

A. Balerica (Balerian); hardy perennial; 3 inches; flowers white, in July; Majorca; 1787. *A. biflora* (two-flowered); hardy perennial; 3 inches; flowers white, in June; Switzerland; 1818. *A. cæspitosa* (tufted); hardy perennial; 3 inches; flowers white, in June; Switzerland; 1826. *A. glandulosa* (having glands); hardy annual; 3 inches; flowers purple, in June; Europe; 1820. *A. nardifolia* (spikenard-leaved); hardy perennial; 6 inches; flowers white, in June; Siberia; 1827.

There are about seventy other species.

ARETHUSA. [Orchidaceæ.] A genus of only two species, of which only one is hardy. The plants are very difficult of cultivation, but their beauty richly repays any care. The root is a small tuber, about the size of a large pea. Soil, peat, very wet.

A. bulbosa (bulbous); hardy perennial; 9 inches; flowers purple and white, in June; North America; in low peaty swamps.

This plant is dying out in many localities where it was once very plenty.

ARETIA. [Primulaceæ.] Pretty little perennials, of easy culture in loam and peat. Propagated by division.

A. Alpina (Alpine); hardy perennial; 3 inches; flowers pink, in June; Switzerland; 1775. *A. Helvetica* (Swiss); hardy perennial; 3 inches; flowers white, in June; Switzerland; 1775. *A. pubescens* (downy); hardy perennial; 3 inches; flowers white, in June; Switzerland; 1824. *A. Vitaliana* (Vital's); hardy perennial; 3 inches; flowers yellow, in June; Pyrenees; 1787. *A. argentea* is half-hardy.

All the species are very impatient of standing water at the roots.

ARGEMONE. [Papaveraceæ.] Annuals and perennials, with white and yellow poppy-like flowers. Common garden soil. They will not bear transplanting. The annuals are propagated by seed, the perennials by suckers. The latter require winter protection in the Northern States.

A. grandiflora (large-flowered); hardy perennial; 2 feet; flowers white, in July; Mexico; 1827. *A. intermedia* (intermediate); hardy perennial; 18 inches; flowers white, in July; Mexico; 1827. *A. Mexicana* (Mexican); hardy annual; 2 feet; flowers yellow, in July; Mexico; 1592. *A. ochroleuca* (yellowish); hardy annual; 2 feet; flowers cream-colored, in July; Mexico; 1827.

ARISÆMA. [Araceæ.] Hardy and half-hardy tuberous-rooted perennials, with a curious and spathaceous inflorescence. Soil, peat and loam. Propagated by division.

A. dracontium (dragon); hardy tuber; 2 feet; flowers green, in June; North America; 1759. *A. ringens* (gaping); half-hardy tuber; 6 inches; flowers in May; Japan; 1800. *A. ternatum* (ternate); half-hardy tuber; 9 inches; flowers purple, in May; Japan; 1774. *A. triphyllum* (three-leaved); hardy tuber; 9 inches; flowers brown, white, purple, and green, in May; North America; 1664.

This latter species is commonly known as "Indian Turnip," "Jack in the Pulpit," or "Wild Arum." In cultivation, it grows very large, and is very curious in flower, and ornamental in fruit.

ARISTOLOCHIA. *Birthwort.* [Aristolochiaceæ.] (Dutchman's Pipe.) Hardy greenhouse or stove herbs or shrubs, often with twining stems. Soil for the hardy sorts, rich loam and sand; plenty of root-room. Propagated by layers. The twining species are rampant climbers, often growing thirty feet high: they should have plenty of room, to appear to advantage. They are increased by layers and division.

The following are the hardy and half-hardy species, of

GARDEN FLOWERS.   49

which *A. sipho* and *tomentosa* are the best. There are also six greenhouse and about twenty stove species. The flowers of all are more curious than beautiful.

A. Bætica (Spanish); deciduous climber; 6 feet; flowers purple, in June; Spain; 1596. *A. Chilensis* (Chilian); deciduous half-hardy; 6 feet; flowers purple and green, in September; West Indies; 1832. *A. clematitis* (clematis-like); herbaceous perennial; 2 feet; flowers yellow, in July; Britain. *A. longa* (long-rooted); deciduous trailer; 2 feet; flowers purple, in July; south of Europe; 1548. *A. pallida* (pale-flowered); herbaceous perennial; 2 feet; flowers white and purple; Italy; 1640. *A. pistolochia* (pistolochia); deciduous trailer; 2 feet; flowers purple, in July; south of Europe; 1597. *A. sagittata* (arrow-shaped); herbaceous perennial; 1 foot; flowers purple, in July; North America; 1819. *A. serpentaria* (snakeroot); deciduous trailer; 1 foot; flowers dark-purple, in July; North America; 1632. *A. sipho* (tube-bearing); deciduous climber; 30 feet; flowers yellow and brown, in July; North America; 1763. *A. tomentosa* (downy); deciduous climber; 20 feet; flowers purple, in July; North America; 1799.

ARMERIA. *Thrift.* [Plumbaginaceæ.] Dwarf herbaceous plants, nearly all hardy. Soil, sandy loam. Increased by dividing the crown, and planting the separate pieces as cuttings under hand-glasses. They are fine rock-plants, and also do well in pots; and some varieties of the common thrift, especially a deep rose and a white one, make pretty edging to flower-beds.

A. cephalotes (headed); hardy perennial; 18 inches; flowers deep rose-pink, in August; Europe; 1800. *A. dianthoides* (pink-leaved); hardy perennial; 1 foot; flowers pale red, in May; Europe; 1810. *A. latifolia* (broad-leaved); hardy perennial; 2 feet; flowers pale-red, in June; Portugal; 1740. *A. plantaginea* (plantain-leaved); hardy perennial; 1 foot; flowers pale-red, in June; Jersey. *A. vulgaris* (common); hardy perennial; 6 inches; flowers pink, in June; England. There is a pretty white-flowered variety of this, called *alba*.

ARONICUM. [Compositæ.] A hardy herbaceous plant allied to Doronicum, flourishing in garden soil, and propagated by division.

A. Altaicum (Altaic); hardy perennial; 1 foot; flowers yellow, in July; Siberia; 1783.

ARROW-HEAD. See SAGITTARIA.

ARTEMISIA. Hardy and greenhouse herbs and shrubs, with a few annuals, remarkable in many cases for a strong heavy odor. *A. Abrotanum*, the Southernwood, is a favorite in cottage gardens; the rest are unimportant. Common soil. Propagated by cuttings.

A. Abrotanum (Southernwood); hardy shrub; 2 feet; flowers greenish, in August; Europe; 1548.

There are about forty other species.

ARUM. [Araceæ.] Curious perennials. The majority hardy, but some requiring a greenhouse, others a stove. It is the floral sheath or spathe of these plants that forms the conspicuous part of the inflorescence. The tender kinds should have rich loam, and plenty of water while growing. For the hardy sorts, any common soil that is deep. Propagated by suckers.

A. dracunculus (dragon); hardy perennial; 3 feet; flowers brown, in July; south of Europe; 1548. *A. Italicum* (Italian); hardy perennial; 1 foot; flowers yellowish, in June; Italy; 1683. *A. tenuifolium* (slender-leaved); hardy perennial; 1 foot; flowers white, in June; south of Europe; 1750.

Many plants formerly belonging to Arum have been referred to Arisæma.

ARUNDO. [Gramineæ.] Hardy perennials, flourishing in rich damp soil. Propagated by division.

A. Donax; hardy perennial; 10 feet; flowers apetalous; south of Europe; 1648 *A. Donax versicolor;* a pretty striped variety.

ASARUM. *Asarabacca.* [Aristolochiaceæ.] Dwarf hardy perennials, more remarkable for the curious structure of their flowers than for their beauty. Cool moist common soil. Propagated by division.

A. Canadense (Canadian); hardy perennial; 6 inches; flowers brown, in April; Canada; 1713. *A. Europæum* (European); hardy perennial; 6 inches; flowers brown, in April; England. *A. Virginicum* (Virginian); hardy perennial; 6 inches; flowers brown, in April; Virginia; 1759.

ASCLEPIAS. *Swallow-wort.* [Asclepiadaceæ.] Herbaceous perennials, including stove, greenhouse, and hardy kinds. For the tender kinds, rich loam and leaf-mould in equal parts. They are best raised from seeds, which are generally produced freely, and the plants should be often renewed: they may also be raised by cuttings in sand in a hot-bed. The seed should be sown in pots in the spring, and the plants pricked out as soon as large enough, afterwards potted singly, and shifted into larger pots as they grow. Most of the hardy sorts grow in good deep garden soil; but *A. tuberosa* should have good loam, but will thrive in garden soil. These are increased by division.

A. amœna (pleasing); hardy perennial; 3 feet; flowers purple, in July; North America; 1732. *A. Curassavica* (Curassoa); stove perennial; 3 feet; flowers orange, in June; South America; 1692. A white variety is called *alba;* a long-leaved deep-red variety is called *rubra:* these are very desirable stove plants, and do well as bedding plants in summer. *A. decumbens* (decumbent); hardy tuberous perennial; 2 feet; flowers orange, in July; North America; 1731. *A. exaltata* (tall); hardy perennial; 6 feet; flowers purple, in July; North America; 1800. *A. nivea* (snowy); hardy perennial; 3 feet; flowers white, in July; North America; 1730. *A. pulchra* (fair); hardy perennial; 2 feet; flowers purple, in July; North America. *A. rubra* (red); hardy perennial; 1 foot; flowers red, in July; Virginia; 1825. *A. Syriaca* (Syrian); hardy perennial; 4 feet; flowers purple, in July; North America; 1629. *A. tuberosa* (tuberous); hardy tuberous perennial; 2 feet; flowers orange-scarlet, in July; North America; 1690.

ASH. See FRAXINUS.

ASPEN. See POPULUS.

ASPERULA. [Galiaceæ.] Very pretty hardy perennials. Grow in cool moist soil; and increased by division.

A. Aparine (marsh); hardy perennial; 2 feet; flowers white, in July; south of Europe; 1818. *A. galeoides* (galium-like); hardy perennial; 6 inches; flowers white, in June; south of Europe; 1710. *A. longifolia* (long-leaved); hardy perennial; 1 foot; flowers red, in July; south of Europe; 1820. *A. odorata* (sweet); hardy perennial; 9 inches; flowers white, in May. *A. tinctoria* (dyer's); hardy perennial; 9 inches; flowers pink, in July; Europe; 1764. *A. trichodes* (hairy); hardy annual; propagated by seeds; flowers white, in July; 1838.

ASPHODELUS. [Liliaceæ.] Hardy herbaceous perennials, growing in common garden soil. Increased by division

A. albus (white); hardy perennial; 3 feet; flowers white, in June; south of Europe; 1820. *A. luteus* (yellow); hardy perennial; 18 inches; flowers yellow, in June; Sicily; 1596. *A. proliferous* (prolific); hardy annual; propagated by seed; flowers white, in August; Armenia; 1824. *A. ramosus* (branching); hardy perennial; 3 feet; flowers white, in June; south of Europe; 1551. *A. tenuior* (more slender); hardy perennial; 2 feet; flowers white, in July; Siberia; 1824.

ASTER. [Compositæ.] Hardy composite perennials. Common garden soil. Propagated by seed and by division. A very large family, of which we enumerate a very small selection. See also CALLISTEPHUS and FELICIA.

A. Alpinus (Alpine); hardy perennial; 9 inches; flowers bluish-purple, in July; Europe; 1658. *A. Amellus* (Amellus); hardy perennial; 2 feet; flowers purple, in August; Italy; 1596. *A. Bessarabicus* (Bessarabian); hardy perennial; 2 feet; flowers purple, in September; Bessarabia; 1834. *A. Novæ Angliæ*

(New England); hardy perennial; 5 feet; flowers purple, in September; North America; 1710. *A. pulcherrimus* (prettiest); hardy perennial; 9 inches; flowers purple, in August; North America; 1800.

There are more than a hundred and fifty other species.

ASTEROCEPHALUS. Hardy annuals and perennials, including the well-known Sweet Scabious, or Mourning Bride. The seeds of this are sown in the flower-borders in May, and merely thinned out when the plants come up, or in a hot-bed, and transplanted. The perennial species are of easy culture in common garden soil, and increase by division.

A. atropurpureus (Sweet Scabious); hardy annual; 2 feet; flowers various colors, in July; India. *A. graminifolius* (grass-leaved); hardy perennial; 1 foot; flowers blue, in July; Switzerland; 1683. *A. incana* (hoary); hardy perennial; 1 foot; flowers red, in June; Europe; 1826. *A. ochroleucus* (yellowish); hardy perennial; 2 feet; flowers pale yellow, in July; Germany; 1517.

There are many other species.

ASTRAGALUS. *Milk Vetch.* [Leguminosæ.] Perennials and annuals, mostly hardy, bearing papilionaceous flowers. The large species are suitable for the common borders, and the smaller ones for rock-work. They are increased by seeds, by division, or by cuttings, according to their habit. It is a very numerous family, containing many species of merely botanical interest.

A. alopecuroides (fox-tail); hardy perennial; 18 inches; flowers yellow, in June; Spain; 1738. *A. Austriacus* (Austrian); hardy perennial; 6 inches; flowers pale-blue, in June; Austria; 1640. *A. hypoglottis* (under-tongue); hardy perennial; 6 inches; flowers purplish-blue and white, in June; England. *A. leontinus* (lion's tail); hardy perennial; 6 inches; flowers blue, in May; Austria; 1816. *A. leptophyllus* (fine-leaved); hardy perennial; 6 inches; flowers white, in June; Barbary; 1811. *A. Monspessulanus* (Montpelier); hardy perennial; 1 foot; flowers purple, in July; France; 1710. *A. odoratus* (sweet); hardy perennial; 1 foot; flowers yellow, in June; Levant; 1820. *A. onobrychis* (Saintfoin); hardy perennial; 18 inches; flowers purple or white, in June; Austria; 1640. *A. Ponticus* (Pontic); hardy perennial; 2 feet; flowers yellow, in July; Tauria; 1820. *A. stipulatus* (stipuled); hardy perennial; 1 foot; flowers yellow, in June; Nepaul; 1822.

There are more than a hundred other species.

ASTRANTIA. [Umbelliferæ.] Elegant herbaceous plants, quite hardy. Common garden soil. Increased by division.

A. Carniolica (Carniolian); hardy perennial; 1 foot; flowers striped, in May; Carniola; 1812. *A. Caucasica* (Caucasian); hardy perennial; 3 inches; flowers pink, in June; Caucasus; 1818. *A. major* (greater); hardy perennial; 2 feet; flowers striped, in June; Europe; 1596. *A. maxima* (greatest); hardy perennial; 2 feet; flowers pink, in July; Caucasus; 1804.

ATRAGENE. [Ranunculaceæ.] Hardy deciduous climbers, resembling Clematis. Soil, rich garden loam. Propagated by cuttings in sand under a bell-glass, or by layers.

A. Americana (American); hardy climbing shrub; 10 feet; flowers purple, in June; North America; 1797. *A. Austriaca* (Austrian); hardy climbing shrub; 12 feet; flowers blue, in June; Austria; 1792. *A. Sibcrica* (Siberian); hardy climbing shrub; 12 feet; flowers white, in June; Siberia; 1753.

AUBERGINE. See SOLANUM, EGG-PLANT.

AUBRIETIA. [Cruciferæ.] Very pretty dwarf evergreen herbaceous perennials, growing in common garden soil, and well suited to rock-work. Propagated by seeds and division, or by cuttings under a bell-glass in sand.

A. deltoidea (three-angled); hardy perennial; 3 inches; flowers purple, in May; Levant; 1710. *A. hesperidiflora* (hesperis-flowered); hardy perennial; 3 inches; flowers purple, in May;

south of Europe; 1823. *A. purpurea* (purple); hardy perennial; 3 inches; flowers lilac-purple, in May; Levant; 1820.

There are varieties with variegated foliage.

ACUBA. [Cornaceæ.] A fine evergreen shrub, conspicuous for its variegated foliage; hardy south of Philadelphia. Common soil. Propagated by cuttings and layers.

A. Japonica (Japan); hardy shrub; 8 feet; flowers chocolate, in May; Japan; 1783.

The plant is diœcious.

AURICULA. See PRIMULA.

AVENS. See GEUM.

AVENA. [Gramineæ.] OAT. Too well known to need description. *A. sterilis* is the common animated oats of the garden. All the species are ornamental in a collection of grasses.

AZALEA. [Ericaceæ.] Handsome, low, hardy, and greenhouse shrubs.

The American or hardy Azaleas *(A. pontica, calendulacea, nudiflora,* and *viscosa,* with hosts of garden varieties bred from them) are inhabitants of all our best shrubberies, and have been so wonderfully improved by seedling culture as to throw into the shade the original species: there are now to be selected twenty or thirty varieties better than the very best of the original species. Every year, too, adds to the diversity of sorts, and to the size of the flowers, which is one of the characteristics of the improved kinds. In many places they thrive in the common soil of the garden, but, in general, they require peat earth to be dug in with the natural soil; and where there is to be any quantity grown, or a nursery of them made, beds of peat earth, or compounds of the greatest part of turfy-peat earth, must be made up. They are raised from seed sown in beds in the open air; but, from its extreme diminutiveness, many prefer sowing in pans and wide-mouthed pots. When they are large enough, they should be planted out in peat-beds six inches apart: the second year every alternate plant may be taken out and planted elsewhere, to make room; and, as they increase in size, they should have more room. They are propagated chiefly by layers; but cuttings of the last year's wood will root readily in sand. The following are some of the hardy species :—

A. arborescens (tree-like); 10 feet; flowers red, in June; North America; 1818. *A. bicolor* (two-colored); 4 feet; flowers scarlet, in June; North America; 1734. *A canescens* (hoary); 3 feet; flowers red, in June; North America; 1812. *A. calendulacea* (marigold-like); 4 feet; flowers orange, in June; North America; 1806. *A. calendulacea chrysolecta* (fine-golden); 4 feet; flowers yellow, in June; North America. *A. calendulacea crocea* (saffron-colored); 4 feet; flowers saffron, in June; North America. *A. calendulacea cuprea* (copper-colored); 4 feet; flowers copper, in June; North America. *A calendulacea flammea* (flame-colored); 4 feet; flowers red, in June; North America; 1812. *A. calendulacea grandiflora* (large-flowered); 4 feet; flowers orange, in June; North America. *A. calendulacea ignescens* (fire-colored); 1 foot; flowers red, in June; North America. *A. calendulacea splendens* (shining); 4 feet; flowers orange, in June; North America. *A. calendulacea triumphans* (triumphant); 4 feet; flowers orange, in June; North America. *A. glauca* (dwarf-glaucous); 2 feet; flowers white, in June; North America; 1734. *A. hispida* (bristly); 5 feet; flowers white, in June; North America; 1734. *A. ledifolium* (ledum-leaved); 2 feet; flowers white, in April; China; 1824. *A. nitida* (shining-leaved); 4 feet; flowers white, in April; North America; 1812. *A. nudiflora* (naked-flowered); 3 feet; flowers deep pink, in June; North America; 1734. *A. nudiflora alba* (early-white); 4 feet; flowers white, in June; North America. *A. nudiflora alba-plena* (double-white); 4 feet; flowers white, in June; North America. *A. nudiflora blanda* (soft); 4 feet; flowers blush, in June; North America. *A. nudiflora carnea* (flesh); 4 feet; flowers pale-red, in June; North America; 1734. *A. nudiflora Caroliniana* (Carolina); 4 feet; flowers scarlet, in June; North America. *A. nudiflora Coburghii* (Coburg's); flowers scarlet, in June; North America. *A. nudiflora coccinea* (scarlet); 4 feet; flowers scarlet, in June; North America. · *A. nudiflora corymbosa* (corymbose); 4 feet; flowers scarlet, in June; North America. *A. nudiflora crispa* (curled); 4 feet; flowers pink, in June; North America. *A. nudiflora cumulata* (bundled); 4 feet; flowers scarlet, pink, in June; North America. *A. nudiflora discolor* (two-colored); 4 feet; flowers white, scarlet, in June; North America. *A. nudiflora fastigiata* (pyramidal); 4 feet; flowers pink, in June; North America. *A. nudiflora florida* (many-flowered); 4 feet; flowers pink, n June; North America. *A. nudiflora globosa* (globe-like); feet; flowers pink, in June; North America. *A. nudiflora glomerata* (round-headed); 4 feet; flowers pink in June; North America. *A. nudiflora incana* (hoary); 4 feet; flowers pink, in June; North America. *A. nudiflora incarnata* (flesh-colored); 4 feet; flowers flesh, in June; North America. *A. nudiflora mirabilis* (wonderful); 4 feet; flowers scarlet, in June; North America. *A. nudiflora magnifica* (magnificent); 4 feet; flowers scarlet, in June; North America. *A. nudiflora montana* (mountain); 4 feet; flowers scarlet, in June; North America. *A. nudiflora pallida* (pale-flowered); 4 feet; flowers pale-red, in June; North America. *A. nudiflora paludosa* (marsh); 4 feet; flowers pale-red, in June; North America. *A. nudiflora papilionacea* (butterfly); 4 feet; flowers striped, in June; North America. *A. nudiflora partita* (five-parted); 4 feet; flowers white and red, in June; North America. *A. nudiflora parviflora* (small-flowered); 4 feet; flowers in June; North America. *A. nudiflora prolifera* (proliferous); 4 feet; flowers in June; North America. *A. nudiflora pumila* (dwarf); 4 feet; flowers white, in June; North America. *A. nudiflora purpurascens* (purplish); 4 feet; flowers purple, in June; North America. *A. nudiflora purpurea* (purple); 4 feet; flowers purple, in June; North America. *A. nudiflora purpureo-pleno* (double-purple); 4 feet; flowers purple, in June; North America. *A. nudiflora rosea* (rosy); 4 feet; flowers red, in June; North America. *A. nudiflora ruberrima* (reddest); 4 feet; flowers dark-red, in June; North America. *A. nudiflora rubescens* (reddish); 4 feet; flowers red, in June; North America. *A. nudiflora rubicunda* (ruddy); 4 feet; flowers red, in June; North America. *A. nudiflora rubra* (red); 4 feet; flowers red, in June; North America. *A. nudiflora rutilans* (shining-red); 4 feet; flowers dark-red, in June; North America. *A. nudiflora semi-duplex* (semi-double); 4 feet; flowers white, in June; North America. *A. nudiflora staminea* (long-stamened); 4 feet; flowers red, in June; North America. *A. nudiflora stellata* (starry); 4 feet; flowers red, in June; North America. *A. nudiflora tricolor* (three-colored); 4 feet; flowers scarlet, white, in June; North America. *A. nudiflora variabilis* (variable); 4 feet; flowers red, in June; North America. *A. nudiflora variegata* (variegated); 4 feet; flowers red and white, in June; North America. *A. nudiflora versicolor* (party-colored); 4 feet; flowers red and white, in June; North America. *A. nudiflora violacea* (violet-colored); 4 feet; flowers violet, in June; North America. *A. Pontica* (Pontic); 6 feet; flowers yellow, in June; Turkey; 1793. *A. Pontica albiflora* (white-flowered); 6 feet; flowers white, in May; Turkey. *A. Pontica coronarium* (garland); 7 feet; flowers yellow, in June; Holland; 1832. *A. Pontica cuprea* (copper-colored); 6 feet; flowers copper, in June; Turkey. *A. Pontica glauca* (milky-green-leaved); 6 feet; flowers yellow, in June; Turkey. *A. Pontica pallida* (pale); 6 feet; flowers pale-

sided); 4 feet; flowers in June; North America. *A. speciosa prunifolia* (plum-leaved); 4 feet; flowers in June; North America. *A. speciosa revoluta* (rolled-back-leaved); 4 feet; flowers in June; North America. *A. speciosa tortulifolia* (twisted-leaved); 4 feet; flowers in June; North America. *A. speciosa undulata* (waved-leaved); 4 feet; flowers in June; North America. *A. viscosa* (clammy); 2 feet; flowers white, in July; North America. *A. viscosa crispa* (curled); 4 feet; flowers white, in July; North America. *A. viscosa dealbata* (whitened); 4 feet; flowers white, in July; North America. *A. viscosa fissa* (cleft); 4 feet; flowers white, in July; North America. *A. viscosa odorata* (scented); 4 feet; flowers white, in July; North America. *A. viscosa pencillata* (pencilled); 4 feet; flowers white, in July; North America. *A. viscosa pubescens* (downy); 4 feet; flowers white, in July; North America. *A. viscosa rubescens* (reddish); 4 feet; flowers white, in July; North America. *A. viscosa variegata* (variegated); 4 feet; flowers white, in July; North America. *A. viscosa vittata* (banded); 4 feet; flowers white, in July; North America. *A. amœna* (bright-flowered); 1 foot; flowers crimson and purple, in April; Shanghæ. This beautiful little species is hardy as far north as Massachusetts, if planted in peat and sand, and protected from the winter's sun by an evergreen bough thrown over it. The foliage is evergreen.

BABY'S BREATH. See MUSCARI.

BAERIA. [Compositæ.] A pretty hardy annual, thriving in any garden soil, from seeds sown in May.

B. chrysostoma (golden-mouthed); hardy annual; 1 foot; flowers yellow, in June; California; 1835.

BALM. See MELISSA.

BALSAMINA. *Balsam.* [Balsaminaceæ.] Tender annuals. The garden Balsam, of which numerous handsome varieties are grown, is *B. hortensis.* This requires a rich compost of loam and vegetable mould. Sow the seeds in pots, about March, and put them in a cucumber-frame or melon-bed. As soon as they are up, and before they have time to draw, let them be potted out, one in a pot three inches across, and put in a declining or very moderate hot-bed, where they must have air to prevent their being drawn up, and must be so placed that the tops shall be near the glass, and the plants must be shifted every time the pots fill with roots; and in this way you go on moving them from one pot to another as they fill with roots. The heat of the bed must not be neglected; and the pots will have to be lowered, or the frame raised, as the plants increase in size. Some of the plants may be hardened off in May, and in June turned into the borders, where, if the soil be rich, and the situation sheltered, they make a very pretty show, and seed freely. Those in pots have to be put into the greenhouse when they have grown too large for the frames; and, if the house is a lean-to, they should be turned every day, that one side may not be drawn more than another. By constant shifting, as the plants fill the pots, and keeping them near the glass, they can be grown very large, much branched, and the flowers will cover the branches. Compared with the double varieties of the common Balsam, the other species are unimportant, though some of the stove species, when well grown, are very beautiful. Balsams also do well if sown in a hot-bed and planted out after the weather has become settled.

B. hortensis (garden); tender annual; 3 feet; flowers various, in July; East Indies; 1596.

There seems to be no reason for making this new genus from *Impatiens*. The plant is better named *Impatiens balsaminea*.

BANEBERRY. See ACTÆA.

BANKSIAN ROSE. See ROSA.

BAPTISIA. [Leguminosæ.] Hardy perennials, with papilionaceous blossoms. Common loamy soil. Multiplied by division and seed.

B. alba (white); hardy perennial; 2 feet; flowers white, in June; North America; 1724. *B. Australis* (southern); hardy perennial; 3 feet; flowers blue, in June; North America; 1758. *B. lanceolata* (lanceolate); hardy perennial; 1 foot; flowers yellow, in July; North America; 1818. *B. mollis* (soft); hardy perennial; 18 inches; flowers blue, in June; North America; 1824. *B. villosa* (villous); hardy perennial; 2 feet; flowers yellow, in June; North America; 1811.

BARRENWORT. See EPIMEDIUM.

BARBAREA. [Cruciferæ.] Hardy herbaceous plants, allied to Arabis, readily increased by seed and division, growing in garden soil; not ornamental.

The species are *B. arcuata, orthocerus, precox, stricta, Taurica,* and *vulgaris*; all with yellow flowers.

BARTONIA. [Loasaceæ.] Half-hardy annuals and biennials. Soil peaty and rather cool. Propagated by seeds: the annuals sown in March in a mild hot-bed, and planted out in May, or sown in the open ground in May; the biennials sown in July, and kept in frames during winter. *B. aurea*, which is the principal sort cultivated, is very pretty.

B. albescens (white); half-hardy annual; 2 feet; flowers white, in July; Chili; 1831. *B. aurea* (golden); half-hardy annual; 2 feet; flowers yellow, in July; California; 1834. *B. ornata* (ornate); half-hardy biennial; 2 feet; flowers white, in August; Missouri; 1811. *B. nuda* (naked); half-hardy biennial; 2 feet; flowers white, in August; Missouri; 1811.

BASTARD INDIGO. See AMORPHA.

BATSCHIA. Hardy perennials. Good loamy garden soil. Increased either by seeds or by division.

B. canescens (hoary); hardy perennial; 18 inches; flowers yellow, in July; North America; 1826. *B. longiflora* (long-flowered); hardy perennial; 6 inches; flowers yellow, in May; Missouri; 1812. *B. sericea* (silky); hardy perennial; 6 inches; flowers yellow, in July; North America; 1825.

BEAD-TREE. See MELIA.

BEAR'S BREECH. See ACANTHUS.

BEAR'S EAR. See ARCTOTIS.

BEAR'S EAR SANICLE. See CORTUSA.

BEAR'S GRAPE. See ARCTOSTAPHYLOS.

BEDSTRAW. See GALIUM.

BEECH. See FAGUS.

BELLADONNA LILY. A beautiful species of Amaryllis *(A. Belladonna)*, occasionally used as a bedding plant. The foliage dies in July, and the spike of pink lily-like flowers is produced on a tall stem in September. After blooming, the bulb should be potted, and the growth of foliage encouraged, as on this depends the bloom of the next year. The bulb is tender, and must not be exposed to frost.

BELL-FLOWER. See CAMPANULA.
BELLWORT. See UVULARIA.
BELLIDIASTRUM. [Compositæ.] Dwarf hardy perennials, with daisy-like flowers. Soil, loam and peat. Increased by division.

B. Michelii (Micheli's); hardy perennial; 1 foot; flowers white, in June; Austria; 1570.

Requires protection in the Northern States.

BELLIS. [Compositæ.] A genus of very pretty half-hardy perennials, growing in common garden soil, and increased by division. The usual mode is to plant them in a frame, and bring them into the house to bloom, or to bloom them in the frame. The flowers are double and single, of various colors. Some have variegated foliage.

B. hybrida (hybrid); half-hardy perennial; 3 inches; flowers white, in spring; Italy; 1824. *B. integrifolia* (entire-leaved); half-hardy perennial; 3 inches; flowers white and pink, in July; Texas; 1801. *B. perennis* (perennial); half-hardy perennial; flowers white, in June; the common Daisy of England. Variety *hortensis*, the garden double red Daisy; variety *fistulosa*, the garden double red quilled Daisy; variety *prolifera*, the garden variety, pink and white, with small flower-heads round the larger one. *B. sylvestris* (wood); half-hardy perennial; 3 inches; flowers white, in June; Portugal; 1797.

This plant offers a wide field for improvement by careful hybridization. All the species require to be shaded from our summer's sun.

BELLIUM. [Compositæ.] A genus of small pretty half-hardy herbaceous perennials, with daisy-like flowers, and grown in sandy peat: the perennials increased by division; the annuals, by seed.

B. bellidioides (daisy-like); hardy annual; 3 inches; flowers white, in June; Italy; 1796. *B. crassifolium* (thick-leaved); half-hardy perennial; 6 inches; flowers white, in June; Sardinia; 1831. *B. intermedium* (intermediate); half-hardy perennial; 3 inches; flowers white, in August; hybrid. *B. minutum* (small); half-hardy perennial; 3 inches; flowers white, in July; Levant; 1772.

BERBERIS. *Barberry*. [Berberiaceæ.] A genus of evergreen and deciduous shrubs, ornamental in foliage, flower, and fruit. The common Barberry *(B. Canadensis)* is a very ornamental but neglected shrub. Although there is not a shrub more decidedly shrubby, it can be formed into a pretty standard. Young suckers may be supported with stakes until they run up to the height required, all their side shoots being removed before they advance much in growth: the top may then be taken off, and a few of the lateral branches encouraged close to the top; these, shortened before they grow much, cause other laterals to grow, and a good head may be formed in a short time. Generally a deep sandy loam is desirable. Propagated by cuttings in autumn, by grafting in the case of rare sorts, and by seeds where large quantities are raised.

One group of the Berberries have been called Mahonias. These are beautiful dwarf evergreen shrubs, with bright shiny foliage, growing thick and rich, and bearing beautiful close bunches of bright yellow flowers in the spring, succeeded by rich purple fruit. There is hardly a prettier set of evergreens in cultivation: they afford a very striking variety in the foliage of a mixed clump; but, as the plants feather down to the ground, there should be nothing to hide them: on this account they make excellent lawn plants. They bear round, bright, purple fruit, which looks as well as the flowers; and the plants, which do not grow higher than three or four feet in general, and are a good while reaching that height, are handsome without either flowers or fruit. They are multiplied by suckers, which may be taken off in the autumn : they also strike freely, and may therefore be raised from cuttings ; but, of late, they have been chiefly raised from seeds, which yield a much greater variety of foliage than the several enumerated sorts exhibit. The seed should be washed out of the soft berries and dried ; then a bed, with a portion of turfy peat dug among the ordinary soil, should be prepared, and the seed sown very thinly indeed upon it, and raked in. When it comes up let it be cleared of weeds, and, in very dry weather, occasionally watered. They may remain until large enough to plant out a foot apart ; for, if they have not room, they soon become drawn. Here they have only to be kept clean till they are large enough to plant where they are to stand. Except where otherwise specified, those named below are evergreen.

B. aquifolium (holly-leaved); evergreen shrub ; 5 feet ; flowers yellow, in May ; North America ; 1823. *B. Beali* (Beal's); evergreen shrub ; 5 feet ; flowers yellow, in March ; China ; 1852. *B. Darwinii* (Darwin's) ; evergreen shrub ; 5 feet ; flowers deep orange, in May ; Chili ; 1847. *B. dealbata* (whitened) ; evergreen shrub ; 5 feet ; flowers yellow, in May ; Mexico ; 1833. *B. dulcis* (sweet) ; evergreen shrub ; 5 feet ; flowers yellow, in May ; Magellan ; 1830. *B. empetrifolia* (empetrum-leaved) ; half-hardy evergreen shrub ; 3 feet ; flowers yellow, in May ; Magellan ; 1827. *B. fasicularis* (bundled) ; half-hardy evergreen shrub ; 6 feet ; flowers yellow, in May ; California ; 1820. *B. Fortuni* (Fortune's) ; evergreen shrub ; 8 feet ; flowers yellow, in July ; China ; 1846. *B. glumacea* (glumaceous) ; evergreen shrub ; 10 feet ; flowers yellow, in May ; North America ; 1822. *B. ilicifolia* (holly-leaved) ; evergreen shrub ; 8 feet ; flowers orange-yellow, in July ; Terra del Fuego ; 1843. *B. Jamiesoni* (Jameson's) ; evergreen shrub ; flowers yellow ; Peru ; 1847. *B. Loxensis* (Loxa) ; half-hardy evergreen shrub ; 4 feet ; flowers yellow ; Loxa ; 1848. *B. macrophylla* (large-leaved) ; evergreen shrub ; 5 feet ; flowers yellow ; Japan ; 1847. *B. Nepalensis* (Nepaul) ; half-hardy evergreen shrub ;

5 feet; flowers yellow, in March; north of India; 1850. *B. repens* (creeping); evergreen shrub; 2 feet; flowers yellow, in May; North America; 1822. *B. trifoliata* (trifoliate); half-hardy deciduous shrub; 5 feet; flowers yellow, in June; Mexico; 1839. *B. trifurca* (three-forked); half-hardy evergreen shrub; 5 feet; flowers unknown; China; 1852. *B. vulgaris* (common); hardy deciduous shrub; 8 feet; flowers yellow, in May; England. *B. Wallichiana* (Wallich's); evergreen shrub; 10 feet; flowers yellow; East Indies; 1820.

Most of the evergreen species require a winter protection of evergreen boughs in the Northern States.

BERGIA. [Elatinaceæ.] Hardy annual, of no great beauty. Sandy soil. Propagated by seeds.

B. verticillata (whorled); hardy annual; 1 foot; flowers white and red, in June; Egypt; 1820.

BERTEROA. [Cruciferæ.] A small family of herbaceous half-hardy plants, allied to Arabis, grown in common garden soil, and increased by division, seed, and cuttings. The species all have whitish flowers and are *B. incana, mutabilis,* and *obliqua.* The former is also known as Alyssum incanum.

BETCKIA. [Valerianaceæ.] A genus of hardy annuals, allied to Valerian. Propagated by seeds sown in a hot-bed, and transplanted to the border.

B. magis (larger); hardy annual; 18 inches; flowers rose, in August; California; 1836. *B. samolifolia* (samolus-leaved); hardy annual; 1 foot; flowers rose, in July; Chili; 1835.

BETONICA. *Betony.* [Labiatæ.] Hardy perennials. Soil, common garden mould. Propagated by division.

B. grandiflora (great-flowered); hardy perennial; 2 feet; flowers purple, in July; Siberia; 1800. *B. incana* (hoary); hardy perennial; 6 inches; flowers flesh-color, in June; Italy; 1759. *B. nivea* (snowy); hardy perennial; 1 foot; flowers red,

in June; Caucasus; 1820. *B. Orientalis* (Oriental); hardy perennial; 1 foot; flowers light-purple, in June; Levant; 1737.
This genus is now united to Stachys, which see.

BETULA. *Betulaceæ*. [Birch.] Hardy trees and shrubs, flourishing in common soil, and propagated by seed. The following are the species:—

B. alba (common white); 40 feet; flowers in April; Britain. *B. alba Dalecarlica* (Dalecarlian); 40 feet; flowers in May; Europe. *B. alba foliis-variegatis* (variegated-leaved); flowers in May. *B. alba macrocarpa* (large-fruited); 40 feet; flowers in June; Europe. *B. alba pendula* (pendulous); flowers in April; Britain. *B. alba Pontica* (Pontic); 70 feet; flowers in May; Turkey. *B. alba urticifolia* (nettle-leaved); 40 feet; flowers in May. *B. alba verrucosa* (warty); 40 feet; flowers in April; Britain. *B. Bhojpattra* (Bhojpattra); 50 feet; flowers in May; Himalayas; 1840. *B. carpinifolia* (horn-beam-leaved); half-hardy; 50 feet; flowers in July; North America; 1759. *B. Daurica* (Daurian); 30 feet; flowers in July; Siberia; 1785. *B. Daurica parvifolia* (small-leaved); flowers in July; Siberia. *B. excelsa* (tall); 60 feet; flowers in July; North America; 1767. *B. fruticosa* (shrubby); 6 feet; flowers in June; Siberia; 1818. *B. glandulosa* (glanded); flowers in May; North America; 1816. *B. grandis* (great); North America; 1834. *B. lanulosa* (woolly); 70 feet; flowers in July; North America; 1817. *B. lenta* (pliant); 50 feet; flowers in July; North America; 1759. *B. lutea* (yellow); 20 feet; flowers in May; North America. *B. mollis* (soft); East Indies; 1840. *B. nana* (smooth-dwarf); 4 feet; flowers in May; North America. *B. nana macrophylla* (large-leaved); 6 feet; flowers in May; Switzerland; 1819. *B. stricta* (upright); flowers in May. *B. nigra* (black); 60 feet; flowers in July; North America; 1736. *B. ovata* (egg-leaved); 6 feet; flowers in May; Hungary; 1820. *B. pallescens* (palish); 6 feet. *B. papyracea* (paper); 50 feet; flowers in June; North America; 1750. *B. papyracea fusca* (blackish-brown); flowers in May; Carolina. *B. papyracea platyphylla* (broad-leaved); 50 feet; flowers in

June; Carolina. *B. papyracea trichoclada* (hairy-twigged); flowers in June; Carolina. *B. pendula* (pendulous); 40 feet; flowers in June; Britain. *B. Pontica* (Pontic); hardy evergreen; 12 feet; flowers in May; Turkey. *B. populifolia* (poplar-leaved); hardy evergreen; 30 feet; flowers in July; North America; 1750. *B. populifolia laciniata* (cut-leaved); 30 feet; flowers in July. *B. populifolia pendula* (pendulous); flowers in July. *B. pubescens* (downy); 30 feet; flowers in June; Germany; 1812. *B. pumila* (hairy-dwarf); 6 feet; flowers in May; North America; 1762. *B. rubra* (red); 60 feet; flowers in July; Canada. *B. Scopolii* (Scopoli's); 6 feet. *B. tristis* (sad); 10 feet; flowers in May; Kamtschatka.

BIDENS. [Compositæ.] Annuals, biennials, and perennials, generally hardy, allied to Coreopsis. Propagated by seed and division. Garden soil.

B. arguta; herbaceous perennial; flowers yellow, in June; Mexico; 1825. *B. bipinnata* (twice-leaved); hardy annual; 2 feet; flowers yellow, in July; North America; 1687. *B. leucantha* (white-flowered); hardy annual; 18 inches; flowers white, in July; South America. *B. macrosperma* (large-seeded); hardy annual; 1 foot; flowers yellow, in July; Siberia; 1829.

There are many other species.

BIGNONIA. *Trumpet-Flower.* See TECOMA.
BINDWEED. See CONVOLVULUS.
BIRTHWORT. See ARISTOLOCHIA.
BITTER VETCH. See OROBUS.
BLADDER SENNA. See COLUTEA.

BISCATELLA. [Cruciferæ.] A genus of hardy perennials and annuals, of little beauty, growing in common soil. Increased by seed and division.

BISERULA. [Fabaceæ.] A hardy annual, growing in sandy soil. Increased by seed.

B. pilecinus; hardy annual; 1 foot; flowers purple, in July; south of Europe; 1640.

BIVONÆA. [Cruciferæ.] A hardy annual, growing from seed in common soil.

B. lutea (yellow); hardy annual; 6 inches; flowers yellow, in July; Italy; 1824.

BLEPHILIA. [Labiatæ.] A family of herbaceous perennials, allied to Monarda. Propagated by seeds and division. Common soil.

B. ciliata (hair-fringed); hardy perennial; 3 feet; flowers red, in July; North America. *B. hirsuta* (hairy); hardy perennial; 3 feet; flowers purple, in August; North America; 1798.

BLITUM. *Strawberry Blite.* [Chenopodiaceæ.] Hardy annuals, with fruit resembling Strawberries. Common soil. Propagated by seeds sown in May where the plants are to grow.

B. capitatum (headed); hardy annual; 2 feet; fruit red, in July; Austria; 1633. *B. virgatum* (twiggy); hardy annual; 2 feet; fruit red, in July; south of Europe; 1680.

BLOODROOT. See SANGUINARIA.
BLUE BELL. CAMPANULA ROTUNDIFOLIA.
BLUE BOTTLE. CENTAURIA CYANUS.

BLUMENBACHIA. [Loasaceæ.] Hardy annuals, grown from seed sown in May in rich loam.

B. insignis (remarkable); hardy annual; 9 inches; flowers white, in July; Monte Video; 1826. *B. multifida* (many-cleft); hardy annual; 1 foot; flowers greenish-red, in July; Buenos Ayres; 1826.

BOG-BEAN. See MENYANTHES.
BUCK-BEAN. See MENYANTHES.

BOLTONEA. [Compositæ.] Hardy herbaceous perennials, with pinkish flowers in September. Common garden soil. Propagated by division. The species are *B. asteroides* and *glastifolia*, natives of North America, introduced in 1758.

BORAGO. *Borage.* [Boraginaceæ.] Hardy annuals,

biennials, and perennials. The common Borage, a gay annual, is one of the best flowers to sow in the neighborhood of bees; for it is said they derive more nourishment from it than from any other flower that grows. Good garden soil. Propagated by seeds, which may be scattered over the surface and raked in, and the plants afterwards thinned where they are too much crowded. The perennials may be multiplied by parting the roots.

B. crassifolia (thick-leaved); herbaceous perennial; 2 feet; flowers pink, in June; Persia; 1822. *B. laxiflora* (loose-flowered); hardy biennial, trailing; flowers blue, in June; Corsica; 1813. *B. officinalis* (common); hardy annual; 3 feet; flowers blue or white, in June; England. *B. Orientalis* (Oriental); hardy perennial; 2 feet; flowers blue, in May; Turkey; 1752.

BOTTLE-GOURD. See LAGENARIA.

BOUVARDIA. [Cinchonaceæ.] Handsome small sub-shrubs, mostly greenhouse plants. Some of the species produce a profusion of scarlet blossoms, when planted out for the summer, in a bed of good peaty earth in the flower-garden. Of this habit are *B. triphylla* and a variety of it called *splendens*. The other greenhouse kinds require similar treatment; the stove species are not of much importance. The roots must be taken up in autumn, and potted and kept rather dry in a greenhouse, and in spring excited in a dung-frame, and hardened off afterwards to plant out as soon as danger from frost is past. These kinds are best propagated by pieces of the thicker roots, an inch or two long, set round against the side of a pot, just covered with soil, and the pots plunged in a dung-frame. When they begin to grow up, they should be potted separately; they grow well in a compost of turfy peat and loam.

B. Cavanillesii (Cavanille's); greenhouse sub-shrub; 3 feet; flowers scarlet, in May; Mexico; 1846. *B. flava* (yellow);

greenhouse sub-shrub; 3 feet; flowers yellow, in July; Mexico; 1845. *B. leiantha* (smooth-flowered); greenhouse sub-shrub; 3 feet; flowers deep scarlet, in June; Mexico; 1850. *B. triphylla* (three-leaved); greenhouse sub-shrub; 2 feet; flowers scarlet, in June; Mexico.

A larger flowered and very fine variety is called *splendens*.

Box. See Buxus.

Box Thorn. See Lycium.

Brachycome. *Swan-River Daisy*. [Compositæ.] Pretty half-hardy annuals. Soil, rich light earth. Propagated by seeds, which may be sown in heat about April, and, when large enough, planted out in the borders or beds six inches apart, or they may be sown thinly out of doors in May, and be thinned out; but the bloom is much later in general than when sown in heat and planted out in May. The plants are very pretty when grown in pots.

B. iberidifolia (iberis-leaved); half-hardy annual; 18 inches; flowers blue, in July; Swan River; 1840.

There is a pure white variety called *alba*, and various shades of blue and pink.

Bramble. See Rubus.

Briza. *Quaking Grass*. [Graminaceæ.] One of the many beautiful grasses which are so ornamental in the flower-garden, bearing roundish, drooping, chaffy-like clusters of flowers. Hardy annuals. The seeds may be sown in common soil in May.

B. maxima (largest); hardy annual grass; 18 inches; flowers in June; south of Europe; 1633. *B. rubra* (red); hardy annual grass; 1 foot; flowers in June; south of Europe; 1820. *B. virens*; hardy annual grass; 18 inches; flowers in July; Spain.

Broussonetia. *Paper Mulberry*. [Moraceæ.] Hardy trees, resembling Mulberry. Propagated by cuttings, suckers, and seeds.

B. papyrifera (paper-bearing); hardy tree; 20 feet; flowers purplish, in June; Japan; 1751. Of this there are varieties, *cucullata*, *dissecta*, *fructu-albo*, *macrophylla*, and *variegata*. This species is hardy as far north as Massachusetts. *B. spatulata* (spatulate); tree; 12 feet; Japan; 1824.

BROWALLIA. [Scrophulariaceæ.] Pretty half-hardy annuals or shrubs. The annuals grow in light rich soil, and are increased by seeds sown in March in a hot-bed, as other tender annuals. The shrubs grow in peat and loam, in equal proportions, and are propagated by cuttings, placed in a gentle heat.

B. demissa (low); half-hardy annual; 1 foot; flowers blue, in July; South America; 1735. There is a white variety. *B. elata* (tall); half-hardy annual; 2 feet; flowers blue, in July; Peru; 1768. There is a white variety. *B. grandiflora* (large-flowered); half-hardy annual; 2 feet; flowers light yellow, in June; Peru; 1829. *B. Jamesoni* (Jameson's); greenhouse sub-shrub, 3 feet; flowers orange, in July; New Grenada; 1846. *B. speciosa* (showy); tender annual; 18 inches; flowers purple, in July; Quindiu; 1846.

BRYANTHUS. [Ericaceæ.] Small evergreen shrubs now united to Menziesia, growing in sandy peat, and increased by cuttings in sand under a bell glass and kept cool. The plants must be kept from heat and drought.

B. erectus (erect); hardy evergreen; 1 foot; flowers blush, in June; a garden hybrid. *B. Gmelini;* hardy evergreen trailer; 6 inches; flowers red, in June; Kamtschatka. *B. Stelleri;* hardy evergreen trailer; 6 inches; flowers pale red, in June; Northwest America.

BRUGMANSIA. See DATURA.
BUCKTHORN. See RHAMNUS.
BUGLE. See AJUGA.
BUGLOSS. See ANCHUSA.
BULBOCODIUM. [Melanthaceæ.] Beautiful dwarf hardy

crocus-like bulbous plants. Soil, sandy loam. Increased by offsets.

B. vernum (spring); hardy bulb; 3 inches; flowers purple, in May; Spain; 1629. *B. versicolor* (various-colored); hardy bulb; 3 inches; flowers lilac and yellow, in September; Russia; 1820.

BUPLEARUM. *Hare's Ear.* [Umbelliferæ.] A genus consisting of about a dozen hardy annuals, as many hardy perennials, and four greenhouse evergreens, growing in sandy loam, and propagated by seeds, divisions, or cuttings. They are not very ornamental or desirable. The general color of the flowers is green and yellow.

BUPTHALMUM. *Ox-eye.* [Compositæ.] Shrubby and herbaceous plants, the former increasing by cuttings, the latter by division or by seeds, and all growing in a soil of equal parts sandy loam and leaf-mould.

B. grandiflorum (large-flowered); hardy perennial; 2 feet; flowers yellow, in August; Austria; 1722. *B. maritimum* (sea); half-hardy perennial; 1 foot; flowers yellow, all summer; Sicily; 1640. *B. salicifolium* (willow-leaved); hardy perennial; 18 inches; flowers yellow, in August; Austria; 1722. *B. speciosissimum* (most showy); hardy perennial; 2 feet; flowers yellow, in July; south of Europe; 1826.

Winter protection is necessary in the Northern States.

BURNET. See SANGUISORBA.
BURNING BUSH. See EUONYMUS.
BUTCHER'S BROOM. See RUSCUS.
BUTOMUS. [Butomaceæ.] Perennial aquatics, very ornamental on the margin of ponds or streams. Planted in rich mud, they soon establish themselves and increase rapidly. They require winter protection in the Northern States.

B. latifolius (broad-leaved); 1 foot; flowers white, in July;

Nepaul; 1823. *B. umbellatus* (umbelled); 3 feet; flowers pink, in August; England.

BUXUS. *Box-Tree*. [Euphorbiaceæ.] A family of ornamental evergreen shrubs and trees, some hardy, others requiring greenhouse protection. Propagated by seed, cuttings, and layers; the small variety used for edging, by division. *B sempervirens* and its varieties are hardy as far north as Massachusetts, though often browned by the winter's sun.

B. Australis (southern); 6 feet; New Holland; 1820. *B. Balearica* (Balearic); 8 feet; flowers yellow, green, in July; Minorca; 1780. *B. Chinensis* (Chinese); 3 feet; flowers yellow, green, in July; China; 1802. *B. sempervirens* (common evergreen); 8 feet; flowers yellow, green, in May; England. *B. sempervirens angustifolia* (narrow-leaved); 8 feet; flowers yellow, green, in May. *B. sempervirens arborescens* (tree-like); 30 feet; flowers yellow, green, in May; Britain. *B. sempervirens argentea* (silver-variegated); 30 feet; flowers yellow, green, in May; Britain. *B. sempervirens aurea* (golden-variegated); 30 feet; flowers yellow, green, in May; Britain. *B. sempervirens marginata* (yellow-edged); 30 feet; flowers yellow, green, in May; Britain. *B. sempervirens myrtifolia* (myrtle-leaved); 8 feet; flowers yellow, green, in May; Britain. *B. sempervirens suffruticosa* (sub-shrubby); 1 foot; flowers yellow, green. *B. sempervirens variegata* (variegated-leaved); 30 feet; flowers yellow, green, in May; Britain.

CACALIA. [Compositæ.] This genus consists partly of curious succulent plants (sometimes called *Kleinia*), and partly of herbaceous plants, among which are two pretty hardy annuals (sometimes called *Emilia*). The former are but seldom grown in this country, though very pretty little plants; the latter, commonly called "Tassel Flowers," are very popular garden flowers, and are propagated by seeds, which may be sown in the open borders in May, and the plants come into bloom during summer.

C. Alpina (Alpine); hardy herbaceous perennial; 2 feet; flowers purple, in July; Austria; 1739. *C. coccinea* (scarlet); hardy annual; 18 inches; flowers orange, in July; South America; 1799. *C. coccinea aurea;* flowers buff-orange; garden hybrid.

CŒLESTINA. [Compositæ.] Pretty half-hardy plants, suitable for bedding, forming fine dense plants in rich loamy soil, requiring greenhouse protection in winter. Propagated by seeds and cuttings.

C. ageratoides (ageratum-like); 1 foot; flowers blue, in August; New Spain; 1824; called also *Ageratum cœlestinum*. *C. cærulea* (sky-blue); 1 foot; flowers blue, in July; North America; 1732; called also *Eupatorium cœlestinum*. *C. micrantha* (small-flowered); 18 inches; flowers blue, in July; South America; 1800.

CAJOPHORA. [Loasaceæ.] Pretty biennial twining plants, which have been separated from Loasa. To be had in perfection, they should be sown in June or July, and kept through the winter in an airy greenhouse, and then planted out in May, to cover trellis-work, or trained around stakes in large pots, if that be preferred. They are readily increased by seed. Like the Loasas, they have stinging hairs. They usually bloom throughout the summer, or, if raised as above directed, they will also be in blossom through the spring months.

C. Herbertii (Herbert's); greenhouse climbing biennial; 6 feet; flowers orange-red, in June; a garden hybrid. *C. lateritia* (brick-colored); greenhouse climbing biennial; 10 feet; flowers brick-red, in May; Tucuman; 1836. *C. Pentlandica* (Pentland's); climbing biennial; 10 feet; flowers orange, in summer; Peru; 1841.

CALAIS. [Compositæ.] A hardy annual, growing in common garden soil. Propagated by seeds.

C. Lindleyi (Lindley's); hardy annual; flowers yellow, in July; North America; 1833.

CALAMINTHA. *Calamint.* [Labiaceæ.] Pretty herbaceous perennials. Common soil. Propagated by division.

C. alba (white); hardy perennial; 1 foot; flowers white, in July; Hungary; 1818. *C. Caroliniana* (Carolinian); hardy perennial; 1 foot; flowers flesh-color, in July; Carolina; 1804. *C. grandiflora* (large-flowered); hardy perennial; 1 foot; flowers, reddish-lilac, in July; Italy; 1596. Of this there is a variegated leaved variety. *C. sylvatica* (wood); hardy perennial; 1 foot; flowers pale rose, in August; England.

CALAMPELIS. [Bignoniaceæ.] Beautiful half-hardy climbers, well suited for arbors or trellises in summer. The blossoms are tubular, orange-colored, in loose panicles and very showy; the seed-pod is ornamental. Light loamy soil. Propagated by seeds and cuttings. Requires greenhouse in winter. The plant is often called Eccremocarpus.

C. scabra (rough); half-hardy climbing perennial; 15 feet; flowers orange, all summer; Chili; 1834.

CALANDRINA. [Portulaceæ.] A family of herbaceous plants which do well treated as annuals. They should be started early from seed in a moderate hot-bed, and planted out in a dry hot situation after the weather has become settled. If sown in August, and wintered in a greenhouse, they flower finely in the border the following summer. They need a sunny exposure, as the flowers only expand in the sun.

C. discolor (two-colored); 2 feet; flowers rosy purple, in July; Chili; 1834. *C. grandiflora* (large-flowered); 2 feet; flowers rose purple, in July; Chili; 1826. *C. procumbens* (procumbent); 3 inches; flowers rose purple, in July; Peru; 1827. *C. speciosa* (showy); 3 inches; flowers rose, in July; California; 1831. *C. umbellata* (umbelled); 6 inches; flowers rose-purple, in July; Peru; 1826.

There are other species some of which are stove plants.

CALCEOLARIA. Shrubs and herbaceous plants, properly greenhouse plants, but doing well in the border in summer. The shrubby varieties are far superior to the herbaceous, and are very useful for summer decoration. Calceolarias are, strictly speaking, greenhouse plants, and will bear no frost. They are generally kept, until they are rising for bloom, in pits, where frost can be kept out by mats or other coverings; for any thing short of frost will not hurt them. They are propagated by cuttings of the side-shoots, which root freely if planted in light sandy peat, about October; but they do not root freely if planted in spring or summer. Seeds may be sown in pans, or wide-mouthed pots, in August, and the seedlings potted off, six or eight in a pot, when large enough; and after this, when they have got forward enough, put singly in small pots, to be changed from time to time for larger: these bloom early the following year. Later blooming plants may be had by sowing in spring. The stems require no support, unless the plants are to be carried out, in which case they require a stake to every stem. The soil should be light rich loam, well drained. *C. integrifolia*, and its varieties *angustifolia* and *viscosissima*, are brilliant flower-garden dwarf shrubby plants, bearing large masses of yellow blossoms from May throughout the summer. The florist's varieties are very numerous, and are constantly undergoing change and improvement.

C. alba (white); greenhouse evergreen sub-shrub; 2 feet; flowers white, in June; Chili; 1844. *C. amplexicaulis* (stem-clasping); greenhouse perennial; 2 feet; flowers yellow, in June; Peru; 1845. *C. arachnoidea* (cobwebbed); greenhouse perennial; 1 foot; flowers purple, in June; Chili; 1827. *C. bicolor* (two-colored); greenhouse evergreen sub-shrub; 2 feet; flowers yellow, in August; Peru; 1829. *C. corymbosa* (corymb-flowered); greenhouse perennial; 18 inches; flowers yellow, in May; Chili; 1822. *C. crenatiflora* (crenate); greenhouse perennial; 18 inches; flowers yellow-spotted, in June; Chili; 1831. *C. integrifolia* (entire-leaved); greenhouse or half-hardy evergreen shrub; 18 inches; flowers deep yellow, all summer; Chili; 1822. The variety *angustifolia* has pale flowers: *viscossissima* is much deeper colored. *C. pinnata* (pinnate); half-hardy annual; 2 feet; flowers yellow, in July; Peru; 1773. *C. purpurea* (purple); greenhouse perennial; 1 foot; flowers purple, in July; Chili; 1827. *C. thyrsiflora* (thyrse-flowered); greenhouse evergreen shrub; 18 inches; flowers yellow, in July; Chili; 1827. *C. violaceæ* (violet); greenhouse evergreen sub-shrub; 2 feet; flowers violet, in June; Chili; 1852.

The shrubby varieties General Outram, Queen of Oude, Kentish Hero, Etna, Little Dorrit, Prince of Orange, Princess Helena, Rubens, General Havelock, Nobey, Ambassador, Beauty of Montreal, Queen, and Victor Emmanuel, do well as bedding plants.

CALENDULA. *Marigold.* [Compositæ.] Showy hardy or half-hardy annuals and greenhouse shrubs. The hardy annual species succeed in common garden soil, and are readily ncreased by seeds, which should be sown in May. The half-hardy sorts should be reared on a slight hot-bed in April, and planted out in May. The common Marigold is very brilliant.

C. hybrida (hybrid) ; great Cape Marigold ; half-hardy annual ; 1 foot ; flowers white and brown, in July; Cape ; 1752. *C. nudicaulis* (naked-stalked) ; hardy annual ; 1 foot ; flowers white and purple, in July ; Cape ; 1731. *C. officinalis* (officinal) ; common Marigold ; hardy annual ; 1 foot; flowers deep orange, in June ; south of Europe ; 1751. *C. officinalis flore-pleno;* a double-flowered variety. *C. pluvialis* (rainy) ; small Cape Marigold ; half-hardy annual ; 1 foot ; flowers white, in July; Cape ; 1693.

CALLICHROA. [Compositæ.] A pretty dwarf hardy annual. It grows in common garden soil, and is increased by seeds, which should be sown in May.

C. platyglossa (broad-rayed) ; hardy annual ; 1 foot ; flowers yellow, in July ; California ; 1835.

CALLIOPSIS. [Compositæ.] Extremely showy hardy annuals, also known as Coreopsis. They may be sown in gentle heat to forward them, pricked out five or six in a pot, and kept growing in the house until the middle of May, when the balls of earth may be turned out whole, the plants being undisturbed. But it is better to sow in the open border. When sown thus, it must be in May, and these will come into flower in July, a month after those turned out of pots in a forward state. This flower ought, of course, to be planted behind shorter things, about even with Sweet Peas, branching Larkspurs, and things of similar growth. It does not make a bad appearance mixed with branching Larkspurs on large borders ; for both show only their flowers, the stems of neither being large enough to interfere with their abundant bloom, and the beautiful blue of the one contrasting well with the orange-yellow black-eyed flowers of the other. *C. Drummondii* is dwarfer, but equally beautiful.

C. bicolor (two-colored); hardy annual; 2½ feet; flowers orange and black, in July; Arkansas; 1822. Of this, formerly called *Coreopsis tinctoria*, there are several varieties. *C. Drummondii* (Drummond's); hardy annual; 2 feet; flowers yellow and brown, in July; Texas; 1834.

There are many new varieties among which we may mention *C. Atkinsonia*, yellow and crimson; *cardiminifolia hybrida*, bright yellow; *coronata*, crimson and yellow; *Burridgii*, crimson golden edge.

CALLIRHOE. [Malvaceæ.] A fine tribe of hardy annuals, flourishing in garden soil, and raised from seed sown in May.

C. involucrata; hardy annual; 1 foot; flowers rosy-crimson, all summer; North America. *C. pedata;* hardy annual; 2 feet; flowers purple, with white eye, all summer; North America; variety *nana*, a dwarf variety. *C. verticillata;* hardy annual; 6 inches; flowers purple, with white eye; North America.

CALLISTEPHUS OR CALLISTEMMA. *China Aster.* [Compositæ.] Callistemma hortense is a favorite annual. The German varieties, with flowers single, semi-double, or double, self-colored, red, pink, dark and light purple, or striped in all ways, form a varied and striking feature towards the end of the summer wherever they are introduced. To have them in perfection, plant them in half well-decomposed dung and half loam, or add plenty of manure to the soil of the garden. Sow them in a hot-bed in March or April; plant them out in May. If planted in beds, — in which way they are very effective, — let the bed be supplied with a good dressing of dung, and plant them a foot apart every way: keep them clear of weeds, and, in dry sultry weather, let them have plenty of water. They will bloom much better treated in this way; though when planted about the borders, wherever there happens to be room, they add greatly to the beauty of the garden, because their colors are so varied. The best flowers should be marked for seeding.

C. Chinensis (Chinese); hardy annual; 1 foot; flowers in July; China; 1731.

There are varieties of various colors, as well as double and quilled flowers.

CALLUNA. *Heather.* [Ericaceæ.] Pretty dwarf hardy evergreen shrubs. Soil, peat. Increased by layers or by seeds.

C. vulgaris (common); hardy evergreen shrub; 1 foot; flowers flesh-color, in April; England.

This plant has lately been found growing wild in Tewksbury, Mass., with every indication of its being indigenous to this continent. The question has provoked much argument, and is of great interest to botanists. See "Silliman's Journal," and "Journal of Boston Society of Natural History," *passim;* also "Proceedings of Massachusetts Horticultural Society for 1861."

The varieties bearing double or white or red or scarlet flowers, or that with variegated leaves, are very pretty plants for the American or peat border.

CALOPHACA. [Leguminosæ.] A hardy deciduous shrub, very ornamental, grafted standard high on the Laburnum. Common light loam. Propagated by seeds or cuttings under a bell glass.

C. Wolgarica (Wolga); hardy shrub; 2 feet; flowers yellow, in June; Siberia; 1780.

CALOPHANES. [Acanthaceæ.] Half-hardy perennial, growing in sandy loam and peat. Propagated by division.

C. oblongifolia (oblong-leaved); tender perennial; 1 foot; flowers blue, in August; Carolina; 1832.

The plant requires winter protection.

CALOPOGON. [Orchidaceæ.] A fine native orchid, but of difficult culture. Soil, moist peat and sand.

C. pulchellum (pretty); hardy perennial; 6 inches; flowers purple, in July; North America; 1771.

CALTHA. *Marsh-marigold.* [Ranunculaceæ.] Hardy perennial water-plants, of easy culture, propagated by dividing the roots. They are suited for planting on the margin of a piece of water, where their bright-colored blossoms are very showy. The most ornamental is the double-flowered variety of our wild species *(C. palustris flore-pleno.)* Though growing best in the immediate vicinity of water, and most appropriate for rough scenery, they do very well in other situations, if the soil is damp; and the variety above named is sufficiently showy to make it worth introducing among hardy perennials in a mixed border.

C. natans (floating); hardy aquatic, floating; flowers yellow, in May; Siberia; 1816. *C. palustris flore-pleno;* hardy perennial; 18 inches; flowers golden, in May; a garden variety. *C. parnassiæfolia* (parnassia-leaved); hardy perennial; 6 inches; flowers yellow, in May; North America; 1815.

There are ten other species.

CALYCANTHUS. *Allspice.* [Calycanthaceæ.] Hardy deciduous shrubs, remarkable for the fragrant spice-like odor of their brownish blossoms. Moist, light, loamy garden soil. Increased by layers.

C. floridus; hardy shrub; 6 feet; flowers brown, in June; Carolina; 1726.

There are several varieties of this species. The other species are *C. fertilis, glaucus, lævigatus, macrophyllus, oblongifolius, occidentalis,* and *Pennsylvanicus,* all with fragrant brownish-purple flowers.

CALYPSO. [Orchidaceæ.] A beautiful and very rare native orchid, growing in rich sandy peat, in a moist cool exposure.

C. borealis (northern); hardy perennial; 6 inches; flowers rose and brown, in May; North America; 1820.

CALYSTEGIA. [Convolvulaceæ.] Convolvulus-like twining or trailing perennial plants, hardy or mostly so. Their culture is extremely simple; a fragment of the perennial root merely requires to be placed in the ground, and it will soon establish itself, and, if not checked, spread, and become a troublesome weed. Sandy loam is most congenial to them. *C. Soldanella* should be occasionally watered with salt water.

C. Catesbiana (Catesby's); flowers rose, in July; Carolina; 1816. *C. Dahurica* (Dahurian); hardy climbing perennial; 18 inches; flowers pink, in July; Dahuria; 1823. *C. pubescens* (pubescent); hardy climbing perennial; 6 feet; flowers pink, double and single, in July; China; 1844. *C. sepium* (great hedge); hardy climbing perennial; 6 feet; flowers white or rose-color, in June; England. *C. Soldanella* (Soldanella); hardy trailing perennial; 1 foot; flowers flesh-color, in June; England. *C. spithamæa*; hardy climbing perennial; 1 foot; flowers white, in July; North America; 1796. *C. sylvestris* (wood); flowers white, in July Hungary; 1815. *C. tomentosa* (woolly); flowers pinkish-white, in June; North America; 1818.

CAMPANULA. [Campanulaceæ.] Very handsome plants, comprising annuals, biennials, and perennials, mostly hardy, with a few greenhouse species. The annuals should be sown in the open border in May, the seed being slightly covered on account of its small size. The perennial hardy kinds are increased by seeds or division, and require no peculiar treatment. The biennials are sown in May and June for blooming the following year. Good garden soil suits them all, but it should be rather rich for the Canterbury-bell. The Chimney Campanula is undoubtedly one of the best for pot culture, and requires the protection of a frame or greenhouse. The compost for it should be loam from rotted turfs one-half, dung from a spent hot-bed one-fourth, and turfy peat one-fourth, well mixed together. Select a small healthy plant, place it in a four-inch pot, and grow it in a frame : if it should throw up a stem for bloom, take off the top at once ; and when the pot is full of roots, change it for a six-inch pot, using the same kind of compost. Thus continue to grow it, changing the pot for a larger as fast as the roots fill up the one it is in. The second season it may bloom ; but continue the changing into larger pots, and, when it is three years old, it will produce many spikes of bloom, which should be spread fan-like on a trellis, and, in this state, it completely covers a fireplace or a window with its numerous beautiful blue flowers. The smaller perennials make beautiful rock-plants.

C. aurea (golden); greenhouse shrub ; 3 feet; flowers yellow, in July; Madeira; 1777. *C. barbata* (bearded); hardy perennial; 2 feet ; flowers light or dark blue, in June ; Italy ; 1752. *C. Carpatica* (Carpathian); hardy perennial ; 18 inches ; flowers blue or white, in June ; Carpathian Alps ; 1774. *C. fragilis* (fragile) ; half-hardy perennial, trailing ; flowers pale-blue, in August ; Alps of Italy ; 1826. *C. Garganica* (Gargangian); half-hardy perennial, trailing ; flowers pale-blue, in July ; Gargania ; 1830. *C. grandis* (large); half-hardy perennial ; 3 feet; flowers purple, in August ; Natolia ; 1842. *C. Loreyi* (Lorey's); hardy annual ; 1 foot ; flowers blue or white, in June ; Italy ; 1824. *C. macrantha* (large-flowered); hardy perennial ; 3 feet; flowers purple, in August ; Russia ; 1822. *C. medium* (Canterbury-bell); hardy biennial ; 3 feet ; flowers blue or white, single or double, in June ; Germany; 1597. *C. nitida* (shining) ; hardy perennial); 1 foot ; flowers blue or white, single or double, in July; North America ; 1731. *C. nobilis* (noble); hardy perennial ; 2 feet ; flowers lilac-purple, in July ; China ; 1844. *C. persicifolia* (peach-leaved); hardy perennial ; 3 feet; flowers dark-blue or white,

single or double, in July; Europe; 1596. *C. pulla* (russet);
hardy perennial; 6 inches; flowers purple, in June; Austria;
1779. *C. pumila* (dwarf); hardy perennial; 6 inches; flowers
blue or white, in June; Switzerland; introduction uncertain.
C. pyramidalis (chimney); perennial; 4 feet; flowers blue or
white, in August; Carniolia; 1594. *C. sylvatica* (wood); hardy
annual; 1 foot; flowers blue, in June; Nepaul; 1840. *C. thyrsoidea* (thyrse-flowered); hardy biennial; 2 feet; flowers blue,
in June; Switzerland; 1785. *C. Vidalii* (Capt. Vidal's); greenhouse or half-hardy shrub; 3 feet; flowers white, in August;
Azores; 1851.

There are more than one hundred and fifty species and
varieties, all worthy of garden culture.

CANARY-BIRD FLOWER. See TROPÆOLUM.
CANDLEBERRY MYRTLE. SEE MYRICA.
CANDYTUFT. See IBERIS.
CANTERBURY BELLS. See CAMPANULA.
CANNA. *Indian Shot.* [Marantaceæ.] Stove perennial
herbs, of considerable stature. The seeds are as large as
sweet peas, and as hard as flint. Stove or hot-bed heat is
required to bring up the plants, which are tall, reed-like, with
showy scarlet or yellow flowers. They grow well in loam
and dung, and require large pots to grow them successfully.
In April fill some well-drained pots with soil, and sow in
them a couple of seeds, not more than half an inch deep.
Place these pots in a hot-bed, and in a few days the plants
will shoot up. Let them have water enough to keep them
moist, and, as they grow, destroy the weakest plant, shifting
the others by removing the balls whole into larger pots; and
having kept them in the hot-bed a day or two to establish
them, remove them to the stove, or, if you have not a stove,
to the greenhouse, and plant in the open border about the
last of May. They perfect their seed in this country. All
the species flower well in warm situations, planted out in

the flower-border, and are very effective both in foliage and blossom. For this purpose the plants are turned out about the middle of May. When once reared, the plants may be perpetuated by division.

C. Achiras (Achiras); 5 feet; flowers dark-red, in August; Isle of Mendoza; 1829. *C. angustifolia* (narrow-leaved); 2 feet; flowers scarlet, in July; South America; 1824. *C. aurantiaca* (orange); 4 feet; flowers orange, in September; Brazil; 1824. *C. carnea* (flesh-colored); 4 feet; flowers flesh-color, in September; Brazil; 1822. *C. coccinea* (scarlet); 2 feet; flowers scarlet, in September; South America; 1731. *C. compacta* (compact); 2 feet; flowers red, in July; East Indies; 1820. *C. crocea* (saffron-colored); 2 feet; flowers red, in July; 1823. *C. denudata* (naked); 2 feet; flowers scarlet, in June; Brazil; 1818. *C. denudata latifolia* (broad-leaved); 3 feet; flowers red, in July; Brazil; 1818. *C. discolor* (two-colored-leaved); 10 feet; flowers scarlet, in September; Trinidad; 1827. *C. edulis* (eatable); 3 feet; flowers red, in September; Peru; 1820. *C. esculenta* (esculent); 4 feet; flowers red, in September; South America; 1822. *C. excelsa* (lofty); 16 feet; flowers scarlet, in September; Brazil; 1820. *C. flaccida* (weak); 5 feet; flowers red, in July; South Carolina; 1788. *C. gigantea* (gigantic); 5 feet; flowers red and yellow, in July; south of Europe; 1809. *C. glauca* (milky-green); 2 feet; flowers yellow, in September; South America; 1730. *C. glauca rubrolutea* (yellow and red); 4½ feet; flowers yellowish-red, in August; Jamaica; 1834. *C. glauca rufa* (reddish-brown); 2 feet; flowers brown, in July; South America. *C. Indica* (Indian); 2 feet; flowers scarlet, in September; India; 1570. *C. maculata* (spotted); 2 feet; flowers reddish-yellow, in September; India. *C. iridiflora* (iris-flowered); 6 feet; flowers red, in September; Peru; 1816. *C. juncea* (rush-like); 1 foot; flowers red, in May; Indies; 1820. *C. Lagunensis* (Laguna); 5 feet; flowers yellow, in September; Laguna; 1828. *C. Lamberti* (Lambert's); 4 feet; flowers scarlet, in July; Trinidad; 1819. *C. lanceolata* (spear-leaved); 3 feet; flowers red, in September; Brazil; 1825. *C. lanuginosa* (woolly); 6 feet; flowers deep scarlet, in July; 1823. *C. latifolia* (broad-leaved); 10 feet; flowers pink, in September; Brazil; 1820. *C. limbata* (bordered); 3 feet; flowers red, in September; Brazil; 1818. *C. lutea* (yellow); 2 feet; flowers yellow, in September; East Indies; 1829. *C. Nepalensis* (Nepaul); 6 feet; flowers straw-color, in August; Nepaul; 1862. *C. Occidentalis* (Western); 3 feet; flowers reddish-yellow, in June; West Indies; 1822. *C. Orientalis* (Eastern); 4 feet; flowers red, in June; East Indies; 1820. *C. Orientalis flava* (yellow); 4 feet; flowers yellow, in June; East Indies; 1820. *C. Orientalis maculata* (spotted); flowers scarlet and yellow, in August; East Indies; 1570. *C. pallida* (pale-flowering); 4 feet; flowers pale-yellow, in June; West Indies; 1820. *C. pallida latifolia* (broad-leaved); 3 feet; flowers yellow, in June; West Indies; 1820. *C. patens* (spreading); 2 feet; flowers reddish-yellow, in June; Rio Janerio; 1778. *C. pedunculata* (long-flower-stalked); 6 feet; flowers orange, in October; 1820. *C. polymorpha* (many-formed); 3 feet; flowers red, in September; South America; 1825. *C. Reevesii* (Reeve's); 5 feet; flowers yellow, in June; China; 1835. *C. rubra* (red); 3 feet; flowers red, in September; West Indies; 1820. *C. rubricaulis* (red-stemmed); 3 feet; flowers red, in July; 1821. *C. sanguinea* (bloody); 4 feet; flowers red, in September; South America; 1820. *C. speciosa* (showy); 3 feet; flowers red, in August; South America; 1820. *C. sylvestris* (wild); 5 feet; flowers scarlet, in September; South America; 1820. *C. variabilis* (variable); 3 feet; flowers red, in September; India; 1822. *C. Warszewiczii* (Warszewicz's); 3¼ feet; flowers scarlet, in September; Costa Rica; 1849.

CANNABIS. *Hemp.* [Urticaceæ.] Hardy, and an annual in this country. Though insignificant in its flowers, the Hemp is yet a stately plant when grown freely, remarkable for its fine palmate foliage. It merely requires to be sown in rich garden soil, and the plants allowed to stand out separately. In wilderness scenery it has a fine appearance.

C. sativa (common); hardy annual; 6 feet; flowers green, in June; India; introduction uncertain.

CAPE MARIGOLD.   See CALENDULA.

CAPRIFOLIUM. *Honeysuckle.* [Caprifoliaceæ.] A genus of mostly deciduous, and some evergreen, climbers, generally hardy, too well known to need description. Propagated by seeds, cuttings, and layers. The hardy species require little care, except pruning; the half-hardy are better laid down and covered with earth in the winter.

C. dioicum (diœcious); 6 feet; flowers purple, in June; North America; 1776.   *C. Douglasii* (Douglas's); 20 feet; flowers orange, in July; North America; 1824.   *C. Etruscum* (Etruscan); 15 feet; flowers orange, in May; Italy. *C. flavum* (yellow); 10 feet; flowers yellow, in May; Carolina; 1810.   *C. gratum* (pleasant); evergreen; 20 feet; flowers red, in July; North America; 1730.   *C. hirsutum* (hairy-leaved); 20 feet; flowers yellow, in May; Canada; 1822.   *C. longiflorum* (long-flowered); climber; flowers yellow, white, in July; China; 1826.   *C. Occidentale* (Western); 20 feet; flowers orange, in July; Fort Vancouver; 1824.   *C. periclymenum* (woodbine); 20 feet; flowers yellow, in June; Britain.   *C. periclymenum Belgica* (Dutch); 20 feet; flowers yellow, in June.   *C. periclymenum quercifolium* (oak-leaved); 20 feet; flowers yellow, red, in June.   *C. periclymenum serotinum* (late-red); 20 feet; flowers yellow, red, in June.   *C. periclymenum variegatum* (variegated); 15 feet; flowers yellow, red, in June; Britain.   *C. sempervirens* (evergreen); 15 feet; flowers scarlet, in June; North America; 1656.   *C. sempervirens Brownii* (Brown's); 20 feet; flowers bright-scarlet, in May.   *C. sempervirens major* (larger-flowered); 20 feet; flowers scarlet, in May.   *C. sempervirens minus* (less trumpet); 15 feet; flowers scarlet, in June; Carolina; 1656.

C. brachypoda (Lonicera) variegata is a very beautiful variety, lately introduced from Japan, with fine variegated foliage, and does well if covered with earth in winter.

CAPSICUM. [Solanaceæ.] Annuals requiring a warm sunny exposure. The plants should be started in a hot-bed in April, and pricked out when all danger of frost is over:

they need a rich soil. The shrubby species thrive in a stove, and are very ornamental. The greater number will ripen fruit in the open air, and, from the different colors of the fruit, white, purple, blue, green, red, and yellow, are attractive in garden or conservatory.

C. annuum (Guinea pepper); half-hardy annual; 1 foot; fruit erect, usually red; India; 1548. *C. baccatum* (bird-pepper); stove shrub; 3 feet; fruit erect, red; India; 1731. *C. bicolor* (two-colored); stove shrub; 3 feet; flowers white and purple; fruit erect, violaceous; West Indies; 1804. *C. cerasiforme* (cherry-pepper); stove shrub; 3 feet; fruit erect, red or yellow; South America; 1739. *C. cereolum* (waxy); stove shrub; 3 feet; fruit pendent, yellow; South America; 1850. *C. cordiforme* (heart-shaped); half-hardy annual; 2 feet; fruit pendent, red or yellow; India; 1548. *C. frutescens* (fruiting); 1 foot; flowers pale-yellow; India; 1656. *C. Millerii* (Miller's); flowers white; West Indies; 1824.

CARAGANA. *Pea-Tree.* [Leguminoseæ.] Pretty, hardy, and chiefly low-growing shrubs; the most interesting of which are kept grafted, as standards in the nurseries, and make beautiful little pendent trees. The stock used is *C. arborescens*, which is increased by seeds. The rest may be increased by layering, and the spreading sorts are suitable for large rock gardens. Sandy, loamy soil.

C. arborescens (tree-like); a small deciduous tree; 15 feet; flowers yellow, in May; Siberia; 1752. *C. var. inesmis* (unarmed); 10 feet; Siberia; 1820. *C. Altagana* (Siberian pea); hardy shrub; 3 feet; flowers yellow, in May; Siberia; 1789. *C. Chamlagu* (Chinese); hardy shrub; 3 feet; flowers yellow, in May; China; 1773. *C. frutescens* (shrubby); hardy shrub; 6 feet; flowers yellow, in May; Russia; 1752. *C. jubata* (crested); hardy shrub; 2 feet; flowers white and red, in May; Siberia; 1796. *C. pygmæa* (pygmy); hardy shrub; 3 feet; flowers yellow, in May; Siberia; 1751. *C. spinosa* (spiny); hardy shrub; 3 feet; flowers yellow, in May; Siberia; 1755.

CARDAMINE. [Cruciferæ.] Hardy perennials, growing in common moist soil. Increased by division.

C. amara (bitter); aquatic; 1 foot; flowers white, in May; Britain. *C. asarifolia* (asarum-leaved); 1 foot; flowers white, in June; Italy; 1710. *C. bellidifolia* (daisy-leaved); 1 foot; flowers white, in May; Scotland. *C. bellidifolia Alpina* (Alpine); 1 foot; flowers white, in May; Austria; 1658. *C. chelidonia* (celandine-leaved); 1 foot; flowers white, in June; Italy; 1739. *C. glauca* (milky-green); 1 foot; flowers white, in June; Calabria; 1827. *C. latifolia* (broad-leaved); marsh plants; 2 feet; flowers purple, in June; Spain; 1710. *C. macrophylla* (large-leaved); 1 foot; flowers purple, in May; Siberia; 1824. *C. pratensis* (meadow); marsh-plant; 1 foot; flowers purple, in May; Britain. *C. pratensis plena* (double-flowered); marsh-plant; 1 foot; flowers purple, in May. *C. pratensis plena-alba* (double white-flowered); marsh-plant; 1 foot; flowers white, in May. *C. thalictroides* (thalictrum-like); annual; 1 foot; flowers white, in June; Piedmont; 1818. *C. trifolia* (three-leaved); 2 feet; flowers white, in May; Switzerland; 1629. *C. uliginosa* (bog); marsh-plant; 1 foot; flowers white, in May; Tauria; 1819.

CARDINAL FLOWER. See LOBELIA.

CARDIOSPERMUM. [Sapindaceæ.] A family of ornamental climbers, commonly known as "balloon vine." They need a light warm soil and a sunny exposure, and are useful for covering arbors and trellisses. Propagated by seed sown in May.

C. Halicacabum (smooth-leaved); tender-annual; 5 feet; flowers white, in July; India; 1594. The other species are *C. Corindum* and *pubescens*.

CARDUUS. *Thistle.* [Compositæ.] A genus of rank-growing plants with showy flowers. Although generally regarded as weeds, some of the species do well in shrubbery, and are not unornamental. They are annual, biennial, and perennial, and are generally propagated by seed.

CARNATION. See DIANTHUS.
CAROLINA ALLSPICE. See CALYCANTHUS.
CARPINUS. *Hornbeam.* [Corylaceæ.] A family of hard-wooded ornamental trees, of rapid growth, hardy and desirable. The European species are used for hedges. Propagated by seed or layers. Grow in rich loamy soil.

C. Americana (American); 20 feet; North America; 1812. *C. betulus* (common); 30 feet; flowers in March; Britain. *C. betulus incisa* (cut-leaved); 15 feet. *C. betulus quercifolia* (oak-leaved); 30 feet; flowers in May; Europe. *C. betulus variegata* (variegated); 20 feet; Britain. *C. betulus aurea-variegata* (golden-variegated-leaved); 20 feet; 1845. *C. Orientalis* (Eastern); 12 feet; Levant; 1739.

CARTHAMUS. [Compositæ.] Hardy annuals. They are best sown on a gentle hot-bed in spring, and transplanted into the open borders in May. Rich garden soil.

C. tinctorius (dyer's); half-hardy annual; 3 feet; flowers orange, in July; Egypt; 1551. *C. oxycantha* (sharp-spined); half-hardy annual; 2 feet; Caucasus; 1818.

CARYA. *Walnut.* [Juglandiaceæ.] A family of hardy deciduous trees, too well known to need description. Propagated by seed. The trees transplant with difficulty, having a long tap-root.

C. alba (white shag-bark hickory); 30 feet; flowers in May; 1629. *C. amara* (bitter-nut); 30 feet; flowers in May; 1800. *C. compressa* (compressed-fruited); 30 feet; flowers in May; 1730. *C. laciniosa* (jagged); 30 feet; flowers in May. *C. microcarpa* (small-fruited); 30 feet; flowers in May. *C. obcordata* (reversed heart-shaped); 30 feet; flowers in May; 1812. *C. olivæformis* (olive-shaped); 30 feet; flowers in May. *C. porcina* (pig-nut); 30 feet; flowers in May; 1799. *C. porcina glabra* (smooth); flowers in May. *C. sulcata* (furrowed); 30 feet; flowers in May; 1804. *C. tomentosa* (woolly); 30 feet; flowers in May. *C. tomentosa maxima* (greatest fruited); 60 feet; flowers in May.

CASSANDRA. See ANDROMEDA.

CASSIA. [Leguminoseæ.] A large genus, mostly stove shrubs. There are, however, some annuals and perennials which do well in the garden. Propagated by seed and division. Good loamy soil. There are more than two hundred species.

C. Burmannii (Burman's); tender annual; 1 foot; flowers yellow, in July; Cape of Good Hope; 1810. *C. Marilandica* (Maryland); hardy perennial; 4 feet; flowers yellow and black, in August; North America. *C. nictitans* (twinkling); hardy annual; 1 foot; flowers yellow, in July; North America; 1800. *C. procumbens* (lying down); hardy annual; 14 inches; flowers yellow, in July; North America; 1806.

CASSIOPE. [Ericaceæ.] Pretty, diminutive heath-like shrubs, related to Andromeda. Peat soil; a moist, cool, shady situation. Propagated by cuttings or layers.

C. fastigiata (fastigiate); hardy evergreen shrub; 1 foot; flowers white, in July; North India; 1852. *C. hypnoides* (hypnum-like); hardy evergreen shrub; 6 inches; flowers white, in June; Siberia; North America; 1798. *C. lycopodioides* (clubmoss-like); hardy evergreen shrub; 6 inches; flowers red, in July; Siberia. *C. tetragona* (four-cornered); hardy evergreen shrub; 6 inches; flowers white, in May; Siberia; 1810.

CASTANEA. *Chestnut.* [Corylaceæ.] Generally hardy trees, ornamental in foliage and flower, and valuable for fruit. The Sweet Chestnut *(C. vesca)* and its varieties are tender in the Northern States, but farther south may become valuable trees.

C. Americana (American); 50 feet; flowers white, in May; America. *C. Chinensis* (China); 50 feet; flowers green, in May; China. *C. pumila* (dwarf); 12 feet; flowers green, yellow, in July; North America; 1699. *C. vesca* (Spanish edible); 50 feet; flowers green, in June; England. *C. vesca asplenifolia* (asplenium-leaved); 50 feet; flowers green, in May; Europe.

C. vesca cochleata (spiral); flowers green, in May. *C. vesca corallina-variegata* (coral-variegated); flowers green, in May; 1846. *C. vesca cucullata* (hooded); flowers green, in May; 1846. *C. vesca foliis-aureis* (golden-leaved); 50 feet; flowers green, in June. *C. vesca glabra* (smooth-leaved); flowers green, in May. *C. vesca glauca* (milky green); flowers green, in June. *C. vesca lucida* (shining-leaved); flowers green, in May; 1846. *C. vesca media* (intermediate); 50 feet; flowers green, in June; Europe. *C. vesca Princei* (Prince's); flowers green, in May; 1846. *C. vesca pumila* (dwarf); flowers green, in May; 1846. *C. vesca variegata* (variegated-leaved); flowers green, in May.

CASTILLEJA. [Scrophulariaceæ.] Pretty annuals and perennials. Sandy peat soil. Increased by seeds, or division of the root.

C. coccinea (scarlet-bracted); hardy annual; 6 inches; flowers yellow, in July; North America; 1787. *C. grandiflora* (large-flowered); half-hardy perennial; 18 inches; flowers purple and yellow, in July; Louisiana; 1811. *C. lithospermoides* (gromwell-like); greenhouse perennial; 2 feet; flowers scarlet, in August; Mexico; 1848. *C pallida* (pale); hardy perennial; 1 foot; flowers light purple; Siberia; 1782. *C. septentrionale* (Northern); hardy annual; 2 feet; flowers white and green, in August; Labrador; 1824.

CATALPA. [Bignoniaceæ.] A family of hardy and tender trees, very ornamental in leaf and flower. They thrive best in rich deep damp soil. Propagated by seeds, root-cuttings, and cuttings.

C. syringifolia (lilac-leaved); tree; 30 feet; flowers white, purple, and orange, in July; North America. *C. Kempferii* (Kempfer's); hardy shrub; 9 feet; flowers yellowish-white, with crimson blotches, in July; Japan; 1860.

CATANANCHE. [Compositæ.] Hardy perennial free-growing plants, requiring ordinary garden soil. They are best propagated by seeds, and treated as biennials.

C. cærulea (blue); hardy perennial; 3 feet; flowers blue or white, in July; south of Europe; 1596. Variety *bicolor*; white and blue; garden hybrid. *C. lutea* (yellow); hardy annual; 1 foot; flowers yellow, in July; Candia; 1640.

CATCHFLY. See SILENE.

CATMINT. See NEPETA.

CEANOTHUS. [Rhamnaceæ.] Hardy or half-hardy evergreen and deciduous shrubs, generally worthy of cultivation in the shrubbery. They are mostly of free growth and neat habit; flowers numerous and showy. Propagated either by cuttings, which should be planted in sandy soil under handglasses, or by layers, which is the readiest way of obtaining strong plants. They are not particular as to soil, but grow well in sandy loam, and, not being very hardy, the situation ought to be a well-drained one. The Californian species may be considered as hardy, in mild winters, south of Philadelphia.

C. Americanus (New-Jersey tea); hardy shrub; 2 feet; flowers white, in August; North America. *C. ovalis* much resembles this in flower. *C. azureus* (azure-flowered) half-hardy evergreen shrub; 10 feet; flowers pale-blue, in August; Mexico; 1818. *C. cuneatus* (wedge-leaved); half-hardy evergreen shrub; 5 feet; flowers white, in April; California; 1848. *C. dentatus* (tooth-leaved); half-hardy evergreen shrub; 5 feet; flowers blue, in May; California; 1848. *C. floribundus* (many-flowered); half-hardy evergreen shrub; 5 feet; flowers deep blue, in June; California; 1852. *C. Lobbianus* (Lobb's); half-hardy evergreen shrub; 5 feet; flowers blue, in June; California; 1852. *C. pallidus* (pale-flowered); half-hardy shrub; 10 feet; flowers pale-blue, in summer; North America; 1838. *C. papillosus* (papillose); half-hardy evergreen shrub; 5 feet; flowers violet-blue, in May; California; 1848. *C. rigidus* (stiff); half-hardy shrub; flowers blue; California; 1848.

CEDRUS. *Cedar.* [Pinaceæ.] Evergreen trees, hardy

GARDEN FLOWERS. 95

south of Philadelphia, growing in deep sandy soil, and increased by seeds and cutting.

C. Africanus (Mount Atlas); Mount Atlas; 1843. *C. Deodora* (Deodar); Nepaul; 1822. Varieties *crassifolia, tenuifolia*. and *viridis*. *C. Libani* (Mount Lebanon); Levant; 1683. Varieties *foliis argenteis, nana, glauca, intermedia, pendula, pyramidalis*, and *pyramidalis argenteis*.

CELASTRUS. [Celastrinæ.] Woody climbers, of which only one (*C. scandens*, the "Staff Tree" or "Roxbury Waxwork") is hardy in the Northern States. It is a rampant climber, ornamental in foliage and fruit, and well worthy more notice than it receives. Soil, rich black loam. Propagated by seeds or cuttings. There are more than thirty tender species.

C. bullatus (blistered); 20 feet; flowers white, in July; Virginia; 1759. *C. scandens* (climbing); 15 feet; flowers yellow, in June; North America; 1736.

CELOSIA. *Cockscomb.* [Amarantaceæ.] The only species at all cultivated is the common Cockscomb, *C. cristata*. All the varieties of this are popular with gardeners. The following is the English method of growing large plants.

The deep crimson-colored varieties are generally the most esteemed; and of these there are tall and dwarf kinds, the latter being generally preferred, the comb at its extremities altogether or nearly touching the sides of the pot. Seeds should be sown in a fresh hot-bed in spring; and unlike the balsam, where splendid specimens are required, they should never be turned out of the hot-bed until the combs are nearly full grown, when they may be set in the greenhouse. Two systems of culture may be adopted. First, as soon as the plants are one inch in height, prick out, and shift successively into larger pots, never allowing the plants to be pot-bound. By this method, the plants are strong before the combs appear, and you have a chance of having many very fine, but with the risk that many others, from their shape, will be fit only for the rubbish-heap. By the second method, the best for those with limited space, the young plants are pricked out a few inches apart into shallow pans, in light, rich earth, encouraged to grow freely, and then checked suddenly by keeping them cooler, and withholding water, which will cause them to show their combs in a few days. Though small, you can easily observe those which are close and well shaped from those which will be upright and straggling. Select the best, pot them, and continue repotting, and encourage with heat and manure-water; and the strength of your culture going chiefly into the combs, these will be large, while your plants will be small. Where extremely dwarf plants are wanted, cut off young plants a little below the comb; insert the part with the comb into a small pot, in sandy soil, in strong heat, and a hand-glass over. Soil, sandy loam and very rotten dung, but sweet. Temperature when growing, 60° to 85° by day; 60° at night.

The variety *aurea* is a fine plumed Indian plant with showy feathery golden flowers. Variety *coccinea*, a native of China, has scarlet crimson flowers. Both, when well grown, are very showy.

CELSIA. [Scrophulariaceæ.] Half-hardy biennials and annuals, the former requiring frame or greenhouse protection in the winter. Light sandy open soil. Propagated by seed.

C. Arcturus (Arcturus); half-hardy biennial; 4 feet; flowers yellow, in August; Candia; 1780. *C. betonicæfolia* (betony-leaved); half-hardy biennial; 2 feet; flowers yellow, in July; North Africa; 1824. *C. Cretica* (Cretan); half-hardy biennial; 6 feet; flowers yellow, in July; Crete; 1752. *C. lanceolata* (lance-leaved); half-hardy biennial; 3 feet; flowers yellow, in July;

Levant; 1816. *C. Orientalis* (Eastern); hardy annual; 2 feet; flowers brown and yellow, in July; Levant; 1713.

CELTIS. *Nettle-Tree.* [Ulmaceæ.] Hardy ornamental trees. Propagated by seed sown as soon as ripe, and by cuttings of the young shoots. Common soil.

C. crassifolia (thick-leaved); 20 feet; flowers green, in May; North America; 1812. *C. lævigata* (polished); 20 feet; flowers green, in May; Louisiana. *C. Occidentalis* (Western); 20 feet; flowers green, in May; North America; 1656. *C. Occidentalis cordata* (heart-leaved); 20 feet; flowers green, in May; North America. *C. Occidentalis scabriuscula* (roughish); 20 feet; flowers green, in May; North America. *C. pumila* (dwarf); 6 feet; flowers green, in May; North America; 1812.

CENIA. [Compositæ.] A family of small hardy annuals, propagated by seed, and thriving in any good garden soil.

C. turbinata (turbinate); hardy annual; 1 foot; flowers white, in August; Cape of Good Hope; 1713. *C. turbinata formosa* (beautiful); hardy annual; 1 foot; flowers yellow, in August; Cape of Good Hope.

CENTAUREA. [Compositæ.] A large family of mostly hardy perennials, comprising, however, some very ornamental annuals, which should have a place in every garden. These may either be sown in the open border about the end of April, and the plants thinned out subsequently to three or four in a patch, to be left for blooming, or they may be sown with other annuals in a seed-bed, or in pots, for facility of transplantation; in the latter case being sown somewhat earlier, and coming earlier into flower. They bloom from June, more or less onwards to September. The very numerous hardy perennial kinds — any of which are worth growing as common border flowers — grow well in the common soil of gardens, and are increased by division.

C. crocodylium (crocodylium); hardy annual; 3 feet; flowers purple, in July; Levant; 1777. *C. cyanus* (corn-bottle); hardy annual; 3 feet; flowers blue, pink, or white, in July; England. *C. depressa* (depressed); hardy annual or biennial; 1 foot; flowers blue, in June; Caucasus; 1818. *C. moschata* (Sweet Sultan); hardy annual; 2 feet; flowers purple, in August; Persia; 1629. *C pulchella* (pretty); hardy annual; 2 feet; flowers purple, in June; Persia; 1836. *C. pulchra* (beautiful); hardy annual; 1 foot; flowers blue and crimson, in June; .Cashmere; 1838. *C. suaveolens* (Yellow Sultan); hardy annual; 2 feet; flowers yellow, in July; Levant; 1683.

CENTAURIDIUM. [Compositæ.] A fine hardy annual. Propagated by seeds, and succeeding in good garden soil.

C. Drummondii (Drummond's); hardy annual; 18 inches; flowers orange, in August; Texas.

CENTRANTHUS. [Valerianaceæ.] Ornamental hardy perennials or annuals. The perennials are best raised from seeds; for, having but few thick woody roots, they do not divide well, like many other hardy perennials. The seeds should be sown in May on a bed of light, not over rich, soil, from which they may be transplanted to a nursery-bed as soon as large enough to handle, and will be fit to be transplanted in the autumn into the positions in which they are required to bloom the following year. The plants grow readily in common light garden soil. The annuals require to be sown in the open border in March or April, and like a rather moist soil.

C. angustifolius (narrow-leaved); hardy perennial; 2 feet; flowers crimson, in June; south of Europe; 1759. *C. macrosiphon* (long-tubed); hardy annual; 2 feet; flowers crimson or white, in July; 1851. *C. ruber* (red Valerian); hardy perennial; 2 feet; flowers crimson, rose, or white, in June; England.

CENTROCARPHA. [Compositæ.] Showy, hardy perennials, requiring good light garden soil, and increased by root-division.

C. chrysomela (yellow and black); half-hardy perennial; 2 feet; flowers yellow, in July; South America; 1821. *C. fulgida* (glowing); hardy perennial; 2 feet; flowers yellow, in July; North America; 1760. *C. gracilis* (slender); hardy perennial; 18 inches; flowers yellow, in August; North America; 1825. *C. grandiflora* (great-flowered); hardy perennial; 3 feet; flowers yellow, in July; North America; 1830. *C. hirta* (hairy); hardy perennial; 2 feet; flowers yellow, in July; North America; 1714.

CEPHALANTHUS. *Button Bush.* [Cinchonaceæ.] A hardy ornamental shrub, native of our river banks, but succeeding in upland, and valuable for blooming at a season when the shrubbery is bare of flowers. Propagated by cuttings and layers. Damp peaty soil, or rich loam.

C. Occidentalis (Western); hardy shrub; 5 feet; flowers white, in August; North America. *C. brachypodus* (short-stalked); hardy shrub; flowers white, in August; North America.

CEPHALOTAXUS. [Taxaceæ.] A fine genus of yews from Japan. Hardy and very ornamental. Propagated by cuttings.

C. drupacea (berry-bearing); hardy evergreen; 20 feet; Japan; 1844. *C. Fortunii* (Fortune's); hardy evergreen; 50 feet; Japan; 1848. *C. pedunculata* (stalked); hardy evergreen; Japan; 1837.

CERASTIUM. [Caryophyllaceæ.] This is a large genus, of which many annuals are of no cultural value; but a few of the perennials are ornamental. All are low-growing plants, with whitish flowers, growing anywhere, and propagated by division. The best are *C. Alpinum, Biebersteinii glaciale, grandiflorum, lanatum, Ledbourii, latifolium, purpurascens, Scarani,* and *tomentosum.*

CERASUS. *Cherry.* [Rosaceæ.] The ornamental part of this genus comprises early-flowering trees and shrubs, all free-growing plants in good garden soil. Propagated by seeds, by layers, or by budding. By some, these are all included under Prunus.

ORNAMENTAL TREES. *C. Padus,* the Bird-cherry, a free-growing, deciduous, small tree, in the early spring, about May, covered with long drooping racemes of white blossoms. *C. sylvestris duracina flore-pleno*, the double French white. *C. vulgaris flore-pleno*, a dwarfer double-flowered tree. *C. semperflorus* (ever-flowering); a remarkably handsome drooping free-flowering tree, when budded standard high. *C. Mahaleb* (perfumed cherry).

All are pretty, and desirable for neat, clean foliage seldom attacked by insects, and for beauty of flowers. There are about seventy-five species and varieties, some with beautifully variegated foliage.

CERATIOLA. [Empetraceæ.] A small family of evergreen diminutive bushes, with heather-like foliage. Propagated by cuttings.

C. ericoides (heath-like); hardy shrub; 18 inches; flowers brown, in June; North America; 1826.

CERCIS. *Judas-tree*. [Leguminosæ.] Deciduous small trees, forming beautiful objects when in flower; the blossoms being produced before the leaves, and appearing about the same time as those of the laburnum, the guelder-rose, the hawthorn, and flowering dogwood, with which they contrast admirably. They prefer a rather rich loamy soil, and require a sheltered situation. The seeds are sown in the spring, and produce plants which come to bloom in six or eight years. The young plants require protection.

C. Canadensis (Canadian); hardy tree; 20 feet; flowers pale red, in May; North America; 1730. *C. siliquastrum* (common); hardy tree; 20 feet; flowers pink or white, in May; south of Europe; 1596.

CERINTHE. [Boraginaceæ.] Hardy annuals of coarse habit, requiring to be sown in May where they are to flower, and thinned out to three or four plants in a patch as soon as they grow large enough to become crowded. Common soil.

C. major (greater); hardy annual; 3 feet; flowers yellow, in

July; south of France; 1596. *C. minor* (lesser); hardy annual; 2 feet; flowers yellow and purple, in July; Austria; 1570.

The other species are *C. Alpina, aspera, maculata,* and *retorta.*

CHÆNOSTOMA. [Scrophulariaceæ.] The *C. polyantha* is a very pretty plant for the decoration of the flower-garden during summer. It is half-hardy, requiring to be kept during winter in a greenhouse, or in a dry frame secure against frost; and in summer it may be planted out in a warm sunny situation, in light, moderately rich soil. It is readily raised from seeds in spring, and may also be increased by cuttings during summer. The flowers are small but numerous. The other perennial species are to be treated similarly. The annuals must be raised in heat, in April, and planted out in June.

C. cordata (cordate); half-hardy perennial; 6 inches; flowers red, in June; Cape; 1816. *C. fœtida* (fetid); half-hardy annual; 18 inches; flowers white, in June; Cape; 1794. *C. polyanthum* (many-flowered); half-hardy perennial; 18 inches; flowers rosy-lilac, in June; South Africa; 1844. *C. villosa* (villous); half-hardy annual; 1 foot; flowers white, in June; Cape; 1783.

CHAMÆCYPARIS. *Bastard Cypress.* [Pinaceæ.] A small genus of evergreens, allied to Cypress, hardy, growing in sandy loam. Propagated by seeds. The species are *C. Nootkanensis, obtusa, pisifera, sphæroides, squarrosa,* and *thurifera.* The last is tender.

CHAMÆNERIUM. [Lythraceæ.] Hardy, ornamental, herbaceous perennials, of the easiest culture in the open ground; formerly called Epilobium. They increase with facility by division of the root.

C. angustifolium (narrow-leaved); hardy perennial; 3 feet; flowers rose or white, in July; England. *C. Halleri* (Haller's); hardy perennial; 1 foot; flowers rose-red, in June; Switzerland;

1798. *C. rosmarinifolium* (rosemary-leaved); hardy perennial; 18 inches; flowers rose-red, in June; Europe; 1800.

CHAMÆRHODES. [Rosaceæ.] Hardy herbaceous perennials. Sandy loam; dry, cold situation. Increased by seeds.

C. grandiflorus (large-flowered); hardy perennial; 6 inches; flowers yellow, in June; Dahuria; 1828. *C. polygynus* (many-pistilled); hardy perennial; 6 inches; flowers yellow, in June; Siberia; 1824.

CHEIRANTHUS. *Wall-flower.* [Cruciferæ.] Half-hardy perennials, of somewhat shrubby habit. *C. Cheiri*, the well known common Wall-flower, has produced various handsome double-flowered varieties, of which the best are the bright yellow, dark brown, and purple. The common single kind bears its yellow or brownish blossoms freely in June, on plants raised from seeds sown in May of the previous year. The seeds should be sown in a bed of light or rather sandy soil, and the plants pricked out, when large enough, into a frame, from whence they may be transplanted, with compact balls of earth about their roots, in the early part of the next May, into the places where they are to flower. When the plants live over to a second year, they are larger; but, in general, the one-year-old plants are preferable. The double varieties are increased by cuttings, planted under a hand-glass in sandy earth about May or June; and are best potted, and protected through the winter in cold frames, though sometimes established plants will survive the winter, if exposed. The other species furnish beautiful dwarf plants, suitable for rock-work, or small beds, or the front parts of borders. They are quite hardy, and are increased by cuttings. *C. mutabilis* is a tall, rather straggling shrub, which has changeable purplish single flowers, and requires the protection of a frame or cool greenhouse.

C. Alpinus (Alpine); hardy perennial; 9 inches; flowers yellow, in May; Norway; 1810. *C. Cheiri* (common); hardy sub-shrub; 18 inches; flowers yellow or brown, in May; Europe. *C. Marshallii* (Marshall's); hardy herbaceous perennial; 9 inches; flowers deep-orange, in June and August; Scotch hybrid. *C. mutabilis* (changeable); greenhouse sub-shrub; 3 feet; flowers purple, changeable, in March; Madeira; 1777. *C. ochroleucus* (pale-yellow); hardy perennial; 9 inches; flowers pale-yellow, in May; Switzerland; 1822.

CHELIDONIUM. *Celandine.* [Papaveraceæ.] Hardy herbaceous well-known perennials, some of which are rather pretty, and desirable from their early flowering. Propagated by seeds and division.

C. grandiflorum (large-flowered); hardy perennial; 2 feet; flowers yellow, in May; Dahuria; 1820. *C. laciniatum* (jagged); hardy perennial; 2 feet; flowers yellow, in May; south of Europe. *C. majus flore-pleno* (large-double-flowered); hardy perennial; 2 feet; flowers yellow, in summer; Hybrid.

CHELONE. [Scrophulariaceæ.] Beautiful herbaceous perennials, closely allied to Pentstemon, and requiring similar treatment.

C. barbata (bearded); hardy perennial; 3 feet; flowers scarlet, in July; Mexico; 1794. Varieties *carnea* and *major* have flesh-colored and orange-striped flowers. *C. glabra* (smooth); hardy perennial; 3 feet; flowers white, in August; North America; 1730. *C. Lyoni* (Lyon's); hardy perennial; 3 feet; flowers purple, in August; North America; 1812. *C. obliqua* (oblique); hardy perennial; 3 feet; flowers rose-purple, in August; North America; 1752.

CHENOPODIUM. [Chenopodiaceæ.] A few plants of this family, which consists mainly of weeds, have of late been introduced into gardens for dark or elegant foliage. They are generally hardy annuals. *C. album* and *atriplicis* are good species.

CHERRY. See CERASUS.

CHILI-PEPPER. See CAPSICUM.

CHESTNUT. See CASTANEA.

CHIMAPHILA. [Pyrolaceæ.] Hardy herbaceous evergreens, of difficult culture. Soil, forest-loam and sand. *C. maculata* is one of our finest native foliaged plants.

C. umbellata (umbelled); hardy perennial; 6 inches; flowers pinkish-white, in June; North America; 1752. *C. maculata* (spotted); hardy perennial; 6 inches; flowers pink, in June; North America; 1752.

CHIMONANTHUS. [Calycanthaceæ.] Half-hardy deciduous shrub, thriving in the Southern States, but tender in the Northern. The flowers of all the varieties are deliciously fragrant, and are produced on the leafless branches in winter.

C. fragrans (fragrant); shrub; 6 feet; flowers yellow and red, in December; Japan; 1766. Variety *grandiflorus* (large-flowered); flowers yellow; 8 feet; China. Variety *parviflorus* (small-flowered); 8 feet; flowers pale-yellow, Japan; 1818.

CHINA ASTER. See CALLISTEPHUS.

CHINESE HOLLYHOCK. See ALTHÆA.

CHINESE PINK. See DIANTHUS.

CHIONANTHUS. *Fringe-tree.* [Oleaceæ.] Fine hardy deciduous small trees or shrubs. Soil, peat-earth in damp situations. Propagated by seeds or layers.

C. maritima (marine); hardy shrub; 10 feet; flowers white, in May; North America; 1736. *C. Virginica* (Virginian); hardy tree; 30 feet; North America; 1736.

There is a narrow-leaved and broad-leaved variety.

CHLORIS. [Gramineæ.] A family of tropical ornamental grasses, thriving in common soil; all half-hardy annuals. The species are *C. barbata, polydactyla, fimbriata,* and *radiata.*

CHRISTMAS ROSE. See HELLEBORUS.

CHLORA. [Gentianaceæ.] A family of hardy annuals, succeeding from seeds sown in May in the open border.

C. imperfoliata ; flowers yellow, in June; Italy; 1823. *C. perfoliata;* flowers yellow, in June; England. *C. serotina* (late); flowers yellow, in September; south of Europe; 1832.

CHRYSANTHEMUM. [Compositæ.] Hardy annuals, perennials, and greenhouse shrubs. The annuals, though free-growing plants, have a strong chamomile smell, and are poor in their flowers, though often grown among collections of annuals. They should be sown in patches for planting out in the borders when large enough, about three in a clump, at equal distances. Sown in heat, and forwarded for planting out in May, the bloom is much earlier than when sown in the open air. Besides being abundant flowerers, these Chrysanthemums continue their bloom until the frost cuts the plant down, and are chiefly useful in large borders where variety is wanted. The greenhouse kinds are straggling shrubs, with deeply jagged leaves, and flowers a good deal resembling those of Mayweed. The annuals are increased by seeds; but the shrubby kinds may be renewed by cuttings, which take root readily. A light loamy soil suits the latter, of which young vigorous plants should be constantly reared. Many of the Pompon varieties are very good; but as new ones are constantly introduced, the florists' latest catalogues will show the best.

C. Arcticum (Arctic); hardy perennial; 6 inches; flowers white and purple, in June; Kamtschatka; 1801. *C. argenteum* (silvery leaved); hardy perennial; 1 foot; flowers white, in July; Levant; 1731. *C. carinatum* (keeled); hardy annual; 18 inches; flowers white, yellow, and purple, in June; Barbary; 1796. *C. coronarium* (garland); hardy annual; 2½ feet; flowers yellow, in June; Sicily; 1629. *C. coronopifolium* (buck's-horn-leaved); greenhouse shrub; 2 feet; flowers white, in April; Madeira; 1815. *C. montanum* (mountain); hardy perennial; 2 feet; flowers white, in June; France; 1752. *C. pinnatifidum* (pinnatifid); greenhouse shrub; 2 feet; flowers yellow, in April; Madeira; 1777. *C. Ruthenicum* (Russian); hardy perennial; 1 foot; flowers pink, in June; Russia; 1827.

CHRYSEIS. See ESCHSCHOLTZIA.

CHYRSOCOMA. *Goldy-locks.* [Compositæ.] A genus of hardy herbaceous and greenhouse evergreen species. The former grow in common soil, and are increased by division; the latter prefer light sandy loam, and are increased by cuttings. They are not very showy.

C. biflora (two-flowered); hardy perennial; 3 feet; flowers blue, in August; Siberia; 1741. *C. cernua* (drooping); greenhouse sub-shrub; 3 feet; flowers white, in July; Cape; 1712. *C. comaurea* (golden-hair); greenhouse sub-shrub; 3 feet; flowers yellow, in July; Cape; 1731. *C. virgata* (twiggy); hardy perennial; 1 foot; flowers yellow, in September; North America; 1821.

CHRYSOGONUM. [Compositæ.] A hardy herbaceous plant, growing in common garden soil, and increased by division.

C. Virginiacum (Virginian); hardy perennial; 1 foot; flowers yellow, in May; North America.

CHRYSOSTEMMA. [Compositæ.] Hardy herbaceous perennials, with showy flowers. Common garden soil. Increased by division.

C. tripteris (three-winged); hardy perennial; 6 feet; flowers yellow, in August; North America; 1837.

CHRYSURUS. [Graminaceæ.] A pretty annual ornamental grass, doing well in the flower border.

C. aureus (golden); hardy annual; 6 inches; Levant.

CINQUEFOIL. See POTENTILLA.

CIMICIFUGA. [Ranunculaceæ.] Hardy herbaceous plants, growing readily in the border, and increased by division.

C. Americana (American); 2 feet; flowers white and yellow, in July; Carolina; 1824. *C. cordifolia* (heart-leaved); 3 feet; flowers white and yellow, in June; North America; 1812. *C. fœtida* (fetid); 4 feet; flowers light-yellow, in June; Siberia; 1777. *C. palmata* (palmate); 4 feet; flowers white and yellow, in July; North America; 1812.

CIRCÆA. *Enchanter's Nightshade.* [Onagraceæ.] Hardy herbaceous perennials. Common soil. Increased by division.

C. Alpina (Alpine); hardy perennial; 6 inches; flowers pink, in July; Britain. *C. Lutetiana* (Parisian); hardy perennial; 1 foot; flowers pink, in July; Britain. *C. intermedia* (intermediate); 1 foot; flowers red, in July; Europe; 1821.

CIRSIUM. [Compositæ.] Hardy thistle-like biennials and perennials: some of them showy. Common soil. Increased by division; or the biennials by seed, from which plants should be raised annually. Some few of the species, among which is *C. Casabonæ*, one of the most ornamental species, require protection.

C. Casabonæ; half-hardy biennial; 2 feet; flowers purple, in July; south of Europe; 1714. *C. tuberosum* (tuberous); hardy perennial; 2 feet; flowers purple, in August; England.

There are more than fifty other species, many of which are mere weeds.

CLADANTHUS. [Compositæ.] A small genus, containing one pretty, hardy annual, which should be sown in a frame in April, and transplanted to the border in May; or in the open border in May.

C. Arabicus (Arabian); hardy annual; 1 foot; flowers yellow, in July; Barbary; 1759.

CLARKIA. [Onagraceæ.] Showy, free-flowering, well-known annuals, flourishing in common garden soil, not very rich, as then the plants run to leaves. Propagated by seed, which should be sown in a frame in April, and the plants set in the border in May; or sown in the border in May. The plants should not be allowed to become crowded. The double varieties are very pretty.

C. elegans (elegant); hardy annual; 2 feet; flowers rose, in June; California; 1822. Of this there is a double-flowered variety. *C. pulchella* (pretty); hardy annual; 18 inches; flowers rose or white, in June; North America; 1826. This latter species has produced the fine varieties *integripetala*, petals entire on the margin, rosy-purple, (a double variety has rich crimson flowers, and a sub-variety has the petals edged with white); *pulcherrima*, petals three-lobed, bright crimson; *striata*, petals three-lobed, white, flaked with rose; *marginata*, petals three-lobed, rosy-purple, tipped with white; *florepleno*, very double, with large rosy-purple or crimson flowers.

CLAYTONIA. [Portulacaceæ.] Hardy annuals and tuberous-rooted perennials, not very showy. Common soil. Increased by seeds, or by division.

C. Caroliniana (Carolina); hardy perennial; 1 foot; flowers pink, in May; North America; 1789. *C. grandiflora* (large-flowered); hardy perennial; 1 foot; flowers pink, in May; North America; 1789. *C. perfoliata* (perfoliate-leaved); hardy annual; 9 inches; flowers white, in June; North America; 1794. *C. Siberica* (Siberian); hardy annual; 1 foot; flowers red, in June; Siberia; 1768. *C. Virginiana* (Virginian); hardy perennial; 1 foot; flowers white, in May; North America; 1740.

There are ten other species.

CLEMATIS. *Virgin's-bower.* [Ranunculaceæ.] A large genus of climbing shrubs, some of which are very ornamental. The hardy kinds are of the simplest culture. They are raised from seeds or layers, and grow freely in any moderately good ground. They are valuable for covering walls, arbors, and trellis-work. The half-hardy kinds are useful for the pillars and rafters of greenhouses and cool conservatories. The stove species are of little importance. *Sieboldii, cærulea, graveolens,* and *Hendersonii,* are worthy of being grown on a large pot trellis, and are manageable in that form. The genus contains some hardy perennials, which are managed like other herbaceous perennials.

C. azurea grandiflora (large-flowered azure); hardy climber; 10 feet; flowers blue, in May, very large; China; 1852. *C. cærulea* (sky-blue); hardy climbing shrub; 10 feet; flowers bluish-lilac. in May; Japan; 1836. *C. calycina* (Minorca); half-hardy evergreen climbing shrub; 12 feet; flowers creamy, in March; Minorca; 1783. *C. crispa* (curled-flowered); hardy climbing shrub; 6 feet; flowers pinkish, in August; North America; 1726. *C. erecta* (upright); hardy perennial; flowers white, in June; Austria; 1597. A double variety of this species is said to be very fine. *C. flammula* (sweet-scented); hardy climbing shrub; 20 feet; flowers white, in July; France; 1596. *C. florida* (flowering); half-hardy climbing shrub; 12 feet; flowers white, in June; Japan; 1776. *C. florida flore-pleno* (double-flowering); half-hardy climbing shrub; 12 feet; flowers white. in June; Japan; 1776. *C. florida Sieboldii* (Siebold's); half-hardy climber; 12 feet; flowers white and purple, in June; Japan; 1836. *C. graveolens* (heavy-smelling); half-hardy climbing shrub; 8 feet; flowers sulphur-color, in July; Tartary; 1845. *C. Hendersonii* (Henderson's); hardy climbing shrub; 20 feet; flowers purple, in June; gardens. *C. indivisa lobata* (lobed); greenhouse evergreen climbing shrub; 12 feet; flowers creamy white, in May; New Zealand; 1847. *C. integrifolia* (entire-leaved); hardy perennial; 2 feet; flowers blue, in June; Hungary; 1596. *C. lanuginosa* (woolly-budded); half-hardy climbing shrub; 8 feet; flowers very large, blue or gray, in June; China; 1850. *C. lathyrifolia* (lathyrus-leaved); hardy perennial; 3 feet; flowers white, in June; doubtful; 1836. *C. montana* (mountain); hardy climbing shrub; 20 feet; flowers large white, in May; Nepaul; 1831. *C. ochroleuca* (yellowish); hardy perennial; 2 feet; flowers yellowish-white, in June;

North America; 1767. *C. tubulosa* (tubular); half-hardy perennial; 6 feet; flowers blue, in July; North China; 1845. *C. viorna* (traveller's joy); hardy climbing shrub; 12 feet; flowers purple, in August; North America; 1730. *C. viticella* (vine-bower); hardy climbing shrub; 20 feet; flowers purple, in June; Spain; 1569.

C. Sophia, with pale lilac and white, and *Helene*, with creamy-white flowers, are fine varieties of *C. patens*, introduced from Japan in 1853, and hardy if laid down in winter. There are double-flowered varieties. *C. reginæ* is a hybrid between *C. azurea grandiflora* and *lanuginosa*. *C. Jackmanii* is a fine hybrid between *C. viticella Hendersonii* and *C. lanuginosa*, producing large royal-purple flowers. *C. rubroviolacea*, a hybrid between *C. viticella atrorubens* and *C. lanuginosa*, has rich velvety violet flowers five inches in diameter. *C. Fortunei*, a recent acquisition from Japan, has very large white fragrant double flowers; and *C. florida Standishii*, also just introduced, has deep violet-blue flowers. We cannot name a class of plants which will give more general satisfaction, or which is more worthy of cultivation.

CLEOME. [Capparidaceæ.] This genus contains several curious and rather pretty annuals. They should be raised from seeds in spring, in a frame, with slight warmth, potted off singly, and hardened subsequently, so as to be planted out in May, when they should be strong, vigorous plants. They like a dry, warm situation. One or two species are stove, soft-wooded shrubs, and there are some stove annual species; but they are not suitable for general cultivation.

C. heptaphylla (seven-leaved); half-hardy annual; 3 feet; flowers white, in June; Jamaica; 1719. *C. Iberica* (Iberian); hardy annual; 6 inches; flowers white, in July; Iberia; 1820. *C. lutea* (yellow); hardy annual; 1 foot; flowers yellow, in July; North America; 1840. *C. speciosissima* (most showy); half-hardy annual; 3 feet; flowers purple in June; Mexico; 1827.

C. violacea (violet); hardy annual; 1 foot; flowers purple, in July; Portugal; 1776. *C. virgata* (twiggy); hardy annual; 1 foot; flowers white, in July; Persia; 1820.

CLETHRA. [Ericaceæ.] A genus of hardy and tender shrubs. The hardy species are natives of North America, and are very valuable summer-flowering shrubs. They are easily propagated by layers.

C. acuminata (acuminate); hardy shrub; 10 feet; flowers white, in August; Carolina; 1806. *C. alnifolia* (alder-leaved); hardy shrub; 4 feet; flowers white, in August; North America; 1731. *C. paniculata* (panicled); hardy shrub; 4 feet; flowers white, in August; North America; 1770. *C. tomentosa* (downy); hardy shrub; 4 feet; flowers white, in August; North America; 1731.

CLINTONIA. [Lobeliaceæ.] Very pretty hardy annuals. They are slender-growing dwarf plants, hanging over the edges of the pots, if grown in pots, but forming very beautiful objects on the ground, being so much covered with blossoms as to hide the stems. Sow the seeds in pots in March; put them in a frame, if with a little warmth, so much the better; set them in feeders of water until germinated, then thin the plants so as to give them room, and keep them growing in frames till May, when those for the borders may be turned out. They will very soon flower, and have a very pretty appearance. To provide a succession, some should be sown in the borders about May: these will flower when those of the first sowing leave off. Many annuals may thus be managed, so as to keep up a succession of bloom during several months, by sowing at different seasons. *C. pulchella*, the best of the two species, is a much more interesting object for pot-culture than nine-tenths of the plants grown in pots. Peaty soil, or a light mixture of leaf-mould, loam, and sand, is the proper soil for them.

C. elegans (elegant); half-hardy annual; 6 inches; flowers blue, in June; Colombia; 1827. *C. pulchella* (pretty); half-hardy annual; 6 inches; flowers blue, white, and yellow, in June; Colombia; 1831.

CLEIOCOCCA. [Linaceæ.] Half-hardy perennial, allied to Linum. Propagated by seeds and division. Light loam and peat.

C. tenuifolia (slender-leaved); 3 inches; flowers purple, in July; Australia; 1837.

CLOVER. See TRIFOLIUM.

CLOVE-PINK. See DIANTHUS.

COBÆA. [Polemoniaceæ.] Greenhouse or half-hardy rapid-growing climbers, covering a large space during the summer season with their herbaceous stems, which, in a greenhouse or conservatory, retain their foliage, and continue to blossom through the winter. They are very useful as well as ornamental out doors during the summer season; but in such situations are killed by the first frost. When grown in a greenhouse, they generally ripen plenty of seeds, by which they are best propagated; though they may be increased by cuttings. They require a rich loamy soil.

C. macrostemma (long-stamened); greenhouse climbing perennial; 20 feet; flowers yellowish-green, in September; Guayaquil; 1839. *C. scandens* (climbing); greenhouse climbing perennial; 20 feet; flowers purple, in July; Mexico; 1792. *C. stipularis* (stipuled); greenhouse climbing perennial; 20 feet; flowers yellow, in August; Mexico; 1839.

COCKSCOMB. See CELOSIA.

COCKSPUR THORN. See CRATAEGUS.

CŒLESTINA. [Compositæ.] A small family, of which *C. ageratoides*, formerly *Ageratum cœlestinum*, is the best. They require a greenhouse or frame in winter, and bloom well in the border in summer. The species are *C. ageratoides* and *cœrulea*.

Coix. [Gramineæ.] Perennial grasses, doing well in the open border in summer.

C. arundinacea (reedy); 2 feet; apetalous, July; Mexico; 1818. *C. lachryma* (tears); 2 feet; apetalous, July; East Indies; 1596.

Colchicum. [Melanthaceæ.] Hardy bulbs, with crocus-like flowers in October, commonly called Autumn Crocuses. The leaf appears and the plant ripens its seed the following spring. Increased by offsets or seeds, which should be sown as soon as they are ripe. Replanting, which is not often necessary, should be done in July, when the bulbs are at rest. They succeed in any garden soil.

C. Alpinum (Alpine); 3 inches; flowers purple, in July; Apennine; 1820. *C. arenarium* (sand); 3 inches; flowers purple, in September; Hungary; 1816. *C. autumnale* (autumnal; common meadow saffron); 1 foot; flowers purple, in September; Britain. *C. autumnale album* (white-flowered); 3 inches; flowers white, in September; Britain. *C. autumnale atro-purpureum* (dark-purple); 3 inches; flowers dark-purple, in September; Britain. *C. autumnale foliis-variegatis* (variegated-leaved); 3 inches; flowers purple, in September; Britain. *C. autumnale flore-pleno* (double-flowered); 3 inches; flowers purple, in September; Britain. *C. autumnale purpureo-striatum* (purple-striped); 3 inches; flowers purple-striped, in September; Britain. *C. autumnale striatum-pleno* (double-striped); 3 inches; flowers lilac-striped, in September; Britain. *C. Byzantinum* (Byzantine); 3 inches; flowers purple, in September; Levant; 1629. *C. Chionense* (Chio); 3 inches; flowers purple, in November; Chio. *C. crociflorum* (crocus-flowered); 18 inches; flowers purple, in August; south of Europe. *C. montanum* (mountain); 3 inches; flowers purple, in August; south of Europe; 1819. *C. tessellatum* (checkered); 3 inches; flowers purple, in August; south of Europe; 1600. *C. umbrosum* (shaded); 3 inches; flowers pink, in September; Guinea; 1819. *C. varie-*

gatum (variegated-flowered); 3 inches; flowers purple, in September; Greece; 1629.

COLEUS. [Labiatæ,] A genus of which some species are used for summer bedding as foliaged plants. The species are properly stove shrubs, but do well in a sunny exposure. More commonly known as Plectranthus. Propagated by cuttings.

C. Verschafeldtii; a very dark foliaged plant, and fine for massing; flowers inconspicuous; the foliage is rich glowing crimson; Java; 1860. *C. Blumeii* is of no value as a bedding plant.

COLIC ROOT. See ALETRIS.

COLLINSIA. [Scrophularineæ.] Pretty dwarf annuals. *C. bicolor* is a very showy plant, in clumps. The culture is simple: in ordinary cases the seeds may be sown in patches in the borders in May; eight or ten plants will be sufficient to form a patch. When they are to form a mass of flowers, they ought to be not more than three inches apart; for this it is best to sow thinly where they are to flower, and, when they are up, thin the plants so that they may be from two to three inches from each other. This gives the appearance of a complete mass of flowers when the spikes of bloom rise. Sowing in pots should be begun in April, and eight or ten plants are enough for a pot. These should be placed in a greenhouse, and, as they grow, if any two should be too close together, remove one. Where patches of this flower are to be at certain distances round borders, the balls may be turned out from the pots as soon as the weather becomes warm. If this cannot be done, they must be sown on a reserve bed, and transplanted when large enough, or else raised and kept in pots till they are wanted; for either of which purposes they should be sown in April on a very gentle hot-bed. *C. grandiflora* is a dwarfish variety, equally pretty, though differing from *bicolor*. It grows six inches high, spreading on the ground instead of growing erect; flowers rose-purple and bright-lilac, in June. There are several other pretty kinds, but differing only in their colors; and every year will add to the number of varieties, which will, in time, perhaps become, like larkspurs, most interesting in mixtures.

C. bartsæfolia (bartsia-leaved); hardy annual; 18 inches; flowers white and red, in June; California; 1850. *C. bicolor* (two-colored); hardy annual; 1 foot; flowers lilac and white. in June; California; 1833. *C. grandiflora* (large-flowered); hardy annual; 9 inches; flowers blue and purple, in June; North-west America; 1826. *C. heterophylla* (various-leaved); hardy annual; 2 feet; flowers lilac, in July; Colombia; 1838. *C. multicolor* (many-colored); hardy annual; 18 inches; flowers white and red-spotted, in June; California; 1850. *C. tinctoria* (dyer's); hardy annual; 18 inches; flowers pinkish-lilac, in June; California; 1848. *C. verna* (spring); hardy annual; 1 foot; flowers purple and blue, in June; North America; 1826.

COLLINSONIA. [Labiatæ.] Hardy herbaceous perennials, increased by division, and growing in moist garden soil.

C. Canadensis (Canadian); hardy perennial; 3 feet; flowers lilac-yellow, in September; North America; 1734. *C. cordata* (heart-leaved); hardy perennial; 3 feet; flowers lilac-yellow, in September; North America; 1735.

COLLOMIA. [Polemoniaceæ.] Hardy free-growing annuals, allied to Gilia, growing in common garden soil. The seeds should be sown in the open borders in May, and the plants not allowed to become crowded.

C. coccinea (scarlet); hardy annual; 1 foot; flowers scarlet, in June; Chili; 1832. *C. gracilis* (slender); hardy annual; 6 inches; flowers pink, in June; North America; 1827. *C. grandiflora* (large-flowered; hardy annual; 18 inches; flowers pinkish-buff, in July; North America; 1826. *C. linearis* (narrow); hardy annual; 1 foot; flowers red, in June; 1826. *C. heterophylla, gilioides*, and *glutinosa* are other species.

COLTSFOOT. See TUSSILAGO.

COLUMBINE. See. AQUILEGIA.

COLURIA. [Rosaceæ.] Hardy herbaceous perennial, allied to Geum, growing in good loam. Propagated by division.

C. potentilloides (like potentilla); hardy perennial; 1 foot; flowers orange, in June; Siberia; 1780.

COLUTEA. *Bladder-Senna.* [Leguminosæ.] Hardy deciduous shrubs, growing in common soil, and increased by seeds and layers.

C. arborescens (tree-like); hardy shrub; 10 feet; flowers yellow, all summer; France; 1548, *C. Haleppica* (Aleppic); hardy shrub; 6 feet; flowers yellow, in June; Levant; 1752. *C. cruenta* (bloody); hardy shrub; 4 feet; flowers scarlet, in June; Levant; 1710. *S. Nepaulensis* (Nepaul); hardy shrub; 5 feet; flowers yellow, in August; Nepaul; 1822.

COMMELINA. A very pretty group of plants, comprising hardy annuals and half-hardy perennials and stove evergreens. Increased respectively by seeds, division, and cuttings. All the herbaceous species, whether from tropical regions or New Holland, if the seeds are sown in a hot-bed early in spring, pricked off, and potted and planted out towards the end of May, will flourish in the flower-garden, and constitute a pleasing feature until the end of autumn. Before frost, the tuberous kinds should be taken up and kept like Dahlias, but not over dry, started a little in spring in heat, and then transplanted at the end of May. Thus treated, they will bloom stronger than the seedlings. The soil should be light and rich, using either rotten dung or leaf-mould, with sandy loam. Summer temperature for stove species, 50° to 75°; winter, 40° to 45°.

C. cœlestis (sky-blue); half-hardy perennial; 2 feet; flowers blue or white, in July; Mexico; 1813. *C. communis* (common); hardy annual; 2 feet; flowers blue-purple, in June; North America; 1732. *C. cucullata* (hooded); greenhouse annual; 2 feet; flowers blue, in July; Brazil; 1825. *C. fasciculata* (fascicled); hardy perennial; 18 inches; flowers blue, in July; Lima; 1817. *C. orchidioides* (orchis-like); half-hardy perennial; 2 feet; flowers blue, in June; Mexico; 1837. *C. tuberosa* (tuberous); half-hardy perennial; 2 feet; flowers blue, in July; Mexico; 1732.

CONVALLARIA. *Lily of the Valley.* [Liliaceæ.] This universally admired plant is a dwarf herbaceous perennial; and its spikes of drooping, white, deliciously fragrant flowers, and broad green leaves, form one of the loveliest of Nature's contrast's in coloring, — rich green and pure white. There are varieties, in one of which the flowers are pinkish, and in the other double white; but the simple form is the most attractive. They grow in common garden soil, and flourish in shady places. The plants are increased by dividing the roots. Planted in pots, they are beautiful subjects for forcing into early bloom.

C. majalis (May); hardy perennial; 6 inches; flowers white, in May; England.

CONVOLVULUS. *Bindweed.* [Convolvulaceæ.] Ornamental plants, with trumpet-shaped flowers, which are great favorites in gardens. The most common are known as the Convolvulus major and the Convolvulus minor of gardens; the former of which belongs to another family, called PHARBITIS (which see); and the hardy annual species, of which *C. tricolor*, and its white and dark-blue varieties are the best, should be sown in pots in April for early bloom, and again in May, in the open borders, for a succession. *C. tricolor* is a fine border plant, and, where the beds are large, it is a good flower for masses; for, though a little straggling, it is not more so than can be controlled. *C. Scammonia*, among the hardy perennial kinds, is a very pretty twiner, and, like the rest, is best increased by seeds, and need only be planted in a dry, well-drained situation, in good lightish garden soil. The half-hardy kinds chiefly need protection at the root against wet during winter. There are some stove and greenhouse shrubby and climbing species which require an open compost of turfy peat and loam, and are increased by cuttings, as the other perennial kinds may also be. The annuals are in all cases perpetuated by seeds.

C. althæoides (althæa-like); half-hardy trailing perennial; 1 foot; flowers pink, in June; Levant; 1759. *C. Bonariensis* (Buenos-Ayrean); half-hardy twiner; 3 feet; flowers white, in July; Chili; 1817. *C. cneorum* (silver-leaved); greenhouse evergreen shrub; 2 feet; flowers blush, in June; Levant; 1640. *C. farinosus* (mealy); greenhouse evergreen twiner; 6 feet; flowers pink, in May; Madeira; 1777. *C. Italicus* (Italian); half-hardy twiner; 3 feet; flowers rose-colored, in May; south of Europe; 1844. *C. lineatus* (lined); hardy perennial; 6 inches; flowers purplish, in June; south of Europe; 1770. *C. Scammonia* (scammony); hardy climbing perennial; 6 feet; flowers creamy-white, in July; Levant; 1726. *C. tricolor* (three-colored); hardy annual; 2 feet; flowers blue, white, and yellow, in June; south of Europe; 1629.

There are numerous other half-hardy greenhouse and stove species.

CORAL-TREE. See ERYTHRINA.

COPTIS. [Ranunculaceæ.] Hardy herbaceous perennial, commonly called Gold-thread from the color of the roots. In moist peaty soil, it will carpet the ground with glossy foliage enlivened with starry white flowers. Propagated by seeds and division.

C. trifolia (three-leaved); hardy evergreen perennial; 4 inches; flowers white, in May; North America; 1782.

CORBULARIA. *Hoop Petticoat Narcissus.* [Amaryllidaceæ.] Hardy bulbs, separated from Narcissus. Garden soil. Increased by offsetts.

C. bulbocodium: hardy bulb; 6 inches; flowers yellow, in May; south of Europe; 1629. *C. conspicua* (showy); hardy bulb; 6 inches; flowers yellow, in May. *C. lobulata* (lobed); hardy bulb; 6 inches; flowers yellow, in May. *C. tenuifolia* (slender-leaved); hardy bulb; 6 inches; flowers yellow, in May; Spain; 1760.

COREOPSIS. [Compositæ.] A genus of showy perennials (for the annuals see Calliopsis), propagated by division, and thriving in garden soil. All the species we describe have yellow flowers in July and August.

C. angustifolia (narrow-leaved); 2 feet; North America; 1778. *C. arguta* (sharp); 2 feet; Carolina; 1786. *C. aurea* (golden); 3 feet; North America; 1785. *C. grandiflora* (large-flowered); 3 feet; North America; 1826. *C. lanceolata* (lance-leaved); 3 feet; Carolina; 1724. *C. tenuifolia* (slender-leaved); 2 feet; North America; 1780. *C. tripteris* (three-winged); 5 feet; North America; 1737. *C. verticillata* (whorl-leaved); 3 feet; North America; 1759.

There are many other species.

CORN-FLAG. See GLADIOLUS.

CORNELIAN CHERRY. See CORNUS.

CORNUS. [Cornaceæ.] Hardy deciduous trees, shrubs, and perennials. Propagated by seeds, cuttings, layers, and division of the root. *C. florida* is a very beautiful ornamental tree. *C. mascula* is the Cornelian cherry. All require a rich loamy soil.

C. alba (white-berried); 10 feet; flowers white, in July; Siberia; 1741. *C. alba Rossica* (Russian); 8 feet; flowers white, in July; Siberia; 1820. *C. alba Siberica* (Siberian); 10 feet; flowers white, in August; Siberia; 1824. *C. alternifolia* (alternate-leaved); 15 feet; flowers white, in July; North America; 1760.

C. Canadensis (Canadian); herbaceous perennial; 1 foot; flowers white, in June; Canada; 1774. *C. circinata* (round-leaved); 6 feet; flowers white, in July; North America; 1784. *C. florida* (flowery); 15 feet; flowers white, in May; North America; 1731. *C. macrophylla* (large-leaved); flowers white, in July; Nepaul; 1827. *C. mascula* (male cornel); 15 feet; flowers yellow, in April; Austria; 1596. *C. mascula variegata* (variegated); 8 feet; flowers yellow, in June; Austria; 1596. There are other varieties of *C. mascula*, which differ only in the color of the fruit. *C. oblonga* (oblong); 15 feet; flowers purple; Nepaul; 1818. *C. paniculata* (panicled); 6 feet; flowers white, in June; North America; 1758. *C. sanguinea* (bloody); 8 feet; flowers white, in June; Britain. *C. sanguinea variegata* (variegated); 8 feet; flowers white, in June; Britain. *C. sanguinea foliis variegatis* (variegated-leaved); 10 feet; flowers white, in June; Britain. *C. sericea* (silky); 5 feet; flowers white, in August; North America; 1683. *C. sericea asperifolia* (rough-leaved); 8 feet; flowers white; Carolina. *C. sericea oblongifolia* (oblong-leaved); 8 feet; flowers white, in August. *C. Sibirica* (Siberian); 8 feet; flowers white, in July; Siberia; 1824. *C. stricta* (erect); 10 feet; flowers white, in June; North America; 1758. *C. stricta asperifolia* (rough-leaved); 10 feet; flowers white. *C. stricta sempervirens* (sub-evergreen); 10 feet; flowers white, in June. *C. stricta variegata* (variegated); 10 feet; flowers white, in June; North America; 1758. *C. Suecica* (Swedish); herbaceous perennial; 1 foot; flowers white, in May; Britain.

CORONILLA. [Leguminoseæ.] Shrubs and herbaceous perennials, of easy culture. Propagated by seed and division. There are many greenhouse species.

C. Cappadocica (Cappadocian); 1 foot; flowers white, in July; Cappadocia; 1800. *C. emerus* (scorpion-senna); shrub; 3 feet; flowers yellow and red, in May; France; 1596. *C. varia* (various); 1 foot; flowers pink, in July; Europe; 1597. *C. globosa*, *Iberica* and *squamata* are other species.

CORTUSA. *Bear's-ear Sanicle*. [Primulaceæ.] A pretty

dwarf herbaceous perennial, suitable to be grown on rockwork, or among alpine plants. Loam and peat. Propagated by division. Should have frame protection in winter.

C. Matthiola (Matthioli's); 6 inches; flowers red, in May; Austria; 1596.

CORYDALIS. [Fumariaceæ.] Pretty, hardy plants, of easy culture, in common soil. The annuals and biennials, which are the least important, may be sown in the borders in April and June. The perennials are increased by division.

C. aurea (golden); hardy biennial; 6 inches; flowers golden-yellow, in May; North America. *C. bulbosa* (bulbous); hardy tuberous perennial; 6 inches; flowers purplish, in May; England. *C. flavula* (yellowish); hardy perennial; 1 foot; flowers yellow, in June; Russia; 1838. *C. longiflora* (long-flowered); hardy tuberous perennial; 9 inches; flowers pale rose, in May; Altai; 1832. *C. lutea* (yellow); hardy perennial; 1 foot; flowers yellow, in May; England. *C. Marshalliana* (Marshall's); hardy tuberous perennial; 6 inches; flowers purple, in May; Tauria; 1824. *C. nobilis* (noble); hardy tuberous perennial; 1 foot; flowers pale yellow, in May; Siberia; 1783. *C. pæonifolia* (peony-leaved); hardy perennial; 1 foot; flowers purple, in May; Siberia; 1820. *C. Siberica* (Siberian); hardy perennial; 6 inches; flowers yellow, in July; Siberia; 1810.

CORYLUS. [Corylaceæ.] The Hazel-nuts, or Filberts, are mostly cultivated for fruit, and seldom for ornament, except the purple foliaged variety. They are all of easy culture in garden soil. Propagated by seeds, division, and layers.

COSMANTHUS. [Hydrophyllaceæ.] Pretty hardy annuals. Rich garden soil. Increased by seeds.

C. fimbriatus (fringed); hardy annual; 1 foot; flowers white and lilac, in June; North America; 1838.

COSMEA. [Compositæ.] Pretty half-hardy annuals and perennials. Rich garden soil. The annuals increased by seeds, which should be sown in gentle heat in spring, and the young plant turned out in May; the perennials, by root division. Also called *Cosmos*.

C. bipinnata (bi-pinnate); half-hardy annual; 3 feet; flowers purple, in July; Mexico; 1799. *C. diversifolia* (various-leaved); half-hardy tuberous perennial; 3 feet; flowers lilac, in September; Mexico; 1835. *C. lutea* (yellow); half-hardy annual; 2 feet; flowers yellow, in September; Mexico; 1811. *C. scabiosoides* (scabious-like); half-hardy tuberous perennial; 4 feet; flowers scarlet, in September; Mexico; 1836. *C. sulphurea* (sulphur); half-hardy annual; 2 feet; flowers yellow, in July; Mexico; 1799. *C. tenuifolia* (slender-leaved); half-hardy annual; 2 feet; flowers red, in September; Mexico; 1836.

COTONEASTER. [Pomaceæ.] Hardy trees and shrubs of an ornamental character. Common soil. Increased by layers and seeds. Most of the species require protection in the Northern States. The evergreens are very ornamental in leaf and berry.

C. acuminata (pointed-leaved); 4 feet; flowers pink, in May; Nepaul; 1820. *C. affinis* (similar); 4 feet; flowers pink, in May; Nepaul; 1820. *C. bacillaris* (rod); Nepaul; 1841. *C. buxifolia* (box-leaved); 3 feet; flowers white, in May; Nepaul; 1824. *C. buxifolia marginata* (white-margined); 3 feet; flowers white, in May; Sahrunpore; 1838. *C. denticulata* (fine-toothed-leaved); 6 feet; flowers white; Mexico; 1826. *C. emarginata* (bordered); flowers white, in May; Nepaul. *C. frigida* (cold); 10 feet; flowers white and green, in May; Nepaul; 1824. *C. laxiflora* (loose-flowered); 4 feet; flowers pink, in May; 1826. *C. laxiflora uniflora* (one-flowered); 3 feet; flowers white, in May; Nepaul. *C. microphylla* (small-leaved); 4 feet; flowers white, in May; Nepaul; 1825. *C. multiflora* (many-flowered); 4 feet; flowers white, in May; Altai; 1837. *C. nummularia* (moneywort-leaved); 10 feet; flowers white and green, in May; Nepaul; 1824. *C. rotundifolia* (round-leaved); 3 feet; flowers white, in May; Nepaul; 1820. *C. Roylei* (Dr. Royle's); flowers white; North India; 1845. *C. tomentosa* (woolly); 4 feet; flowers pink, in May; 1759. *C. vulgaris* (common); 4 feet; flowers pink, in May; Europe; 1656. *C. vulgaris depressa* (depressed); flowers white, in May; Europe. *C. vulgaris erythrocarpa* (red-fruited); 4 feet; flowers white, in May; Europe. *C. vulgaris melanocarpa* (black-fruited); 8 feet; flowers white, in May; Europe.

COTTON GRASS. See ERIOPHORUM.

COUSINEA. [Compositæ.] A family of not very ornamental hardy plants. The annuals increased by seed, the perennials by division. Common soil. The species are *C. carduiformis, cynaroides, Hohenakeri, hystrix, macrocephala, tenella,* and *Volgensis.*

COW PARSNIP. See HERACLEUM.

COWSLIP. See PRIMULA.

CRANE'S BILL. See GERANIUM.

CRATÆGUS. *Hawthorn.* [Pomaceæ.] The most ornamental genus of the smaller trees. It is a very extensive family. The majority grow from twelve to twenty feet high, forming small trees of considerable diversity of habit. The flowers are for the most part white, in bunches, so familiar in the common Hawthorn; but there are some with pink blossoms. The trees are, however, no less valuable on account of their flowers than their fruit, which is very ornamental in the autumn; the flowers being developed in the spring, or between May and June. The thorns all grow freely in good garden soil, preferring that of a loamy texture. They are, in ordinary cases, better known as small standards, or trees, than as bushes. It is usual to graft all the kinds upon stocks of the common Hawthorn: an upright leading shoot is then trained up to a sufficient height for the stem, which may be four or six feet high, when they are pruned to form the head. The common kind for stocks, or for the purpose of forming hedges,—for which it is one of the best of deciduous subjects, — is raised from the seeds or haws, sown broadcast in beds, and transplanted when a year old into nursery-beds. Fences are best planted with two-year-old plants. The stocks for grafting should be four years old ; and, if they are not placed where the trees are to remain, they should have been transplanted annually previously to grafting them.

The species are all desirable ; but the following are selected in regard to their different qualities and properties : —

FOR FLOWERS. — *C. cordata;* flowers white, in large corymbs. *C. Mexicana;* flowers white, succeeded by large yellowish apple-like fruit. *C. Oxyacantha flore-pleno;* with double white flowers. *C. Oxyacantha præcox;* the Glastonbury thorn ; white, the earliest of all, blooming in early May. *C. Oxyacantha punicea;* with crimson flowers. *C. Oxyacantha rosea flore-pleno;* with double crimson flowers.

FOR FRUIT. — *C. Aronia;* fruit yellow. *C. Azarolus;* fruit scarlet. *C. coccinea;* fruit scarlet. *C. Douglasii;* fruit dark purple. *C. Mexicanus;* fruit pale yellowish-green. *C. Orientalis;* fruit coral-colored. *C. Oxyacantha melanocarpa;* fruit black. *C. tanacetifolia Leeana;* fruit yellow.

FOR HABIT OF GROWTH. — *C. Crusgalli;* spreading. *C. glandulosa;* compact. *C. Oxyacantha pendula;* drooping. *C. purpurea;* upright, rigid. *C. Oxyacantha stricta;* fastigiate.

C. Crusgalli pyracanthifolia is a remarkable grotesque little tree, like a miniature cedar of Lebanon. *C. pyracantha* is an evergreen trailing species, with bunches of fiery berries in winter. It is one of the best of plants for training against a wall or building.

CRAWFORDIA. [Gentianaceæ.] Beautiful half-hardy perennial twiner, thriving in loamy peat. Increased by cuttings or division.

C. fasciculata (fascicled) ; 4 feet ; flowers blue, in August ; Himalaya ; 1855.

GARDEN FLOWERS. 125

CREPIS. See TOLPIS.

CRISTARIA. [Malvaceæ.] Hardy herbaceous perennial, thriving in peat, and increased by division.

C. coccinea (scarlet); hardy perennial; 6 inches; flowers scarlet, in August; Missouri; 1811.

CROCUS. Beautiful dwarf hardy bulbs, with grassy leaves and showy flowers, of easiest culture in common garden soil. The bulbs should be planted in October or November, about two inches deep, in clumps, or rows. They should not be planted singly, as they are far more effective if put in groups of six, twelve, or even more, the groups being proportionately distant. There is another race of Crocuses, the autumn-bloomers, comprising some very splendid species, which bloom in the end of October and through November, and are equally useful, as ornaments, with the spring Crocuses, in consequence of blooming when other flowers are out of bloom. Many of these, however, are very scarce. They should be planted in June and July, and in other respects require precisely the same treatment as the others.

C. argenteus (silvery); hardy bulb; 4 inches; flowers white and brown, in April; Pisa; 1842. *C. Asturicus* (Asturian); hardy bulb; 4 inches; flowers purple, in October; Asturia; 1842. *C. aureus* (golden); hardy bulb; 4 inches; flowers yellow, in April; Greece. *C. biflorus* (two-flowered); hardy bulb; 6 inches; flowers white and purple, in spring; Crimea; 1629. *C. Boryanus* (Bory's); hardy bulb; 6 inches; flowers white, in autumn; Greek Islands; 1842. *C. Cartwrightianus* (Cartwright's); hardy bulb; 6 inches; flowers white and purple, in autumn; Crete; 1842. *C. Caucasicus* (Caucasian); hardy bulb; 4 inches; flowers purple, in September; Caucasus. *C. chrysanthus* (golden-flowered); hardy bulb; 4 inches; flowers golden, in April. *C. Imperatorius* (Imperato's); hardy bulb; 4 inches; flowers lilac, in April; Naples; 1830. *C. luteus* (common yellow); hardy bulb; 4 inches; flowers yellow, in April; Turkey;

1629. *C. Mæsiacus* (Mæsian); hardy bulb; 6 inches; flowers orange or saffron, in spring; Greece; 1629. *C. medius* (intermediate); hardy bulb; 6 inches; flowers violet, in autumn; Liguria; 1842. *C. nivalis* (snowy); hardy bulb; 4 inches; flowers white, in May; Morea. *C. odorus* (sweet-scented); hardy bulb; 6 inches; flowers lilac and gold, in autumn; Naples; 1830. *C. Pallasianus* (Pallas'); hardy bulb; 4 inches; flowers lilac, in October; Crimea; 1821. *C. pulchellus* (neat); hardy bulb; 6 inches; flowers pale-bluish, pearl-colored, in autumn; Mount Atlas; 1843. *C. Pyrenæus* (Pyrenæan); hardy bulb; 4 inches; flowers purple, in September; England. *C. sativus* (saffron); hardy bulb; 4 inches; flowers violet, in September; England. *C. serotinus* (late); hardy bulb; 4 inches; flowers violet, in October; south of Europe; 1629, *C. speciosus* (showy); hardy bulb; 6 inches; flowers blue, in autumn; England. *C. Susianus* (Susian); hardy bulb; 6 inches; flowers deep yellow, in spring; Turkey, 1605. *C. Thomasianus* (Thomas's); hardy bulb; 4 inches; flowers blue, in September; Naples; 1830. *C. vallecola* (valley); hardy bulb; 4 inches; flowers white, in October; Trebizond Alps; 1842. *C. versicolor* (many-colored); hardy bulb; 6 inches; flowers white and blue, in spring; south of Europe; 1629.

There are numerous other species and varieties, all plants of much beauty and interest. The following are good named varieties. WHITE.— *Caroline Chisholm, Ecossais, Grootvorst, Countess de Morny, Queen Victoria.* BLUE.— *Albion, Argus, David Rizzio, Grande Vidette, Grand Lilas, Lilaceus, Vulcan, Walter Scott.* YELLOW.— *Grande jaune, Drap d'or, Scotch.*

CROSSWORT. See CRUCIANELLA.

CROWFOOT. See RANUNCULUS.

CRUCIANELLA. [Galiaceæ.] Hardy annuals and perennials, with a few stove species. The annuals are of no floricultural importance. *C. stylosa* is a pretty trailing species, desirable for rock-work, growing in garden soil, and propagated by cuttings or division.

C. stylosa (long-styled); hardy perennial; 1 foot; flowers pink, in July; Persia; 1836. *C. suaveolens* (sweet); hardy perennial; 1 foot; flowers yellow, in July; Russia; 1838.

CRYPTOMERIA. *Japan Cedar.* [Pinaceæ.] A very ornamental evergreen tree, thriving best in pure and rather sandy loam, but not hardy in the Northern States, though occasionally surviving the winter. Propagated by seeds and cuttings.

C. Japonica (Japan); half-hardy evergreen; 100 feet; Japan; 1844. There is a dwarf variety.

CUCUMIS. *Cucumber.* [Cucurbitaceæ.] Half-hardy trailing annuals, requiring a warm exposure and rich soil. A few species are grown for their ornamental fruit.

C. flexuosus (snake); flowers yellow; fruit in autumn; East Indies; 1597. Some of the other species are *C. dipsaceus, melochito,* and *perennis.*

CUCURBITA. *Gourds.* [Cucurbitaceæ.] Half-hardy trailing annuals, requiring the same treatment as *Cucumis.* *C. digitata, leucantha, Angora, melopeto variegata, maxima, sipho,* are desirable.

CUNILA. [Lamiaceæ.] Hardy herbaceous perennials. Peat and loam. Propagated by division.

C. coccinea (scarlet); hardy perennial; 18 inches; flowers scarlet, in September; North America; 1823. *C. Mariana* (Maryland); hardy perennial; 1 foot; flowers red, in September; North America; 1759.

CUPHEA. [Lythraceæ.] Pretty shrubby or herbaceous perennials and procumbent annuals, comprising both tender and hardy species. The hardy annual kinds should be sown along with the annuals in April on a slight hot-bed, or in frames, for the earliest bloom, and again in May in the open borders. They prefer a rich light soil. The greenhouse and tender species grow in a mixture of two parts leaf-mould to one of loam, with a sixth of sand added; and are increased by cuttings in sand, in a brisk hot-bed, during the spring or summer. *C. ignea*, better known as *platycentra*, an almost ever-blooming shrubby species, with bright scarlet tubes, just tipped with a ring of black and white, is well suited for the flower-garden during summer. It scarcely grows more than a foot high in the course of a season : but the larger the plants, the better they look; so that the old plants should be preserved.

C. ignea (fiery) ; greenhouse sub-shrub ; 18 inches ; flowers scarlet and black, all the year ; Mexico ; 1845. *C. Melvillii* (Melville's) ; stove sub-shrub ; 3 feet ; flowers scarlet and green, in July ; Guinea ; 1823. *C. miniata* (vermilion) ; greenhouse sub-shrub ; 18 inches ; flowers scarlet and purple, in June ; South America ; 1845. *C. procumbens* (procumbent) ; hardy annual ; 1 foot ; flowers pale-purple, in July ; Mexico ; 1816. *C. silenoides* (silene-like) ; hardy annual ; 18 inches ; flowers lilac-edged purple, in July ; Mexico ; 1836. *C. strigillosa* (coarse-haired) ; greenhouse sub-shrub ; 18 inches ; flowers red and yellow, in June ; Mexico ; 1844. *C. viscosissima* (clammiest) ; hardy annual ; 18 inches ; flowers pale-purple, in July ; America ; 1776.

C. eminens is of no value as a bedding plant.

CUPRESSUS. *Cypress.* [Pinaceæ.] Handsome evergreen shrub-like trees, mostly of pyramidal growth. They are mostly large trees when full grown, but, being erect-growing, may be kept for many years in a moderate space. Good loamy soil is best for them ; and they are best increased by seeds, but sometimes by cuttings and by grafting.

ORNAMENTAL EVERGREENS.— *C. sempervirens* (common evergreen) ; *C. Lusitanica* (cedar of Goa) ; *C. torulosa* (Bhotan cypress) ; *C. thurifera* (frankincense-bearing) ; *C. funebris* (funebral) ; *C. Goveniana* (Gowen's) ; *C. macrocarpa* (large-fruited) ; *C. Udheana* (Udhe's).

Most of the species are tender in the Northern States.

GARDEN FLOWERS. 129

CURRANT. See RIBES.

CYANANTHUS. [Polemoniaceæ.] Pretty little hardy herbaceous plants, requiring sandy soil. Increased by division and cuttings, which must be rooted under a bell-glass.

C. lobatus (lobed); hardy perennial; 10 inches; flowers purple or blue, in August; Chinese Tartary; 1844.

CYDONIA. *Quince.* [Pomaceæ.] A genus of trees and shrubs, including *C. Japonica*, once known as *Pyrus Japonica*, which is one of the most brilliant of deciduous flowering shrubs, blooming in early spring. The large scarlet flowers grow in clusters on the branches, and are very conspicuous. It is a free-growing plant, and does well trained against a wall as a shrub, or as a hedge-plant. There are varieties, with pink, citron-yellow, cream-colored, dark-red, and semi-double flowers, some of which are very fine. The fruit is very fragrant. Propagated by root-cutting, seeds, division, and layers.

C. Japonica (Japan); hardy shrub; 6 feet; flowers scarlet, in May; Japan; 1815. *C. sinensis* (Chinese); hardy tree; 15 feet; flowers pink, in May; China; 1816.

CYNANCHUM. [Asclepiadaceæ.] Mostly hardy herbaceous perennials, not very showy, growing in common soil, and propagated by division. The species are *C. acutum, cirrhosum, excelsum, luteum, medium, melanthus, nigrum, roseum, villosum,* and others.

CYNARA. *Artichoke.* [Compositæ.] Large plants with ornamental foliage, suitable for large borders. Common soil. Increased by division.

C. cardunculus (cardoon); 5 feet; flowers blue, in August; Candia; 1658. *C. ferox* (fierce); 5 feet; flowers blue, in July; Italy; 1820. *C. glomerata* (clustered); half-hardy; 3 inches; flowers blue, in August; Cape of Good Hope; 1824. *C. horrida* (horrid); greenhouse; 6 feet; flowers purple, in August;

9

Madeira; 1768. *C. integrifolia* (whole-leaved); 4 feet; flowers blue, in July; Spain. *C. pygmæa* (pigmy); 1 foot; flowers purple, in July; Spain; 1820. *C. Scolymus* (common); *Artichoke;* 8 feet; flowers purple, in August; south of Europe; 1548. *C. spinosissima* (most spiny); 4 feet; flowers blue, in July; Sicily; 1826.

CYNOGLOSSUM. *Hound's Tongue.* [Boraginaceæ.] A large genus of hardy annuals, biennials, and perennials, generally coarse-growing, and not desirable. *C. canescens, diffusum, hirsutum,* and *lanceolatum,* are annuals; *C. amplexicaule, anchusoides, Australe, grandiflorum, longiflorum, Magellense, tomentosum,* and *Virginicum,* are perennials; and there are about twenty biennial species.

CYPRESS. See CUPRESSUS.

CYPRESS VINE. See QUAMOCLIT.

CYPRIPEDIUM. *Lady's-Slipper.* [Orchidaceæ.] Beautiful herbaceous perennials, comprising about a dozen hardy and some two dozen stove species. The latter are easily cultivated in a moist heated atmosphere, such as the Orchideous family generally require, and may be potted in rough turfy peat. They must not be over-watered at the root, nor should cold water be poured about their roots or hearts at any time. They increase by division. The hardy ones are more difficult to cultivate, and can only be well managed in a cold, shady situation, in a bed of peat earth. They may be kept in pots of peat soil, and set into a frame. Whether grown in pots, or planted out, they do not at all like to be disturbed, and should therefore be replanted or repotted as seldom as possible. It is a remarkable as well as beautiful family, and is worth any trouble to secure its successful cultivation.

C. album (white); hardy perennial; 1 foot; flowers white, in May; North America; 1800. *C. arietinum* (ram's-head); hardy perennial; 6 inches; flowers white and green, in May;

North America; 1808. *C. barbatum* (bearded); stove perennial; 1 foot; flowers purple and green, in July; Mount Ophir; 1838. *C. calceolus* (common slipper); hardy perennial; 1 foot; flowers yellow and brown, in May; England. *C. candidum* (white); hardy perennial; 1 foot; flowers white, in May; North America; 1826. *C. guttatum* (spotted); hardy perennial; 2 feet; flowers white and rose, in May; Siberia; 1829. *C. humile* or *acaule* (humble); hardy perennial; 6 inches; flowers purple and white, in June; North America; 1786. *C. insigne* (striking); stove perennial; 1 foot; flowers green, white, and purple, in July; Nepaul; 1819. *C. Irapeanum* (Irapean); stove perennial; 18 inches; flowers yellow, in June; Mexico; 1844. *C. Lowii* (Low's); stove perennial; 18 inches; flowers purple and green, in May; Borneo; 1847. *C. pubescens* (pubescent); hardy perennial; 1 foot; flowers yellow and purple, in May; North America; 1790. *C. spectabile* (showy); hardy perennial; 18 inches; flowers purple and white, in June; North America; 1731. *C. ventricosum* (bellied); hardy perennial; 9 inches; flowers purple, in May; Siberia; 1828. *C. venustum* (handsome); stove perennial; 1 foot; flowers green and red, in July; Nepaul; 1816.

CYTISUS. [Leguminosæ.] Elegant, and, for the most part, showy shrubs, and small trees. *C. Laburnum* and *Alpinus* are well-known free-flowering trees, and, though the most familiar and common, are the most beautiful of the whole family. They may be raised from seeds, which need only be sown on the common open ground and raked in, where they may be thinned to proper distances, two or three inches apart, and remain the first season; the next, they may be planted out in rows, a foot from plant to plant, and two feet from row to row. As all these trees are wanted as standards, whether for their own sakes or for stocks on which to graft or bud other varieties, the side-shoots, except the top two or three, should be rubbed off while merely buds. When they are tall enough, their heads may be allowed to grow and bloom, because those with the largest and handsomest racemes of flowers may be saved for Laburnums, and the others may be worked with the different species of Cytisus, some of which are white, others yellow, and many are of different forms and habits; but all make good standards. Some of them have small racemes of flowers, others bloom all the way along the branches; some are pendulous, others shrubby and upright; but all very pretty, and worth growing in collection among ornamental shrubs. Most of the hardy kinds may be grown as dwarf shrubs in any common soil, and are readily increased either by seeds or by layers. The greenhouse species are handsome shrubs, growing freely in peat and loam, and increased by seeds, by grafting, or by cuttings.

ORNAMENTAL TREES. — *C. Laburnum* (common Laburnum); *C. Alpinus* (Scotch Laburnum); *C. Adami* (purple Laburnum).

ORNAMENTAL SHRUBS. — *C. purpureus* (purple); *C. albus* (Portugal Broom); *C. nigricans* (black); *C. sessilifolius* (sessile-leaved); *C. patens* (spreading); *C. scoparius* (broom), and its varieties; *C. nanus* (dwarf); *C. multiflorus* (many leaved); *C. spinosus* (spiny).

There are some thirty other species.

CZACKIA. See ANTHERICUM LILIASTRUM.

DAHLIA. [Compositæ.] The florists' varieties of this flower require good rich soil, and a moist, open situation. In this country, the plant is falling out of favor, and is by no means as extensively grown as formerly; the attention of florists being directed to Hollyhocks and Gladiolus. The flower, though showy, has a set, rosette appearance, and is a rank-smelling thing; and in a small garden a hundred flowers can be found any one of which will well fill its place. For ordinary gardens, where no great increase is required, the tubers may be placed in any warm situation — a hot-bed for instance, or a warm kitchen or other apartment — about the month of April, and in a few days the eyes, or incipient shoot-buds, will appear; then separate the tubers into as many pieces as are wanted, with at least a sound eye and tuber to each piece. These pieces may be potted, and placed in the greenhouse or dwelling-house, or in a common frame, or any place from which frost can be excluded, and they will begin growing. In potting, the tubers may be freely cut to lessen their size for the convenience of using moderate sized pots. Those who want to increase their stock considerably may pot the whole tubers, and put them in a hot-bed, and as fast as any shoots come and have grown two inches long, cut them off at the base, pot them singly in the smallest sized pots, and put them in the hot-bed to strike. Plants reared in either of these ways may be put in the open ground about the middle of May, in the places where they are to flower. The plants should be six feet apart, and they must be tied up as they grow, or the wind will break them down. Seeds may be sown in April in a hot-bed, and the young plants potted and kept growing till the middle of May; they may then be planted in rows, two feet apart in the row, and three from row to row. The florists' varieties have been obtained by years of crossing and seed-saving, from *D. variabilis*, and are now almost endless in variety of colour, and vary in height from three to six feet. The other kinds of Dahlias are small tuberous-rooted perennials, requiring to be protected in winter, and planted out in summer in good garden soil.

D. Barkeriæ (Miss Barker's); half-hardy tuber; 2 feet; flowers blush, in August; Mexico; 1838. *D. frustranea* (barren-rayed); half-hardy tuber; 6 feet; flowers scarlet or orange, in September; Mexico; 1802. *D. glabrata* (smooth); half-hardy tuber; 3 feet; flowers lilac, in July; Mexico; 1838. *D. scapigera* (scape-bearing); half-hardy tuber; 2 feet; flowers lilac, in July; Mexico; 1837. *D. variabilis* (variable); half-hardy perennial; 3 to 6 feet; flowers various, in September; Mexico; 1789.

The florists' varieties are very numerous, and a selection can be readily made from any florist's catalogue. The pompon varieties are rather pretty if well pegged down in a bed.

DAFFODIL. See NARCISSUS.

DAISY. See BELLIS.

DALIBARDA. [Rosaceæ.] A pretty, low-growing family of plants, suitable for rock-work. Increased by seed and division.

D. repens (creeping); hardy perennial; 6 inches; flowers white, all summer. North America.

DAPHNE. [Thymelaeæ.] A genus of well-known plants, of which only two, *D. cneorum* and *mezereon*, are hardy in the Northern States. They thrive in any good garden soil, and are propagated by division, layers, or seeds. The latter require two years to vegetate.

D. Fortuni (Fortune's); hardy shrub; 3 feet; flowers lilac, in April; China, 1844. *D. mezereon* (hardy shrub); 2 feet; flowers pink, in April; England. Variety *album* has white flowers; *rubrum* has red flowers; *autumnale* has red flowers, in August. *D. cneorum* (garland flower); hardy evergreen; 1 foot; flowers pink, in May. A variety has variegated foliage.

DATURA. [Solanaceæ.] The greenhouse species, usually known as Brugmansias, do well planted in a rich, moist, sunny border, in summer, and often flower profusely. The annuals are rank-growing plants, but have showy flowers. They are easily raised from seed, which should be sown in May in the border, or in a frame in April, and transplanted.

D. bicolor (two-colored); greenhouse shrub; 10 feet; flowers orange and red, in August; Peru; 1833. *D. candida* (white); greenhouse shrub; 10 feet; flowers white, in August; Peru, 1813. *D. ceratocaulon* (horn-stemmed); half-hardy annual; 2 feet; flowers white, in July; South America; 1805. *D. cornigera* (horn-bearing); greenhouse shrub; 10 feet; flowers white, in July; Brazil; 1846. *D. fastuosa* (purple); half-hardy annual; 2 feet; flowers purple, in July; Egypt; 1629. *D. Gardneri* (Gardner's); greenhouse shrub; 10 feet; flowers white, in July; South America; 1733. *D. Knightii* (Knight's); greenhouse shrub; 10 feet; flowers white, in August; gardens. *D. lutea* (yellow); greenhouse shrub; 10 feet; flowers yellowish, in August. *D. Metel* (downy); half-hardy annual; 2 feet; flowers white, in July; Asia; 1596. *D. Stramonium* (Stramonium); hardy annual; 3 feet; flowers white, in July; England. *D. suaveolens* (sweet-scented); greenhouse shrub; 10 feet; flowers white, in August; Peru; 1733. *D. Tatula* (blue); half-hardy annual; 2 feet; flowers purple, in July; North America; 1629.

DAY LILY. See HEMEROCALLIS.

DELPHINIUM. *Larkspur*. [Ranunculaceæ.] An extensive genus of hardy plants, chiefly perennials, but containing some annuals and biennials. Mostly plants of considerable beauty, and favorites in gardens. The perennials are increased by dividing the roots in spring, and need not be disturbed oftener than once in three years, to part the roots. The double variety of *D. grandiflorum* has beautiful flowers of an intense blue color. The best of the annuals, *D. consolida* and *Ajacis*, should be sown where they are to bloom, and thinned to three or four inches apart. They ought to be grown in every garden, and require only good garden soil. The branching Larkspur is often hardy enough to stand the winter if sown in autumn.

D. aconiti (aconite-like); hardy annual; 1 foot; flowers purplish, in June; Levant; 1801. *D. Ajacis* (rocket); hardy annual; 18 inches; flowers pink, blue, or white, in June; Switzerland, 1573. *D. amænum* (pleasing); hardy perennial; 3 feet; flowers light-blue, in July; Siberia; 1818. *D. azureum* (azure); hardy perennial; 5 feet; flowers light-blue, in July; Carolina; 1805. *D. Barlowi* (Barlow's); hardy perennial; 3 feet; flowers deep-blue, double, in June; gardens. *D. cheilanthum* (lip-flowered); hardy perennial; 3 feet; flowers dark-blue. in June; Siberia; 1819. *D. Chinense* (Chinese); hardy perennial; 2 feet; flowers deep-blue, in July; Tartary; 1818. *D. consolida* (branching); hardy annual; 2½ feet; flowers blue, pink, or white, in June; England. *D. divaricatum* (straggling); hardy annual; 18 inches; flowers purple, in July; Asia; 1836. *D. grandiflorum* (large-flowered); hardy perennial; 2 feet; flowers deep-blue, in July; Siberia; 1816. *D. grandiflorum flore-pleno;* hardy perennial; 2 feet; flowers deep-blue, double, in July; gardens. *D. speciosum* (showy); hardy perennial; 4 feet; flowers blue, in July; Caucasus; 1816.

There are numerous other showy species, among which *D. Hendersoni* and *formosum*, garden varieties, are conspicuous. For common cultivation, we should select as the best, *D. formosum, sinense* (white, light, and deep blue), *sinense plenum, Hendersoni, elatum,* varieties *cœlestinum, grandiflorum, bicolor plenum, azureum grandiflorum, bicolor* and *plenum.*

DESERT ROD. See EREMOSTACHYS.

DENTARIA. [Cruciferæ.] A family of hardy herbaceous plants, comprising some dozen species, easily propagated by seeds and division. They are of little horticultural importance.

DEUTZIA. [Philadelphaceæ.] Handsome hardy deciduous shrubs, very ornamental in both garden and shrubbery. Propagated by suckers and layers. The smaller species, especially *D. gracilis*, are valuable for forcing in the greenhouse.

D. corymbosa (corymbed); hardy shrub; 5 feet; flowers white, in June; Himalayas; 1838. *D. gracilis* (graceful); hardy shrub; 2 feet; flowers white, in May; Japan; 1850. *D. scabra* (rough); hardy shrub; 5 feet; flowers white, in June; Japan; 1833. *D. staminea* (broad-stamened); hardy shrub; 3 feet; flowers white, in June; Himalayas; 1831. The double-flowered species are desirable. *D. crenata flore-pleno* is a fine species, introduced from Japan in 1863

DEVIL IN A BUSH. See NIGELLA.

DIANTHOIDIS. See FENZLIA.

DIANTHUS. *Pink.* [Caryophyllaceæ.] The majority of the Pinks are highly ornamental hardy perennials, particularly suited for rock-work, and almost all the species are alike desirable in such situations. All the hardy perennials prefer a light, dryish soil, and are increased by cuttings or pipings, and also by seeds, which should be sown as soon as ripe. There are a few half-hardy, sub-shrubby kinds, which may be kept in a dry frame or greenhouse, and should be potted in sandy loam and peat : they propagate by cuttings. The Indian pink *(D. Chinensis)* is a richly colored hardy biennial, and does well treated as an annual.

Pink (Dianthus plumarius, vars.). — The fancy or florist's race of pinks is extensive: they require every year to be struck from pipings, which are the shoots that spring out round the base of the stem; these are taken off at blooming time, or rather later, and each shoot is cut across just below the third joint; the lower pair of leaves from the heart being cut clean away. A bed is made of rich sandy loam and dung, and the surface is made quite soft with water, in which state pipings or shoots are inserted all over it not more than an inch apart. After drying for an hour or two, it is covered with a hand-glass, which is not disturbed for some days, and then only to water the pipings if they require it. A good deal can be done towards moistening them by watering outside the glass. In three weeks they will have struck root, and the glass may then be tilted a little to admit some air, and in a few days more may be taken away, that they may have full benefit of the air. After a few days, they may be taken up, and planted out in four-feet beds: six inches apart every way will be the proper distance for the plants. The soil in which they grow should be the loam from rotted turfs; or, if ordinary garden soil be used of necessity, a good dressing of dung should be forked in before the pinks are planted. In May, when they send up their bloom-stalks, remove all but the best from each plant, and, as these advance, take off all but two or three buds from each stalk; and when these have swelled almost to bursting, but not quite, tie them fast round the middle with a piece of bass-matting, and tear the bud-cover down to the tie at its five natural divisions. After the bloom is over, the grass, as it is called, — that is, the young shoots, — will be ready to strike for the next year. The best double Pinks do not seed freely, but they do occasionally; and such seed should be prized as a means towards obtaining new varieties of merit. The seed should be sown in wide-mouthed pots or seed-pans, not too thick, and placed in a cold frame: if not too much crowded when they come up, the plants may remain there till they are large enough to plant out, in like manner with the pipings or cuttings, and the treatment is the same throughout. As they bloom, throw away instantly every one that is semi-double or single, and all that are not as good or better than the varieties already in cultivation. A very few of the seedlings may be worth trying again, and of these a few cuttings should be reared. The flowers of seedlings should be examined daily, almost hourly, in order to destroy at once those that are good for nothing; for single and semi-double kinds can only spoil the seed of the better sorts. It is not to be expected, with every care and advantage in seed-saving, to get one improved variety out of fifty, or even a larger number of seedlings. For list of the best varieties see the latest trade catalogues.

Carnation and Picotee (Dianthus Caryophyllus, vars.). — These superb and highly scented flowers are precisely similar as to the requirements of their cultivation. They are propagated chiefly by layering. The shoots at the bottom of the stems, being longer than those of the pink, can be pegged under the surface to strike root, which they do when half divided from the parent; for by cutting them half-way through, and pegging the cut part firmly under the surface, the supply of nourishment from the parent plant being diminished, they endeavor to compensate for their loss by forming roots. The shoots in this case do not droop, because the connection with the old plant is not cut off, as in the removal of a piping; consequently, there is not so much risk of losing any of them. In cutting these stems, the knife should go in slanting just under a joint (about the third joint from the top); and, when nearly half through, they should be split up half an inch above the joint, the sloping piece below the joint being cut off even. The half-joint thus separated, will, when pegged down, send forth roots. These layers, as they are called, may be all cut off in September, and potted in four-inch pots, two in a pot, with nothing but clean good loam from rotted turfs, no dung. In February, prepare rich mould to bloom them in, — half loam from rotted turfs, a fourth decomposed dung, and the other fourth turfy peat and silver, or other very clean sand, mixed well and left in a heap. In the beginning of April, get twelve-inch pots; fill one-third with sherds of broken pots, then a third of the proper soil, then turn out the ball of earth with the pair of plants in it; and, having placed it in the middle at the proper depth, fill up all round, press the soil to the ball of earth, and after adjusting it properly, and filling up to within half-an-inch of the top edge, place the pot on a dry hard flooring, the object being twofold, — to prevent worms entering at the bottom hole and disarranging the soil, and to keep this hole, which is essential for drainage, from getting filled up, or in any way stopped, to prevent the egress of whatever superfluous water may reach the soil. Go through the whole in this way, and then water freely, taking all possible precaution to prevent vermin from getting to the pots: one plan is to raise shelves, with their supports standing in pans of water. When the stems rise for bloom, treat them in the same way as Pinks, in every respect, even to the flowering. The Carnation differs from the Picotee only in the disposition of the coloring; the Carnation is striped or ribboned outwards, the Picotee is edged or feathered inwards. It is a prevalent practice to put cards on the buds of the flowers, that the petals may be displayed on them as they open. For a list of the best varieties of these flowers, see the latest trade-lists.

Sweetwilliam (D. barbatus). — This hardy perennial is best treated as a biennial, and raised annually from seeds, except in the case of distinct and particularly handsome varieties, which can only be increased by propagating from the shoots produced from the root, and which may be either treated as cuttings or layers. The seeds should be sown in June in a bed of light open soil; and, when the seedlings have formed a pair or two of leaves, they may be pricked out three inches apart on a bed of light rich earth, in which they may grow till autumn, and will gain strength for flowering. In September or early in October, remove them with good balls of earth to the borders or beds where they are to flower. For beds, this should be done annually; the old roots being either destroyed after seed is secured, or transplanted to the borders, or, in the case of new and striking varieties, removed and carefully propagated. In borders, the old roots, if vigorous enough, may be left to bloom again. Young plants reared from cuttings or layers may be treated exactly like seedlings. The best soil for the blooming plants is a sandy loam well manured with decayed leaf-mould and stable-dung. The varieties of different colors of Sweetwilliam are now numerous; but they are hardly advanced enough for selection by name.

D. arboreus (tree); half-hardy evergreen sub-shrub; 2 feet; flowers pink, in July; Greece; 1820. *D. arbuscula* (small tree); half-hardy evergreen sub-shrub; 18 inches; flowers red, in July; China; 1824. *D. barbatus* (Sweetwilliam); hardy perennial; 18 inches; flowers various, in July; Germany; 1573. *D. caryophyllus* (clove-pink); hardy perennial; 2 feet; flowers flesh-color, in June; England *D. Chinensis* (Indian pink); half-hardy biennial; 1 foot: flowers various, in July; China; 1713. *D. Heddewigii* is a gigantic form of *D. Chinensis*, introduced from Japan in 1859. *D. fruticosus* (shrubby); half-hardy evergreen sub-shrub; 3 feet; flowers pink, in July;

Greece; 1815. *D. Hendersonianus* (Henderson's); hardy perennial; 1 foot; flowers crimson, in July; gardens. *D. plumarius* (garden pink); hardy perennial; 9 inches; flowers white and purple, in June; England. *D. suffruticosus* (half-shrubby); half-hardy evergreen sub-shrub; 18 inches; flowers pink, in August; Siberia; 1804.

There are about one hundred hardy perennial kinds, varying in height from 6 to 18 inches, and with flowers usually white, pink, or flesh-colored. All of these are more or less ornamental. *D. deltoides* is a fine plant for rockwork: *D. cruentus* has brilliant red flowers; *D. Verschafeldtii* and *Veitchii* are very showy species if carefully grown.

DIAPENSIA. [Polemoneaceæ.] A dwarf Alpine evergreen, of difficult culture.

D. Lapponica (Lapland); hardy shrub; 4 inches; flowers white, in July; Lapland; North America; 1801.

DICTAMNUS. *Fraxinella.* [Rutaceæ.] Showy hardy perennials, with leaves something like those of an ash-tree; hence the name *fraxinella*, or little *Fraxinus*, the latter being the name of the Ash. They grow in common garden soil, preferring loam. Propagated slowly by dividing the roots; or more readily by seeds, which should be sown as soon as ripe, in open beds.

D. albus (white); hardy perennial; 3 feet; flowers white, in June; Germany; 1596. *D. angustifolius* (narrow-leaved); hardy perennial; 3 feet; flowers lilac, in June; Altai; 1821. *D. fraxinella* (fraxinella); hardy perennial; 3 feet; flowers purple, in June; Germany; 1596.

DIDISCUS. [Umbelliferæ.] A very pretty half-hardy annual. Sow in April in a hot-bed, and plant out in the border in May. Rich light soil. Propagated by seed.

D. cœruleus (sky-blue); half-hardy annual; 2 feet; flowers pale-blue, in July; New South Wales; 1827.

DIELYTRA. [Fumariaceæ.] Hardy herbaceous perennials, with showy flowers, formerly called "Fumaria." Rich garden soil. Increased by division. *D. spectabilis* the most showy of all, is propagated readily by cuttings of the young shoots in spring, managed as dahlia cuttings, or by dividing its tuberous roots.

D. bracteosa (bracted); hardy perennial; 1 foot; flowers white, in June; North America; 1823. *D. Canadensis* (Canadian); hardy perennial; 1 foot; flowers white, in June; North America; 1819. *D. cucullaria* (hooded); hardy perennial; 9 inches; flowers whitish, in May; North America; 1731. *D. eximia* (choice); hardy perennial; 1 foot; flowers red, in June; North America; 1812. *D. formosa* (handsome); hardy perennial; 1 foot; flowers red, in June; North America; 1796. *D. speciosa* (showy); hardy perennial; 1 foot; flowers flesh-color, in June; 1810. *D. spectabilis* (beautiful); hardy tuberous perennial; 2 feet; flowers pink, in April; north of China; 1846. *D. tenuifolia* (slender-leaved); hardy perennial; 1 foot; flowers pink, in June; Kamtschatka; 1820.

There is a white variety of *D. spectabilis*.

DIERVILLA. [Caprifoliaceæ.] A hardy native shrub, growing freely anywhere, and increasing rapidly by suckers.

D. lutea (yellow); hardy shrub; 3 feet; flowers yellow, in June; North America; 1739.

DIGITALIS. *Foxglove.* [Scrophulariaceæ.] Hardy perennials, with a few biennial species, mostly showy or pretty plants for the borders. The common Foxglove *(D. purpurea)* is much esteemed as a garden flower, and is a very handsome plant. They are all increased readily by seeds. Sow in August if the seeds are ripe; if not, in April, on moderately good ground, and rather thinly; thin the plants to six inches apart; those taken up, if required, may be planted elsewhere six inches apart; but those not removed will be the strongest. The autumn-sown ones may be removed in spring, with good balls of earth, to the places where they are to flower : the summer-sown crop are better transplanted early in autumn. If the object is to *improve* the common or any other sorts, sow in beds, and thin out the plants as before, but leave the rest to bloom : when they come into flower, pull up and destroy every thing common-place and mark the best for seed.

D. ambigua (ambiguous); hardy perennial; 3 feet; flowers light-yellow, in July; Switzerland; 1596. *D. aurea* (golden); hardy perennial; 3 feet; flowers yellow, in July; Greece; 1816. *D. eriostachya* (woolly-spiked); hardy biennial; 3 feet; flowers brown and yellow, in July; Russia; 1827. *D. ferruginea* (rusty); hardy biennial; 4 feet; flowers red-brown, in July; Italy; 1597. *D. fucescens* (tawny); hardy perennial; 2 feet; flowers red, in July; Hungary; 1823. *D. laciniata* (cut-leaved); hardy perennial; 2 feet; flowers yellow, in June; Spain; 1827. *D. lanata* (woolly); hardy perennial; 2 feet; flowers white and brown, in June; Hungary; 1789. *D. ochroleuca* (yellowish); hardy perennial; 4 feet; flowers light-yellow, in July; Europe; 1816. *D. Orientalis* (Eastern); hardy perennial; 2 feet; flowers white, in June; Levant; 1820. *D. purpurea* (common); hardy biennial; 3 feet; flowers rose-purple or white, in June; England. *D. Thapsi* (mullein); hardy perennial; 2 feet; flowers purple, in June; Spain; 1752. *D. tomentosa* (woolly); hardy perennial; 3 feet; flowers red, in July; Portugal; 1818.

DINETUS. [Convolvulaceæ.] A pretty little convolvulus-like twiner, thriving in light rich soil in summer. Propagated by seeds.

D. racemosa (branched); annual climber; 12 feet; flowers white, in August; Nepaul; 1823.

D. paniculata is a greenhouse evergreen climber.

DIOSCOREA. [Dioscoriaceæ.] Tuberous-rooted perennials, mostly stove plants, but including two hardy species.

D. batatas (the Chinese Yam) is a very ornamental climber with cinnamon-scented flowers and neat glossy foliage. Propagated by offsets from root and bulblets produced on branches.

D. batatas (Chinese Yam); hardy perennial herbaceous climber; 20 feet; flowers greenish-white, in July; China.
D. villosa (wild Yam); hardy perennial herbaceous climber; 6 feet; flowers greenish-yellow, in July; North America.

DIOSPYROS. [Ebenaceæ.] The Persimmon of the Middle and Southern States, useful as an ornamental tree, and of some value for fruit. The trees differ much in the quality of the fruit, and this tree offers much opportunity for improvement to the culturist; and the time may come when the Persimmon will be a market-fruit. Rich deep soil. Increased by seed.

D. Virginiana (Virginia); hardy tree; 25 feet; flowers greenish-yellow, in June.

The family is diœcious. There are many tender species.

DIPHYLLEIA. [Berberidaceæ] A pretty hardy herbaceous perennial, allied to Jeffersonia. Soil, sandy peat. Increased by division. Requires a shady situation.

D. cymosa (cyme-flowered); hardy perennial; 6 inches; flowers white, in May; North America; 1812.

DIPLACUS. [Scrophulariaceæ.] Greenhouse or half-hardy showy shrubs, related to Mimulus, and blooming tolerably well in the borders during summer if well established, or if old plants are employed. Cuttings root readily in sandy soil, put in a frame or hand-glass, and the striking is hastened by a little warmth. They may be potted in compost of loam, lightened with turfy soil, or leaf-mould and sand. Like other free-growing subjects, the young plants must be shifted on, and frequently topped to keep them bushy, until they get to a blooming size, or as large as may be required. If good plants are required, strong young plants should be prepared through one summer for blooming the following spring. Smaller plants, to bloom the same year, may be raised in spring.

D. glutinosus (clammy); greenhouse sub-evergreen shrub; 4 feet; flowers orange-yellow, in summer; California; 1794. *D. puniceus* (scarlet); greenhouse sub-evergreen shrub; 4 feet; flowers deep crimson, in summer; California; 1837.

DIPLOPAPPUS. [Compositæ.] Hardy or half-hardy perennials, some of them sub-shrubby, related to Aster. Common loamy soil. Increased by cuttings or by division.

DIRCA. [Thymelaceæ.] A hardy deciduous shrub, commonly called Leatherwood, valuable for its early blooming. Common damp soil. Increased by layers.

D. palustris (marsh); hardy shrub; 5 feet; flowers yellow, in early spring; North America; 1750.

DISPORUM. [Melanthaceæ.] Half-hardy perennial, requiring winter protection. Soil, sandy peat. Propagated by division and seed.

D. fulvum (tawny); half-hardy perennial; 18 inches; flowers brown, in autumn; China; 1801. *D. parviflorum* (small-flowered); half-hardy perennial; 3 feet; flowers yellow, in July; Nepaul; 1820.

DITTANY. See ORIGANUM.

DODECATHEON. *American Cowslip.* [Primulaceæ.] Very pretty, early flowering, dwarf, perennial, herbaceous plants, quite hardy; preferring to be planted in a soil where there is a good proportion of loam and peat earth, and requiring a cool situation. The flowers are in shape like a half-opened inverted parasol. They are increased without difficulty by dividing the roots. Seeds are also produced, from which young plants may be raised by the same process as in raising seedlings of the Auricula, except that, when large enough, these may be planted out in the open ground. There are several varieties of the Common or Mead's Virginian Cowslip, differing in the size and color of their flowers.

D. integrifolium (entire-leaved); hardy perennial; 6 inches; flowers pale-purple, in May; North America; 1829. *D. Media* (Mead's); hardy perennial; 1 foot; flowers rose-lilac, in May; Virginia; 1744.

DOG'S-BANE. See APOCYNUM.

DOG'S-TOOTH VIOLET. See ERYTHRONIUM.

DORONICUM. *Leopard's-Bane.* [Compositæ.] Showy hardy herbaceous plants, with large yellow flowers. They are propagated easily by dividing the roots in autumn or spring, and grow in any ordinary garden soil. Except for the variation of the blooming season, there is scarcely difference enough in their appearance to render it necessary to cultivate more than one species.

D. Altaicum (Altaic); hardy perennial; 1 foot; flowers white, in June; Siberia; 1783. *D. Austriacum* (Austrian); hardy perennial; 1 foot; flowers yellow in May; Austria; 1816. *D. Caucasicum* (Caucasian); hardy perennial; 1 foot; flowers yellow, in June; Caucasus; 1815. *D. cordifolium* (heart-leaved); hardy perennial; 1 foot; flowers yellow, in May; Russia; 1838. *D. macrophyllum* (large-leaved); hardy perennial; 2 feet; flowers yellow, in July; Caucasus; 1828. *D. Pardalianches* (great); hardy perennial; 2½ feet; flowers yellow, in May; England. *D. plantagineum* (plantain-leaved); hardy perennial; 2 feet; flowers yellow, in May; south of Europe; 1570.

DORYCNIUM. [Leguminosæ.] Hardy and half-hardy perennial and sub-shrubby plants, of little beauty. Soil, common loam. Propagated by seeds.

D. herbaceum (herbaceous); hardy perennial; 18 inches; flowers white, in July; south of Europe; 1802. *D. hirsutum* (hairy); hardy evergreen sub-shrub; 3 feet; flowers red and white, in July; south of Europe; 1682. *D. suffruticosum* (sub-shrubby);

half-hardy sub-shrub; 18 inches; flowers white, in July; south of Europe; 1640. *D. tomentosum* (woolly); hardy evergreen sub-shrub; 3 feet; flowers red and white, in July; south of Europe; 1817.

DRABA. [Cruciferæ.] Hardy perennials, of low growth and easy culture, well suited for rock-work. Increased by division. There are about forty perennial species, all dwarf, mostly with white flowers.

DRACOCEPHALUM. *Dragon's-Head.* [Labiatæ.] The hardy perennial species of this genus are pretty border flowers, not particular as to soil. They are propagated by division of the root. The hardy annual species may be sown in the open border in May.

D. Altaiense (Altaian); hardy perennial; 6 inches; flowers purple, in July; Georgia; 1787. *D. Argunense* (Fischer's); hardy perennial; 18 inches; flowers blue, in July; Siberia; 1822. *D. Austriacum* (Austrian); hardy perennial; 1 foot; flowers blue, July; Austria; 1547. *D. canescens* (hoary); hardy annual; 2 feet; flowers blue, in July; Levant; 1711. *D. grandiflorum* (large-flowered); hardy perennial; 1 foot; flowers blue, in July;. Siberia; 1759. *D. Mexicanum* (Mexican); hardy perennial; 2 feet; flowers blue, in June; Mexico; 1832. *D. Moldavicum* (Moldavian Balm); hardy annual; 2 feet; flowers blue or white, in July; Moldavia; 1596. *D. peregrinum* (foreign); hardy perennial; 9 inches; flowers blue, in July; Siberia; 1759. *D. pinnatum* (pinnate-leaved); hardy perennial, prostrate; flowers blue, in June; Siberia; 1822. *D. Ruyschianum* (Ruysch's); hardy perennial; 2 feet; flowers blue, in July; north of Europe; 1699.

DRACOPIS. [Compositæ.] A hardy annual, allied to Rudbeckia. Propagated by seeds sown in May in good garden soil.

D. amplexicaulis (stem-clasping); hardy annual; 3 feet; flowers yellow, in July; Louisiana; 1793.

DRACUNCULUS. [Araceæ.] Hardy herbaceous perennials, with a very curious-looking inflorescence. Loamy soil. Propagated by division of the roots.

D. crinitum (hairy); half-hardy perennial; 1 foot; flowers brownish-purple, in April; Minorca; 1777. *D. vulgare* (common Dragon; hardy perennial); 2 feet; flowers brownish-purple, in June; south of Europe; 1548.

DRAGON'S-HEAD. See DRACOCEPHALUM.

DROSERA. *Sundew.* [Droseraceæ.] Curious little herbaceous plants, seldom seen in cultivation. There are four native species, and numerous others inhabiting various parts of the world. They should be planted in chopped sphagnum moss mixed with a third part of sandy peat soil, and should always be kept wet. Propagated by seeds.

DRUMMONDIA. [Saxifragaceæ.] A hardy herbaceous perennial, suitable for rock-work. Soil, dryish sandy loam. Increased by division of the plant.

D. mitelloides (mitella-like); hardy herbaceous perennial; 6 inches; flowers yellowish, in July; Rocky Mountains; 1827.

Also called Metellopsis.

DRYAS. [Rosaceæ.] Small hardy or half-hardy sub-herbaceous plants, with white flowers. Peat soil, with slight protection in winter. Propagated by cuttings under a hand-glass, by division, or by seeds.

ECHINACEA. [Compositæ.] Large-growing, half-hardy perennials, of the habit of Rudbeckia, and requiring similar treatment. Common garden soil. Propagated by division.

E. Dicksoni (Dickson's); hardy perennial; 1 foot; flowers lilac, in August; Mexico; 1836. *E. heterophylla* (various-leaved); hardy perennial; 2 feet; flowers purple, in October; Mexico; 1829. *E. intermedia* (intermediate); hardy perennial; 3 feet; flowers rose-purple, in July; Mexico; 1826. *E. purpurea* (purple); hardy perennial; 4 feet; flowers red, in September; North America, 1699.

ECCREMOCARPUS. See CALAMPELIS.

ECHINOPS. *Globe Thistle*. [Compositæ.] Coarse hardy perennials or biennials, remarkable for their spheroidal thistle-like flower-heads. Common soil. The perennials increased by division; the biennials by seeds.

E. Barmaticus albus (Hungarian white); hardy biennial; 4 feet; flowers white, in August; Hungary; 1832. *E. exaltatus* (tall); hardy perennial; 6 feet; flowers white, in July; Austria; 1817. *E. Persicus* (Persian); hardy perennial; 3 feet; flowers white, in August; Persia; 1821. *E. Ritro* (small); hardy perennial; 3 feet; flowers blue, in July; Europe; 1570. *E. Ruthenicus* (Russian); hardy perennial; 3 feet; flowers blue, in July; Russia; 1816. *E. spinosus* (spiny); hardy perennial; 4 feet; flowers white, in July; Egypt; 1597. *E. tenuifolius* (slender-leaved); hardy perennial; 2 feet; flowers blue, in August; Russia; 1820.

There are many other species.

ECHIUM. *Viper's Bugloss.* [Boraginaceæ.] A large genus of hardy annuals, biennials, and perennials, and of greenhouse evergreen shrubs. The hardy sorts grow in common garden soil, and are all best propagated by seeds. The greenhouse species require sandy loam and peat, and are increased by seeds or cuttings, and require to be kept in a rather dry atmosphere during winter. Some of the greenhouse kinds are showy, though not of good habit; but the hardy kinds are of little value for ornamental purposes.

HARDY ANNUALS. — *E. angustifolium* (narrow-leaved); flowers blush, in July; Spain; 1826. *E. arenarium* (sand-inhabiting); flowers purple, in July; Calabria; 1826. *E. calycinum* (large-calyxed); flowers blue and yellow, in July; south of Europe; 1829. *E. macranthum* (large-flowered); 1 foot; flowers violet, in July; Barbary; 1818. *E. Simsii* (Sims'); flowers red and blue, in August; south of Europe; 1816.

HARDY BIENNIALS. — *E. amœnum* (agreeable); flowers blue, in July; Caucasus; 1826. *E. asperrimum* (very rough); flowers blue, in July; Caucasus; 1826. *E. Dahuricum* (Dahurian); flowers blue, in July; Dahuria; 1827. *E. Italicum* (Italian); 4 feet; flowers white, in July; Jersey. *E. Sibthorpii* (Sibthorp's); 1 foot; flowers red, in June; Europe; 1824. *E. tenue* (slender); 1 foot; flowers blue, in July; Sicily; 1824. *E. tuberculatum* (pimpled); 1 foot; flowers violet, in August; Spain; 1820. *E. violaceum* (violet-flowered); 3 feet; flowers blue, in June; Austria; 1658. *E. vulgare flore-albo* (common white-flowered); 1 foot; flowers white, in July; Britain.

EGG-PLANT. See SOLANUM.

EGLANTINE. See ROSA.

ELÆAGNUS. *Oleaster.* [Elæagnaceæ.] A genus of shrubs with silvery foliage, consisting chiefly of hardy deciduous species, with a few greenhouse evergreens. For the former, which are useful in shrubberies, the common garden soil will suffice; and they are increased by seeds, cuttings, or layers. The latter should have loam, with a third peat or leaf-mould, and a portion of sand, and are increased by cuttings.

E. argenteus (silvery); hardy shrub; 10 feet; North America; 1813.

ELDER. See SAMBUCUS.
ELECAMPANE. See INULA.
ELM. See ULMUS.
ENCHANTER'S NIGHTSHADE. See CIRCÆA.

EPIGÆA. [Ericaceæ.] A lovely little procumbent evergreen shrub. The plant has a creeping stem, which spreads by degrees over the ground, rooting as it extends. It requires a bed of peat soil, and a cool, shady, somewhat moist situation. If planted between Rhododendrons, in situations where these thrive, if they do not too far shade the surface, the Epigæa would flourish.

E. repens (creeping); hardy evergreen shrub; 6 inches; flowers white, in April; North America; 1736. The variety *rubicunda* has flowers of a beautiful rose-red, and blooms in April.

EPILOBIUM. See CHAMŒNERIUM.

EPIMEDIUM. *Barrenwort.* [Berberidaceæ.] Dwarf hardy perennials, suitable for rock-work or for pot culture. They like a soil of mellow loam and peat, in equal proportions, mixed with an eighth of sand. On rock-work, they should be planted in similar soil. They are quite hardy. Division of the root is the most ready means of propagating them, and this should be attended to soon after they have done flowering, that the plants may get well established before winter.

E. Alpinum (Alpine); hardy perennial, 9 inches; flowers red and yellow, in May; England. *E. diphyllum* (two-leaved); hardy perennial; 6 inches; flowers white, in May; Japan; 1830. *E. hexandrum* (six-anthered); hardy perennial; 9 inches; flowers lilac, in May; North America; 1827. *E. macranthum* (large-flowered); hardy perennial; 9 inches; flowers whitish, in May; Japan; 1835. *E. Musschianum* (Mussch's); hardy perennial; 1 foot; flowers white, in May; Japan; 1838. *E. pinnatum* (pinnate); hardy perennial; 9 inches; flowers yellow, in May; Persia; 1848. *E. violaceum* (violet); hardy perennial; 9 inches; flowers violet-color, in May; Japan; 1835.

EQUISETUM. *Horsetail.* [Equisetaceæ.] Hardy herbaceous perennials of singular appearance, associating well with Ferns and Lycopodiums about damp, shady rock-work. They mostly prefer peaty soil and a damp situation, and are increased by division of the root.

ERAGROSTIS. [Graminaceæ.] A family of ornamental grasses, succeeding in common garden soil. *E. elegans, Namaquensis, cylindrifolia,* and *megastachya* are the species.

ERANTHIS. *Winter Aconite.* [Ranunculaceæ.] The Winter Aconite is one of those simple flowers which please more on account of the season of their appearance than their beauty. It begins to bloom in earliest spring, often amidst frost and snow, and for a long time continues to decorate the garden and shrubbery. It is altogether not more than three inches high, the flowers being seated one on each pair of flat-lobed leaves, which terminate the stalk. They look like little yellow cups with their bases surrounded by green frills. It is tuberous, and only requires to be planted in the soil and left to itself. Planted just within the margin of a flower-bed, it interferes with nothing; and, if placed thick enough, makes a conspicuous edging for some time. It is also very well placed in patches among shrubs, or in any other wilderness scenery, which it serves to enliven at a dreary season.

E. hiemalis (winter); hardy tuberous perennial; 3 inches; flowers yellow, in April; England. *E. Sibcrica* (Siberian); hardy tuberous perennial; 3 inches; flowers yellow, in April; Siberia; 1826.

EREMOSTACHYS. *Desert Rod.* [Labiatæ.] Hardy herbaceous perennial, requiring protection from wet in winter, and a sandy loamy soil. It is best to preserve some plants in pots in a dry frame during winter. Increased only by seeds.

E. laciniata (jagged); hardy perennial; 4 feet; flowers sulphur-yellow and orange-brown, in July; Caucasus; 1731.

ERIGERON. [Compositæ.] Hardy plants, comprising annuals, biennials, and perennials. Some of the latter may be grown in borders or on rock-work, but they are not very important. All grow freely in common garden soil. The perennials are increased by division, the annuals and biennials by seeds.

E. armeriæfolium (thrift-leaved); hardy perennial; 1 foot; flowers purple, in June; Dahuria; 1829. *E. asperum* (rough); hardy perennial; 2 feet; flowers white, in August; North America; 1828. *E. Chinensis* (Chinese); hardy annual; 1 foot; flowers white, in July; China; 1818. *E. glabellum* (smoothish); hardy perennial; 1 foot; flowers bluish, in July; North America; 1825. *E. humile* (dwarf); hardy perennial; 3 inches; flowers flesh-color, in August; North America; 1828. *E. Lehmanni* (Lehmann's); hardy annual; 2 feet; flowers lilac, in July; Egypt; 1828. *E. pubescens* (downy); hardy perennial; 1 foot; flowers white, in July; Mexico; 1827. *E. Villarsii* (Attic); hardy perennial; 18 inches; flowers purple, in July; Attica; 1816.

ERINOSMA. [Amaryllidaceæ.] A beautiful little hardy bulb. Soil, sandy loam. Increased by offsets. More commonly called Leucojum.

E. verna (spring); hardy bulb; 9 inches; flowers white, in February; Germany; 1596. There are two varieties, called *Carpatica* and *multiplex*.

ERINUS. [Scrophulariaceæ.] This genus contains some dwarf hardy perennials, which form beautiful objects for pot-culture among alpine plants, as well as for rock-work.

They prefer light and rather sándy soil. When grown in pots, they should have the protection usually given to alpines, which consists mainly in plunging the pots to prevent frosts from acting on the roots, and in shielding off heavy rains, which saturate the soil, and sometimes, if the drainage gets deranged, become conducive to the decay of the plants by rotting the roots and root-stocks. They are increased by division, which should be done about July or August, or by seeds sown as soon as they ripen. The greenhouse subshrubby species are referred to Nycterinia.

E. Alpinus (smooth); hardy perennial; 3 inches; flowers rose-purple, in April; Pyrenees; 1739. *E. Hispanicus* (hairy); hardy perennial; 6 inches; flowers rose-color, in March; Spain; 1739.

These plants are half-hardy in the Northern States.

ERIOGONUM. [Polygonaceæ.] Half-hardy herbaceous perennials, increased by division and seed. Soil, peaty loam.

E. compositum (compound); hardy perennial; 18 inches; flowers yellowish-white, in May; North America. *E. longifolium* (long-leaved); hardy perennial; 2 feet; flowers yellow, in June; North America; 1824. *E. sericeum* (silky); hardy perennial; 1 foot; flowers yellow, in July; Missouri; 1811. *E. tomentosum* (downy); hardy perennial; 2 feet; flowers white, in May; Carolina; 1811.

ERIOPHORUM. *Cotton-grass.* [Cyperaceæ.] Very pretty hardy herbaceous perennials, producing heads of silvery white plumes, which might be effective planted in low ground. Increased by division and seed. Soil, wet loamy peat.

EROPHILA. [Cruciferæ.] Hardy annuals, allied to Draba, growing from seed, in garden soil. Flowers white. The species are *E. Americana, precox,* and *vulgaris.*

ERYNGIUM. [Umbelliferæ.] A curious genus of perennials, generally hardy, remarkable for the colored bracts of the involucre, which constitute the showy part of their inflorescence. They are desirable among hardy herbaceous subjects, the prevailing color being blue. They belong, in truth, to the umbelliferous order, without having any external resemblance to that class of forms so familiar in the Parsley, the Celery, the Carrot, and the Fennel. They are raised from seeds, which, like those of other perennials, may be sown in May either in pots or in a bed. The young plants, if nursed into strength, will bloom the following year; but, usually, the old plants are the best if they are kept in vigor. They are not very particular as to soil; but a deep sandy loam is best.

E. Alpinum (Alpine); hardy perennial; 2 feet; flower-heads blue, in July; Switzerland; 1597. *E. amethystinum* (amethystine); hardy perennial; 3 feet; flower-heads blue, in July; Styria; 1648. *E. Bourgati* (Bourgati's); hardy perennial; 2 feet; flower-heads blue, in July; south of France; 1731. *E. cæruleum* (sky-blue); hardy perennial; 2 feet; flower-heads blue, in July; Caspian; 1816. *E. giganteum* (giant); hardy perennial; 4 feet; flower-heads blue, in July; Caucasus; 1820. *E. planum* (flat-leaved); hardy perennial; 3 feet; flower-heads blue, in July; Europe; 1596.

There are numerous other hardy perennial species.

ERYSIMUM. *Hedge Mustard.* [Cruciferæ.] Hardy plants, chiefly biennial, those which are cultivated being treated as annuals: the majority are uninteresting objects. *E. Peroffskianum* is, however, a very brilliant-flowered plant, well adapted for beds in gardens: indeed, there is hardly any other plant which furnishes the color, — an intense orange. It is perfectly hardy, and, if sown in the spring, will bloom in June and July. It will bloom much earlier if sown in pots like a half-hardy annual, and turned out in May; for it will then begin flowering in the pots in May. The plant is too small for planting out, but should be sown where it is to flower. If it comes up too thick, let it be properly thinned; but, unless it is tolerably close, it makes no show, and would fail as a bed plant. It looks well in patches round a border, and in pots among other dwarf blooming plants, because its color is uncommon: indeed, but for its color, it would not be cultivated; for its habit is weed-like.

E. Peroffskianum (Peroffski's); hardy annual; 18 inches; flowers orange, in May; Palestine; 1838.

ERYTHRINA. *Coral-tree.* [Leguminosæ.] These showy stove shrubs will bloom well if planted in a rich sunny border in spring. On the approach of frosty weather, place the plants in the cellar, or under a greenhouse stage.

E. Bidwillii (Bidwill's); greenhouse or stove perennial; 3 feet; flowers crimson, in June; Sydney; 1840. *E. crista-galli* (cock's-comb); stove shrub; 10 feet; flowers crimson, in June; Brazil; 1771. *E. herbacea* (herbaceous); half-hardy perennial; 3 feet; flowers crimson, in July; Carolina; 1824. *E. laurifolia* (laurel-leaved); stove sub-shrub; 6 feet; flowers scarlet, in July; South America; 1800.

E. Maria Belanger is a fine hybrid species, with dazzling scarlet flowers. *E. Belangeri, floribunda*, and *ruberrima* are new hybrids.

ERYTHROLÆNA. [Compositæ.] The prettiest of all the Thistles. Sow the seeds in April. It should be treated as a biennial, or not allowed to seed. The young plants should be kept over the winter in frames, and planted out in May in beds, where they will rise with numerous branches crowned with scarlet thistle-looking flowers.

E. conspicua (conspicuous); 8 feet; flowers scarlet and orange, in September; Mexico; 1825.

ERYTHRONIUM. *Dog's-tooth Violet.* [Liliaceæ.] Pretty dwarf, hardy, spring-flowering herbaceous perennials, with tuberous roots. They grow in good garden soil, preferring a good proportion of peat earth. Increased readily by offsets.

E. albidum (whitish); hardy tuber; 3 inches; flowers white, in April; North America; 1824. *E. Americanum* (American); hardy tuber; 3 inches; flowers yellow, in April; North America; 1665. *E. Dens-canis* (Dog's-tooth); hardy tuber; 3 inches; flowers purplish or whitish, in March; Europe; 1596. *E. grandiflorum* (large-flowered); hardy tuber; 3 inches; flowers yellow, in April; North America; 1826.

ESCHSCHOLTZIA. [Papaveraceæ.] Hardy perennials, which may be cultivated as annuals. The plants are procumbent, and form a low dense branching mass, abundantly furnished with large poppy-like flowers, much more showy than neat. It is one of those flowers which always look untidy, and owes its place in the garden to its bright color and large blossoms. The seed may be sown in early spring where it is to grow, and, when the plants come up too close together, they must be thinned out. The plant has a tap-root like a small carrot. There may be two complete seasons of bloom; for, if the seed be sown in autumn, it will come up, and, unless the frost be very severe, stand through the winter, and bloom early. If the plants are allowed to shed their seed, the place will be overrun as with a weed; and, where it has once been sown or planted, it will afterwards require only to be thinned; for hundreds of plants will come up. It makes a very brilliant appearance in fine weather, and especially when contrasted with the blue of the Convolvulus or Larkspur, and the scarlets and purples of other flowers. The genus has been called Chryseis.

E. Californica (California); hardy perennial; 18 inches; flowers yellow and orange, or white, in June; California; 1826. A white-flowered variety of this is in cultivation; and it is indeed probable that the plants called *E. crocea* and *compacta* are new varieties of *E. Californica*. *E. compacta* (compact); hardy perennial; 1 foot; flowers yellow, in July; California; 1833. *E. crocea* (saffron-colored); hardy perennial; 18 inches; flowers orange, in June; California; 1833. *E. tenuifolia* (slender); hardy annual; 1 foot; flowers yellow, in July; California; 1853.

EUCHARIDIUM. [Onagraceæ.] Hardy annuals, allied to Clarkia, and requiring the same treatment. Sow in the open border in May.

E. concinnum (neat); hardy annual; 1 foot; flowers rosy, in June; North America; 1836. *E. grandiflorum* (large-flowered); hardy annual; 1 foot; flowers rose-colored, in June; garden variety.

EUCNIDE. [Loasaceæ.] A pretty half-hardy annual, succeeding well in garden soil. Sow in May, or in a frame, and transplant.

E. bartonoides (bartonia-like); half-hardy annual; 1 foot; flowers yellow, in August; Mexico.

EUONYMUS. *Spindle-tree.* [Celastraceæ.] A genus of hardy shrubs, of which *E. Japonicus*, and a striped variety, are fine evergreens with ornamental foliage, but are not hardy in the Northern States. They grow in common garden soil, and increase by layers or cuttings planted under hand-glasses. The deciduous kinds are proper for shrubberies: they are not remarkable for beauty in the flowers, but are ornamental in autumn, from the profusion of three-cornered scarlet fruit which they produce.

ORNAMENTAL EVERGREENS. — *E. Chinensis; E. grandiflorus; E. Japonicus*, and its varieties *maculatus* and *variegatus*.

ORNAMENTAL DECIDUOUS SHRUBS. — *E. Americanus; E. atropurpureus; E. Europæus; E. Hamiltonianus; E. latifolius; E. verrucosus*.

EUPATORIUM. [Compositæ.] A family of stove and hardy herbaceous plants. The hardy species do well in any rich garden soil, and are propagated by division.

E. ageratoides (ageratum-like); 4 feet; flowers white, in August; North America; 1640. *E. altissimum* (tallest); 5 feet; flowers pink, in September; North America; 1699. *E. aromaticum* (aromatic); 4 feet; flowers white, in July; North America; 1739. *E. cannabinum* (hemp-like,) (Agrimony); 4 feet; flowers pink, in July; Britain. *E. coronopifolium* (coronopus-leaved); 3 feet; flowers white, in August; Carolina; 1824. *E. fœniculaceum* (fennel-leaved); 4 feet; flowers pale yellow, in August; North America; 1807, *E. Fraseri* (Fraser's); 18 inches; flowers white, in August; Carolina; 1820. *E. hyssopifolium* (hyssop-leaved); 1 foot; flowers white, in August; North America; 1699. *E. lanceolatum* (spear-head-leaved); 3 feet; flowers white, in July; North America; 1819. *E. maculatum* (spotted-stalked); 3 feet; flowers purple, in July; North America; 1656. *E. perfoliatum* (pierced-leaved); 2 feet; flowers white, in July; North America; 1699. *E. pubescens* (downy); 4 feet; flowers white, in July; North America; 1819. *E. purpureum* (purple-stalked); 5 feet; flowers pink, in August; North America; 1610. *E. rotundifolium* (round-leaved); 1 foot; flowers white, in July; North America; 1699. *E. sessilifolium* (stalkless-leaved); 1 foot; flowers white, in September; North America; 1777. *E. Syriacum* (Syrian); 4 feet; flowers purple, in August; Syria; 1807. *E trifoliatum* (three-leaved); 6 feet; flowers purple, in August; North America; 1768. *E truncatum* (cut-off); 18 inches; flowers white, in September; North America; 1800. *E. verticillatum* (whorl-leaved); 5 feet; flowers purple, in August; North America; 1811.

EUPHORBIA. [Euphorbiaceæ.] A very large family, including some hardy herbaceous perennials, and a few hardy annuals. They thrive in common garden soil, and are increased by seed or division, but are not very desirable. *E. variegata* is a showy annual.

EUPHRASIA. *Eye Bright.* [Scrophulariaceæ.] Hardy annuals, thriving in the border, from seeds sown in May.

E. Alpina (Alpine); hardy annual; 1 foot; flowers purple, in

July; Europe; 1827. *E. linifolia* (flax-leaved); hardy annual; 9 inches; flowers purple, in August; France; 1826. *E. lutea* (yellow); hardy annual; 18 inches; flowers purple, in August; south of Europe; 1818.

EUSTOMA. [Gentianaceæ.] A genus comprising a greenhouse herbaceous plant, a border half-hardy biennial, and an annual; growing in loamy soil, and propagated by division and seeds.

E. exaltatum; greenhouse herbaceous plant. *E. Russelleanum* (Russell's); half-hardy biennial; flowers purple, in August; Texas; 1835. *E. silenefolia* (catchfly-leaved); hardy annual; 1 foot; flowers white, in July; Isle of Providence; 1804.

EUTOCA. [Hydrophyllaceæ.] Hardy annual plants, of easy culture. Sow in April on a slight hot-bed, for transplanting, and in May in the open borders.

E. divaricata (straggling); hardy annual; 1 foot; flowers bluish-lilac, in June; California; 1834. *E. Menziesii* (Menzies'); hardy annual; 1 foot; flowers bluish-lilac, in May; North America; 1826. *E. viscida* (clammy); hardy annual; 2 feet; flowers blue, in June; California; 1834. *E. Wrangeliana* (Wrangel's); hardy annual; 1 foot; flowers dark bluish-lilac, in June; California; 1835.

EVENING PRIMROSE. See ŒNOTHERA.

EVERLASTING FLOWER. See GNAPHALIUM and HELICHRYSUM.

EVERLASTING PEA. See LATHYRUS.

EXACUM. [Gentianaceæ.] A family of hardy annuals, allied to Chironia, flourishing in peaty moist soil, and propagated by seed sown in May. The species are *E. macranthum, pulchellum, tetragonum,* and *bicolor.*

EXOGONIUM. [Convolvulaceæ.] A division of the old family Ipomœa. *E. purga,* a very handsome slender climber, bearing rosy-purplish blossoms through the autumn months, is the source of the drug Jalap. The plant has a fleshy root, which is very liable to decay in winter, if kept too damp. The best place to keep the root is in a cool part of the greenhouse, in the soil, which should be nearly, but not quite, dry. In the spring, the crown may be excited slowly in a greenhouse, or close frame; but, as the summer draws on, the plant will grow freely enough in the open air, where it should have a branchy stake, or a trellis six or eight feet high. It may be kept in a pot trained around stakes, cylinder-fashion, and may be increased by cuttings. The flowers of this kind are less funnel-shaped than is usual among the plants of this order.

E. filiforme (thread-shaped); stove twining perennial, 10 feet; flowers purple, in October; West Indies; 1823. *E. purga* (purgative); jalap; tuberous twining perennial; 10 feet; flowers rose-color, in September; Mexico; 1838. *E. repandum* (wavy-edged); stove twining perennial; flowers red, in August; West Indies; 1793.

FAGUS. *Beech.* [Corylaceæ.] A family of well-known ornamental trees, propagated by seed, and the varieties by grafting. They thrive in any good soil. The species and varieties are —

EVERGREENS. — *F. betuloides* (birch-like); hardy; 50 feet; Magellan; 1830. *F. Cunninghamii* (Cunningham's); half-hardy; New Zealand; 1843.

HARDY DECIDUOUS. — *F. antarctica* (antarctic); 50 feet; Magellan; 1830. *F. castanæfolia* (chestnut-leaved); flowers in June; North America; *F. comptoniæfolia* (comptonia-leaved); flowers in May. *F. ferruginea* (American rusty); 30 feet; flowers in June; North America; 1766. *F. ferruginea Caroliniana* (Carolina); Carolina. *F. purpurea* (purple); flowers in April; Germany. *F. sylvatica* (common wood); 70 feet; flowers in June; Britain. *F. sylvatica Americana* (American); 100 feet; flowers in May; North America. *F. sylvatica atrorubens* (dark-red-leaved); 30 feet; flowers in June. *F. sylvatica cristata* (crested-leaved); 30 feet; flowers in May. *F. sylvatica cuprea* (copper-colored-leaved); 70 feet; flowers in May. *F. sylvatica foliis argenteis* (silver-leaved); flowers in May. *F. sylvatica foliis aureis* (golden-leaved); flowers in June. *F. sylvatica heterophylla* (various-leaved); 40 feet; flowers in April and May. *F. sylvatica incisa* (cut-leaved); 10 feet; flowers in June. *F. sylvatica pendula* (pendulous); flowers in May; gardens.

FEATHER-GRASS. See STIPA.

FEDIA. [Valerianaceæ.] A genus of hardy annuals, allied to Centranthus, which are rather pretty garden plants. Sown in pots about April, and planted out subsequently, the plants bloom in June; but if sown in the open ground, in May, they bloom in July: in either case continuing in flower for some time. Planted moderately thick, they form good bedding-plants. Light, rich garden soil.

F. graciliflora (slender-flowered); hardy annual; 1 foot; flowers pinkish, in June; Algiers; 1845. *F. cornucopiæ* (cornucopia); hardy annual; 1 foot; flowers red, in July; south of Europe; 1796.

FELICIA. [Compositæ.] A small genus, containing a neat dwarf half-hardy annual. Soil, rich light garden mould. Increased by seeds. Sow in April, in pots, in a frame, and in May in the borders. It is known as *Aster tenellus*.

F. tenella (slender); half-hardy annual; 9 inches; flowers bluish-lilac, in June; Cape; 1769.

FENNEL-FLOWER. See NIGELLA.

FENZLIA. [Polemoniaceæ.] A pretty hardy annual from California, sometimes called Dianthoidis. Soil, sandy loam. The plants may be sown in a hot-bed in April, and transplanted to the border, or in the open border in May. Propagated by seed.

F. dianthiflora (pink-flowered); hardy annual; 4 inches; flowers purple and yellow, in June; California; 1833.

FERULA. *Giant Fennel.* [Umbelliferæ.] Large-growing hardy perennials, not often seen in cultivation, but, on account of their noble appearance, well adapted for conspicuous positions in mixed borders, or even as specimen plants on a lawn. The foliage of several of the kinds is very large, and is made up of an immense number of little parts, varying in width and shape in different kinds. The flower-stems rise from a large tuft of these leaves to the height of six to eight feet, and bear numerous umbels of yellow flowers. The species especially alluded to as deserving of cultivation are *F. Tingitana, Ferulago,* and *glauca,* the former having the divisions of the leaf small but egg-shaped, with notched margins, and a shining surface; the two latter, smaller and narrower. They like a dryish deep soil, the roots being large, fleshy, and penetrating deeply, and abounding moreover in a gum-resinous matter, which, in several of the species, is employed medicinally.

F. Ferulago (Ferulago); hardy perennial; 6 feet; flowers yellow, in June; south of Europe. *F. glauca* (glaucous); hardy perennial; 8 feet; flowers yellow, in June; Italy; 1596. *F. Tingitana* (Tangiers); hardy perennial; 8 feet; flowers yellow, in June; Barbary; 1680.

There are some twenty other species.

FEVERFEW. See PYRETHRUM.

FICARIA. [Ranunculaceæ.] A genus of pretty little early-flowering plants, allied to Ranunculus. Easily propagated by division of the tuberous roots in spring. A moist shady situation is best adapted for them.

F. verna (spring); hardy perennial; 6 inches; flowers yellow in May; England. *F. verna pallida* (pale-flowered); has pale yellow flowers. *F. verna plena* (double-flowered); has double flowers.

FILBERT. See CORYLUS.

FIR. See ABIES, PINUS, PICEA.

FITZROYA. [Coniferæ.] Fine hardy evergreen trees. Soil, sandy loam. Increased by seeds or cuttings.

F. Patagonica (Patagonian); hardy evergreen tree; Patagonia; 1849.

FLAX. See LINUM.

FLOS ADONIS. See ADONIS.

FLOWER (FLEUR) DE LUCE. See IRIS.

FLOWERING FERN. See OSMUNDA.

FLOWERING RUSH. See BUTOMUS.

FORGET-ME-NOT. See MYOSOTIS.

FORSYTHIA. [Oleaceæ.] Beautiful hardy deciduous shrubs. Soil, sandy loam. Propagated by layers or cuttings. *F. viridissima* is a valuable shrub for early forcing; but, from its early blooming habit, it requires to be in a sheltered position, or its blossoms become disfigured.

F. viridissima (very green); hardy deciduous shrub; 6 feet; flowers yellow, in May; north of China; 1845. *F. suspensa* (pendulous); hardy deciduous shrub; grafted high, it is pretty; flowers yellow, in May; Japan; 1858.

FOTHERGILLA. [Hamamelidaceæ.] Pretty little hardy shrubs, with white flowers. Soil, sandy peat. Propagated by seeds and layers. All are natives of North America.

F. alnifolia (alder-leaved); hardy shrub; 4 feet; flowers in May; 1765. The varieties *acuta*, *major*, *obtusa*, and *serotina*, differ only in foliage and season of flowering.

FOXGLOVE. See DIGITALIS.

FRAXINELLA. See DICTAMNUS.

FRAXINUS. *Ash.* [Oleaceæ.] Hardy deciduous trees, of which many of the varieties are desirable. Those with cut or variegated foliage, or of weeping habit, are ornamental on the lawn or in the shrubbery.

F. acuminata (pointed; green); 40 feet; flowers in May; North America; 1723. *F. alba* (white); 30 feet; flowers green, in May; North America; 1823. *F. amarissima* (bitterest); 20 feet; flowers in May. *F. Americana* (American-white); 20 feet; flowers in May; North America; 1723. *F. Americana latifolia* (broad-leaved); 20 feet; flowers in May. *F. angustifolia* (narrow-leaved); flowers in May; Spain; 1825. *F. appendica* (appendaged); 20 feet; flowers in May. *F. appendiculata* (appendiculate); 20 feet; flowers in May. *F. argentea* (silvery); 15 feet; flowers in June; Corsica; 1825. *F. atro-virens* (dark-green); 4 feet; flowers in May; Britain. *F. atro-virens aurea* (golden); flowers in April. *F. Caroliniana* (Carolina); 30 feet; flowers in June; North America; 1783. *F. cinerea* (gray); 30 feet;

flowers in May; North America; 1824. *F. elliptica* (oval);
30 feet; flowers in May; North America; 1825. *F. epiptera*
(dotted stalked); 30 feet; flowers in May; North America;
1823. *F. excelsior* (taller; common Ash); 80 feet; flowers in
May; Britain. *F. excelsior argentea* (silver-barked); 20 feet;
flowers in May; Britain. *F. excelsior aurea* (golden-barked);
20 feet; flowers in May; Britain. *F. excelsior aurea pendula*
(yellow-pendulous); flowers in May; Britain. *F. excelsior
crosa* (gnawed); 20 feet; flowers in May; Britain. *F. excelsior
fungosa*; 26 feet; flowers in May; Britain. *F. excelsior horizontalis* (horizontal); 20 feet; flowers in May; Britain. *F. excelsior jaspidea* (jasper-like; yellow-barked); 30 feet; flowers
in May. *F. excelsior Kincairniæ* (Kincairney); 40 feet; flowers
in May; Kincairney. *F. excelsior lutea* (yellow-edged); 20 feet;
flowers in May; Britain. *F. excelsior nana* (dwarf); 10 feet;
flowers in May; Britain. *F. excelsior pendula* (pendulous); 20
feet; flowers in May. *F. excelsior striata* (streaked); 20 feet;
flowers in May; Britain. *F. excelsior verrucosa* (warted-barked);
60 feet; flowers in May; England. *F. excelsior verrucosa pendula* (pendulous-warted); flowers in May; England. *F. excelsior verticillaris* (whorled); 20 feet; flowers in May; Britain.
F. expansa (expanded); 30 feet; flowers in May; North America; 1824. *F. fusca* (dark-brown); 30 feet; flowers in May;
North America; 1823. *F. heterophylla* (various-leaved); 30
feet; flowers in May; England. *F. heterophylla variegata* (varieagated-leaved); 12 feet; flowers in May; Ireland; 1836. *F.
juglandifolia* (walnut-leaved); 40 feet; flowers in May; North
America; 1783. *F. juglandifolia subintegerrima* (nearly entire);
40 feet; flowers in May. *F. laciniata* (jagged-leaved); flowers
in May; North America. *F. lancea* (lance-leaved); 30 feet;
flowers in May; North America; 1820. *F. lentiscifolia* (lentiscus-leaved); 6 feet; flowers in May; Aleppo; 1710. *F. letiscifolia pendula* (pendulous); 20 feet; flowers in June; Germany;
1833. *F. longifolia* (long-leaved); 30 feet; flowers in May;
North America; 1824. *F. lucida* (shining); 20 feet; flowers
in May. *F. macrophylla* (large-leaved); 40 feet; flowers in
May; 1823. *F. mixta* (mixed); 30 feet; flowers in May;

North America; 1824. *F. monstrosa* (monstrous); flowers in July; Britain. *F. nana* (dwarf); 6 feet; flowers in June. *F. nigra* (black-branched); 30 feet; flowers in May; North America; 1825. *F. ovata* (egg-shaped); 30 feet; flowers in May; North America. *F. oxycarpa* (sharp-fruited); 20 feet; flowers in May; Caucasus; 1815. *F. oxycarpa oxyphylla* (sharp-leaved); 20 feet; south of Europe; 1821. *F. pallida* (pale); 30 feet; flowers in May; North America. *F. pannosa* (cloth-leaved); 30 feet; flowers in May; Carolina; 1820. *F. parvifolia* (small-leaved); 20 feet; flowers in May; Levant; 1822. *F. platycarpa* (broad-fruited); 30 feet; flowers in May; North America; 1820. *F. polemonifolia* (great-valerian-leaved); flowers in April; North America; 1812. *F. pubescens* (downy); 20 feet; flowers in April; North America; 1811. *F. pubescens latifolia* (broad-leaved); 20 feet; flowers in May. *F. pubescens longifolia* (long-leaved); 20 feet; flowers in May. *F. pulverulenta* (powdery); 30 feet; flowers in May; North America; 1824. *F. quadrangulata* (four-angled, blue); 30 feet; flowers in May; North America; 1822. *F. quadrangulata nervosa* (nerved); 30 feet; flowers in May. *F. rubicunda* (ruddy-veined); 30 feet; flowers in May; North America; 1824. *F. rufa* (rusty); 30 feet; flowers in May; North America; 1822. *F. sambucifolia* (elder-leaved); 30 feet; flowers in May; North America; 1800. *F. sambucifolia crispa* (curled); 30 feet; flowers in May. *F. versicolor* (many-colored); flowers in May; Britain. *F. virens* (green); 20 feet; flowers in May. *F. virens variegata* (variegated); 20 feet; flowers in May. *F. viridis* (green); 30 feet; flowers in May; North America; 1824.

All of the above species are seldom found in any collection; but all the larger species are fine trees for street-planting.

FRENCH MARIGOLD.   See TAGETIS.

FRINGE-TREE.   See CHIONANTHUS.

FRITILLARIA. *Fritillary.* [Liliaceæ.] A genus of hardy bulbs, of easy culture, propagated without difficulty by means of offsets. The bulbs should be planted in sandy, loamy soil; when taken up for transplanting, it should be about August. All the speciæs propagate by offsets, and grow freely in the open ground, without protection. They mostly flower in May, and are thus very useful in gardens as spring flowers. The most stately species is the Crown Imperial, which bears a whorl of drooping flowers, surmounted by a tuft, or crown, of leaves. The smaller species bear one or two drooping cup-shaped flowers. The bulbs of the Fritillarias are scaly, and of a soft texture, like those of lilies, consequently they must not be dried by being left long exposed at the period of replanting.

F. alba (white); hardy bulb; 9 inches; flowers white, in May; North America. *F. cuprea* (coppery); half-hardy bulb; 18 inches; flowers copper-colored, in July; Mexico; 1834. *F. imperialis* (Crown-imperial); hardy bulb; 4 feet; flowers yellow or red, in May; Persia; 1596. *F. lanceolata* (spear-leaved); hardy bulb; 9 inches; flowers dark-purple, in May; Kamtschatka; 1759. *F. latifolia* (broad-leaved); hardy bulb; 1 foot; flowers reddish-purple, in May; Caucasus; 1604. *F. leucantha* (white-flowered); hardy bulb; 1 foot; flowers white, in May; Siberia; 1822. *F. lutea* (yellow); hardy bulb; 1 foot; flowers yellow, in May; Caucasus; 1812. *F. meleagris* (guinea-fowl-like); hardy bulb; 1 foot; flowers purple-checkered or white, in May; England. *F. minor* (small); hardy bulb; 1 foot; flowers dark-purple, in April; Altai; 1830. *F. nervosa* (nerved-leaved); hardy bulb; 18 inches; flowers dark-purple, in May; Caucasus; 1826. *F. obliqua* (oblique-leaved); hardy bulb; 1 foot; flowers brown-purple, in April; Caucasus; 1596. *F. Persica* (Persian); hardy bulb; 2 feet; flowers brown-purple, in May; Persia; 1596. *F. præcox* (early); hardy bulb; 1 foot; flowers white, in May; Europe. *F. pudica* (chaste); hardy bulb; 1 foot; flowers pale-yellow, in May; North America; 1824. *F. Pyrenaica* (Pyrenæan); hardy bulb; 18 inches; flowers dark-purple, in June; Spain; 1605. *F. Ruthenica*

(Russian); hardy bulb; 1 foot; flowers purple, in May; Caucasus; 1826. *F. tenella* (slender); hardy bulb; 1 foot; flowers purple, in May; Caucasus; 1826. *F. verticillata* (whorled); hardy bulb; 1 foot; flowers purple, in May; Crimea; 1823.

FUMARIA. See DIELYTRA.

FUNKIA. [Liliaceæ.] Very pretty hardy herbaceous perennials. They grow freely in any light common soil, and require no particular culture; but they must have a warm and rather dry situation to induce them to bloom freely. Increased by division of the roots.

F. albo-marginata (white-margined); hardy perennial; 18 inches; flowers lilac in July; Japan; 1837. *F. lancifolia* (lance-leaved); hardy perennial; 1 foot; flowers lilac, in July; Japan; 1824. *F. ovata* (ovate-leaved); hardy perennial; 18 inches; flowers bluish-lilac, in June; Japan; 1790. *F. Sieboldiana* (Siebold's); hardy perennial; 1 foot; flowers lilac, in June; Japan; 1830. *F. sub-cordata* (sub-cordate-leaved); hardy perennial; 1 foot; flowers white, in August; Japan; 1790. *F. undulata* (wavy-leaved); half-hardy perennial; 1 foot; flowers lilac, in August; Japan; 1834.

GAGEA. [Liliaceæ.] Hardy bulbs, closely related to Ornithogalum. Light sandy soil. Increased by offsets.

G. Bohemica (Bohemian); hardy bulb; 6 inches; flowers yellow, in April; Bohemia; 1825. *G. bracteolaris* (bracteolate); hardy bulb; 6 inches; flowers yellow, in April; Europe; 1817. *G. chlorantha* (yellow-flowered); hardy bulb; 6 inches; flowers yellow, in April; Siberia; 1819. *G. glauca* (glaucous); hardy bulb; 6 inches; flowers yellow, in March; Switzerland; 1825. *G. Liotardi* (Liotard's); hardy bulb; 6 inches; flowers yellow, in May; south of Europe; 1825. *G. lutea* (yellow); hardy bulb; 6 inches; flowers yellow, in May; England. *G. minima* (least); hardy bulb; 3 inches; flowers yellow, in May; Switzerland; 1826. *G. Podalica* (Podalian); hardy bulb; 6 inches; flowers yellow, in May; Podalia; 1827. *G. pusilla* (small); hardy bulb; 3 inches; flowers yellow, in April; Bohemia; 1825. *G. spathacea* (sheathed); hardy bulb; 6 inches; flowers yellow, in May; Germany; 1759. *G. uniflora* (one-flowered); hardy bulb; 6 inches; flowers yellow, in May; Siberia; 1781. *G. villosa* (shaggy); hardy bulb; 6 inches; flowers yellow, in April; Caucasus; 1825.

GAILLARDIA. [Compositæ.] Showy hardy and half-hardy perennials. Soil, sandy loam, or light garden soil. Increased by division. *G. picta*, a soft-stemmed plant, used for flower-garden decoration, requires protection from frost in a dry frame during winter, and is raised from seeds or cuttings in autumn, for planting out in the following May.

G. aristata (awned); hardy perennial; 2 feet; flowers deep-yellow, in July; North America; 1812. *G. bicolor* (two-colored); hardy perennial; 2 feet; flowers deep-yellow, in August; North America; 1787. *G. picta* (painted); half-hardy perennial; 18 inches; flowers yellow and red, in July; Louisiana; 1833. *G. Richardsoni* (Richardson's); hardy perennial; 18 inches; flowers deep-yellow, in July; North America; 1827. *G. grandiflora* is a garden hybrid; flowers rich red, with yellow border, very large; 1855.

GALANTHUS. *Snowdrop.* [Amaryllidaceæ.] Well-known hardy bulbs, dwarf, pretty, and very general favorites, partly perhaps from the season at which they appear, as the heralds of spring. *G. plicatus* is the finest species, but is rare. The bulbs require planting in October, in common soil, and should be left undisturbed for several years; they then form thick patches, and are more showy when in flower. They should be planted in patches, instead of single rows along the edging of borders.

G. nivalis (common); hardy bulb; 4 inches; flowers white and green, in March; England. *G. plicatus* (plaited); hardy bulb; 9 inches; flowers white and green, in March; Crimea; 1818. *G. reflexus* (reflexed); hardy bulb; 6 inches; flowers white and green, in March; Mount Gargarus; 1844.

GALAX. [Pyrolaceæ.] Hardy perennials. Soil, peat, kept rather damp. Increased by division.

G. aphylla (leafless); hardy perennial; 6 inches; flowers white, in July; North America; 1786.

GALEGA. *Goat's-Rue.* [Leguminosæ.] Large growing hardy or half-hardy perennials. Common soil. Increased by division or by seeds.

G. biloba (two-lobed); hardy perennial; 3 feet; flowers blue, in July; native country uncertain; 1823. *G. officinalis* (officinal); hardy perennial; 3 feet; flowers blue or white, in July; Spain; 1568. *G. Orientalis* (Eastern); hardy perennial; 3 feet; flowers blue, in July; Levant; 1801. *G. Persica* (Persian); hardy perennial; 3 feet; flowers white, in July; Persia; 1826.

GARDEN FLOWERS.   173

GALIUM. [Galiaceæ.] A genus of coarse, not very showy plants, thriving in any soil, and propagated by division. *G. suavolens* is an annual: the rest of those we mention are herbaceous perennials, generally hardy.

G. campanulatum (bell-flowered); 6 inches; flowers white, in June; south of Europe; 1821. *G. capillipes* (hairy-stalked); 1 foot; flowers white, in October; Russia; 1838. *G. Græcum* (Grecian); 6 inches; flowers purple, in July; Candia; 1798. *G. Persicum* (Persian); flowers yellow, in July; Persia; 1837. *G. purpureum* (purple); 1 foot; flowers purple, in July; Switzerland; 1831. *G. rubrum* (red); 1 foot; flowers purple, in July; Italy; 1597. *G. suavolens* (sweet-scented); 1 foot; flowers white, in July; north of Europe; 1821. *G. Tauricum* (Taurian); 6 inches; flowers yellow, in July; Tauria; 1818. *G. Vaillantii* (Vaillant's); 2 feet; flowers green, in May; England.

GAULTHERIA. [Ericaceæ] Pretty dwarf, procumbent, hardy evergreens, growing in moist peaty soil, and increased by layers and seeds.

G. procumbens (procumbent); hardy trailing evergreen shrub; flowers white, in July; North America; 1762. *G. Shallon* (Shallon); hardy evergreen shrub; 1 foot; flowers white, in May; North America; 1826.

There are evergreen greenhouse species.

GAURA. [Onagraceæ.] Showy plants, mostly biennials. Soil, sandy loam. Increased by seeds. *G. Lindhiemeriana* is a very elegantly branched free-blooming plant, and, though perennial, is perhaps best treated as a biennial: it blooms freely, however, the first year from the seed, if sown in May with the half-hardy annuals. The species are not hardy in the Northern States.

G. biennis (biennial); hardy biennial; 6 feet; flowers white and red, in September; North America; 1762. *G. coccinea* (scarlet); hardy perennial; 1 foot; flowers scarlet, in August; Louisiana; 1811. *G. Lindhiemeriana* (Lindheimer's); half-hardy perennial; 2 feet; flowers white and pink, in July; Texas; 1851. *G. mutabilis* (changeable); half-hardy perennial; 2 feet; flowers yellow, in July; North America; 1795. *G. œnotheræfolia* (œnothera-leaved); hardy biennial; 2 feet; flowers purple, in July; South America; 1816.

GAZANIA. [Compositæ.] Greenhouse herbaceous plants, producing large and very showy yellow or orange-colored composite flowers. Soil, loam, leaf-mould, and sand. Increased by division or by cuttings. They require little care beyond ordinary routine greenhouse management, and to be occasionally repotted as they become thickly rooted. *G. uniflora* is of a different habit from the rest, producing numerous branching stems, and forms a good bedding-out plant for the flower-garden in summer if planted in a dryish situation. Cuttings struck about August in one season, form good blooming plants for the next summer: they should be frequently stopped while young.

G. pavonia (peacock); greenhouse perennial; 1 foot; flowers orange and black, in June; Cape; 1804. *G. rigens* (stiff); greenhouse perennial; 1 foot; flowers orange and black, in June; Cape; 1735. *G. splendens* (showy); greenhouse perennial; 1 foot; flowers orange with black centre, in August. This species is a fine bedding plant, and is a hybrid between *G. uniflora* and *rigens*; gardens; 1860. *G. uniflora* (one-flowered); greenhouse perennial; 1 foot; flowers pale-yellow, in June; Cape; 1816.

GENISTA. *Broom.* [Leguminoseæ.] A large genus, of which some are hardy. They do well in common soil, and are very conspicuous for their bright yellow flowers in June. Propagated by seeds.

G. aphylla (leafless); hardy shrub; 4 feet; flowers violet, in July; Siberia; 1800. *G. diffusa* (spreading); hardy shrub; 3 feet; flowers yellow, in June; Hungary; 1816. *G. Siberica* (Siberian); hardy shrub; 2 feet; flowers yellow, in June; Siberia; 1785. *G. tinctoria* (dyer's); hardy shrub; 3 feet; flowers yellow, in June; England.

There are double-flowered varieties.

GENTIANA. [Gentianaceæ.] Beautiful hardy herbaceous plants. They should be planted in good rich soil, and most of them prefer a considerable proportion of peat earth. They are propagated readily by dividing the plant in autumn or spring. The hardy annual and biennial species are of much less horticultural importance.

G. acaulis (Gentianella); hardy perennial; 3 inches; flowers blue, in May; Wales. *G. algida* (cold); hardy perennial; 6 inches; flowers white, in June; Siberia; 1808. *G. Altaica* (Altaic); hardy perennial; 1 foot; flowers purple, in May; Siberia; 1824. *G. asclepiadea* (asclepias-like); hardy perennial; 1 foot; flowers blue or white, in July; Austria; 1629. *G. aurea* (golden); hardy perennial; 6 inches; flowers yellow, in August; Norway; 1823. *G. Bavarica* (Bavarian); hardy perennial; 3 inches; flowers blue, in July; Germany; 1775. *G. Catesbæi* (Catesby's); hardy perennial; 18 inches; flowers blue, in June; North America; 1803. *G. ciliata* (hair-fringed); hardy perennial; 9 inches; flowers blue, in July; Germany; 1759. *G. crinita* (fringed); hardy perennial; flowers sky-blue, in October; North America; 1804. *G. cruciata* (crossed); hardy perennial; 1 foot; flowers blue, in June; Austria; 1596. *G. fimbriata* (fringed); hardy perennial; 6 inches; flowers blue, in August; Caucasus; 1818. *G. Fortuni* (Fortune's); hardy perennial; 18 inches; flowers deep-blue, spotted with white, in July; north of China; 1852. *G. frigida* (frigid); hardy perennial; 1 foot; flowers white, in July; Carpathian Mountains; 1817. *G. glacialis* (icy); hardy biennial; 1 foot; flowers blue, in August; north of Europe; 1819. *G. lutea* (yellow); hardy perennial; 4 feet; flowers yellow, in July; Alps; 1596. *G. macrophylla* (large-leaved); hardy perennial; 1 foot; flowers blue, in July; Siberia; 1796. *G. Pannonica* (Pannonian); hardy perennial; 1 foot; flowers purple, in July; Alps. *G. pneumo-*

nanthe (Calathian-violet); hardy perennial; 1 foot; flowers blue or white, in August; England. *G. pumila* (dwarf); hardy perennial; 3 inches; flowers blue, in May; Switzerland; 1817. *G. punctata* (spotted); hardy perennial; 3 feet; flowers yellow, in July; Alps; 1795. *G. saponaria* (soapwort-leaved); hardy perennial; 2 feet; flowers blue or white, in August; North America; 1796. *G. septemfida* (seven-cleft); hardy perennial; 9 inches; flowers blue, in June; Persia; 1804. *G. verna* (vernal); hardy perennial; 3 inches; flowers blue, in April; England.

There are many other showy species.

GERANIUM. *Crane's-bill.* [Geraniaceæ.] Ornamental herbaceous plants. Common garden soil. Increased readily by division or by seeds.

G. aconitifolium (aconite-leaved); hardy perennial; 18 inches; flowers white, in June; Switzerland; 1775. *G. cristatum* (crested); hardy perennial; 18 inches; flowers veined with red, in July; Iberia; 1820. *G. Dahuricum* (Dahurian); hardy perennial; 1 foot; flowers purple, in June; Dahuria; 1820. *G. Ibericum* (Iberian); hardy perennial; 18 inches; flowers blue, in July; Levant; 1802. *G. Lancastriense* (Lancaster); hardy perennial; 9 inches; flowers striped, in June; Britain. *G. Mexicanum* (Mexican); hardy perennial; 2 feet; flowers pale purple, in August; Mexico; 1832. *G. pratense* (meadow); hardy perennial; 18 inches; flowers blue or white, or blue and white striped, single or double, in June; Britain. *G. rubifolium* (bramble-leaved); hardy perennial; 1 foot; flowers pink, in July; Himalayas; 1839. *G. sanguineum* (bloody); hardy perennial; 1 foot; flowers crimson, in July; Britain.

There are many other species.

GERARDIA. [Scrophulariaceæ.] A family of annuals, biennials, and perennials, mostly natives of North America, and of difficult culture. Soil, leaf-mould and sand.

G. flava (yellow); hardy perennial; 18 inches; flowers yellow, in August; North America; 1796. *G. quercifolia* (oak-leaved);

hardy perennial; 1 foot; flowers yellow, in August; North America; 1812. *G. purpurea* (purple); hardy annual; flowers purple, in August; North America; 1772.

GEUM. *Avens.* [Rosaceæ.] Hardy perennials, some of which are ornamental. Soil, sandy loam. Propagated by division or by seeds.

G. album (white); hardy perennial; 1 foot; flowers white, in July; North America; 1730. *G. Canadense* (Canadian); hardy perennial; 18 inches; flowers yellow, in July; Canada; 1810. *G. Chilense* (Chili); hardy perennial; 2 feet; flowers copper-color, in July; Chili; 1826. The variety *atro-sanguineum* has the flowers dark blood-colored; variety *grandiflorum*, scarlet. *G. macrophyllum* (large-leaved); hardy perennial; 2 feet; flowers yellow, in July; Kamtschatka; 1804. *G. Pyrenaicum* (Pyrenæan); hardy perennial; 18 inches; flowers yellow, in July; Pyrenees; 1804. *G. Virginianum* (Virginian); hardy perennial; 18 inches; flowers white, in July; North America; 1730.

GIANT-FENNEL. See FERULA.

GILIA. [Polemoniaceæ.] Favorite hardy annuals, with small cup-like, but very pretty simple flowers. There are several varieties, and but little to distinguish them from each other save the different shades of color. *G. tricolor* is the best for general purposes; it is neat, dwarf, and free flowering. Being as hardy as most of the annuals, it may be sown in May where it is to bloom, and should not be too much crowded. It will bloom from June onwards in succession.

G. achilleæfolia (milfoil-leaved); hardy annual; 1 foot; flowers purple-blue, in June; California; 1833. *G. capitata* (round-headed); hardy annual; 2½ feet; flowers gray-blue or white, in June; Columbia; 1826. *G. gracilis* (slender); hardy annual; 6 inches; flowers pink, in July; North America; 1826. *G. tenuiflora* (slender-flowered); hardy annual; 2 feet; flowers rose and violet, in July; California. *G. tricolor* (three-colored); hardy annual; 1 foot; flowers lilac, yellow, and black, in June; California; 1833. Of this there are the varieties *nivalis*, white, with yellow throat; *albiflora*, white, with yellow and black; and *splendens*, pink, with yellow and black.

GILLENIA. [Rosaceæ.] Hardy herbaceous perennials. Peaty soil, rather moist. Propagated by division.

G. stipulacea (large-stipuled); hardy perennial; 2 feet; flowers white and red, in July; North America; 1803. *G. trifoliata* (three-leaved); hardy perennial; 2 feet; flowers white and red, in July; North America; 1713.

GLADIOLUS. [Iridaceæ.] A large family of showy bulbs, mostly tender. The hybrids of *G. Gandavensis* have of late attracted much attention. Though less delicate, they are not excelled in beauty by any of the rarer species. They will often endure the winter in the open air as far north as Massachusetts; but the safest and best way is take up the bulbs after the leaves are killed by the frost, dry them rapidly in the sun, and preserve them in a dry, cool, frost-proof cellar until spring. Seeds ripen freely, but produce new varieties, the older being propagated by division of the bulbs and by bulblets. Seedlings bloom the second year.

For a list of varieties consult the florists' newest catalogues. Some of the best, however, are: *Light* — El Dorado, Penelope, Madame Leseble, Junon, Madame Binder, Ceres, Vesta, Calypso, Queen Victoria, Canari, Samuel Walker, Rebecca, and Imperatrice. *Dark* — Pluton, Napoleon III., Mars, Brenchleyensis, Anatole Levanneur, Premice de Mont-Rouge, Vulcain, Mrs. Basseville, La Poussin, Count de Morny.

G. communis and *Byzanthium* are hardy bulbs, requiring to be treated like crocuses.

GLAUCIUM. [Papavaraceæ.] A family of annuals and biennials, grown from seed sown in the open borders in May. The chief species are *G. Arabicum, Persicum, Phœnicium, rubrum*, and *tricolor*, all annuals; and *G. flavum* and *fulvum* biennials.

GLEDITSCHIA. [Leguminoseæ.] Hardy ornamental deciduous trees. Common soil. Propagated by seed.

G. horrida; hardy tree; 10 feet; flowers green, in July; China; 1774. *G. sinensis;* hardy tree; 20 feet; flowers green, in June; China; 1812. The varieties are *inermis, major, nana,* and *pendula*. *G. tricanthos* (three-thorned); Honey Locust; hardy tree; 30 feet; flowers green, in July; 1700. Variety *inermis* differs in having no thorns.

GLOBE-AMARANTH. See GOMPHRENA.
GLOBE-FLOWER. See TROLLIUS.
GLOBE-THISTLE. See ECHINOPS.

GLOBULARIA. [Selaginaceæ.] Dwarf herbaceous plants, nearly or quite hardy, except in the Northern States. Soil, sandy loam and peat. Increased by cuttings of the young shoots under a hand-glass in summer.

G. Alypum (three-toothed); half-hardy perennial; 2 feet; flowers pale-red, in August; south of Europe; 1640. *G. bellidifolia* (daisy-leaved); hardy perennial; 3 inches; flowers red, in July; Italy; 1825. *G. cordifolia* (heart-leaved); hardy perennial; 6 inches; flowers blue, in July; Germany; 1683. *G. vulgaris* (common); hardy perennial; 6 inches; flowers blue, in June; Europe; 1640.

GLOSSOCOMIA. [Campanulaceæ.] Half-hardy herbaceous perennials. Common soil. Increased by seeds or division.

G. lurida (lurid); half-hardy perennial; 2 feet; flowers green and purple, in May; North India; 1838. *G. ovata* (ovate); half-hardy perennial; 18 inches; flowers white, in July; North India; 1839.

GNAPHALIUM. [Compositæ.] A pretty family of plants commonly known as Everlastings, comprising greenhouse perennials and hardy annuals and biennials. Soil, sandy loam and leaf-mould. Propagated by seeds. The annual species are *G. obtusifolium* and *undulatum*.

GOAT'S BEARD. See SPIREA ARUNCUS.

GOAT'S RUE. See GALEGA.

GODETIA. [Onagraceæ.] Showy hardy annuals, nearly related to Œnothera. Sow in the open beds or borders in May, to flower in June, July, and August. As soon as the plants come up, they should be thinned; for, if crowded, they grow weakly, and do not flower so well. Six or eight, plants may be left in a patch. If they are required early, they may be sown in pots in April, to be forwarded in frames, and turned out in May. In this case, the pots must be kept near the light, and beyond the reach of frost, which, while the plants are young and tender, will injure them. Several of the species are too much alike. When vigorous, the plants remain some time in bloom.

G. albescens (whitish); hardy annual; 18 inches; flowers pinkish-purple, in June; Columbia; 1841. *G. grandiflora* (large-flowered); hardy annual; 2 feet; flowers white and red, in July; Columbia; 1841. *G. lepida* (pretty); hardy annual; 18 inches; flowers pink, in June; California; 1835. *G. Lindleyana* (Lindley's); hardy annual; 18 inches; flowers pale-rose and crimson, in June; North America; 1826. *G. quadrivulnera* (four-spotted); hardy annual; 18 inches; flowers pink, in July; North America; 1826. *G. Romanzovii* (Romanzow's); hardy annual; 1 foot; flowers bluish-purple, in June; North America; 1817. *G. rosea-alba* (red and white); hardy annual; 18 inches; flowers red and and white, in June; Nepaul; 1827. *G. rubicunda* (ruddy); hardy annual; 2 feet; flowers rosy-lilac, in June; California; 1834. *G. tenella* (slender); hardy annual; 6 inches; flowers purple, in May; Chili; 1822. *G. tenuifolia* (fine-leaved); hardy annual; 9 inches; flowers pinkish, in June; Chili; 1828. *G. viminea* (twiggy); hardy annual; 2½ feet; flowers purple, in June; California; 1826. *G. vinosa* (wine-stained); hardy annual; 18 inches; flowers bluish, in June; California; 1835.

GOLDEN FLOWER. See CHRYSANTHEMUM.

GOLDEN-ROD. See SOLIDAGO.

GOLDYLOCKS. See CHRYSOCOMA.

GOMPHRENA. *Globe Amaranth.* [Amaranthaceæ.] Pretty plants, usually grown as annuals. The chief kind is *G. globosa* commonly called Globe Amaranth. The seeds should be thinly sown in a hot-bed in April. As soon as the young plants are large enough to be handled, they should be transplanted to a frame, and set four inches apart, or into pots, where they may grow until all danger of frost is over, when they may be transplanted to the garden. They seed freely; and the flowers continue beautiful a long time after they are gathered and dried, the petals being chaffy, or scaly, like those of Everlasting flowers. *G. pulchella*, another pretty annual kind, though not as yet very commonly grown, deserves to be so.

G. globosa (globe); stove annual; 18 inches; flowers purple or white, in July; India; 1714. *G. pulchella* (pretty); stove annual; 18 inches; flowers rose-red, in July; Brazil; 1843.

There are varieties with white, pink, and orange flowers.

GOODYERA. [Orchidaceæ.] A genus of pretty terrestrial orchids, with pretty variegated foliage. They need a sandy peat or leaf-mould, and a shady situation. Propagated by offsets.

G. pubescens (downy); hardy perennial; 6 inches; flowers white, in July; North America; 1802. *G. repens* (creeping); hardy perennial; 4 inches; flowers white, in July; North America.

GOURD ORNAMENTAL. See CUCURBITA.

GRAPE HYACINTH. See MUSCARI.

GRAMMANTHES. [Crassulaceæ.] Pretty annual plants with starry flowers, flourishing in warm sunny situations. Propagated by seed sown in sandy loam, and transplanted to garden.

G. chloræflora (yellow-flowered); half-hardy annual; 6 inch-

es; flowers yellow and red, in July; Cape of Good Hope; 1774.
G. gentianoides (gentian-like); half-hardy annual; 6 inches; flowers pinkish-red, in July; Cape of Good Hope; 1848.

Other varieties are *reflexa, cinnabarina, lilacina,* and *lutea.*

GREEK VALERIAN. See POLEMONIUM.

GRATIOLA. [Scrophulariaceæ.] A family of low-growing plants of but little beauty, but useful in rich moist soil. Propagated by division. The best species are *G. aurea, megalocarpa, officinalis, pilosa, quadridentata,* and *Virginica.*

GROMWELL. See LITHOSPERMUM.

GROUNDSEL. See SENICIO.

GROUND IVY. See NEPETA.

GUELDER-ROSE. See VIBURNUM.

GUIZOTIA. [Compositæ.] Hardy annual. Cultivated in southern Europe as an oil plant. Soil, light rich loam. Increased by seeds.

G. oleifera (oil-yielding); hardy annual; 3 feet; flowers yellow, in July; Abyssinia; 1775.

GYMNOCLADUS. [Leguminosæ.] A fine hardy ornamental tree, very conspicuous in summer for its plumes of foliage. It thrives in any good soil, but in deep mellow loam it grows with great rapidity. Propagated by seeds and cuttings of the root.

G. Canadensis (Canadian); hardy tree; 20 feet; flowers white, in June; North America.

GYMNODISCUS. [Compositæ.] A hardy annual, growing in common garden soil, and propagated by seeds sown in the open border in May.

G. capillaris (hair-like); hardy annual; flowers yellow, in June; Cape of Good Hope; 1822.

GYNANDROPSIS. [Capparidaceæ.] Hardy and stove annuals and biennials, allied to Cleome. The hardy species should be sown in a gentle hot-bed in April, and transplanted to the border in May.

G. candelabrum (chandelier); hardy annual; 1 foot; flowers red, in July; South America; 1824. *G. sessiliflora* (sessile-flowered); hardy annual; 1 foot; flowers white, in July; West Indies; 1820. *G. triphylla* (three-leaved); hardy annual; 1 foot; flowers white in July; West Indies; 1816.

GYNERIUM. *Pampas Grass.* [Gramineæ.] A noble plant from the Pampas of South America. The plumes of nodding feathers are very ornamental. The plant is half-hardy, needing a cold frame or cellar protection during winter, but thrives well planted out in summer. Soil, rich loam. Propagated by division and seed.

G. argenteum (silvery); half-hardy perennial; 15 feet; flowers apetalous, in August; South America; 1852.

GYPSOCALLIS. [Ericaceæ.] Beautiful little evergreen half-hardy shrubs, formerly known as Ericas. They require to be planted in a bed of peat earth, with Rhododendrons, Ledums, and like plants, and should occupy the outer parts. If the situation is rather moist, it is preferable; otherwise they require to be abundantly watered in spring, while making their new growth. Increased by layers.

G. carnea (flesh-colored); evergreen shrub; 6 inches; flowers pinkish, in January; Germany; 1763. *G. Mediterranea* (Mediterranean); evergreen shrub; 4 feet; flowers purple, in April; Portugal; 1648. *G. multiflora* (many-flowered); evergreen shrub; 1 foot; flowers flesh-color, in June; France; 1731. *G. vagans* (wandering); evergreen shrub; 1 foot; flo*ers red or pink, or white, in July. Britain.

These plants are tender in the Northern States.

GYPSOPHILA. [Caryophyllaceæ.] Hardy herbaceous perennials, with one or two exceptions. Some of them are pretty, producing a number of small flowers, usually white,

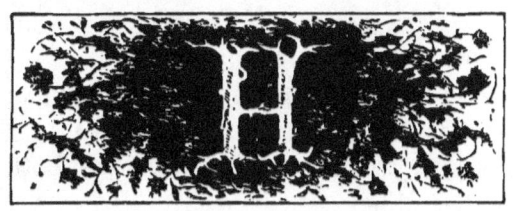

HABENARIA. [Orchidaceæ.] A genus of herbaceous perennials, containing one or two hardy species. Soil, moist peat. Propagated by division.

H. procera (tall); hardy perennial; 2 feet; flowers green, in August; North America; 1822.

There are many stove and tender species.

HACQUETIA. [Umbelliferæ.] A small hardy herbaceous perennial. Soil, sandy loam and peat. Increased by division.

H. epipactis; hardy perennial; 3 inches; flowers yellow, in April; Alps; 1823.

HALESIA. *Snowdrop-Tree.* [Styracaceæ.] Hardy deciduous shrubs, ornamental in flower and foliage, thriving best in deep, rich, rather moist loam. Propagated by layers, seeds, and cuttings. *H. diptera* is not hardy north of Massachusetts.

H. tetraptera (four-winged); hardy shrub; 10 feet; flowers white, in June; North America; 1756. *H. parviflora* (small-flowered); hardy shrub; 8 feet; flowers white; North America; 1827. *H. diptera* (two-winged); hardy shrub; 8 feet; flowers white, in May; North America; 1758.

HALIMODENDRON. [Leguminosæ.] Hardy deciduous shrubs, usually grafted as standards on Laburnum, thus forming a graceful drooping tree. Soil, sandy loam. Propagated by seeds, cuttings, and layers.

H. argenteum (silvery); hardy shrub; 6 feet; flowers pink, in June; Siberia; 1779.

The varieties *brachysema* and *subvirescens*, both with pink flowers, are desirable.

HAMAMELIS. *Witch-Hazel.* [Hamamelidaceæ.] Hardy deciduous shrubs, very showy from the abundance of yellow flowers produced in November after the leaves have fallen, and imparting a gay appearance to the shrubbery at that dreary season. Propagated by root cuttings, layers, and seeds, the latter requiring two years to vegetate. Soil, moist loam. The female flowers are the more showy.

H. Virginica (Virginian); hardy shrub; 10 feet; flowers yellow, in November; North America; 1812.

HAREBELL. See CAMPANULA.
HARE'S EAR. See BUPLEURUM.
HAWTHORN. See CRATAEGUS.
HAWKWEED. See TOLPIS.
HAZEL-NUT. See CORYLUS.
HEATHER. See CALLUNA.
HEART'S EASE. See PANSY, VIOLA.

HEDEOMA. [Lamiaceæ.] Hardy annuals, growing readily from seed sown in spring in common garden soil.

H. puligioides (pennyroyal-like); hardy annual; 6 inches; flowers blue, in July; North America. *H. thymoides* (thyme-like); hardy annual; 3 inches; flowers red, in July; France.

HEDERA. *Ivy.* [Araliaceæ.] A well-known hardy evergreen climber, of which there are several varieties. The tender Ivies are of little interest. Common garden soil suits the Ivy, but it grows quicker if it be rich and deep. Increased by cuttings in autumn, in a moist sandy soil. The best of the varieties for general purposes are the *Irish* and *H. Rægneriana*, the latter with large heart-shaped leaves.

H. Helix (common). The principal varieties are, *arbores-*

cens (tree-like); *Canariensis* (Irish); *chrysocarpa* (yellow-berried); *digitata* (finger-leaved); *foliis argenteis* (silver-striped); *foliis aureis* (gold-striped); *Rægneriana* (Rægner's).

HEDGE-HYSSOP. See GRATIOLA.
HEDGE-MUSTARD. See ERYSIMUM.
HEDGE-NETTLE. See STACHYS.

HEDYSARUM. [Leguminosæ.] Hardy or half-hardy herbaceous plants, including annuals, biennials, and perennials. Common garden soil. Increased by seeds or division.

H. Altaicum (Altaic); hardy perennial; 6 inches; flowers purple, in July; Siberia; 1818. *H. Caucasicum* (Caucasian); hardy perennial; 1 foot; flowers purple, in July; Caucasus; 1820. *H. coronarium* (French honeysuckle); hardy biennial; 3 feet; flowers scarlet, in June; Italy; 1596. *H. grandiflorum* (large-flowered); hardy perennial; 18 inches; flowers purple, in June; Tauria; 1821. *H. Ibericum* (Iberian); hardy perennial; 6 inches; flowers purple, in July; Iberia; 1818. *H. lasiocarpum* (woolly-podded); hardy perennial; 1 foot; flowers purple, in July; Siberia; 1816. *H. roseum* (rosy); hardy perennial; 6 inches; flowers pink, in August; Caucasus; 1803. *H. splendens* (shining); hardy perennial; 6 inches; flowers cream-color, in July; Siberia; 1819. *H. varium* (variable); hardy perennial; 1 foot; flowers white, in July; south of Europe; 1820. *H. venustum* (lovely); hardy perennial; 6 inches; flowers purple, in June; Attica; 1828.

HELENIUM. [Compositæ.] Hardy, herbaceous, yellow-flowered perennials, growing in common soil, and increased by division.

H. autumnale (autumnal); 3 feet; flowers in September; North America; 1729. *H. atropurpureum* (dark-purple); hardy annual; 1 foot; flowers, orange, black, and yellow, in August; Texas; 1845. *H. caniculatum* (channelled); 3 feet; flowers in August; North America; 1800. *H. pubescens* (downy); 3 feet; flowers in August; North America; 1776. *H. pumilum* (dwarf); 1 foot; flowers in August; 1818.

HELIANTHEMUM. [Cistineæ.] A large family of ornamental trailing plants. A few of the herbaceous perennials are hardy. The annuals should be sown from seed in spring in the open border.

ANNUALS.—*H. Ægyptiacum* (Egyptian); 9 inches; flowers white, in June; Egypt; 1764. *H. eriocaulon* (woolly-stemmed); 9 inches; flowers yellow; Spain; 1817. *H. guttatum* (spotted); 6 inches; flowers yellow, in June; England. *H. ledifolium* (ledum-leaved); 6 inches; flowers yellow, in June; England. *H. Niloticum* (Nile); 6 inches; flowers yellow, in June; south of Europe; 1817. *H. Niloticum majus* (larger); 1 foot; flowers yellow; Europe; 1817. *H. plantagineum* (plantain-like); 6 inches; flowers yellow, in June; south of Europe; 1823. *H. punctatum* (dotted); 6 inches, flowers yellow, in July; south of France; 1816. *H. salicifolium* (willow-leaved); 6 inches; flowers yellow, in July; south of Europe; 1759. *H. sanguineum* (bloody); 3 inches; flowers yellow, in July; Spain; 1826. *H. villosum* (shaggy); 6 inches; flowers yellow, in July; Spain; 1823.

HERBACEOUS PERENNIALS.—*H. Canadense* (Canadian); 1 foot; flowers yellow, in June; North America; 1799. *H. Carolinianum* (Carolina); 1 foot; flowers yellow, in July; Carolina; 1823. *H. rosmarinifolium* (rosemary-leaved); 1 foot; flowers pale-yellow, in June; Canada; 1823.

HELIANTHUS. *Sun-flower.* [Compositæ.] These tall-growing, coarse-flowered perennials are well adapted for shrubberies. The annual species are showy, and should be cultivated where there is room.

H. annuus (annual); hardy annual; 6 feet; flowers yellow, in August; South America; 1596. *H. Indicus* (Indian); hardy annual; 6 feet; flowers yellow, in July; Egypt; 1785. *H. multiflorus* (many-flowered); hardy perennial; 5 feet; flowers yellow, single, or double, in August; North America; 1597. *H. tuberosum* is the Jerusalem Artichoke.

There are some thirty other species.

HELICHRYSUM. [Compositæ.] A genus comprising many species, including the well-known annual Everlastings, and a few half-hardy perennials. The common annual Everlasting, and some allied plants, though introduced from New Holland, are treated as half-hardy annuals, being sown in the open borders in May, or, for earlier blooming, on a gentle hot-bed in March, and transplanted in May. They come into bloom at an advanced period of the summer, and continue a succession of blossoms until destroyed by the frosts of autumn.

H. arenarium (sand); half-hardy perennial; 9 inches; flowers yellow, in July; Europe; 1739. *H. bracteatum* (bracted); half-hardy annual; 2 feet; flowers yellow or white, in July; New Holland; 1799. *H. candidissimum* (whitest); half-hardy perennial; 2 feet; flowers pale-yellow, in June; Caspian; 1823. *H. macranthum* (large-flowered); half-hardy annual; 2 feet; flowers white, with rosy tips, in July; New Holland; 1837. *H. robustum* (robust); half-hardy annual; 3 feet; flowers white and yellow, in July; Swan River; 1839. *H. spectabile* (showy); half-hardy annual; 2 feet; flowers cream-color, in July; Swan River; 1840.

There are numerous other species; and fine varieties with various colored flowers may be obtained of florists and seedsmen. *H. incurvum* is a variety of *bracteatum*, producing flowers of every shade of yellow, sulphur, cream, white, pink, rose, red, and crimson.

HELIOPHILA. [Cruciferæ.] Hardy annuals, some of which are pretty flower-border plants. They should be sown in the open ground in May, or, for earlier blooming, in April, under cover, and afterwards planted out. Rather sandy soil is preferable, and they like exposure to sun. Two or three are delicate greenhouse shrubs, but not of much importance.

H. araboides (arabis-like); hardy annual; 1 foot; flowers

blue, in June; Cape; 1768. *H. pilosa* (hairy); hardy annual; 1 foot; flowers blue, in July; Cape; 1768. *H. stricta* (erect); hardy annual; 1 foot; flowers blue, in June; Cape; 1823. *H. trifida* (three-cleft); hardy annual; 1 foot; flowers blue, in June; Cape; 1819.

HELIOTROPE. See HELIOTROPIUM.

HELIOTROPIUM. *Heliotrope.* [Boragineæ.] A genus comprising stove and hardy annuals, and stove and greenhouse shrubs, of little importance, except the Peruvian Heliotrope *(H. Peruvianum)*, which is a great favorite in flower-gardens, and bears very fragrant blossoms, prized chiefly for their perfume. This species is, strictly speaking, a greenhouse low shrub. The young shoots will strike freely in light sandy soil during summer, under a frame or handglass, but more readily with slight warmth. When well rooted, they may be potted into small pots, and placed in a frame or in the greenhouse, where they may grow till their roots show through the bottom of the pots, and then be changed into those of the next larger size. Top the leading shoots to produce laterals. They must be wintered in a dryish part of the greenhouse. If intended for beds and borders, they must be hardened in cold frames in the spring, and planted out in May after danger from frost is over. It is sometimes preferred to keep an old plant or two through the winter, and to put them into a hot-bed or warm house about February, when they will produce plenty of young shoots, the tops of which are quickly struck in a hot-bed; and, if potted and gradually hardened, make good plants for turning out in May. Where there are no such conveniences, the plants may be kept in a warm part of the greenhouse in spring, and the young shoots taken off as soon as they grow, planted in sandy soil, and covered by a glass. When rooted, they may be potted, or at once planted out, according to the season. There are now several varieties of the Peruvian Heliotrope; the principal variations consisting in the larger size of the blossoms, and the deepening of the color, which, in the variety *Voltaircanum*, is of a deep purple. *H. corymbosum*, and many other varieties, are worth growing. Both for flower-beds and for bouquets, the Heliotrope may be considered indispensable. Seed of the annual kinds may be sown in March, in a frame or greenhouse; the plants, when large enough, may be pricked out three or four in a pot, and, as they advance, potted singly, or planted out where they are to remain.

H. corymbosum (corymbose); greenhouse shrub; 4 feet; flowers lilac, in July; Peru; 1800. *H. Peruvianum* (Peruvian); greenhouse shrub; 18 inches; flowers lilac or purple, in July; Peru; 1757.

HELLEBORE. See HELLEBORUS.

HELLEBORUS. *Hellebore.* [Ranunculaceæ.] Showy hardy perennials, of easy culture, growing in good garden soil, and a rather shady situation, and increasing by dividing the roots in the dormant season. It is a desirable family. *H. niger*, called the Christmas Rose, is a favorite dwarf species, which flowers all through the winter. *H. Olympicus*, and some others of the Oriental species, are the better for slight protection; their early blossoms being otherwise disfigured. These, and *H. atrorubens*, with purple flowers, are the most desirable.

H. atrorubens (dark-red); hardy perennial; 1 foot; flowers purple, in May; Hungary; 1820. *H. fœtidus* (bear's-foot); hardy perennial; 18 inches; flowers green, in May; England. *H. lividus* (livid); hardy perennial; 1 foot; flowers purplish, in May; Corsica; 1710. *H. niger* (Christmas Rose); hardy perennial; 1 foot; flowers white, in January; Austria; 1596. *H. odorus* (sweet-scented); hardy perennial; 18 inches; flowers green, in May; Hungary; 1817. *H. Olympicus* (Olympian);

hardy perennial; 1 foot; flowers pinkish-white, in May; India; 1840. *H. Orientalis* (Eastern); hardy perennial; 1 foot; flowers purplish, in May; India; 1839. *H. purpurascens* (purplish); hardy perennial; 18 inches; flowers purplish, in May; Hungary; 1817. *H. vernalis* (spring); hardy perennial; 6 inches; flowers white, in May; Austria; 1596.

HELONIAS. [Melanthaceæ.] Hardy herbaceous perennials. Soil, peat, and a damp shady situation. Increased by division.

H. angustifolia (narow-leaved); hardy perennial; 1 foot; flowers white, in May; North America; 1823. *H. bullata* (bossed); hardy perennial; 1 foot; flowers purple, in April; North America; 1758. *H. erythrosperma* (red-seeded); hardy perennial; 6 inches; flowers white, in June; North America; 1770.

HEMEROCALLIS. *Day-lily*. [Liliaceæ.] Hardy, coarse-looking, but gay, herbaceous perennials, producing showy flowers that last but one day; hence the common name. They are of the simplest culture, growing readily in ordinary garden soil, and are propagated by dividing the plants. The flowers are pretty, and freely produced from June to August.

H. disticha (two-rowed); half-hardy perennial; 2 feet; flowers orange, in May; China; 1798. *H. flava* (yellow); hardy perennial; 2 feet; flowers yellow, in summer.

HEMLOCK. See ABIES.
HEMP. See CANNABIS.
HENBANE. See HYOSCYAMUS.
HEPATICA. [Ranunculaceæ.] Pretty dwarf hardy herbaceous perennials. The common Hepatica *(H. triloba)* is one of the earliest of the spring flowers. These plants require a well-drained border, — sandy loam with one-third peat is preferable, — and never succeed well in soil where there is

stagnant moisture. They deserve a place in every choice garden for their dwarf habit, bright colors, and early flowers. The plants increase by side-shoots, which spread into a moderate-sized tuft in a season or two if undisturbed; they are increased in number by separating these tufts, so that each heart, or side-shoot, with roots attached, may become a plant. This is done in spring, the roots being separated into pieces not too small; for, although the smallest bit would in time spread, they would be two or three seasons before they were fit to plant in the borders: these should be planted in nursery-beds, about six inches apart, and, after one season's growth, they will be large enough to plant out where they are to remain. The beds must be kept clear from weeds. These plants are rather impatient of extreme drought. The double varieties are superior to the single, and therefore are mostly cultivated; but the double white is very scarce, if not altogether lost, and therefore the single white is grown.

The single varieties are natives of our woods, and are among the first flowers of spring. The double varieties must be imported from England or Germany. *H. acutiloba* is only a variety of *H. triloba*.

H. acutiloba (acute-lobed); hardy perennial; 6 inches; flowers blue, in March; North America; 1818. *H. triloba* (three-lobed); hardy perennial; 9 inches; flowers blue, white, or pink, single or double, in April; Europe; 1573. *H. angulosa* is a fine species from Hungary, with blue flowers twice as large as the common species, on tall footstalks, in May; 1864.

HERACLEUM. *Cow Parsnip.* [Umbelliferæ.] Large coarse-growing hardy perennials and biennials, bearing large umbels of white flowers. The larger sorts are admirable plants for rough borders, rock-work on a large scale, wilderness scenery, or wherever a bold, striking, picturesque effect is required. Soil, deep rich loam. Increased abundantly by seeds. *H. giganteum* and *Persicum* are some of the best for these purposes.

HESPERIS. *Rocket.* [Cruciferæ.] A genus of hardy plants, annual, biennial, and perennial. Some of the varieties of the common Rocket *(H. matronalis)*, especially the double white and double purple, are very great favorites in the flower-gardens. They are rather difficult to manage, especially in old gardens or in confined situations; for they love fresh soil and an open situation. A light rich loam is the best for them; but if an artificial compost has to be made up, as it should be if they are required in perfection, a third part of sandy peat mixed with two-thirds of mellow loam will grow them very well. Next to soil, the great secret of success is, not to let them stand too long in a place, for under such circumstances they are sure to dwindle. They ought to be taken up and divided every second year, soon after they have done flowering, — that is, early in autumn, — and replanted in fresh soil. To have a display of healthy plants every year, they should be divided into two sets: those plants respectively which have bloomed in their second year, if taken up in each successive autumn and divided, will furnish a constant supply of young plants, the flowering of which should be prevented in the following summer, and they will then bloom vigorously in the second year from their transplantation. One reason why this constant transplantation is necessary is, that the plant, in its original state, is naturally a biennial, perishing after it has produced flowers. The other species, most of which are also biennials, are unimportant compared with the varieties above alluded to.

H. grandiflora (large-flowered); hardy biennial; 3 feet; flowers white and purple, in July; native country not known; 1820.

H. matronalis (matronly); hardy perennial; 2 feet; flowers white or purple, single or double, in June; Europe; 1597. *H. speciosa* (showy); hardy perennial; 6 inches; flowers rose-purple, in April; Siberia; 1829.

HEUCHERA. [Saxifragaceæ.] Hardy herbaceous perennials, with simple-looking flowers. Common soil. Increased by division. The species are *H. Americana, cylindracea, glabra, hispida, Menziesii, pubescens, Richardsonii*, and *villosa.*

HIBISCUS. [Malvaceæ.] A very large genus, comprising hardy and stove annuals, hardy herbaceous perennials, and hardy greenhouse and stove shrubs. The hardy annuals may be sown in the border in May. They do well in any garden soil, and only require to be thinned properly after they are up. The plants taken up to thin the others may be planted out carefully in other places. The hardy shrubs are splendid objects toward the end of summer when planted in dryish soil. They are increased by layers. The hardy perennials requre peaty soil and a moist, sheltered situation.

H. Africanus (African); hardy annual; 1 foot; flowers cream-color and black, in June; Africa; 1826. *H. grandiflorus* (large-flowered); half-hardy perennial; 3 feet; flowers flame-color, in July; Georgia; 1816. *H. incanus* (hoary); half-hardy perennial; 3 feet; flowers yellow, in September; Carolina; 1806. *H. moschatus* (mallow-rose); hardy perennial; 4 feet; flowers white and pink, in August; North America; 1759. *H. palustris* (marsh); hardy perennial; 3 feet; flowers pink, in July; North America; 1759. *H. roseus* (rosy); hardy perennial; 4 feet; flowers pink, in July; France; 1827. *H. speciosus* (showy); hardy perennial; 2 feet; flowers scarlet, in July; North America; 1804. *H. Syriacus* (Syrian); hardy deciduous shrub; 8 feet; flowers white or purple spotted, single or double, in August; Syria; 1596. *H. Trionum* (bladder ketmia); hardy annual; 2 feet; flowers cream-color and black, in July; Italy; 1596. *H. Virginicus* (Virginian); hardy perennial; 2 feet; flowers yellow, in July; Virginia; 1798.

HICKORY. See CARYA.

HIERACEUM. [Compositæ.] A large genus of yellow-flowered composite plants, none of which are of much horticultural importance. Common soil. Increased by division or by seeds.

HIPPOPHAE. *Sea Buckthorn.* [Elæagnaceæ.] Hardy shrubs, allied to Shepherdia, doing well in sandy soil, and propagated by layers and suckers. The species is *H. rhamnoides*, with the varieties *angustifolia* and *Siberica*.

HOLLY. See ILEX.

HOLLYHOCK. See ALTHÆA.

HOLOGYMNE. See LASTHENIA.

HONESTY. See LUNARIA.

HONEY-LOCUST. See GLEDITSCHIA.

HONEYSUCKLE. See LONICERA and CAPRIFOLIUM.

HONEYWORT. See CERINTHE.

HOOP-PETTICOAT. See CORBULARIA.

HOP. See HUMULUS.

HORMINUM. [Labiatæ.] A showy dwarf hardy herbaceous perennial, requiring a dry situation and a sandy soil, or else to be kept in a dry cool frame in winter. Increased by seeds or division. Not hardy in the Northern States.

H. Pyrenaicum (Pyrenean); hardy perennial; 1 foot; flowers blue-purple, in June; Pyrenees; 1820.

HORNBEAM. See CARPINUS.

HORN-POPPY. See GLAUCIUM.

HORSE-CHESTNUT. See ÆSCULUS.

HORSE-TAIL. See EQUISETUM.

HOTEIA. [Saxifragaceæ.] A very handsome hardy perennial, formerly called *Spiræa Japonica*. Soil, sandy loam and peat. Increased by division.

H. Japonica (Japan); hardy perennial; 3 feet; flowers white, in May; Japan; 1835.

HOUND'S-TONGUE. See CYNOGLOSSUM.

HOUSE-LEEK. See SEMPERVIVUM.

HOUSTONIA. [Cinchonaceæ.] Pretty little tufted perennial herbs. Soil, a sandy mixture of three parts peat to one of loam. Increased by division.

H. cærulea (blue); hardy perennial; 3 inches; flowers bluish-lilac, in May; North America; 1785. *H. purpurea* (purple); hardy perennial; 1 foot; flowers purple, in May; North America; 1800. *H. serpyllifolia* (thyme-leaved); tender perennial; 6 inches; flowers white, in May; North America; 1826.

These plants are now called Oldenlandia, and are rather insignificant singly, but in the mass are showy. *H. cærulea* is the species which in spring almost whitens the pastures. *H. serpyllifolia*, a Southern species, is tender and of little value.

HAGELIA. [Polemoniaceæ.] Dwarf hardy annuals, allied to Gilea, and thriving under the same treatment. Sow in light border soil in May.

H. densiflora (dense-flowered); hardy annual; 1 foot; flowers blue, in July; California; 1833. *H. elongata* (lengthened); hardy annual; 1 foot; flowers deep-blue, in July; California; 1833. *H. lanata* (woolly); hardy annual; 1 foot; flowers light-blue, in July; California; 1847. *H. lutea* (yellow); hardy annual; 6 inches; flowers yellow, in July; California; 1833. *H. virgata* (twiggy); hardy annual; 1 foot; flowers deep-blue, in July; California; 1833.

HUMEA. [Compositæ.] A greenhouse biennial of singular grace and beauty. The seeds should be sown in May, and for a year potted from smaller to larger pots, wintered in a cold frame, and in May turned into the border in a sheltered situation. They will grow from eight to ten feet high. Others may be potted in twelve-inch pots, with loam and dung in equal parts for the compost. Those in pots must be regularly supplied with water, because they will grow fast, and take a good deal: indeed, if weak manure-water is given twice a week, when they have nearly reached their full growth, they will be benefited. The plant looks richer when not overgrown.

H. elegans (elegant); greenhouse biennial; 8 feet; flowers reddish-brown, in June; New South Wales; 1800.

HUMULUS. *Hop.* [Cannabinaceæ.] Hardy perennial twiner, stem herbaceous; a useful plant for covering unsightly objects, as it grows very rapidly, and in fruit is ornamental. Propagated by divisions of the root. Soil deep loam.

H. lupulus; 15 feet; flowers greenish-yellow, in July. A variety has foliage striped.

HUNNEMANIA. [Papaveraceæ.] A half-hardy herbaceous perennial, with the habit and appearance of Eschscholtzia. Soil, rich sandy loam. Increased by seeds.

H. fumariæfolia (fumitory-leaved); half-hardy perennial; 1 foot; flowers yellow, in July; Mexico; 1827.

HYACINTHUS. *Hyacinth.* [Liliaceæ.] Beautiful and well-known bulbs. *H. amethystinus* is a charming little hardy species, which should be planted in sandy loam. The cultivated varieties of Hyacinth are the progeny of *H. Orientalis.* Immense numbers of the bulbs of these odoriferous and showy plants are annually imported from Holland, and, after having been once bloomed, are thrown by, or planted in common borders to degenerate from neglect. To grow the Hyacinth properly, the soil should be composed of one-half turfy loam of mellow texture, one-fourth old cow-dung, or cow-dung mixed with leaf-mould, and one-fourth clean but coarse sand. For beds, loam, sand, and dung, rotted to mould, in equal quantities, may be used. In soil such as this, the offsets of the Hyacinth will grow, till, in two or three seasons, they come to full size and perfection; and bulbs thus grown annually will not degenerate. They must be planted in October, and be taken up when the leaves die down. The beds must be protected against severe frosts and heavy rains in winter, and against all that may damage the foliage in spring. Hyacinths flower beautifully in pots as well as in glasses for the greenhouse and window. Deep pots, five inches in diameter, should be used, the soil made very firm beneath the bulb, and the top of the bulb about level with the surface. The medium-sized, plump-looking, full-crowned bulbs should be chosen, and potted early in October. After potting, plunge the pots in old tan or coal-ashes, so as to cover them two or three inches, and let them remain until removed in succession to a warm room or house to forward the blooms. When grown in glasses of water, the dark-colored glasses should be preferred, and the more opaque the better. November is soon enough to put the bulbs in the glasses. First keep them a week or so in damp sand or moss, then put them in the hollowed top of the glass, and at first allow the water but just to touch their base. Rain-water, quite clean, should be used, and this changed once a week. The glasses should be set in the dark until the roots have grown an inch or two in length. When the flower-stem is advancing, two drops of spirits of hartshorn may be put into the water each time it is changed, with advantage. Tye's hyacinth-glasses are the best, and these are provided with an elegant support for the stem. Bulbs grown in water should be put in the ground when their flowers have decayed; for they derive considerable strength from it, and, besides that, perfect their offsets, if they have any. Hyacinths will grow well in wet sand, and when it is covered with moss the plants look very pretty.

H. amethystinus (amethyst-colored); hardy bulb; 9 inches; flowers bright-blue, in April; south of Europe; 1759. *H. Orientalis* (Oriental); hardy bulb; 1 foot; flowers blue, white, red, or yellowish; single or double, in April; Levant; 1596.

FLORISTS' VARIETIES. — The following are superior varieties: *Double Red* — Acteur, Prince of Wales, Sans Souci, Waterloo. *Double Blush* — Bouquet Royale, Comtesse de la Coste, Grootvoorst. *Double Blue* — Bonaparte, Bouquet Pourpre, Grand Sultan, Laurens Koster, Lord Wellington, Orondatus. *Double White* — Anna Maria, Don Gratuit, La Déesse, Nannette, Ne Plus Ultra, Prince of Waterloo. *Double yellow* — Bouquet Orange, La Grandeur, Louis d'Or, Ophir. *Single Red* — Aimable Rosette, Appelius, L'Ami du Cœur, Mars, Paix d'Amiens, Panorama, Temple d'Apollon. *Single Blue* — Bellerophon, Grande Vidette, L'Ami du Cœur, Nimrod, Orondatus, Othello, Prince Albert, Vulcan. *Single White* — Grand Vainqueur, Grande Vidette, La Candeur, Queen Victoria, Triomph Blandina, Virgo. *Single Yellow* — Héroine, La Belle Jaune, Ida, Duc de Malakoff, San Francisco.

HYDRANGEA. [Saxifrageæ.] Hardy or half-hardy deciduous shrubs, most of them showy plants. *H. hortensis*, the most popular of this family, has been long familiar as one of the commonest of market plants. Grown in the ordinary way it is very showy, but with pains it may be made a very noble object. There are two very different ways of growing it, — the one to form a shrubby plant; the other a single stem, and a large flower-head. The latter is the favorite mode of growing it for show, the aim being to produce as large a head as possible. For this purpose, take cuttings in July of the strongest shoots, and plant them in sandy soil under a hand-glass; when rooted, pot them in five-inch pots, in a compost of one-third loam, one-third dung, and one-third peat, well mixed together, and passed through a very coarse sieve. Such of them as branch out will make pretty little shrubby plants; whilst those whose growth is confined to a single stem, will, in all probability, form a large flower-head. When the general set of plants drop their leaves, and indicate by their terminal buds the strongest heads, some of the most promising cuttings may be taken off, and struck in slight bottom-heat, under a bell-glass, and grown in the stove at once. This will give a change of season, as well as a difference in growth; but all will be fine. The plants may be grown into good-sized bushes by shifting every season into large pots or tubs, which may be wintered in a cold house free from frost. When growing as an outdoor shrub, the Hydrangea must be protected in some way, either by matting, or covering with litter; otherwise the points of the shoots will be killed, and with them the incipient bloom-buds. It is, indeed, sometimes, in severe winters, killed down close to the ground; but it will spring up from the roots, and grow vigorously to make up for its lost wood. It should have a moist sheltered situation. The potted plants struck in July should be bloomed in the greenhouse; but any of them may be turned out into the borders in May. The Hydrangea, like many other plants, blooms finer when young than when it has grown three or four years; for though the plant is larger, and has more heads of flowers, the heads and the individual flowers also are smaller. The plant forces well, and is one of the prettiest forced flowers in spring. The *H. Japonica* is very distinct, and, though it does not bloom in such large heads as the other, its appearance is more picturesque, especially when grown as a bush. *H. hortensis* is not hardy in the Northern States.

H. Belzonii (Belzoni's); half-hardy shrub; 3 feet; flowers white and blue, in July; Japan; 1848. *H. hortensis* (garden); half-hardy shrub; 3 feet; flowers pink, in July; China; 1740. *H. Japonica* (Japan); half-hardy shrub; 3 feet; flowers white and blue, in July; Japan; 1843. *H. nivea* (snow-white-leaved); hardy shrub; 4 feet; flowers white, in August; Carolina; 1786.

HYDRASTIS. [Ranunculaceæ.] A hardy herbaceous perennial, not very showy. Increased by division of the root. Soil, moist peaty loam.

H. Canadensis (Canadian); hardy perennial; 6 inches; flowers greenish, in May; North America; 1759.

HYDROPELTIS. [Podophylleæ.] A very pretty hardy aquatic, useful for the edges of ponds. Propagated by divisions.

H. purpurea (purple); hardy aquatic perennial; flowers dull-purple, in July; North America; 1798.

Now called Brasenia peltata.

HYDROPHYLLUM. [Hydrophyllaceæ.] Hardy herbaceous perennials, of easy culture in moist peaty loam. Increased by division.

H. appendiculatum (appendaged); hardy perennial; 9 inches; flowers blue, in May; North America; 1812. *H. Canadense* (Canadian); hardy perennial; 9 inches; flowers white, in May; North America; 1759. *H. Virginicum* (Virginian); hardy perennial; 9 inches; flowers blue, in June; North America; 1739.

HYMENOXYS. [Compositæ.] A simple dwarf yellow-flowered annual. Common soil. Increased by seeds.

H. Californica (Californian); hardy annual; 6 inches; flowers yellow, in June; California; 1838.

HYOSCYAMUS. *Henbane.* [Solanaceæ.] Annuals and sub-shrubby plants, not very showy. Common light dry soil. Increased by seeds.

H. Camerarii (Camerarus's); hardy annual; 1 foot; flowers yellow and purple, in July; south of Europe. *H. Canariensis* (Canary); half-hardy evergreen sub-shrub; 2 feet; flowers yellow and brown, in September; Canaries; 1816. *H. niger* (black); hardy annual; 1 foot; flowers yellow, with purple veins, in July; Europe.

HYPECOUM. [Fumariaceæ.] Hardy annuals, increased by seeds sown in the open border in May.

H. erectum (erect); hardy annual; 6 inches; flowers yellow, in July; Siberia; 1759. *H. pendulum* (pendulous); hardy annual; 6 inches; flowers yellow, in July; France; 1640. *H. procumbens* (lying down); hardy annual; 1 foot; flowers yellow, in July; south of Europe; 1596.

HYPERICUM. *St. John's Wort.* [Hypericaceæ.] A large genus, containing many hardy species, both perennial herbs and shrubs, as well as some greenhouse species. The hardy perennials and shrubs all grow readily in common sandy soil, and are increased, the former by division, the latter by layers. Yellow is almost universally the color of the flowers in this genus.

H. Ascyron (St. Peter's Wort); hardy perennial; 2 feet; flowers yellow, in June; Siberia; 1774. *H. calycinum* (large-calyxed); half-hardy shrub; 1 foot; flowers large, yellow, in June; Ireland. *H. elatum* (tall); hardy sub-evergreen shrub; 5 feet; flowers yellow, in July; North America; 1762. *H. empetrifolium* (empetrum-leaved); half-hardy evergreen shrub; 2 feet; flowers yellow, in June; south of Europe; 1820. *H. Kalmianum* (Kalm's); hardy deciduous shrub; 2 feet; flowers yellow, in June; North America; 1759. *H. macrocarpum* (long-seeded); hardy perennial; 2 feet; flowers yellow, in August; North America; 1828. *H. pulchrum* (pretty); hardy perennial; 18 inches; flowers yellow, in July; England.

There are many other species.

HYSSOPUS. [Lamiaceæ.] Hardy perennials, flourishing in garden soil, and increased by division and seeds.

H. discolor (two-colored); hardy perennial; flowers blue, in June; Siberia; 1818. *H. officinalis* (officinal); hardy perennial; 2 feet; flowers blue, in June; south of Europe; 1548.

There are varieties *angustifolia, canescens, flore-rubro,* and *variegatus;* the two last being garden hybrids.

IBERIS. *Candytuft.* [Cruciferæ.] A genus containing some well-known hardy annuals, and a few greenhouse and hardy sub-shrubs. The annuals are showy and useful border plants, perfectly hardy, growing in any kind of soil, and need only to be sown where they are to flower. They will sometimes shed the seed in the borders; and the plants come up in autumn, and stand the winter if it be not too severe. Candytuft makes a good clump-plant for a geometrical garden, because it does not grow higher than six or nine inches, and forms a complete mass of flowers in its season, being literally covered with bloom. The natural blooming season may be prolonged by sowing some in pots as early as February, thinning them as they come up, and nursing them in the greenhouse or frames till May, when they will be almost in flower. The seed sown in the borders will be a month or six weeks later before it flowers; and a later sowing toward the end of May will carry on the succession. The sub-shrubby evergreen species thrive in light soil, and the hardy ones are very beautiful for rock-work, or, for early blooming small groups in the flower-garden. They are propagated freely by cuttings in sandy soil under hand-glasses, in a shady place, early in the summer.

I. corifolia (coris-leaved); hardy evergreen sub-shrub; 6 inches; flowers white, in May; south of Europe; 1739. *I. coronaria* (garland); hardy annual; 1 foot; flowers white, in June; gardens. *I. Gibraltarica* (Gibraltar); frame evergreen sub-shrub; 1 foot; flowers whitish-pink, in June; Gibraltar; 1732.

I. odorata (sweet-scented); hardy annual; 1 foot; flowers white, in June; Crete; 1806. *I. saxatilis* (rock); hardy evergreen sub-shrub; 6 inches; flowers white, in May; south of Europe; 1739. *I. sempervirens* (evergreen); hardy evergreen sub-shrub; 9 inches; flowers white, in April; Candia; 1731. *I. Tenoreana* (Tenore's); hardy perennial; 6 inches; flowers pale purple, in June; Naples; 1802. *I. umbellata* (common); hardy annual; 1 foot; flowers purple, rose, crimson, or white, in June; south of Europe; 1596.

There are several other species.

ILEX. *Holly.* [Aquifoliaceæ.] Beautiful evergreen trees, with prickly foliage and red berries. The English Holly in its many beautiful varieties is not hardy in the Northern States. The American Holly, although found native as far north as Maine, is often winter-killed in the New England States: to the southward, it forms a splendid tree. Soil, moist loam, sandy. Propagated by berries, which do not vegetate for two years.

I. opaca (dark); American Holly; hardy trees; 10 to 30 feet; flowers greenish, in June.

I. Cassine, myrtifolia, Dahoon, are Southern species. *I. verticillata* and *lævigata* (Black Alder), and *I. glabra* (Ink Berry), are fine ornamental shrubs, perfectly hardy, which are worthy of general cultivation. The latter is evergreen. These latter are often called Prinos.

ILLICIUM. *Anised-tree.* [Magnoliaceæ.] Half-hardy evergreen shrubs, with good foliage and curious flowers. Soil, peat and loamy. Increased by cuttings of young ripened shoots in sand, or by layers, which take two years to get well established.

I. anisatum (Star Anise); half-hardy evergreen shrub; 6 feet; flowers red, in May; Japan; 1790. *I. Floridanum* (Florida); half-hardy evergreen shrub; 8 feet; flowers red, in May; Florida; 1766. *I. religiosum* (holy); half-hardy evergreen shrub; 4 feet; flowers green, in May; Japan; 1842.

IMPATIENS. *Touch-me-not.* [Balsaminaceæ.] Annual or perennial fleshy-stemmed plants, mostly requiring the assistance of artificial heat, and a moist sheltered climate. The tender annuals should be raised in hot-frames, from seeds, in February or March, and grown on until summer, near the glass, in hot-frames or hot-houses, and may then be bloomed in a greenhouse after its usual occupants are placed out doors. Most of these may be raised from cuttings, or made biennial by removing all flower-buds the first year. Some of them, if reared in a mild heat, and carefully inured to exposure, will flower out doors in a moderately sheltered situation; but they require a moist atmosphere, and moisture at the roots, as well as a warm exposure. *I. glanduligera*, *macrochila*, and *candida* are the best for this treatment: these have a fine pyramidal habit, and bloom abundantly. The hardy annuals may be sown in the open border, in a dampish sheltered place; and there they will spring up abundantly from scattered seeds. See BALSAMINA for culture of the annual kinds.

I. candida (white); half-hardy (or tender) annual; 6 feet; flowers white, in July; Himalayas; 1839. *I. fulva* (tawny, spotted); hardy sub-aquatic annual; 4 feet; flowers yellow, in July; North America. *I. glanduligera* (gland-bearing); half-hardy (or tender) annual; 6 feet; flowers rose-color, in July; Himalayas; 1839. *I. macrochila* (large-lipped); half-hardy (or tender) annual; flowers pale-purple, in August; India; 1839.

INDIAN-CRESS. See TROPÆOLUM.
INDIAN-PINK. See DIANTHUS.
INDIAN-SHOT. See CANNA.
INK-BERRY. See ILEX.
INULA. [Compositæ.] A genus containing many hardy

perennials and annuals : the latter are not worth cultivating ; the former are of coarse habit, and of little horticultural importance. The flowers are yellow. Common soil. Increased by division.

IONOPSIDUM. *Violet Cress.* [Cruciferæ.] A pretty dwarf, half-hardy annual, forming a beautiful plant for rockwork in a shady situation, or an undergrowth for a peat border, or for pot-culture. It forms close to the soil a compact tuft, studded with numerous lilac, cross-shaped flowers.

I. acaule (stemless); half-hardy annual; 1½ inches; flowers lilac, at various seasons; Portugal; 1845.

IPOMŒA. [Convolvulaceæ.] A large genus of showy convolvulus-like plants, consisting mostly of climbing species, of which the greater number require a stove temperature. The sub-shrubby and perennial kinds are increased by cuttings of the short lateral shoots in sandy soil, under glasses. Those which have fleshy roots are more difficult to propagate, unless cuttings of the young shoots, which break from the crown of the tuber are taken : they require brisk bottom-heat. The tuberous, fleshy-rooted sorts may sometimes be increased by division, but not readily : portions of the roots, however, of the commoner sorts serve as stocks on which the rarer and more difficult may be grafted with success by what is called herbaceous grafting ; a good heat and a close frame being indispensable. The annuals are raised by seeds sown in a hot-bed in early spring. The soil for them should be turfy peat and sandy loam, with plenty of gritty sand added, and the roots well drained. The fleshy-rooted kinds require to be kept moderately dry in winter. Their habit is various. Some bloom in the axils along the branches ; and others, including *I. Horsfalliæ*, which is one of the best, bloom only at the end of the shoots. With these latter, it is a practice to top the shoots when five or six feet long, to cause several laterals to branch out; and the result is, that, though the blossoming is retarded, there are many more flowers produced in the end. Stopped in this way, and trained over the roof, or the wall of a stove, this is one of the finest of all creepers. Many of the tender species do well in a warm sunny exposure in the garden.

I. ficifolia (fig-leaved); twining perennial; 15 feet; flowers rosy-purple, in August; Buenos Ayres; 1840. *I. lacunosa* (starry); hardy twining perennial; 10 feet; flowers white, in June; North America; 1640. *I. Michauxii* (Michaux's); greenhouse twining tuberous perennial; 15 feet; flowers white, in August; Georgia; 1815. *I. pandurata* (Virginian); hardy twining perennial; 12 feet; flowers white and purple; North America; 1732. *I. rubra-cærulea* (reddish-blue); half-hardy twining annual; 10 feet; flowers blue, fading red, in September; Mexico; 1833. *I. Tweedici* (Tweedie's); stove twining perennial; 10 feet; flowers reddish-purple, in July; Parana; 1838.

There are numerous other species in cultivation.

IPOMOPSIS. [Polemoniaceæ.] Splendid-flowered biennials, of rather difficult culture. The seeds should be sown in July, thinly, in small pots set into a cold dry frame; the plants are to be thinned to three or four, and removed to a shelf in the greenhouse, near the glass, where they remain during winter, being very moderately and carefully watered. In spring, they are shifted into five-inch pots with as little disturbance to their roots as possible; but one or two of the plants should be cut away, leaving the strongest. They require throughout very careful watering, being very impatient of moisture. A compost of equal proportions of sandy peat and sandy loam, mixed with lumps of charcoal to keep it open and porous, suits them; and they are multiplied by seeds only.

I. elegans (elegant); half-hardy biennial; 3 feet; flowers scarlet, in July; North America; 1826. *I. picta* (painted); half-hardy biennial; 3 feet; flowers scarlet, blotched white, in July; Carolina; 1726.

IRESINE. [Amarantaceæ.] A very fine dark-foliaged plant, more hardy than Coleus and brighter than Perilla, very useful for summer bedding, and easily propagated by cuttings. As a decorative plant it has no rival. Achyranthes of French florists.

I. Herbstii (Herbst's); soft-wooded shrub; 1 foot; not yet flowered in cultivation; Peru and La Plata; 1863.

IRIS. *Flower de Luce.* [Iridaceæ.] Beautiful hardy perennials, of very simple culture. They prefer a loamy soil somewhat moist, and thrive best when not too frequently disturbed, as they then spread into good-sized patches, and produce a greater abundance of flowers. They are propagated without the least difficulty by dividing the plants. There are one or two bulbous-rooted species, *I. Xiphium* and *Xiphioides*, the latter commonly called English, and the former Spanish Iris, the varieties of which are extensively cultivated as florists' flowers. The varieties of color among these bulbous kinds is very great, including white, yellow, blue, purple, and many indescribable tints. These should be planted a foot apart, in a rich bed of loam, dung, and sand, and should be removed only once in two years; the transplanting taking place in September. They are increased by offsets.

I. amœna (pleasing); hardy perennial; 1 foot; flowers white and purple, in June; Europe; 1821. *I. cristata* (crested); hardy perennial; 3 inches; flowers pale-blue, in May; North America; 1756. *I. Florentina* (Florentine); hardy perennial; 2 feet; flowers white, in May; south of Europe; 1596. *I. Germanica* (German); hardy perennial; 2 feet; flowers dark-blue, in May; Germany; 1573. *I. lutescens* (yellowish); hardy perennial; 6 inches; flowers yellow, in May; Germany; 1748. *I. notha* (hybrid); hardy perennial; 18 inches; flowers blue, in June; Italy; 1820. *I. ochroleuca* (yellowish); hardy perennial; 2 feet; flowers pale-yellow, in July; Levant; 1757. *I. pallida* (pale); hardy perennial; 3 feet; flowers pale-blue, in June; Turkey; 1596. *I. Persica* (Persian); hardy bulb; 6 inches; flowers pale-blue, orange and black, in May; Persia; 1629. *I. pumila* (dwarf); hardy perennial; 3 inches; flowers purple, yellow, or white, in May; Austria; 1596. *I. Ruthenica* (Russian); hardy perennial; 1 foot; flowers blue, in May; Siberia; 1804. *I. sambucina* (elder-scented); hardy perennial; 2½ feet; flowers purple and white, in June; south of Europe; 1658. *I. Sibirica* (Siberian); hardy perennial; 3 feet; flowers blue or white, in June; Siberia; 1596. *I. sub-biflora* (sub-two-flowered); hardy perennial; 1 foot; flowers blue, in May; Portugal; 1596. *I. Susiana* (Susian); hardy perennial; 2 feet; flowers striped, in May; Levant; 1596. *I. Swertii* (Swert's); hardy perennial; 18 inches; flowers white, in May; Hungary; 1819. *I. Xiphioides* (great bulbous); hardy bulb; 18 inches; flowers various, in June; Spain; 1571. *I. Xiphium* (small bulbous); hardy bulb; 18 inches; flowers various, in June; Spain; 1596.

Many other species are in cultivation, and many very fine named varieties may be obtained of florists. The last few years have witnessed a great improvement in this plant. *I. Persica* is one of the most beautiful early-flowering spring bulbs. The flowers are of a most delicate texture, bright purple and yellow, with pearl-colored ground. They only require to be planted in a rich soil in the autumn, and may remain for years undisturbed.

ISANTHUS. [Lamiaceæ.] Hardy annual. Propagated by seeds sown in the border in May, or earlier in a frame, and transplanted.

I. cæruleus (blue); hardy annual; 1 foot; flowers blue, in July; North America; 1818.

ISOTOMA. [Lobeliaceæ.] A pretty dwarf blue flowering plant, resembling a Lobelia, requiring greenhouse protection in winter, but blossoming freely as a bedding-plant in summer. Soil, sandy loam, in a warm exposure. The plants should be raised from seed in summer, and wintered in the greenhouse ready to plant out the following May.

I. axillaris; 1 foot; flowers blue, in July; New South Wales; 1824.

ITEA. [Escalloniaceæ.] A pretty white-flowering native shrub, not hardy in the Northern States. Soil, moist sandy peat. Propagated by suckers and layers.

I. Virginica (Virginian); hardy shrub; 6 feet; flowers white, in July.

IVY. See HEDERA.

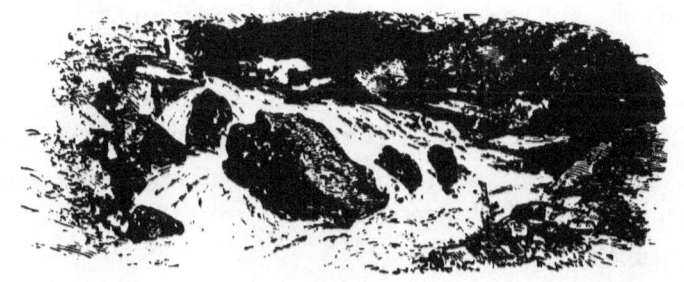

JACOBEA. See SENICIO.
  JACOBEAN LILY. See SPREKELIA.
  JACOB'S LADDER. See POLEMONIUM.
  JAPAN ALLSPICE. See CHIMONANTHUS.
  JAPAN CEDAR. See CRYPTOMEREA.
  JAPAN YEW. See CEPHALOTAXUS.
  JASIONE. *Sheep's-scabious.* [Campanulaceæ.] Pretty dwarf herbs, bearing blue flowers collected in heads. The annuals may be sown in the borders in May, and require no other care than thinning if the plants come up too thick. The perennials are increased by seeds, or by division, and require but to be planted in a warm border, in sandy soil, and winter protection in the Northern States.

J. montana (mountain); hardy annual; 1 foot; flowers pale-blue, in June; England. *J. perennis* (perennial); half-hardy perennial; 1 foot; flowers blue, in June; France; 1787.

JEFFERSONIA. [Podophyllaceæ.] A neat hardy herbaceous perennial. Soil, sandy loam. Increased by division of the plant, which should be done in spring, or by seeds.

J. diphylla (two-leaved); hardy perennial; 6 inches; flowers white, in May; North America; 1792.

JOB'S TEARS. See COIX.
  JONQUIL. See NARCISSUS.
  JUDAS-TREE. See CIRCIS.
  JUGLANS. [Juglandaceæ.] Hardy or half-hardy deciduous ornamental trees. Soil, deep loam. Propagated by seed; the rarer sorts by grafting and budding.

J. cinerea (gray; Butternut); 30 feet; North America; 1656.
J. fraxinifolia (ash-leaved); 40 feet; North America. *J. nigra* (black); 30 feet; North America; 1629. *J. pterocarpa* (winged-fruited); 40 feet; North America. *J. regia* (common; royal); 50 feet; Persia; 1562. *J. regia laciniata* (cut-leaved); 50 feet; Persia. *J. regia maxima* (largest-fruited); 50 feet; Persia. *J. regia pendula* (weeping). *J. regia serotina* (late-vegetating); 50 feet; Persia. *J. regia tenera* (thin-shelled); 50 feet; Persia.

JUNIPERUS. *Juniper.* [Pinaceæ.] Evergreens, many of which are remarkably ornamental in habit, forming light, spreading, more or less pendulous, bushes or low trees. The Junipers prefer a light, loamy soil, but are not difficult of culture in any that is moderately good, and not wet or heavy. Increased with most facility by seeds; but the rarer kinds may be propagated by grafting, or by cuttings of the firm young shoots, planted in sandy soil, on a shady border, and covered by a hand-glass. Most of the species are hardy as far north as Massachusetts, though often requiring protection from the winter's sun and cutting winds.

J. Chinensis (Chinese); 10 feet; flowers in May; China; 1804. *J. communis* (common); 5 feet; flowers in May; Britain. *J. communis Canadensis* (Canadian); 20 feet; flowers in May; Canada; 1820. *J. communis nana* (dwarf); 2 feet; flowers in May; Siberia. *J. communis oblonga* (oblong-fruited); flowers in June. *J. communis oblonga pendula* (oblong-weeping); 5 feet; flowers in May; Britain. *J. Suecica* (Swedish); 12 feet; flowers in May; North of Europe. *J. Cracovia* (Cracovian); 4 feet; flowers in May; Poland; 1820. *J. Daurica* (Dahurian); 8 feet; flowers in July; Dahuria; 1791. *J. drupacea* (drupe-fruited); 4 feet; flowers in May; Syria; 1820. *J. excelsa* (tall); 20 feet; Siberia; 1806. *J. glauca* (milky-green); flowers in May; China; 1814. *J. hemisphærica* (half-globe-headed); flowers in May; Mount Etna; 1844. *J. Hermanni* (Hermann's); flowers in May. *J. Lycia* (Lycian); 10 feet; flowers in May; south of Europe; 1759. *J. macrocarpa* (large-fruited); flowers in May; Greece. *J. oblonga* (oblong); flowers in May; America; 1829. *J. oxycedrus* (sharp-cedar); 15 feet; flowers in May; Spain; 1739. *J. Phœnicea* (Phœnician); 20 feet; flowers in May; south of Europe; 1683. *J. recurva* (curved); 4 feet; flowers in May; Nepaul; 1817. *J. religiosa* (religious); flowers in May. *J. sabina* (common savin); 4 feet; flowers in May; south of Europe; 1548. *J. sabina Alpina* (Alpine); 18 inches; flowers in May; Britain. *J. sabina cupressifolia* (cypress-leaved); 4 feet; flowers in May; south of Europe; 1548. *J. sabina foliis variegatis* (variegated-leaved); 4 feet; flowers in May; Europe. *J. prostrata* (prostrate); 9 inches; flowers in May; North America. *J. tamariscifolia* (tamarisk-leaved); 4 feet; flowers in May; south of Europe; 1562. *J. tamariscifolia variegata* (variegated); 5 feet; flowers in May; south of Europe. *J. Smithii* (Smith's); flowers in May; Nepaul. *J. squamata* (scaly); 4 feet; flowers in May; Nepaul; 1824. *J. thurifera* (incense-bearing); 10 feet; flowers in May; Spain; 1572. *J. uvifera* (grape-bearing); Cape Horn. *J. Virginiana* (Virginian); Red Cedar; 30 feet; flowers in May; North America; 1664. *J. Virginiana Caroliniana* (Carolinian); flowers in May; Carolina. *J. Virginiana humilis* (humble); 12 feet; flowers in May; North America; 1800.

JURINEA. [Compositæ.] Hardy herbaceous perennials. Common soil. Increased by division of the root.

J. spectabilis (showy); hardy perennial; 2 feet; flowers purple, in June; Europe; 1837. *J. subacaulis* (short-stemmed); hardy perennial; 1 foot; flowers purple, in June; Caucasus; 1837.

KALMIA. [Ericaceæ.] Beautiful evergreen shrubs, readily forced into early blossom by the stimulus of artificial heat. The proper soil for them is sandy peat earth. It is, in fact, the usual and the best practice to plant Kalmias, together with Rhododendrons, Azaleas, and other plants of like nature, in separate beds or patches, prepared with peat-soil. They are usually increased by layers made at the end of summer, but may also be raised from seeds, in which case the seeds require to be sown in shallow pans of sandy peat, and kept close in a frame: the seedlings are transplanted to other pans as soon as large enough to be handled, and again kept close for a time until established, when they are gradually inured to exposure.

K. angustifolia (narrow-leaved); hardy evergreen shrub; 2 feet; flowers red, in June; North America; 1736. *K. glauca* (glaucous); hardy evergreen shrub; 3 feet; flowers red, in May; North America; 1767. *K. hirsuta* (hairy); hardy evergreen shrub; 18 inches; flowers red, in August; North America; 1786. *K. latifolia* (broad-leaved); hardy evergreen shrub; 6 feet; flowers pink, in June; North America; 1734.

There are many garden varieties of *angustifolia*. *K. rosmarinifolia* is a variety of *K. glauca*, and *K. myrtifolia* of *K. latifolia*.

KAULFUSSIA. [Compositæ.] A pretty dwarf hardy annual. Sow the seeds in May on finely pulverized soil, or in a frame in April, and transplant. If late-flowering plants are required, the seed may be sown during the summer.

K. amelloides (amellus-like); hardy annual; 1 foot; flowers blue, in July; Cape of Good Hope; 1819. *K. æsculifolia* (horse-chestnut-leaved); hardy annual; 1 foot; flowers brown and yellow, in July.

KENTROPHYLLUM. [Compositæ.] Hardy annuals of little importance. Common soil. Increased by seeds, or, in the case of a half-hardy evergreen shrubby species, by cuttings. The species are *K. arborescens* (half-hardy, shrubby), *Cretica, lanata,* and *Taurica.*

KENTUCKY COFFEE-TREE. See GYMNOCLADUS.

KERRIA. [Rosaceæ.] A hardy deciduous shrub, with green stems and yellow flowers, often seen against walls and fences in old gardens. It is a free-growing plant, adapted for such situations; growing best in light soils. Readily increased by suckers, or by cuttings, under a hand-light. The double-flowered variety is the most ornamental. There is a fine variety with beautifully white variegated foliage.

K. Japonica (Japan); hardy shrub; 3 feet; flowers yellow, in May; Japan; 1700.

KIDNEY-BEAN. See PHASEOLUS.

KŒLREUTERIA. [Sapindaceæ.] A small hardy deciduous tree, with elegant pinnate foliage, and upright panicles of yellow blossoms. It is suitable for a pleasure-ground or shrubbery. Will grow in ordinary garden soil, and is increased by seeds, or by cuttings of the roots or branches.

K. paniculata (panicled); hardy tree; 12 feet; flowers yellow, in August; China; 1763.

KONIGA. [Cruciferæ.] A simple, but useful dwarf hardy annual. Sow the seeds in spring in the borders where the plants are to bloom. The flowers have a rather peculiar, strong, but not disagreeable scent, resembling that of honey.

K. maritima (sea-side, or Sweet Alyssum); hardy annual; 1 foot; flowers white, in May; England.

LABRADOR-TEA. See LEDUM.
LABURNUM. See CYTISUS.
LADY'S MANTLE. See ALCHIMILLA.
LADY'S SLIPPER. See CYPRIPEDIUM.
LADY'S SMOCK. See CARDAMINE.
LAGENARIA. *Bottle Gourd.* [Cucurbitaceæ.] Annual trailing plants, requiring to be raised in heat in spring, and hardened off previously to their being planted out about the end of May in sheltered places, such as against walls and palings, or on a raised beds in a warm corner of the garden. Rich light soil. Increased by seeds. The curious bottle-shaped fruits are the objects for which they are cultivated; but the white flowers are also very pretty.

L. idolatrica (idol-like, pear-fruited); flowers white, in June. *L. vittata* (banded); flowers white, in June. *L. vulgaris* (common); 10 feet; flowers in August; 1597. *L. vulgaris clavata* (club-shaped); 10 feet; flowers in August; 1597. *L. vulgaris depressa* (depressed); 10 feet; flowers in August; 1597. *L. vulgaris courgourda* (courgourde); 10 feet; flowers in August; 1597. *L. vulgaris turbinata* (top-shaped); 10 feet; flowers in August; 1597.

LAGERSTRŒMIA. [Lythraceæ.] A genus of handsome shrubs, containing some greenhouse species. Soil, peat and loam. Propagated by cuttings of the small half-ripened lateral shoots in sand, under bell-glasses in heat. These plants bloom finely, planted out in the flower border in summer, and wintered in a cool frost-proof cellar.

L. Indica (Indian); warm greenhouse evergreen shrub; 12 feet; flowers white or rose-colored, in August; China; 1816.
L. speciosa (showy); warm greenhouse evergreen shrub; 6 feet; flowers rose-colored, in August; China; 1826.

LAGURUS. [Gramineæ.] A hardy annual ornamental grass, growing in any garden soil.

L. ovatus (ovate); hardy annual; 1 foot; apetalous, August; Guernsey.

LAMIUM. [Labiaceæ.] Hardy plants, of which some of the dwarf perennial varieties, and *L. maculatum*, with variegated foliage and white or red blossoms, are pretty subjects for rock-work. Common soil. Increased by division.

LANTANA. [Verbenaceæ.] Stove shrubs, many of the more showy of which, however, may be considered as greenhouse plants, if they can be started in spring, in a frame or warmer house. The larger species should be kept rather dry in winter, when they will be induced to rest, and will lose their foliage; but, if they are excited at that season, they continue growing, and remain evergreen. In spring, or in February, they are to be pruned close back, and started to grow in a stove or warm pit. They are free growers, and require to be shifted into larger pots as their roots become numerous. They should have a free rich loamy soil, consisting of loam, peat, and leaf-mould, equal parts, with sand added if necessary. The young shoots in spring should be freely stopped, to produce bushy growth. *L. Sellowiana* should have three parts sandy peat-earth in the compost, and, though rested by comparative dryness and coolness in winter, ought not to be dried so much as the larger sorts. They do not require the temperature of the stove: that of an intermediate house suits them best. In warm and dry sitations, where the soil is rather sandy, *L. Sellowiana* forms good beds in the flower-garden, looking like a purple verbena; and most of the larger species succeed under the same treatment. Cuttings root very readily in sand, planted in the usual way, and set in a hot-bed. Young plants should be raised from cuttings during summer, to be shifted on for flowering the following spring. The following are selected from the numerous kinds as being the most useful.

L. aculeata (prickly); stove shrub; 3 feet; flowers yellow, changing to deep orange-red, in May; West Indies; 1692. *L. Camara* (Camara); stove shrub; 5 feet; flowers golden, changing to deep-orange or vermilion; South America; 1691. *L. crocea* (saffron); stove shrub; 3 feet; flowers yellow, changing to saffron, in May; West Indies; 1691. *L. mutabilis* (changeable); stove shrub; 3 feet; flowers lilac, changing to rose, in May; East Indies. *L. nivea* (white); stove shrub; 3 feet; flowers white, in May; East Indies; 1732. *L. purpurea* (purple); stove shrub; 2 feet; flowers pale-rose, changing to rosy lilac; South America; 1820. *L. Sellowiana* (Sellow's); cool stove shrub; 2 feet; flowers purple, all summer; Monte Video; 1828.

LARIX. *Larch.* [Pinaceæ.] A family of hardy well-known trees, flourishing in any soil. Propagated by seeds.

L. Gmelini (Gmelin's); Northern Siberia. *L. Griffithi* (Griffith's); 50 feet; Nepaul; 1854. *L. Kamtschatika* (Kamtschatka). *L. larix* (larch); 100 feet; Alps. *L. larix repens* (creeping). *L. larix pendula* (drooping). *L. Ledebourii* (Ledebour's). *L. leptolepis* (slender-scaled); north of Japan. *L. microcarpa* (small-coned); 100 feet; North America. *L. pendula* (drooping); North America. *L. Sibirica* (Siberian); Siberia.

LARKSPUR. See DELPHINEUM.

LASTHENIA. [Compositæ.] Hardy annuals; thriving in poor soil, and increased by seed.

L. Californica (Californian); hardy annual; 1 foot; flowers yellow, in July; California; 1834. *L. glabrata* (smooth); hardy annual; 1 foot; flowers yellow, in July; California; 1834. *L.*

obtusifolia (blunt-leaved); hardy annual; 1 foot; flowers yellow, in July; Chili; 1833.

LATHYRUS. [Leguminosæ.] A genus of showy hardy plants, annual and perennial, mostly climbers. The best of them is the Sweet-pea *(L. odoratus);* and there is not among the annuals a better nosegay flower than this, nor, now that there are many varieties, is there a more lively garden ornament. It has been attempted to grow the different colored varieties separate, and a majority will sometimes prove like the parent, but they do not look so well any way as mixed. They may be sown in pots, in a warmish frame, in March, for early bloom ; and two months afterwards they may be sown in the borders of the open ground : others may be sown in May and June if a succession is desired. They grow in any good light soil, and all the attention they require is to be furnished with a few bushy branches stuck in the ground for them to cling to. If they are not allowed to seed, and the decayed blooms are removed as fast as they decline, the bloom will continue some time ; but, if they are allowed to swell their pods, the bloom goes off much sooner. The perennials may be raised by seeds or by division, and merely require to be planted in the position they are to occupy permanently, and to have pea-stakes put to them annually for their branches to climb over.

L. Altaicus (Altaic); hardy perennial; 2 feet; flowers violet, in June; Altai; 1832. *L. Armitageanus* (Armitage's) ; hardy climbing perennial ; 8 feet; flowers purple-blue, in May ; Brazil; 1824. *L. decaphyllus* (ten-leaved); hardy climbing perennial ; 4 feet; flowers red and lilac, in June ; North America ; 1827. *L. grandiflorus* (large-flowered); hardy climbing perennial ; 4 feet ; flowers pale and deep rose, in July ; south of Europe ; 1814. *L. latifolius* (broad-leaved); hardy perennial ; 5 feet ; flowers pink, in August ; England. *L. Macræi* (McRae's); hardy climbing perennial ; 3 feet ; flowers purple and white, in

October; Chili; 1824. *L. Magellanicus* (Magellan); hardy climbing perennial; 6 feet; flowers blue, in July; Cape Horn; 1744. *L. odoratus* (sweet-pea); hardy annual; 4 feet; flowers various, in July; Sicily; 1700. *L. Tingitanus* (Tangier); hardy annual; 4 feet; flowers dark rose-purple, in July; Barbary; 1680.

LAVANDULA. *Lavender.* [Labiaceæ.] Evergreen shrubs, well known from the fragrance of their flowers. Some of the species require greenhouse protection. Sandy loam for the hardy kinds, and light loamy soil for the tender ones. Increased by cuttings.

L. dentata (tooth-leaved); greenhouse evergreen shrub; 18 inches; flowers lilac, in August; south of Europe; 1597. *L. spica* (common spike); hardy evergreen shrub; 2 feet; flowers lilac, in July; south of Europe; 1568. *L. Stæchas* (Stæchas); hardy evergreen shrub; 18 inches; flowers lilac, in June; south of Europe; 1568. *L. vera* (true); hardy evergreen shrub; 2 feet; flowers gray-blue, in July; south of Europe; 1568. *L. viridis* (green); greenhouse evergreen shrub; 18 inches; flowers purple, in June; Madeira; 1777.

LAVATERA. [Malvaceæ.] Hardy and half-hardy plants of the Mallow tribe. The annuals should be sown in the borders in March, and are increased by seeds. The others are increased by seeds, and require to be planted in a sheltered situation, in which they are sometimes destroyed, sometimes uninjured by the winter. The shrubby kinds may also be propagated by cuttings. A light dry soil suits all of them. There are several species, but, excepting those named below, they are not of much interest, being coarse.

L. arborea (tree); hardy biennial; 6 feet; flowers pale rose-purple, in August; Britain. *L. Neapolitana* (Neapolitan); hardy perennial; 6 feet; flowers purple, in July; Italy; 1818. *L. phœnicea* (red); half-hardy shrub; 5 feet; flowers pink, in July; Canaries; 1816. *L. Thuringiaca* (Thuringian); hardy perennial; 4 feet; flowers pale-blue, in July; Germany; 1731. *L. trimestris* (three-month); hardy annual; 2 feet; flowers flesh-color, in June; Spain; 1633.

LAVENDER. See LAVANDULA.
LAUREL MOUNTAIN. See KALMIA.
LEADWORT. See PLUMBAGO.
LEATHERWOOD. See DIRCA.
LEDUM. See AMMYRSINE.
LEDUM. *Labrador Tea.* [Ericaceæ.] Pretty hardy evergreen American plants. Soil, a rather sandy peat. Increased by layers. They are well suited for the margins of peat-beds.

L. Canadense (Canadian); hardy evergreen shrub; 18 inches; flowers white, in April; Canada; 1763. *L. latifolium* (broad-leaved); hardy evergreen shrub; 3 feet; flowers white, in April; North America; 1763. *L. palustre* (marsh); hardy evergreen shrub; 2 feet; flowers white, in April; Europe; 1762.

LEMON VERBENA. See ALOYSIA.
LEONOTIS. *Lion's-Ear.* [Labiacea.] A genus containing some annual species, and some soft-wooded greenhouse shrubs. *L. leonurus*, one of the latter, and the most common is, when grown vigorously, very ornamental; rich orange-colored flowers being produced in profusion in the axils of the leaves. Cuttings may be planted early in spring, and root readily in bottom-heat. When rooted, they should be potted into a light, rich, loamy, soil, hardened off as soon as possible to the greenhouse temperature; continually stopped to induce bushiness of growth, and shifted, as fast as the pots fill with roots, to give strength to the plants. By the beginning of May, they may be transferred to cold frames; and during the summer they are quite as well grown exposed in the open air, so that care be taken that they do not become parched, which destroys their foliage. After the be-

ginning of August, the shoots should not be topped, but allowed to grow tall for blooming; or, if stronger spikes of bloom are required, the stopping may be discontinued earlier. The object of stopping is, however, to produce a very bushy plant, that may yield a large number of flowering shoots. There is no difficulty in cultivating the plant, which, when established, should be grown in rich loam. With this, and other similar free-growing plants, it is better to raise young ones annually than to attempt to prune back or otherwise renovate the old specimens, which are chiefly to be preserved to furnish cuttings in the spring.

L. leonurus (lion's-tail); greenhouse sub-shrub; 2 feet; flowers deep-orange, in October; Cape; 1812.

LEONURUS. *Motherwort.* [Labiaceæ.] Hardy perennials and biennials. Common soil. Increased by seeds.

L. cardiaca (common); hardy perennial; 3 feet; flowers red, in July; England. There are varieties *crispus* and *villosus*. *L. lanatus* (woolly); hardy perennial; 2 feet; flowers yellow, in June; Siberia; 1752. *L. Sibericus* (Siberian); hardy biennial; 2 feet; flowers red, in June; Siberia; 1759.

LEOPARD'S BANE. See DORONICUM.

LEPECHINIA. [Lamiaceæ.] Hardy herbaceous perennial, comprising one Siberian and one Mexican species, of which the latter is not hardy. Common soil. Increased by division.

L. chenopodifolia (chenopodium-leaved); hardy perennial; 6 inches; flowers red, in July; Siberia; 1818. *L. spicata*, the Mexican species, has pale-yellow flowers.

LEPTANTHUS. [Pontedereæ.] A hardy aquatic plant, with grassy leaves, useful in a small pond. Called also Schollera.

L. gramineus (grassy); hardy perennial; 1 foot; flowers yellow, in July; North America; 1823.

LEPTANDRA. See VERONICA.

LEPTOSIPHON. [Polemoniaceæ.] Beautiful dwarf annuals, forming very pretty objects in clumps and beds, but not very long lived; and, moreover, the blooms look untidy as soon as they begin to decline. The seeds may be sown in the open air in May, and should be sown thinly, because they then grow much more vigorously. They will grow in poor soil, and do as well as any of the annuals in the common borders; but, to have them in perfection, they should be grown in a very light rich soil, such as one-half very rotten cow-dung mixed with good garden earth. In the beds of geometrical gardens, where they have to show a mass of flowers, they should be thinned very evenly to about two inches apart all over the space, because in beds which form parts of a connected figure, there must not be vacancies, nor must the plants be too much drawn by being close together. In patches, the least quantity is about what could be sown in a pot. Many adopt the very good plan of sowing annuals in pots, and bedding them out afterwards for the sake of having the patches uniform.

L. androsaceus (androsace-like); hardy annual; 1 foot; flowers bluish-lilac, or white, in June; California; 1833. *L. densiflorus* (cluster-flowered); hardy annual; 1 foot; flowers rosy-lilac, or white, in June; California; 1833. *L. grandiflorus* (large-flowered); hardy annual; 1 foot; flowers blue and gold, in July; California; 1833. *L. luteus* (yellow); hardy annual; 1 foot; flowers deep-yellow, in July; California; 1833. *L. pallidus* (pale-yellow); hardy annual; 1 foot; flowers pale-yellow, in July; California; 1833. *L. parviflorus* (small-flowered); hardy annual; 1 foot; flowers yellow, in July; California; 1833.

LEUCOJUM. *Snow-flake.* [Amaryllidaceæ.] Pretty hardy bulbs, in foliage much like a Narcissus, in the flowers like a Snow-drop, as the name Snow-flake suggests. They multiply by offsets in spring, and prefer sandy loam, though they may be planted in ordinary garden soil, like common Narcissus and Hyacinths.

L. æstivum (summer); hardy bulb; 18 inches; flowers white, in May; Europe. *L. pulchellum* (pretty); hardy bulb; 18 inches; flowers white, in April; England.

LEUCOTHOE. [Ericaceæ.] Hardy evergreen shrubs, forming part of the old genus Andromeda, which see.

LEUZEA. [Compositæ.] Hardy herbaceous purple-flowered perennials, allied to Serratula. Common soil. Increased by division or by seeds.

LEWISIA. [Crassulaceæ.] Hardy perennial. Sandy loam. Propagated by seeds and division.

L. rediviva (revived); hardy perennial; 6 inches; flowers white, in July; North America; 1827.

LEYCESTERIA. [Caprifoliaceæ.] Half-hardy sub-evergreen shrub. Sandy loam. Increased by cuttings of the young shoots in spring under a hand-glass, or by seeds. Tender in the Northern States. The bark being bright green, forms a good winter contrast to Cornus sanguineus.

L. formosa (handsome), half-hardy shrub; 4 feet; flowers white, with purple bracts, in August; Nepaul; 1824.

LIATRIS. [Compositæ.] Elegant hardy or half-hardy herbaceous perennials, of easy culture. Soil, sandy loam and peat. Increased by division. The half-hardy kinds require slight protection against wet in winter.

L. bellidifolia (daisy-leaved); hardy perennial; 2 feet; flowers pink, in August; North America. *L. corymbosa* (corymbose); half-hardy perennial; 3 feet; flowers purple, in August; Carolina; 1825. *L. elegans* (elegant); hardy perennial; 4 feet; flowers purple, in September; North America; 1787. *L. gracilis* (slender); half-hardy perennial; 18 inches; flowers purple, in August; Carolina; 1818. *L. intermedia* (intermediate); hardy perennial; 2 feet; flowers purple, in August; North America; 1823. *L. paniculata* (panicled); half-hardy perennial; 3 feet; flowers purple, in August; Carolina; 1826. *L. spicata* (spiked); hardy perennial; 5 feet; flowers purple, in August; North America; 1732. *L. squarrosa* (rough-cupped); hardy perennial; 3 feet; flowers purple, in July; North America; 1732. *L. tenuifolia* (fine-leaved); half-hardy perennial; 18 inches; flowers purple in August; Carolina; 1820. *L. turbinata* (turbinate); hardy perennial; 2 feet; flowers purple, in August; North America; 1823.

There are several other species.

LIBOCEDRUS. See THUYA.

LIGULARIA. [Compositæ.] Hardy herbaceous perennials, allied to Cineraria. Common soil. Increased by division.

L. Caucasia (Caucasian); hardy perennial; 18 inches; flowers yellow, in June; Caucasus; 1816. *L. Sibirica* (Siberian); hardy perennial; 4 feet; flowers yellow, in June; Siberia; 1784. *L. speciosa* (showy); hardy perennial; 6 feet; flowers yellow, in June; Siberia; 1815. *L. thyrsoidea* (thyrsoid); hardy perennial; 4 feet; flowers yellow, in July; Russia; 1832.

LIGUSTRUM. *Privet.* [Oleaceæ.] Hardy evergreen or sub-evergreen shrubs. The common sort, *L. vulgare*, is a valuable hedge-plant; the rarer sorts require a sheltered situation, and are very handsome plants for conservatory walls. Privet-hedges should be kept cut back very closely while young, and require to be clipped at least twice a year. Soil, sandy or chalky loam. Increased abundantly by seeds or cuttings; the rarer sorts, by grafting on the common.

L. Japonicum (Japan); hardy sub-evergreen shrub; 6 feet; flowers white, in July; Japan; 1845. *L. lucidum* (shining); hardy evergreen shrub; 12 feet; flowers white, in August; China; 1794. *L. spicatum* (spiked); hardy evergreen shrub; 8 feet; flowers white, in July; Nepaul; 1823. *L. vulgare* (common); hardy sub-evergreen shrub; 8 feet; flowers white, in June; Britain.

The variety *sempervirens* is the best.

LILAC. See SYRINGA.

LILIUM. *Lily.* [Liliaceæ.] Beautiful hardy or half-hardy bulbous-rooted perennials, containing many distinct species, nearly, perhaps quite, all of which are sufficiently hardy to admit of their being cultivated in the open garden. The most beautiful of all is the *Lilium speciosum,* and its superb varieties, *punctatum, roseum, rubrum,* and *album,* some of which are variegated as if rubies were strewn all over their petals. To cultivate these in pots, a compost of one-half turfy peat, one-third turfy loam, and one-third decayed cow-dung, with sand, one-sixth of the whole, added, is suitable. Pot them in February; use large pots; and choose very strong double-crowned bulbs, two or three of which may go in a pot a foot in diameter: drain them well, and plant the bulbs three or four inches below the rims; place them in a cold frame, and cover them from frost and heavy rains, but otherwise give all the air possible. When the stems are five or six inches long, fill up the pots with the compost, which will cause them to root up the covered part of their stems. As they rise too high for the frame, remove them to the greenhouse, where they will flower in great perfection, and retain their beauty a long time if shaded from the heat of the sun. Plants are easily raised from seeds sown an inch apart in pans, and placed in heat; when up, let them be removed to the greenhouse, and be undisturbed two seasons: they may then be placed in three-inch pots, and removed to larger, as they grow, until they flower. They are more generally multiplied by offsets, which form round the old roots, and such plants sooner reach a flowering size. These Japan lilies are, however, sufficiently hardy to be grown in prepared beds in the open air if the beds are covered with some light compost in winter; and, grown thus, they form fine autumn-blooming subjects. The hardy European and North-Asian kinds grow generally well in a rich sandy loam ; but the American, like the Japanese kinds, prefer a compost containing a considerable proportion of peat. They are all increased from offsets, which are generally produced abundantly, or by separating the scales of the bulbs, and planting them as offsets. Some propagate from little bulb-buds which are formed in the axils of their leaves ; and most of them may be multiplied from seeds, when it is worth while to raise them by this more tedious process. The seeds should be sown as soon as ripe. The bulbs of lilies should not be suffered to dry when they are taken out of the ground for transplanting. One of the most striking modern additions to this family is the Indian *L. giganteum*, a stately plant eight to ten feet high, with large heart-shaped leaves. It may be grown as directed for *L. speciosum*, requiring that each bulb, if of flowering size, should have a separate pot of from twelve to eighteen inches diameter.

L. atrosanguineum (dark-red) ; hardy bulb ; 2 feet ; flowers dark-red, in July ; Japan ; 1835. *L. aurantium* (orange) ; hardy bulb ; 3 feet ; flowers dark-orange, in July ; Italy ; 1596. This species readily produces varieties from seed. *L. Canadense* (Canadian) ; hardy bulb ; 4 feet ; flowers light-orange, in July ; North America ; 1629. *L. candidum* (white) ; hardy bulb ; 3 feet ; flowers white, in June ; Levant ; 1596. *L. Carolinianum* (Carolinian) ; hardy bulb ; 2 feet ; flowers orange, in July ; North America ; 1819. *L. Catesbæi* (Catesby's) ; hardy bulb ; 1 foot ; flowers scarlet-spotted, in July ; Carolina ; 1787. *L. Chalcedonicum* (Chalcedonian) ; hardy bulb ; 3 feet ; flowers scarlet, in July ; Levant ; 1596. *L. concolor* (one-colored) ; hardy bulb ; 2 feet ; flowers red, in July ; China ; 1806. *L. croceum* (saffron) ; hardy bulb ; 3 feet ; flowers saffron ; in July ; Italy ; 1596. *L. eximium* (splendid) ; hardy bulb ; 4 feet ; flowers white, in July ; Nepaul ; 1824. *L. giganteum* (gigantic) ; half-hardy bulb ; 8 to 10 feet ; flowers red and white, in June ; Nepaul ; 1851. *L. Japonicum* (Japanese) ; hardy bulb ; 2 feet ; flowers white, in July ;

Japan; 1804. *L. longifolium* (long-leaved); hardy bulb; 2 feet; flowers white, in June; China; 1820. *L. Martagon* (Turk's-cap); hardy bulb; 3 feet; flowers lilac or white, in July; Germany; 1596. *L. monadelphum* (monadelphous); hardy bulb; 2 feet; flowers yellow, in July; Caucasus; 1820. *L. Pomponium* (Pompone); hardy bulb; 3 feet; flowers scarlet, in May; Siberia; 1659. *L. pumilum* (dwarf); hardy bulb; 1 foot; flowers scarlet, in July; Russia; 1816. *L. Sibiricum* (Siberian); hardy bulb; 2 feet; flowers yellow, in July; Siberia; 1829. *L. speciosum* (showy); hardy bulb; 3 to 4 feet; flowers crimson, in August; Japan; 1833. The varieties *punctatum, rubrum,* and *Kœmpferi* are rose, spotted with crimson; *album* is white. *L. spectabile* (showy); hardy bulb; 2 feet; flowers light-orange, in June; Dahuria; 1754. *L. tenuifolium* (fine-leaved); hardy bulb; 2 feet; flowers scarlet, in June; Siberia; 1820. *L. testaceum* (testaceous); half-hardy bulb; 3 feet; flowers pale yellow, in June; Japan; 1841. *L. Thunbergianum* (Thunberg's); hardy bulb; 3 feet; flowers orange-scarlet, in July; Japan; 1835. *L. tigrinum* (tiger); hardy bulb; 3 feet; flowers red, with black spots, in July; China; 1804. *L. auratum;* this superb lily is doubtless the finest of the family; the flowers are white, banded with orange, and often a foot in diameter. In England, it has been grown with twenty-seven flowers on a plant. It requires the same treatment as the Japan Lilies, and is probably as hardy. Introduced from Japan in 1864.

LILY OF THE VALLEY. See CONVALLARIA.

LIMNANTHES. [Tropæolaceæ.] Hardy annuals, of trailing habit, with neat but not showy flowers. They may be sown in the open borders in May, and again in June, for succession. They are not very particular as to soil, but prefer a moist situation. They flower in about six weeks from the time of sowing.

L. alba (white); hardy annual, 9 inches; flowers white, in June; California; 1848. *L. Douglasii* (Douglas's); hardy annual, 9 inches; flowers white and yellow, in June; California;

1833; *L. rosea* (rosy); hardy annual, 9 inches; flowers pale rose, in June; California; 1848.

LIMNOCHARIS. [Butomaceæ.] Stove aquatics, one of which, *L. Humboldtii*, succeeds in the open air, in ponds or tanks. It bears beautiful yellow flowers all the summer. Propagated by its runners, which strike root in the muddy soil.

LINANTHUS. [Polemoniaceæ.] A hardy annual, growing in garden soil from spring-sown seeds.

L. dichotomus (forked); hardy annual; 18 inches; flowers pink, in July; California; 1838.

LINARIA. *Toad-flax.* [Scrophulariaceæ.] Hardy annual and perennial herbs, the numerous species of which display considerable diversity of character and habit: about half are annuals, and a few require protection. *L. Alpina* and *tristis* are pretty minute plants for pot-culture; *L. cymbalaria* and *pilosa* are suitable for rock-work. They all grow best in a dryish sandy loam, and are propagated, the perennials by cuttings in summer, or division of the plants in spring, and the annuals by seeds. Most of them are suitable for rock-work, especially the smaller growers. The half-hardy sorts should be grown in pots, and protected in cold frames in winter.

L. æquitriloba (equal three-lobed); hardy perennial; 3 inches; flowers purple, in June; Sardinia; 1829. *L Alpina* (Alpine); half-hardy perennial; 6 inches; flowers blue, in July; Austria; 1750. *L. bipartita* (two-parted); hardy annual; 1 foot; flowers purple, in June; north of Africa; 1815; sometimes known as *L. speciosa*. *L. cymbalaria* (ivy-leaved); hardy perennial; 3 inches; flowers lilac, in May; England. *L. Dalmatica* (Dalmatian); half-hardy perennial; 2 feet; flowers yellow, in June; Levant; 1731. *L. delphinioides* (larkspur-like); hardy biennial; 18 inches; flowers blue, in August; Russia; 1838. *L. genistæfolia* (genista-leaved); hardy perennial; 2 feet; flowers yellow, in July; Austria; 1704. *L. Monspessulana* (Montpelier); hardy perennial; 2 feet; flowers purple, in July; France. *L. Pelisseriana* (Pelisser's); hardy annual; 1 foot; flowers purple, in June; south of Europe; 1640. *L. Perezii* (Perez's); hardy annual; 1 foot; flowers yellow, in June; Italy. *L. pilosa* (hairy); hardy perennial; 3 inches; flowers lilac, in June; Pyrenees; 1800. *L. purpurea* (purple); hardy perennial; 2 feet; flowers purple, in July; south of Europe; 1648. *L. reticulata* (net-veined); half-hardy biennial; 18 inches; flowers brown and purple, in July; Portugal and Algiers; 1788. *L. spartea* (broom); hardy annual; 1 foot; flowers yellow, in June; Spain; 1772. *L. triornithophora* (three-birds); half-hardy perennial; 18 inches; flowers purple, in July; Portugal; 1710. *L. tristis* (sad); half-hardy perennial; 6 inches; flowers brown, in July; Spain; 1727. *L. villosa* (shaggy); half-hardy perennial; 1 foot; flowers blue, in July; Spain; 1786. *L. vulgaris Peloria* (Peloria); hardy perennial; 18 inches; flowers yellow, in June; England.

The other species are numerous.

LINNÆA. [Caprifoliaceæ.] A hardy trailing sub-shrubby plant, commemorating the name of Linnæus. Soil moist peat, in a shady sheltered situation. Increased by separating portions of its rooting trailing stems.

L. borealis (northern); hardy sub-shrub, trailing; flowers flesh-color, in June; North America and Europe.

LINUM. *Flax.* [Linaceæ.] A showy genus, consisting principally of annual or perennial herbs, which grow freely in ordinary garden soil, preferring sandy loam, and are propagated by seeds, which are readily perfected. There are some shrubby greenhouse kinds, which should be grown in a compost of two parts peat and one of loam, with enough sand added to make it open; and are propagated by cuttings put in a hot-bed. The common cultivated flax is *L. usitatissimum.*

L. Alpinum (Alpine); hardy perennial; 6 inches; flowers blue, in July; Austria; 1739. *L. Altaicum* (Altaic); hardy perennial; 1 foot; flowers blue, in July; Altai; 1829. *L. angustfolium* (narrow-leaved); hardy perennial; 1 foot; flowers pale blue, in July; England. *L. Austriacum* (Austrian); hardy perennial; 1 foot; flowers blue, in June; Austria; 1775. *L. Berendieri* (Berendier's); half-hardy annual; 2 feet; flowers yellow and orange, in September; Texas; 1835. *L. bicolor* (two-colored); hardy annual; 18 inches; flowers yellow and blue, in June; Morocco; 1820. *L. flavum* (yellow); half-hardy sub-shrub; 3 inches; flowers yellow, in June; Austria; 1793. *L. grandiflorum* (large-flowered); hardy annual; 18 inches; flowers crimson, in July; Algiers; 1852. *L. monogynum* (one-styled); half-hardy perennial; 18 inches; flowers white, in July; New Zealand; 1832. *L. montanum* (mountain); hardy perennial; 1 foot; flowers blue, in June; Switzerland; 1817. *L. Narbonense* (Narbonne); half-hardy perennial; 2 feet; flowers blue, in May; south of France; 1759. *L. nervosum* (nerved); hardy perennial; 18 inches; flowers blue, in June; Hungary; 1822. *L. Sibiricum* (Siberian); hardy perennial; 2 feet; flowers blue, in June; Siberia; 1775. *L. suffruticosum* (sub-shrubby); greenhouse sub-shrub; 1 foot; flowers pink, in August; Spain; 1759. *L. Tauricum* (Taurian); hardy sub-shrub; 1 foot; flowers yellow, in June; Tauria; 1818. *L. tenuifolium* (slender-leaved); hardy perennial; 18 inches; flowers pink, in June; Europe; 1789. *L. trigynum* (three-styled); greenhouse shrub; 2 feet; flowers yellow, in June; India; 1799. *L. usitatissimum* (common); hardy annual; 18 inches; flowers blue, in June; England.

There are several other species in cultivation.

LION'S EAR. See LEONOTIS.

LISIANTHUS. See EUSTOMA.

LIQUIDAMBER. *Gum-tree.* [Hamamelaceæ.] A hardy well-known deciduous tree, very ornamental and desirable. Rich loamy soil. Propagated by seeds. Hardy as far north as Massachusetts.

L. styracifera (styrax-flowing); hardy tree; 50 feet; North America; 1863. *L. imberbe* is a species from the Levant.

LIRIODENDRON. *Tulip-tree.* [Magnoliaceæ.] A fine hardy ornamental tree. Flowers yellow and red, in May. Propagated by seed, layers, grafting, or budding. Deep, moist, loamy soil.

L. tulipfera (tulip-bearing); hardy tree; 60 feet; North America; 1663. Variety *obtusifolia* has blunt leaves.

LITHOSPERMUM. *Gromwell.* [Boraginaceæ.] Hardy annuals and perennials. Dryish sandy loam. Increased by division, cuttings, or seeds.

L. Orientale (Eastern); hardy perennial; 2 feet; flowers yellow, in June; Levant; 1713. *L. purpureo-cæruleum* (purplish-blue); hardy perennial; 1 foot; flowers purple-blue, in May; England. *L. rosmarinifolium* (rosemary-leaved); half-hardy sub-shrub; 2 feet; flowers bright blue, in September; Italy; 1833. *L. villosa* (shaggy); hardy perennial; 1 foot; flowers blue, in July; south of France; 1817.

LLOYDIA. [Liliaceæ.] Hardy perennial. Dry sandy loam. Division.

L. striata (streaked); hardy biennial; 9 inches; flowers white striped, in May; Siberia; 1789.

LOASA. [Loasaceæ.] Hardy annuals, with pretty flowers, the stems and leaves invested with poisonous stinging hairs. They may be sown in the borders about the middle of April, and again, if necessary, at the end of May. Increased by seeds.

L. alba (white); hardy annual; 2 feet; flowers white, in July; Chili; 1831. *L. grandiflora* (large-flowered); hardy annual; 2 feet; flowers yellow, in July; Peru; 1825. *L. lucida* (clear); greenhouse perennial; 3 feet; flowers white and red, in June. *L. nitida* (shining); hardy annual; 2 feet; flowers yellow and red, in June; Chili; 1822. *L. picta* (painted); half-hardy annual; 2 feet; flowers white, yellow and red, in June; South America; 1848. *L. Placei* (Place's); hardy annual; 3 feet; flowers yellow, in June; Chili; 1822.

LOBELIA. [Lobeliaceæ.] An extensive genus of very showy plants, comprising stove, greenhouse, and hardy species, and consisting principally of perennial herbs, with a few annuals and biennials. Peat and loam in equal quantities, with a sixth part sand, form a good compost for the smaller and more delicate species. The strong-growing perennial kinds flourish best in rich moist loam; but they must be wintered in a dry cold frame. The annuals should be raised in a slight heat in March, and pricked off into small pots, hardened, and planted out in May: they are better for a liberal mixture of peat-earth. The shrubby and sub-shrubby kinds are increased by cuttings, planted in sand, and put in a hot-bed; the perennials by division in early spring, the shoots being first excited into growth in a mild heat, and then separated into single pots of the smallest size, and put in a warm frame until they are well established, when they may be hardened to bear the open air. For blooming in pots, the herbaceous kinds must be shifted into larger pots progressively: a very rich loamy compost should be used, with abundance of moisture. The more tender of these are best kept nearly dry, under a greenhouse stage, during winter, being very liable to rot from exposure to damp. *L. gracilis* is a dwarf kind, bearing a profusion of small blue flowers throughout the summer, if treated like a half-hardy annual, and planted in the open ground in May. Of the same habit are *L. erinus* and its varieties, *grandiflora*, *compacta*, and *L. decumbens*, perennials employed for the summer decoration of flower-gardens, all bearing blue flowers in profusion, and suitable from their dwarf habit for planting close by the edges of flower-beds and borders. The perennial kinds are annually augmented by cross-bred varieties, which are constantly giving place to new variations. The New-Holland perennial species enumerated below are beautiful plants, most conveniently grown as annuals, and suitable either for pots or beds; raised in autumn, and wintered near the glass in a cool greenhouse, they make beautiful pot-plants.

L. amœna (pleasing); hardy perennial; 3 feet; flowers blue, in July; North America; 1812. *L. bellidifolia* (daisy-leaved); half-hardy perennial; 6 inches; flowers blue, in August; Cape; 1790. *L. cardinalis* (cardinal-flower); hardy perennial; 3 feet; flowers scarlet, in July; Virginia; 1629. *L. cœlestis* (heavenly); hardy perennial; 9 inches; flowers pale blue, in May; North America; 1831. *L. coronopifolia* (coronopus-leaved); half-hardy perennial; 6 inches; flowers pale blue, in July; Cape; 1752. *L. decumbens* (decumbent); half-hardy perennial; 6 inches; flowers blue, in August; Cape; 1820. *L. densiflora* (dense-flowered); half-hardy perennial; 1 foot; flowers blue, in June. *L. erinus* (ascending); half-hardy perennial; 6 inches; flowers blue, in June; Cape; 1752. *L. fulgens* (shining); half-hardy perennial; 3 feet; flowers vivid scarlet, in June; Mexico; 1809. *L. gracilis* (slender); half-hardy annual; 1 foot; flowers blue, in June; New South Wales; 1801. *L. heterophylla* (various-leaved); half-hardy perennial; 18 inches; flowers blue, in May; New Holland; 1837. *L. ignea* (fiery); half-hardy perennial; 3 feet; flowers orange-scarlet, in June; Mexico; 1838. *L. thapsoidea* (mullein-like); half-hardy perennial; 6 feet; flowers rosy-purple, in July; Organ Mountains; 1843. *L. ramosa* (branched); half-hardy perennial; 18 inches; flowers blue, in May; New Holland; 1838. *L. syphilitica* (syphilitic); half-hardy perennial; 2 feet; flowers blue, in September; Virginia; 1665. *L. speciosa* (showy); half-hardy perennial; 3 feet; flowers purple, in June; gardens. *L. splendens* (shining); half-hardy perennial; 3 feet; flowers scarlet, in June; Mexico; 1814.

There are many others in gardens. The tall-growing perennials are generally showy plants; but many of the dwarf kinds are unimportant, and the annuals are often insignificant.

LOCUST. See ROBINIA.

LONDON PRIDE. See LYCHNIS.

LONICERA. [Caprifoliaceæ.] Hardy deciduous shrubs, usually known as Tartarian Honeysuckle. Good garden soil. Increased by cuttings, layers, or seeds.

L. Alpigena (Alpine); 6 feet; flowers yellow, in May; south of Europe; 1596. *L. Alpigena Sibirica* (Siberian); 5 feet; flowers yellow, in May; Siberia; 1810. *L. angustifolia* (narrow-leaved); 5 feet; flowers pale-yellow, in May; North India; 1847. *L. cærulea* (blue-berried); 4 feet; flowers yellow, in May; Switzerland; 1629. *L. Canadensis* (Canadian); flowers yellow, in May; Canada; 1812. *L. canescens* (hoary); 10 feet; May; Europe. *L. ciliata* (hair-fringed); 4 feet; flowers white and red, in May; North America; 1824. *L. ciliata alba* (white-berried); 4 feet; flowers white and red, in May; North America; 1824; *L. discolor* (two-colored); 4 feet; flowers yellow and crimson, in June; East Indies; 1844. *L. diversifolia* (various-leaved); 4 feet; flowers yellow, in May; Himalaya; 1843. *L. flexuosa* (curved); 15 feet; flowers orange, in July; Japan; 1806. *L. Iberica* (Iberian); 6 feet; flowers orange, in May; Iberia; 1824. *L. involucrata* (involucred); 3 feet; flowers yellow, in May; Hudson's Bay; 1824. *L. Ledebourii* (Ledebour's); 3 feet; flowers yellow and red, in June; California; 1833. *L. microphylla* (small-leaved); 4 feet; Siberia; 1818. *L. nigra* (black); 4 feet; flowers pale-yellow, in May; Switzerland; 1597. *L. nigra campaniflora* (bell-flowered); 4 feet; flowers yellow, in May; North America. *L. oblongifolia* (oblong-leaved); 3 feet; flowers white, in May; North America; 1823. *L. Orientalis* (Eastern); 6 feet; flowers yellow, in June; Iberia; 1825. *L. Orientalis puniceus* (crimson); flowers crimson, in May; North America; 1822. *L. Pyrenaica* (Pyrenean); 4 feet; flowers white; Pyrenees; 1739. *L. Tartarica* (Tartarian); 10 feet; flowers pink, in May; Russia; 1752. *L. Tartarica albiflora* (white-flowered); 10 feet; flowers white, in May; Pyrenees; 1739. *L. Tartarica latifolia* (broad-leaved); 10 feet; flowers pink, in May. *L. Tartarica lutea* (yellow-flowered); 10 feet; flowers yellow, in May. *L. Tartarica rubriflora* (red-flowered); 10 feet; flowers red, in May; Russia; 1752. *L. villosa* (shaggy); 4 feet; flowers yellow, in May; Canada; 1820. *L. xylosteum* (fly); 8 feet; flowers yellow, in June; England. *L. xylosteum leucocarpum* (white-berried); 8 feet; flowers yellow, in June; Britain. *L. xylosteum melanocarpum* (black-berried); 8 feet; flowers yellow, in June; Britain. *L. xylosteum xanthocarpum* (yellow-berried); 8 feet; flowers yellow, in June; Britain. A fine new climber, with golden netted foliage, is known as *L. brachypoda fol. aureo reticulata*. It is a very striking plant, but needs to be laid down in winter; Japan; 1860.

LOOSE-STRIFE. See LYSIMACHIA.

LOPEZIA. [Onagraceæ.] Hardy annuals of straggling growth, forming a pretty mass when in flower. They are increased by seeds, which may be sown in March, with the half-hardy annuals, for transplanting, and again in May where they are intended to bloom. The perennials are propagated by cuttings in summer. Common soil.

L. cordata (heart-leaved); hardy annual; 18 inches; flowers purplish, in July; Mexico; 1821. *L. coronata* (crowned); hardy annual; 18 inches; flowers rose-red, in July; Mexico; 1805. *L. hispida* (hairy); hardy annual; 6 inches; flowers red, in August; Mexico; 1826. *L. lineata* (lined); half-hardy perennial; 2 feet; flowers red, in May; Mexico; 1839. *L. racemosa* (racemed); hardy annual; 18 inches; flowers rose-red, in July; Mexico; 1792.

LOPHOSPERMUM. [Scrophulariaceæ.] Showy evergreen greenhouse climbers, adapted also for planting in the flower-garden during the summer season, and for covering trellis-work. These plants all bloom pretty freely throughout the summer, and ripen seeds freely in fine seasons, from which they are best propagated: they also strike readily from cuttings. Planted out for the summer, they flourish in ordinary good garden soil; but if kept in pots, being large-growing plants, they must have tolerably large pots of good rich loamy soil, which, as the plants become large, and begin blooming, may be enriched by applications of dilute liquid manure, or by spreading a layer of dung on the surface, to be washed in by the ordinary waterings. The old plants may be kept through the winter in a greenhouse or frost-proof frame, if their fleshy roots are kept tolerably dry. *L. scandens* is a pretty plant for planting around the edges of raised rustic or other flower baskets, balconies, or similar places.

L. erubescens (blushing); greenhouse climbing perennial; 12 feet; flowers rose, in June; Jalapa; 1830. Of this species there are some improved garden varieties, of which the best are *Cliftoni*, deep bright rose; *Hendersoni*, with the flowers rich deep rose; and *spectabilis*, in which the rosy flowers are usually spotted with white. *L. scandens* (climbing); greenhouse climbing perennial; 6 feet; flowers purplish-rose, in June; Mexico; 1834.

LOTUS. *Bird's-foot Trefoil.* [Leguminosæ.] A family containing many hardy annuals and perennials, none of which are of great horticultural importance. They flourish in good garden soil, and are propagated by seed. There are some fine greenhouse and half-hardy species.

LOUSEWORT. See PEDICULARIS.

LOVE LIES BLEEDING. See AMARANTHUS.

LUNARIA. *Honesty.* [Brassicaceæ.] Hardy border plants, of easy culture, very showy in blossom in May, and in seed in August. Propagated by seeds.

L. biennis (biennial); hardy biennial; 1 foot; flowers light-purple, in May; 1570. A variety has white flowers. *L. rediviva* (revived); hardy perennial; 2 feet; flowers light-purple, in May; 1796.

LUNGWORT. See PULMONARIA.

LUPINUS. *Lupine.* [Leguminosæ.] An extensive genus, comprising annuals, perennial herbs, and some few sub-shrubby species, nearly all hardy, easily cultivated, and possessing considerable general resemblance; so that, in a limited garden, but a few of the kinds are required. The perennials, *L. polyphyllus* and *grandifolius*, throw up long pyramidal closely set spikes of flowers, from two to four feet in height, according to the strength of the plant. The Lupines will all grow freely in good garden soil, which they very much impoverish. The annuals should be sown in March and April where they are to flower. The perennials are increased by parting the roots, but much more freely by seeds, which ripen abundantly, and may be sown in June; in which case the strongest of the plants will blossom the following year. The half-hardy sub-shrubby species are also best raised from seeds, and require to be wintered in a dry protected frame, and planted out about May. *L. mutabilis*, and its variety *Cruikshanksii*, form beautiful objects if raised in August, wintered singly in small pots in a frame or airy greenhouse shelf, shifted about March, and kept in a cold frame till the end of May, and then planted out in good soil in the flower-garden. All the biennials may be treated as annuals.

L. arboreus (tree); half-hardy shrub; 8 feet; flowers yellow, in July; California; 1793. *L. argenteus* (silvery); hardy perennial; 3 feet; flowers white, in June; North America; 1826. *L. arvensis* (field); half-hardy biennial; 18 inches; flowers lilac, purple, and white, in July; Peru; 1842. *L. Barkeri* (Barker's); half-hardy annual or biennial; 3 feet; flowers blue and pink, in July; Mexico; 1839. *L. grandifolius* (large-leaved); hardy perennial; 4 feet; flowers purple, in May; North America; 1834. *L. Hartwegii* (Hartweg's); hardy annual; 2 feet; flowers blue, in June; Mexico; 1838. *L. hirsutus* (hairy); hardy annual; 2 feet; flowers blue, in July; south of Europe; 1629. *L. insignis* (remarkable); a fine hybrid, with bright-rosy pink and yellow flowers; 1857. *L. luteus* (yellow); hardy annual; 2 feet; flowers yellow, in June; south of Europe; 1596. *L. mutabilis* (changeable); half-hardy shrub; 5 feet; flowers white, tinged with blush, changing to blue, with a yellow centre, in July; Bogota; 1819. Best treated as a biennial. A very beautiful variety named *Cruikshanksii* has the flowers deep-blue with yellow, changing to red. *L. nanus* (dwarf); hardy annual; 1 foot; flowers blue, in June; California; 1833. *L. ornatus* (ornate); hardy perennial; 2 feet; flowers purple-lilac, in May; Columbia; 1826. *L. perennis* (perennial); hardy perennial; 2 feet; flowers blue, in June; North America; 1658. *L. pilosus* (shaggy); hardy annual; 2 feet; flowers pink, in July; south of Europe; 1710. *L. polyphyllus* (many-leaved); hardy perennial; 3 feet; flowers blue or white, in May; Colombia; 1826. *L. pubescens* (downy); half-hardy biennial; 3 feet; flowers violet blue, in June; Quito; 1844. *L. tomentosus* (thick downy); half-hardy sub-shrub; 4 feet; flowers pink and white, in July; Peru; 1825. *L. versicolor* (party-colored); half-hardy sub-shrub; 3 feet; flowers pink and blue, in July; Mexico; 1825.

LYCHNIS. [Caryophyllaceæ.] Hardy herbaceous perennials, some of which are very ornamental. This may be said of *L. Chalcedonica*, commonly called Scarlet Lychnis, of which both double and single have been known in gardens for many years, and are as common as the Stock or the Sunflower. They require to be frequently transplanted and divided, giving them fresh good compost, rich sandy loam at each planting, or they soon run out; and this is more particularly the case with the double than single-flowered varieties; it should be done in spring. They develop a dense head of brilliant scarlet blooms at the top of the stem. *L. fulgens* and *L. coronata* are smaller, but very showy plants; their roots require to be protected from wet in winter, by taking them up in autumn, potting them, and placing them in a dry frame. The dwarf hardy kinds are proper for dry rock-work. They are propagated by parting the roots, and also from seeds, which should be sown in pans, or on prepared beds, about May, merely thinning out the young plants until they are large enough to transplant, when they may be placed in nursery-beds, nine inches apart, where they should remain till they are strong enough to produce blossoms. See also AGROSTEMMA and VISCARIA.

L. Alpina (Alpine); hardy perennial; 6 inches; flowers pink, in April; Scotland; suitable for rock-work. *L. Chalcedonica* (Chalcedonian); hardy perennial; 2 feet; flowers scarlet, in July; Russia; 1596. Of the varieties of this plant, the double-flowered scarlet and white are the best. *L. Corsica* (Corsican); hardy perennial; 6 inches; flowers red, in June; Corsica; 1818. *L. fulgens* (shining); hardy perennial; 18 inches; flowers scarlet, in July; Siberia; 1822. *L. grandiflora* (large-flowered); half-hardy perennial; 18 inches; flowers orange-red, in July; China; 1774. *L. Haagena* is a fine hybrid between *L. fulgens* and *L. Sieboldii*, with brilliant crimson-red flowers; hardy and desirable. Seedlings are, however, very apt to revert to *L. Sieboldii*, which, is a pretty white-flowered species; 1860. *L. læta* (lively); hardy perennial; 6 inches; flowers flesh-color, in May; Portugal; 1778. *L. viscaria* (clammy); hardy perennial; 1 foot; flowers red, single, or double, in May; Britain.

LYCIUM. *Box-thorn.* [Solanaceæ.] Hardy rambling shrubby plants, requiring to be trained against a wall or pillar, or supported by poles. They are free-flowering, but not showy, and, from their free growth, rather adapted for covering arbors and unsightly buildings, than desirable for their ornamental properties. *L. Europæum* is especially useful for this purpose, rapidly covering walls or buildings, and growing to a considerable height, producing long, rambling shoots, and an abundance of suckers: these long shoots, if produced from the higher parts of the plant, will assume a drooping position, and in the second year will bear a profusion of changeable veined purple-lilac flowers; so that a succession of such branches should be annually maintained. Root-suckers ought to be destroyed continually. They are all indifferent as to soil, provided it is moderately well-drained and porous; and are increased without difficulty either by cuttings, by layers, or by suckers.

L. Afrum (African); half-hardy trailing shrub; 10 feet; flowers dull-violet, in June; North Africa and Syria; 1712. *L. Barbarum* (Barbary); hardy trailing shrub; 20 feet; flowers livid, in May; south of Europe, and Africa; 1696. *L. Europæum* (European); hardy trailing shrub; 20 feet; flowers purple-lilac, in May; south of Europe; 1730. *L. Ruthenicum* (Russian); hardy climbing shrub; 20 feet; flowers white, in July; Siberia; 1804.

LYONIA. [Ericaceæ.] Hardy ornamental shrubs allied to Andromeda. Soil, sandy peat. Propagated by seeds and layers. There is much confusion in the divisions on the Andromeda family. See ANDROMEDA.

LYSIMACHIA. *Loose-strife.* [Primulaceæ.] Hardy perennials, of the easiest culture, of little importance in a flower-garden. The genus contains a few half-hardy sub-shrubby species, which are increased by cuttings in a gentle hot-bed, in sand. *L. nummularia,* Moneywort, is a pretty trailing plant, adapted for damp rock-work, or for planting in a pot for the side of a shady window. Sandy soil. All multiplied by division.

L. Azorica (Azorian); hardy perennial; 6 inches; flowers yellow, in June; Azores; 1831. *L. ciliata* (fringed); hardy perennial; 18 inches; flowers yellow, in July; England. *L. candida* (white); half-hardy sub-shrub; 18 inches; flowers white, in June; China; 1846. *L. ephemerum* (transient); hardy perennial; 2 feet; flowers white, in August; Spain; 1730. *L. Leschenaultii* (Leschenault's); half-hardy sub-shrub; 18 inches; flowers rose-colored, in June; Neilgherries; 1852. *L. lobelioides* (lobelia-like); hardy perennial; 1 foot; flowers white, in July; North India; 1840. *L. nummularia* (Moneywort); hardy trailing perennial; 6 inches; flowers yellow, in June; England. *L. verticillata* (whorled); hardy perennial; 18 inches; flowers yellow, in July; Crimea; 1820.

LYTHRUM. [Lythraceæ.] Hardy annuals or perennials; the former of little interest, the latter ornamental; often thriving in damp and even wet situations. *L. alatum* is a showy half-hardy plant, with long slender scarcely branched stems, bearing purple flowers throughout the summer, and not unsuited for a good-sized bed. The hardy perennials grow in ordinary soil, and are increased by division; the half-hardy ones grow from cuttings, and should be potted in a soil of three parts peat to one of loam. The annuals may be sown in the open border in May.

L. alatum (winged); half-hardy perennial; 3 feet; flowers purple, in July; Georgia; 1812. *L. lineare* (linear); hardy perennial; 18 inches; flowers white, in July; North America; 1812. *L. myrtifolium* (myrtle-leaved); hardy perennial; 2 feet; flowers purple, in July; North America; 1820. *L. Purshianum* (Pursh's); hardy perennial; 18 inches; flowers purple, in July; North America; 1800. *L. salicaria* (willow-like); hardy perennial; 4 feet; flowers purple, in July; England. *L. tomentosum* (woolly); hardy perennial; 3 feet; flowers purple, in July; Caucasus; 1828. *L. virgatum* (twiggy); hardy perennial; 3 feet; flowers purple, in June; Austria; 1776.

MACHÆRANTHERA. [Compositæ.] A very pretty tender biennial, but which succeeds in the border in summer. Soil, sandy loam. Propagated by cuttings.

M. tanacetifolia (tansy-leaved); 1 foot; flowers purple, in July; Mexico; 1851.

MACLEAYA. [Papaveraceæ.] Half-hardy herbaceous perennials. Good garden soil. Increased by division, in spring.

M. cordata (heart-leaved); hardy perennial; 6 feet; flowers yellowish-pink, in June; Chili; 1795.

MACLURA. [Moraceæ.] This small genus contains one hardy species, *M. aurantiaca*, which, under the name of the Osage-orange, is much used for hedges. Propagated by seeds. This tree is barely hardy in Massachusetts.

M. aurantiaca; 20 feet; North America; 1828.

MADIA. See MADARIA.

MADARIA. [Compositæ.] A family of showy hardy annuals; the flowers golden, with a brownish rim round the disk. May be sown in frames, and transplanted, or in the open border in May. Increased by seeds. Common soil.

M. corymbosa (corymbed); hardy annual; 2 feet; flowers white, in July; California; 1847. *M. elegans* (elegant); hardy annual; 2 feet; flowers yellow, in July; California; 1831. *M. sativa;* flowers yellow, in July; Chili; 1794.

MAGNOLIA. [Magnoliaceæ.] Noble and beautiful hardy and half-hardy shrubs and trees, some among the handsomest of evergreens, others deciduous, and all beautiful as flowering plants. The soil for these plants should be deep and good, of open texture, neither subject to parching, nor liable to excessive wet at any season. The Magnolias all grow finely in peat earth; but this is not essential to them. They are greatly benefited, however, when planted in a young state, by having a bushel or so of good compost placed about their roots: this compost may be of equal parts light turfy loam and peat. Layering is the most usual mode of propagating the Magnolia, the layers being put down in autumn, and requiring a couple of seasons to get well established. Many of the species do not transplant well, except when quite young, unless they are kept in pots: on this account, it is usual to keep them in pots; but when this has been the case, the roots must be carefully uncoiled, and spread out in straight lines, when they are permanently planted. Seeds may be often obtained; and the plants raised from them are the most vigorous, but do not blossom so early. They should be sown in sandy loam, placed in a warm frame, potted as they appear, and kept for several years in a cold pit during winter until they get well established. The arboreous species are only suited for large gardens. *M. grandiflora*, and its varieties, are evergreen trees, which should find a place in every garden. Wherever there is a shrubbery, or a clump of peat-earth shrubs, one or two of the hardy deciduous species should also be grown for their large fragrant blossoms in the early spring months. *M. fuscata*, a small evergreen, something like a camellia in its foliage, is a greenhouse plant, and in May bears blossoms exquisitely fragrant, though not very conspicuous. This should be potted in turfy loam and peat, and is increased by grafting, or inarching on the commoner kinds, as *M. obovata*, which mode of propagation is also resorted to with the other weaker and more tender kinds.

M. acuminata (pointed-leaved); hardy deciduous tree; 40 feet; flowers creamy, in June; North America; 1736. *M. auriculata* (ear-leaved); hardy deciduous tree; 20 feet; flowers white, in May; North America; 1786. *M. conspicua* (showy); hardy deciduous tree; 20 feet; flowers white, in April; China; 1789. *Soulangeana* is a very beautiful variety of this, with the flowers tinged with purple. *M. fuscata* (brown); greenhouse evergreen shrub; 3 feet; flowers brown, in April; China; 1789. *M. glauca* (glaucous); hardy deciduous tree; 15 feet; flowers whitish, in June; North America; 1688. *M. grandiflora* (large-flowered); hardy evergreen tree; 15 feet; flowers white, in July; North Carolina; 1737. Of this there are several varieties, among which that known as *Exoniensis* is the most desirable, on account of its early and free blooming habit. *M. macrophylla* (large-leaved); hardy deciduous tree; 20 feet; flowers white and purple, in June; North America; 1800. *M. purpurea* (purple); hardy deciduous shrub; 6 feet; flowers purple, in April; Japan; 1790. *M. tripetala* (three-petalled); hardy deciduous tree; 20 feet; flowers white, in May; North America; 1752. *M. Thompsoniana* (Thompson's); hardy tree; 20 feet; flowers white, in June; hybrid between *M. glauca* and *tripetala*.

There are many varieties of *M. conspicua*, but they are not very distinct. *M. Norbetiana* is a very deep-colored variety. *M. grandiflora* and its varieties are not hardy north of Philadelphia. *M. Lenne* is a fine hybrid between *M. conspicua* and *purpurea;* color, deep reddish-purple; April, 1860.

MAHONIA. See BERBERIS.

MAIDEN-HAIR TREE. See SALISBURIA.

MALCOLMIA. [Cruciferæ.] Hardy annuals, of which one species — *M. maritima*, the Virginian stock — is a favorite dwarf ornament for the flower-border, very easily grown, but not durable: in good-sized patches, it forms a showy mass of simple flowers. If sown by the middle of May, it will, in favorable seasons, be in bloom early in June; but, to have a good succession of flowers, it ought to be sown monthly, from May to August. It is quite hardy, and forms a pretty edging-plant for large borders. The other species may be similarly cultivated. The best are *M. maritima, littorea, incrassata,* and *arenaria.*

M. arenaria (sand); hardy annual; 1 foot; flowers violet, in June; Algiers; 1804. *M. Chia* (Chian); hardy annual; 1 foot; flowers purple, in June; Greece; 1732. *M. incrassata* (thickened); hardy annual; 6 inches; flowers purplish, in June; islands of the Ægean Sea; 1820. *M. littorea* (shore); hardy annual, or half-hardy biennial; 1 foot; flowers purple, in June; south of Europe; 1683. *M. maritima* (sea-side); hardy annual; 1 foot; flowers rosy-lilac or white, all summer; south of Europe; 1713. *M. triloba* (three-lobed); hardy annual; 6 inches; flowers yellowish, in June; south of Europe; 1780.

MALLOW. See MALVA.

MALOPE. [Malvaceæ.] Showy mallow-like annuals, of very simple culture. The seeds may be sown in March, and again in April, in the open border; the plants to be thinned out when large enough, leaving about three of the strongest in a patch. To get plants to bloom earlier than usual, they may be sown in pots along with half-hardy annuals, and planted out as early in May as the season will admit.

M. malacoides (mallow-like); hardy annual; 2 feet; flowers purple, in June; south of Europe; 1710. *M. trifida* (three-cleft); hardy annual; 2 feet; flowers crimson, in July; Barbary; 1808. Of this there is a variety with white flowers called *alba*, and another with larger flowers called *grandiflora.*

MALVA. *Mallow.* [Malvaceæ.] A large genus, of which the majority are weedy: a few, however, of which a selection is enumerated below, are ornamental. The half-hardy sorts will grow during summer in the borders in good garden soil, or in a mixture of loam, leaf-mould, and sand, and are increased by cuttings in sand, in a frame, during summer. The greenhouse kinds also propagate by cuttings, and grow in similar soil. The hardy annuals may be sown in patches, in the open border, in May.

M. amœna (pleasing); greenhouse shrub; 3 feet; flowers purplish, in May; Cape; 1796. *M. Capensis* (Cape); greenhouse shrub; 3 feet; flowers pink, in June; Cape; 1713. *M. crispa* (curled); hardy annual; 3 feet; flowers white, in June; Syria; 1573. *M. fragrans* (fragrant); greenhouse shrub; 3 feet; flowers red, in June; Cape; 1759. *M. lateritia* (brick-red); half-hardy perennial; 1 foot; flowers red, in September; Buenos Ayres; 1840. *M. Mauritiana* (Mauritanian); hardy-annual; 4 feet; flowers rose-color or white, and purple striped, in July; south of Europe and North Africa; 1768. *M. miniata* (vermilion); half-hardy shrub; 3 feet; flowers vermilion-red, in May; Mexico; 1798. In the borders, it blooms through the autumn. *M. Monroana* (Monro's); half-hardy perennial; 2 feet; flowers scarlet, in August; Colombia; 1828. *M. Morenii* (Moreni's); half-hardy perennial; 3 feet; flowers red, in July; Italy; 1820. *M. moschata* (musk); hardy perennial; 2 feet; flowers flesh-color or white, in June; Britain. *M. purpurata* (purple); half-hardy perennial; 2 feet; flowers dull-red, in July; Chili; 1825.

MAPLE. See ACER.
MARIGOLD. See CALENDULA.
MARJORAM. See ORIGANUM.
MARSH-MALLOW. See ALTHÆA.
MARSH-MARIGOLD. See CALTHA.
MARTAGON. See LILIUM.
MARTYNIA. [Sesameæ.] Greenhouse or half-hardy annuals, with a somewhat coarse habit and showy flowers. The seeds should be sown in a hot-bed in March, and the young plants potted singly, and kept growing in heat near the glass, in the way balsams are managed. As they grow they must be shifted, and hardened off to bloom in a cool stove or greenhouse or frame. *M. fragrans*, the best of the species, will also succeed in a sheltered place, planted out for the summer. They require rich light soil.

M. Craniolaria (white-flowered); greenhouse annual; 18 inches; flowers white spotted, in July; South America; 1733. *M. diandra* (two-stamened); greenhouse annual; 18 inches; flowers red, in July; Mexico; 1731. *M. fragrans* (fragrant); greenhouse, or half-hardy annual; 2 feet; flowers rose-purple, in July; Mexico; 1840. *M. lutea* (yellow); greenhouse annual; 18 inches; flowers yellowish, in July; Brazil; 1824. *M. proboscidea* (proboscis-like); greenhouse annual; 1 foot; flowers pale-violet, with saffron dots, in July; Mexico; 1738.

MARVEL OF PERU. See MIRABILIS.

MATHIOLA. *Stock.* [Cruciferæ.] A favorite genus of hardy plants, among the sweetest and gayest of garden flowers, of which one familiar species, *M. annua*, the Ten-weeks Stock, is an annual; another, *M. simplicicaulis*, the Brompton, or Giant Stock, is a biennial; and *M. incana*, the Queen Stock, is a sub-shrubby kind, though best treated as a biennial. The varieties of these, especially of the first, are very numerous, and, as imported from Germany, very fine. Of the ordinary hoary-leaved Ten-weeks, or Annual Stock, there are a score or more different colors, which the German seed-growers save distinct. Of the Ten-weeks Stock having smooth green, or wallflower-like leaves, there are also many varieties of color; and, besides these, there are variations of habit which have become perpetuated by careful seed-saving. The biennial Stock, that is, those sown one year to bloom the next, varies as much as the annual, in regard to habit, but not in respect to color. The Brompton and the Queen Stock are well-known distinctions in this class. When once possession is obtained of a good strain of Stock, which produces but few single-flowered ones out of a great number, there is not much difficulty in keeping it, for the Stock has a strong disposition to go double; and, when a few single ones only escape this tendency, they may be expected to yield seed equally disposed to produce double flowers. On the other hand, if we remove a single Stock from among hundreds of others equally single, and of a strain which has no disposition to go double, that single one would not yield in its progeny one more double variety for being planted among a thousand double ones; so that the common advice to save seed from such single-flowered plants as grow near many double ones is good for nothing, unless the single ones come from the same "strain," and have the same disposition, as the double ones themselves; that is to say, are of the same progeny. In other words, the planting of a thousand double stocks around a single one does not change the nature of its seed: but the tendency to produce double flowers is an inherent property brought about in certain plants by careful culture and seed-saving, as all other floral improvements have been; and is not shared by other plants though of the very same kind, which have not been influenced in this manner. The single-flowered plants only bear seed. The tendency to produce double flowers is sometimes indicated by the production of flowers with more than the usual number of petals (four): and, when this is observed, it may be taken as a favorable indication; and such blossoms should be marked, and their seed kept separate. The Ten-weeks Stocks should be sown in March, April, and May, for summer and autumn blooming plants: they may be sown in boxes, in a frame, or on prepared sheltered beds; when up, give plenty of air, and no more water than is just enough to keep them from flagging; when they have formed six good leaves, plant them out in a bed of rich soil, or pot them off in rich soil, and give plenty of water until they bloom. For earlier spring-bloom, they, as well as what is called the Intermediate Stock, should be sown in August and September, and wintered in pots in dry cold frames. The Brompton and Queen Stocks may be sown in the open border, thinly, in

June, and the plants, when large enough, planted out in sheltered places where they are to bloom, or some of them may be potted and kept in frames during winter, to be planted out in spring. They will bloom the following May and June. Cuttings may be struck from these two-year stocks, when they are fine enough to be worth it, under a glass in the common borders, like Wallflowers. *M. tristis*, the night-smelling stock, is a greenhouse shrub; and though not showy, the flowers being of a dull livid color, yet it is desirable on account of its powerful evening fragrance: this grows in a light sandy loamy compost, and is propagated by cuttings.

M. annua (annual, or ten-weeks); hardy annual; 1 foot; flowers scarlet, purple, white, yellow, and pink, all summer; south of Europe; 1731. *M. glabrata* (wall-flowered-leaved); hardy sub-shrub; 2 feet; flowers purple, scarlet, or white, in June; native country unknown. *M. Græca* (smooth-leaved annual); hardy annual; 1 foot; flowers purple, white, and pink, all summer; Greece. *M. incana* (hoary, or queen's); hardy sub-shrub; 2 feet; flowers scarlet, purple, and white, in June; south of Europe. *M. odoratissima* (sweetest); greenhouse sub-shrub; 2 feet; flowers cream-colored, changing to purplish-brown, sweet in the evening, in June; Tauria; 1795. *M. simplicicaulis* (single-stemmed or Brompton or Giant); half-hardy biennial; 3 feet; flowers purple, scarlet, or white, in July; native country unknown. *M. tristis* (sad); greenhouse sub-shrub; 18 inches; flowers livid, in June; south of Europe; 1768.

MATRICARIA. [Compositæ.] Weedy hardy annuals for the most part, with single white daisy-like flowers. The only exception worth cultivating is a double-flowered variety of *M. chamomilla*, called *grandiflora*, which, as it does not bear seed, may, if frequently renewed, be continued as a perennial; its double white blossoms render it deserving of being grown in a mixed border. The young shoots should be taken off from near the root, and treated like cuttings. Common garden soil.

M. chamomilla grandiflora (double-flowered); hardy perennial; 1 foot; flowers white, in July; gardens.

MAURANDIA. [Scrophularinæ.] Ornamental greenhouse climbers of slender habit, and also suitable for planting in the open air during the summer, for the purpose of covering wire-fences, and pillars. They are best raised from seeds, which, to insure strong-blooming plants, should be sown about June, and the young plants potted singly, and kept in small pots during winter in a greenhouse. These, if shifted into larger pots in February or March, will be strong and vigorous by the planting-out time, — May. For the greenhouse, they require shifting into large pots of rich soil, of which the basis is sandy loam, and training about pillars, short rafters, or suitable trellises. They grow to a considerable size when their roots have free scope. They may be increased from cuttings, which root readily in sand, in a hotbed.

M. antirrhiniflora (snapdragon-flowered); greenhouse climbing perennial; 10 feet; flowers purple, all summer; Mexico; 1814. *M. Barclayana* (Barclay's); greenhouse climbing perennial; 12 feet; flowers purple, rose-color, or white, all summer; Mexico; 1825. *M. semperflorens* (ever-flowering); greenhouse climbing perennial; 12 feet; flowers pale rose-color, all summer; Mexico; 1796.

MAZUS. [Scrophularinæ.] Small-flowered half-hardy annuals. Light sandy soil. Increased by seeds.

M. pumilus (dwarf); half-hardy annual; 6 inches; flowers pale-purplish, in June; Van Diemen's Land; 1823. *M. rugosus* (wrinkled); half-hardy annual; 6 inches; flowers white and yellow, in July; China; 1780.

MEADOW-RUE. See THALICTRUM.

MEADOW-SAFFRON. See COLCHICUM.

MECONOPSIS. [Papaveraceæ.] Hardy poppy-like herbaceous perennials. Soil, sandy loam. Increased by seeds, sown in May, or by division.

M. Cambrica (Welsh); hardy perennial; 1 foot; flowers buff-yellow, in June; England. *M. crassifolia* (thick-leaved); hardy perennial; 1 foot; flowers orange-red, in June; California; 1833. *M. heterophylla* (various-leaved); hardy perennial; 1 foot; flowers orange-red, in June; California; 1833. *M. Wallichii* (Wallich's); half-hardy perennial; 2 feet; flowers pale-blue, in June; Sikkim; 1851.

MEDEOLA. [Trilliaceæ.] Hardy herbaceous perennial. Soil, free turfy peat. Increased by division, in spring.

M. Virginica (Virginian); hardy perennial; 9 inches; flowers yellow, in June; Virginia; 1759.

MEDICAGO. *Medick.* [Leguminosæ.] A large genus of hardy plants, of no horticultural importance.

MEDLAR. See MESPILUS.

MELIA. [Meliaceæ.] A genus of showy small trees, one of which succeeds well in the Southern States.

M. Azedarach; flowers lilac, in June; Syria; 1656.

MELILOTUS. *Melilot.* [Leguminosæ.] A genus of hardy plants, of little importance as objects of ornament. They are, however, useful as food for bees. *M. arborea*, a shrubby kind, with white flowers; *M. leucantha*, a biennial, also with white flowers; and *M. suaveolens*, a perennial, with yellow blossoms, — are the most desirable.

MELISSA. *Balm.* [Lamiaceæ.] Hardy herbaceous perennials. Common soil. Increased by division.

M. polyanthos (many-flowered); hardy perennial; 1 foot; flowers white, in July; native country unknown. *M. Pyrenaica* (Pyrenæan); hardy perennial; 1 foot; flowers purple, in July; Pyrenees; 1800.

MELITTIS. *Bastard Balm.* [Lamiaceæ.] Hardy herbaceous perennials, of easy culture, propagated by division, and growing in ordinary garden soil. They are rather pretty.

M. grandiflora (large-flowered); hardy perennial; 1 foot; flowers creamy-white and red, in May; England. *M. melissophyllum* (balm-leaved); hardy perennial; 1 foot; flowers pale reddish-purple, in June; England.

MENIOCUS. [Cruciferæ.] Hardy annual. Common soil. Increased by seeds.

M. linifolius (flax-leaved); hardy annual; 6 inches; flowers yellow, in July; Caucasus; 1717.

MENISPERMUM. *Moon-seed.* [Menispermaceæ.] The genus contains one or two hardy deciduous climbers, with ornamental foliage.

M. Canadense (Canadian); hardy climber; 20 feet; flowers white, in June; North America; 1691. *M. Carolinum* (Carolinian), otherwise called *Cocculus Carolinus*, is not hardy in the Northern States. *M. lobatum* is a variety of Canadense.

MENTHA. *Mint.* [Lamiaceæ.] A genus of hardy herbaceous perennials, thriving in any soil, and increased by division. There are some twenty species, of little horticultural importance.

MENTZELIA. [Loasaceæ.] Half-hardy herbaceous perennials and annuals. Soil, sandy loam and peat. Increased by cuttings in sand, in a hot-bed, or by seeds in a slight heat.

M. aspera (rough); hardy annual; 18 inches; flowers yellow, in July; America; 1733. *M. stipitata* (stalked-flowered); half-hardy perennial; 2 feet; flowers yellow, in September; Mexico; 1835.

MENYANTHES. *Buck-bean.* [Gentianaceæ.] Hardy aquatic perennial. Moist boggy soil, or in shallow water. Increased by division.

M. trifoliata (three-leaved); hardy aquatic; 1 foot; flowers white and pink, in June; Britain.

M. var. Americana, our native variety, seems to differ but little from the European species.

MENZIESIA. [Ericaceæ.] Pretty dwarf hardy deciduous shrubs. Sandy peat soil. Increased by layers, or by cuttings under a hand-glass.

M. ferruginea (rusty); hardy deciduous shrub; 3 feet; flowers rust-color, in June; North America; 1811. *M. globularis* (globular); hardy deciduous shrub; 3 feet; flowers yellowish-brown, in June; North America; 1806.

MERENDERA. [Melanthaceæ.] Hardy crocus-like bulb. Soil, peat and loam. Increased by offsets.

M. Caucasica (Caucasian); hardy bulb; 3 inches; flowers purple, in August; Caucasus; 1823.

MESPILUS. *Medlar.* [Pomaceæ.] Hardy deciduous trees, with white flowers and worthless fruit. In bloom, the tree is ornamental, and deserves a place in the shrubbery. Propagated by grafting on thorn, by seeds, and layers. *M. Germanica* is the chief species, of which there are many varieties.

MEZEREON. See DAPHNE.

MIGNONETTE. See RESEDA.

MIKANIA. [Compositæ.] A very neat climbing plant, with Eupatorium-like flowers, flourishing in rather damp, deep loam. This plant is very beautiful, and is covered with white blossoms in August, a season when few climbers bloom. It is a native of river banks.

M. scandens (climbing); hardy climbing herbaceous perennial; 10 feet; flowers white, in August.

There are other stove species.

MILFOIL. See ACHILLEA.

MILK-VETCH. See ASTRAGALUS.

MILKWORT. See POLYGALA.

MIMOSA. This large family contains the sensitive plants, *M. sensitiva* and *M. pudica*, two stove shrubs, the foliage of which is endowed with a very remarkable and interesting sensibility, for the sake of which they are cultivated. The flowers of both are purplish, — little globular balls of colored threads, — not at all showy; but the leaves are very elegant. The peculiarity which obtains for them both their name and popularity is the shrinking of the branches, and folding-up of the leaves, at the slightest touch or disturbance. If a leaf be touched, it falls down, and the leaflets close; and if the whole plant be shaken, or jerked, all the leaves immediately close, and hang down. The seeds are sown in a hot-bed in April, and potted off, as soon as they are large enough to handle, into small-sized three-inch pots, in a light soil of sandy peat and loam. They are best kept in a hot-frame till June, when they may be planted out in a warm exposure. They seed freely enough; but, when they are grown for seed, they are sown in February, and potted off in March. They are also increased by cuttings in sand under bell-glasses, in heat. *M. sensitiva* is not so irritable as *M. pudica*. They are only grown as curiosities. There are many other Mimosas, chiefly shrubs of little interest.

M. pudica (chaste or humble plant); stove shrub; 2 feet; flowers purplish-lilac, in June; Brazil; 1638. *M. sensitiva* (sensitive); stove shrub; 2 feet; flowers pinkish-lilac, in June; Brazil; 1648.

MIMULUS. *Monkey-flower.* [Scrophularinæ.] Showy herbaceous plants, mostly perennial; some small musk plants are annuals. The ornamental garden Mimuluses are mostly seedling varieties raised by florists, the offspring of *M. luteus, guttatus* and *variegatus* on the one hand, and of *M. cardinalis* and *roseus* on the other; and little trace of the originals now remains. These races are fugitive, the varieties of to-day continually giving place to others of some supposed superiority. Rich loamy soil, or, indeed, ordinary garden soil, if good, will grow them well; but they like a damp, cool, and somewhat shady situation in summer. A supply should be kept in pots, protected in cold frames through the winter. *M. moschatus* is a favorite pot-plant for the window: it is quite hardy in sheltered situations, and grows readily in pots of rich mould. The varieties are multiplied by division, and new varieties are obtained from seeds, which, if sown in heat in March, and grown in frames, will come into bloom in the course of the summer. Seeds are freely produced.

M. cardinalis (cardinal); half-hardy perennial; 3 feet; flowers scarlet, in July; California; 1835. *M. guttatus* (spotted); hardy perennial; 1 foot; flowers yellow-spotted, in June; North America; 1812. *M. Harrisonii* (Harrison's); half-hardy perennial; 3 feet; flowers rose, in June; garden variety. *M. luteus* (yellow); hardy perennial; 18 inches; flowers yellow, in June; Chili; 1826. *M. McLainii* (McLain's); half-hardy perennial; 3 feet; flowers rose-crimson, in June; garden variety. *M. moschatus* (musk); hardy perennial; 6 inches; flowers yellow, in June; Columbia; 1826. *M. roseus* (rose); half-hardy perennial; 2 feet; flowers rose, in June; California; 1831. *M. tricolor* (three-colored); half-hardy annual; 9 inches; flowers pink, with yellow and crimson spots, in June; California; 1848. *M. variegatus* (variegated); hardy perennial; 1 foot; flowers white and purple, in June; Chili; 1831. The garden varieties are of two classes: 1, with rosy-colored flowers, and a branching habit, from *E. roseus*, and *cardinalis*; 2, dwarfer, and more herbaceous, with yellow flowers, variously blotched with rich brown-red, from *M. guttatus*, and *luteus*.

MINT. See MENTHA.

MIRABILIS. *Marvel of Peru.* [Nyctaginaceæ.] Showy

half-hardy perennials, with thick fusiform roots. These plants are deservedly great favorites in gardens, where they make towards autumn a splendid appearance. The branching stems bear roundish flowers with rather a long tube; and, as these come at every joint, when fairly open they cover the plant. The individual blooms are in one respect like the Convolvulus, — they shut up on dull days, so that it is not a handsome plant in bad weather. In some kinds, the tubes of the flowers are two or three inches long; in others they are shorter. The colors vary from yellow to red, white, and all shades between them, and sometimes two of the colors are disposed in stripes. To have choice varieties, sow the best seed that can be got, and select each year the best that are produced, for seed-bearing. Sow the seed in a hot-bed in March, and, as soon as the plants are large enough, pot them three or four, or half a dozen, in a pot, to grow until the middle of May, when they may be planted out in the beds or borders a foot apart. Here they will only require to be kept clear of weeds, and be watered in the event of the weather proving more than usually parching, but not if the weather be at all seasonable. The foliage will be touched by the first frost, after which the roots may be dug up, and stored away amongst dry sand, where the frost cannot reach them. In May, they may be put in the ground where they are to flower, whether that be in beds or borders; or, if any good ones are worth propagating, put them in heat in March, and strike the shoots like those of the Dahlia. To effect improvements, a few seeds from the very best should be saved every year, and these plants are then best grown in beds, as they can then be more readily examined, and the worthless ones destroyed. It is in the size, colors, and markings of the flowers, that improvements are chiefly to be effected.

M. Jalapa (Jalap); half-hardy perennial; 2 feet; flowers various, in June; West Indies; 1596. *M. longiflora* (long-flowered); half-hardy perennial; 2 feet; flowers white, in June; Mexico; 1759. *M. suaveolens* (sweet); half-hardy perennial; 2 feet; flowers white, in June; Mexico; 1823.

MITCHELLA. [Cinchonaceæ.] A pretty little evergreen trailing plant, usually known as Checkerberry, ornamental in flower, foliage, and fruit. The whole plant has a rich aromatic taste. For covering the surface of Rhododendron-beds, this little plant is most suitable, as it delights in a soil of peat and leaf-mould.

M. repens (creeping); 2 inches; flowers pinkish-white, in June.

MITELLA. [Saxifragaceæ.] Hardy herbaceous perennials, suitable for rock-work. Common soil. Increased by division.

M. cordifolia (heart-leaved); hardy perennial; 6 inches; flowers white, in May; North America; 1812. *M. diphylla* (two-leaved); hardy perennial; 6 inches; flowers white, in May; North America; 1731. *M. pentandra* (five-stamened); hardy perennial; 6 inches; flowers yellow, in June; North America; 1827. *M. prostrata* (prostrate); hardy perennial; 6 inches; flowers white, in May; North America; 1818.

MOCK-ORANGE. See PHILADELPHUS.

MODIOLA. [Malvaceæ.] Half-hardy annuals and perennials. Common soil. Increased by seeds or divisions.

M. Caroliniana (Carolinian); hardy annual; 1 foot; flowers red, in June; Carolina; 1723. *M. decumbens* (decumbent); half-hardy perennial; 1 foot; flowers red, in June; South America; 1815. *M. prostrata* (prostrate); half-hardy perennial; 1 foot; flowers red, in June; Monte Video; 1806.

MOMORDICA. [Cucurbitaceæ.] A genus of tender plants, for the most part uninteresting for garden culture. One or two of them are, however, elegant and curious, somewhat slender, free-growing creepers, often grown in a greenhouse, or in sheltered places out doors in summer. The fruit is the remarkable part of the plant; and this, which is highly colored orange, splits when ripe, and turns back like a Turk's-cap lily, the deep red seeds attached to its inner surface looking like crimson spots. Sow in a hot-bed in April, in light rich soil, and treat like a cucumber. They are desirable for rafters of a stove. The species referred to are *M. balsamina* and *charantia*, both growing ten or twelve feet in length, and covering a considerable surface. The flowers are yellow, small, and inconspicuous. Both are natives of India.

MONARDA. [Lamiaceæ.] Handsome hardy herbaceous perennials, the plants having an odor compared to Bergamot. They are increased by division of the root, and flourish in the ordinary soil of gardens, preferring a cool and rather moist situation.

M. didyma (Oswego tea); hardy perennial; 3 feet; flowers scarlet, in June; North America; 1752. *M. fistulosa* (hollow); hardy perennial; 4 feet; flowers purple or red, in June; North America; 1656. *M. Kalmiana* (Kalm's); hardy perennial; 4 feet; flowers purple, in June; North America; 1813. *M. punctata* (dotted); hardy perennial; 18 inches; flowers yellowish, dotted with brown, in June; Virginia; 1714. *M. purpurea* (purple); hardy perennial; 3 feet; flowers purple, in June; North America; 1789.

MONEYWORT. See LYSIMACHIA.
MONKEY-FLOWER. See MIMULUS.
MONKSHOOD. See ACONITUM.
MONOLOPIA. [Compositæ.] Pretty hardy annuals. Good garden soil. Increased by seeds.

M. major (greater); hardy annual; 3 feet; flowers yellow, in July; California; 1834.

This plant was formerly called *Helenium Douglasii*.

GARDEN FLOWERS. 261

MOONSEED. See MENISPERMUM.

MONOPSIS. [Lobeliaceæ.] ' A pretty little annual, formerly called *Lobelia speculum*. Seeds sown in a hot-bed in April, and pricked out in May, make a pretty summer show.

M. conspicua (showy); hardy annual; 6 inches; flowers blue, in July; Cape of Good Hope; 1812.

MORNA. [Compositæ.] Showy greenhouse plants. The annual species should be raised from seeds in autumn, about September, and again in spring, about April; the former blooming the following spring, the latter during summer and autumn. Prick out the seedlings, and pot when large enough, three or four in a pot. Shift them as required for blooming in pots in the greenhouse; or a portion may be planted out in a warm situation towards the end of June. Light rich compost should be used, as loam, leaf-mould, and sand. The perennial kinds are increased by cuttings as well as by seeds.

M. nitida (shining); half-hardy perennial; 2 feet; flowers yellow, in June; Swan River; 1835. *M. nivea* (snowy); half-hardy annual; 18 inches; flowers white, in July; New South Wales; 1836.

MORUS. *Mulberry*. [Moraceæ.] Well-known hardy trees, valuable for fruit and flowers. Garden soil. Propagated by seed, cuttings, and layers.

M. alba (white); 30 feet; flowers in June; China; 1596. *M. alba Italica* (Italian); 20 feet; flowers in June; Italy; 1817. *M. alba multicaulis* (many-stemmed); flowers in June; China. *M. Constantinopolitana* (Constantinople); 15 feet; flowers in June; Turkey; 1818. *M. nigra* (common-black); 20 feet; flowers in June; Italy; 1548. *M. nigra laciniata* (cut-leaved); 30 feet; flowers in June. *M. rubra* (red); 10 feet; flowers in June; North America; 1629. *M. scabra* (rough); 20 feet; flowers in June; North America; 1817. *M. Tatarica* (Tartarian); 20 feet; flowers in June; Tartary; 1780.

MORNING-GLORY. See CONVOLVULUS and IPOMEA.

MOTHERWORT. See LEONURUS.

MOUTAN. *Tree Peony*. [Ranunculaceæ.] These are well-known and highly ornamental shrubs. Soil, peat and loam. They are multiplied by grafting on the fleshy roots of the herbaceous peonies, and also by layers. The plants are hardy; but are suitable for growing as large pot plants, to be set in any effective sheltered position while they remain in bloom. Any of the numerous varieties are worth cultivating.

M. officinalis (common); hardy shrub; 3 feet; flowers various colored in the numerous varieties, in April; China; 1789. Among the most desirable are the varieties named *atropurpurea* (deep-purple), *Berenice* (white), *Emperor of China* (rosy-red), *globosa* (white), *Glory of Shanghae* (white), *lilacina* (pale-purple), *picta* (rose-striped), *punicea* (crimson), *Robert Fortune* (bright-red), *salmonea* (pale-salmon), *speciosa* (pink), and *sulphurea* (primrose).

There are, besides, varieties with the flowers white, flesh-color, pale-pink, pale-rose, purple, and of mixed colors. For a longer list see PEONIA.

MULGEDIUM. [Compositæ.] A pretty half hardy perennial, suitable for dry rock-work, or a very dry border. Soil, sandy loam, well drained. Increased by seeds, cuttings, or division.

M. macrorhizon (large-rooted); hardy perennial; 9 inches; flowers pale-blue, in August; Cashmere; 1844.

MULBERRY. See MORUS.

MULLEIN. See VERBASCUM.

MUSCARI. *Grape Hyacinth*. [Liliaceæ.] Dwarf hardy bulbs, which multiply readily by means of offsets. The bulbs should remain in the soil from year to year, and not be taken up and dried; but every fourth year, they may be taken up and replanted in September, or early in October, before they begin to grow. Common garden soil; but a sandy loam is most congenial to these, as to all other bulbs.

M. botryoides (bunch-flowered); hardy bulb; 6 inches; flowers blue or white, in May; Italy; 1596. *M. ciliatum* (hair-fringed); hardy bulb; 9 inches; flowers brown-purple, in May; Crimea; 1822. *M. commutatum* (dark-purple); hardy bulb; 6 inches; flowers dark-blue, in May; Italy; 1836. *M. comosum* (feathered); hardy bulb; 6 inches; flowers purple, in May; south of Europe; 1596. *M. glaucum* (glaucous); hardy bulb; 9 inches; flowers purple and green, in May; Persia; 1825. *M. moschatum* (musky); hardy bulb; 9 inches; flowers pale dingy-brownish, in May; Levant; 1596. *M. racemosum* (racemed); hardy bulb; 6 inches; flowers dark-blue, in May; Europe; 1780.

MYOSOTIS. [Scrophularineæ.] A genus of pretty annuals and herbaceous plants, many of them hardy. *M. palustris* is the true Forget-me-not; a pretty well-known flower, delicate blue, with golden eye. It needs a moist soil, and, in a congenial situation, will become naturalized. Some of the species are not hardy in the Northern States. The perennials are increased by seed and division; the annuals by seed.

HARDY HERBACEOUS. — *M. Alpestris* (Alpine); 6 inches; flowers blue, in July; Switzerland; 1818. *M. Azorica* (Azorean); 1 foot; flowers dark-blue, in August; Azores; 1846. *M. azurea* (light-blue); flowers blue, in June; Corvo; 1842. *M. cæspitosa* (tufted); 9 inches; flowers blue, in June; Britain. *M. cæspitosa macrocalyx* (large-calyxed); 9 inches; flowers blue, in June; Britain. *M. intermedia* (intermediate); 6 inches; flowers blue, in April; Britain. *M. nana* (dwarf); 6 inches; flowers blue, in July; Europe; 1800. *M. palustris* (marsh); 1 foot; flowers blue and yellow, in July; Britain. *M. repens* (creeping); 1 foot; flowers pale-blue, in June; Britain. *M. rupicola* (rock); flowers blue; Scotland. *M. sparsiflora* (scattered-flowered); 18 inches; flowers blue, in May; south of France; 1822.

HARDY ANNUALS. — *M. arvensis alba* (white corn-field); 6 inches; flowers white, in June; Britain. *M. Australis* (southern); flowers blue, in June; New South Wales; 1824. *M. Californica* (Californian); 18 inches; flowers white, in August; California; 1837. *M. clavata* (club-leaved); flowers blue, in June; Siberia; 1829. *M. collina* (hill); 3 inches; flowers blue, in May; Britain. *M. commutata* (changed); flowers blue, in June; Europe; biennial. *M. litoralis* (sea-shore); flowers blue and yellow, in April; Caspian Sea; 1836. *M. peduncularis* (long-flowered-stalked); 18 inches; flowers blue, in June; Astracan; 1824. *M. ungulata* (clawed); flowers blue, in June; Siberia; 1822.

MYRICA. *Wax Myrtle.* [Myricaceæ.] Hardy deciduous shrubs, thriving in any soil, and increased by seeds and layers.

M. cerifera (wax-bearing); 6 feet; *M. gale* (sweet-gale); 4 feet; *M. latifolia* (broad-leaved); 4 feet; are all very ornamental in the shrubbery.

NARCISSUS. [Amaryllidaceæ.] A very large genus of showy, hardy, well-known bulbous-rooted plants, all species of which are ornamental and desirable spring border flowers. Under the name of Polyanthus Narcissus, great numbers of some florists' varieties are imported annually, like the Hyacinth and early Tulips; and these may be forced in pots, or bloomed in water, or planted in the borders. They require in every respect the same treatment as the Hyacinth. If grown in pots, they may be planted in any rich, light soil. If bloomed in glasses, they want a change of water once a week. When put out in the borders, they should be in patches of three, put in pretty close to each other, forming a triangle, with one in front and two behind : a sandy loam is preferable for them. They require no protection except a covering of tan over the bed in the Northern States, and will bear a good deal of frost without injury. The plant has grassy or leek-like leaves : the flower-stem comes up in the centre, and from a sheath at the top bursts on one side the bunch of flowers, which are white or yellow, with a yellow or orange cup in the centre. The Jonquil is a species of Narcissus, considerably smaller than the Polyanthus Narcissus, and very sweet-scented : there are varieties with both double and single flowers. There is considerable variety among the other species of Narcissus, all of which are worth growing as border-flowers. The following very limited selection comprises a few of the most distinct plants.

N. aurantius (orange); hardy bulb; 1 foot; flowers yellow, in March; south of Europe; 1629. There is a double-flowered variety, with yellow and orange blossoms. *N. bicolor* (two-colored); hardy bulb; 1 foot; flowers white and yellow, in April; Spain; 1629. *N. cernuus* (drooping); hardy bulb; 1 foot; flowers creamy white, in March; Spain; 1818. *N. incomparabilis* (incomparable); hardy bulb; 1 foot; flowers yellow, in April; France; 1629. *N. Italicus* (Roman); hardy bulb; 1 foot; flowers pale-yellow, in March; Italy. The double variety has creamy flowers. *N. jonquilla* (jonquil); hardy bulb; 9 inches; flowers yellow, single or double, in April; Spain; 1596. *N. montanus* (mountain); hardy bulb; 1 foot; flowers white, in April; Spain. *N. odorus* (sweet); hardy bulb; 1 foot; flowers yellow, in May; south of Europe; 1629. *N. papyraceus* (paper); hardy bulb; 1 foot; flowers white, in March; Asia Minor. *N. poeticus* (poet's); hardy bulb; 1 foot; flowers white, with orange eye, in May; Europe. *N. pulchellus* (pretty); hardy bulb; 9 inches; flowers yellow, in May; south of Europe. *N. recurvus* (recurved-leaved); hardy bulb; 1 foot; flowers white, with orange eye, in May; south of Europe. *N. Tazetta* (polyanthus); hardy bulb; 1 foot; flowers white and yellow, in March; Spain; 1759. *N. Trewianus* (Trew's); hardy bulb; 1 foot; flowers white and yellow, in March; Spain. This is cultivated under the name of *Bazelman major*.

FLORISTS' VARIETIES. The following are superior kinds: *Bazleman major*, white and yellow; *Grand Monarque*, white and citron; *Grand Primo*, white and citron; *Grand Prince*, white and lemon; *Soleil d'or*, yellow and orange; *Gloriosa*, white and orange, the best for pot-culture.

NARDOSMIA. [Compositæ.] Hardy perennial. Common soil. Increased by division. Allied to Colt's-foot.

N. fragrans (fragrant); hardy perennial; 6 inches; flowers white, in very early spring, fragrant like Heliotrope; south of Europe; 1806.

NASTURTIUM. The vulgar name often given to *Tropæolum*, instead of the proper one of *Indian Cress.*

NAVARETTIA. See ÆGOCHLOA.

NEAPOLITAN VIOLET; *Viola odorata pallida plena.*

NEGUNDO. [Aceraceæ.] Hardy deciduous trees, thriving in sandy loam. Propagated by seed and layers.

N. fraxinifolium (ash-leaved maple); 40 feet; flowers in May; 1688. *N. fraxinifolium crispum* (curled-leaved); 30 feet; flowers, in May; 1688. *N. fraxinifolium violaceum* (purple); 30 feet; flowers in May. *N. fraxinifolium variegatum* is a beautiful plant.

NEJA. [Compositæ.] Half-hardy sub-shrub, suitable for summer beds. Light rich soil. Increased by cuttings.

N. gracilis (slender); half-hardy sub-shrub; 1 foot; flowers yellow, all summer; Mexico; 1828.

NEMESIA. [Scrophularineæ.] Half-hardy annuals or perennials. Sandy loamy soil. Increased by seeds or cuttings.

N. floribunda (many-flowered); half-hardy annual; 1 foot; flowers white and yellow, in July; Cape; 1837.

NEMOPHILA. [Hydrophyllaceæ.] Hardy annuals. The best is *N. insignis*, of which the flowers are very bright blue, with a white eye, and cover the plant: it is on this account a most beautiful plant for clumps and beds. *N. maculata* is another showy species. For beds, the seedlings should be put out four inches apart, and the plants will then present a dense mass of flowers. The soil should not be too rich; for, if the plants grow rank, they become straggling, and flower less abundantly.

N. atomaria (speckled); hardy annual; 9 inches; flowers white, speckled with purple, in May; California; 1836. A variety called *discoidalis* has flowers very dark-brown, narrowly margined with white. *N. aurita* (eared); hardy annual; 1 foot; flowers purple, in June; California. *N. insignis* (showy); hardy annual; 9 inches; flowers blue and white, in May; California; 1833. There are seedling variations with larger, and with speckled flowers. *N. maculata* (blotched); hardy annual; 9 inches; flowers white and purple, in May; California; 1848.

N. phaceloides (phacelia-like); hardy annual; 1 foot; flowers blue, in June; North America.

NEOTTIA. [Orchidaceæ.] A genus containing some hardy perennial, as well as tender species. Soil, peat and loam. Increased by division. *N. æstivalis, autumnalis*, and *cernuus* are worth growing as curiosities.

NEMOPANTHES. [Aquifoliaceæ.] An ornamental, hardy, deciduous, upright-growing shrub, very little known, but very desirable. It was called *Ilex Canadensis* and *Prinos lucida*. The flowers are small and white; but the berries are large, beautiful crimson, and very ornamental. Common shrubbery soil; but it will do better with an addition of sandy peat or leaf-mould. Propagated by layers and seeds in autumn, and by seeds in spring.

N. Canadensis (Canadian); 3 feet; flowers in May; North America; 1812.

NEPETA. *Catmint.* [Lamiaceæ.] A rather large genus of hardy perennials, few of which are ornamental. Sandy garden soil. Increased by division.

N. grandiflora (large-flowered); hardy perennial; 6 feet; flowers blue, in July; Caucasus; 1817. *N. Sibirica* (Siberian); hardy perennial; 2 feet; flowers purple, in July; Siberia; 1804.

NETTLE-TREE. See CELTIS.

NEW-JERSEY TEA. See CEANOTHUS.

NICANDRA. [Solanaceæ.] Robust half-hardy annual, with blue and white flowers; pretty, but running too much to foliage. It should be sown in a mild hot-bed with other annuals towards the end of April, and the plants planted out in May; or it may be sown in the border in May, and all the plants in each patch pulled away but the strongest. When a little stunted, it looks pretty in a large border; the blossoms then being developed in a greater proportion to the leaves.

N. physaloides (physalis-like); hardy annual; 4 feet; flowers blue and white, in July; Peru; 1759.

NICOTIANA. *Tobacco.* [Solanaceæ.] An extensive genus, the species mostly hardy annuals. The most interesting is the *N. Tabacum*, or Virginia tobacco, of which several varieties, all having rose-colored flowers, are pretty enough to be introduced sparingly into large miscellaneous flower-borders: they grow from three to six feet high, according to the soil and climate. *N. Langsdorffii*, with green flowers and blue anthers, is rather pretty. Of the common annual species, the seeds may be scattered over the borders in May, and a single plant left here and there where there is room for them. The Virginian tobacco must be sown in a warm frame in April, and treated like a half-hardy annual, being planted out in May, to produce fine blooming plants. From the size to which these plants grow, with their ample foliage, they should always be planted singly. Seeds are produced in abundance, by which they are increased.

N. Langsdorffii (Langsdorff's); hardy annual; 3 feet; flowers green, in July; Chili; 1819. *N. paniculata* (panicled); hardy annual; 3 feet; flowers green, in July; Peru; 1752. *N. Persica* (Persian); half-hardy annual; 2 feet; flowers white and green, in September; Persia; 1831. *N. Tabacum* (Virginian); half-hardy annual; 4 feet; flowers pink, in July; America; 1570. *N. undulata* (wavy); half-hardy perennial, may be cultivated as an annual; 2 feet; flowers white, in July; New South Wales; 1800.

NIEREMBERGIA. [Solanaceæ.] Pretty half-hardy herbs, suitable for the flower-garden, and for small beds. Sandy loam and peat. Propagated by cuttings in sand, during summer. The plants must be wintered in a dry airy greenhouse, with precaution against damp. They may be planted out in May.

N. calycina (large-calyxed); half-hardy perennial; 6 inches;

flowers white, in July; Uruguay; 1834. *N. filicaulis* (thread-stemmed); half-hardy perennial; 9 inches; flowers white and lilac, in July; Buenos Ayres; 1832. *N. gracilis* (slender); half-hardy perennial; 6 inches; flowers white and lilac, in July; Uruguay; 1831. *N. intermedia* (intermediate); half-hardy perennial; 9 inches; flowers purple, black, and yellow, in July; Buenos Ayres; 1832.

NIGELLA. *Fennel-flower*, or *Devil-in-a-bush*. [Ranunculaceæ.] Hardy annuals, requiring only to be sown in the open border in May, and the plants thinned to three or four inches apart, six or eight being left in a patch. The flowers have a singular form and curious appearance.

N. aristata (awned); hardy annual; 2 feet; flowers blue, in July; Greece. *N. coarctata* (compressed); hardy annual; 9 inches; flowers white, in July; south of Europe; 1793. *N. damascena* (common); hardy annual; 18 inches; flowers blue, single or double, in June; south of Europe; 1570. *N. Hispanica* (Spanish); hardy annual; 18 inches; flowers blue or white, in June; Spain; 1629. *N. Orientalis* (Eastern); hardy annual; 18 inches; flowers yellow, in July; Syria; 1699.

NIGHTSHADE. See SOLANUM.

NOLANA. [Nolanaceæ.] Pretty annuals, of prostrate trailing habit, with convolvulus-shaped blossoms. They may be sown in the open ground in May; or may be sown in March, in pots for planting out, and the plants kept in a cold frame till the middle of May. They will flourish in good light garden soil, and are increased by seeds.

N. atriplicifolia (atriplex-leaved); hardy annual; 6 inches; flowers blue, white, and yellow, in July; Peru; 1834. *N. paradoxa* (violet); hardy annual; 6 inches; flowers blue, in July; Chili; 1825. *N. prostrata* (prostrate); hardy annual; 6 inches; flowers blue, in July; Peru; 1761. *N. tenella* (slender); hardy annual; 6 inches; flowers blue, in July; Chili; 1824. Variety *subcærulea* is a fine free-flowering variety, with pale mauve-colored flowers. Variety *lanceolata* is a vigorous grower, with blue flowers.

NORWAY SPRUCE. See ABIES EXCELSA.

NUPHAR. [Nymphæaceæ.] Hardy water-plants, with large floating leaves, like those of *Nymphæa*, but having yellow flowers. The species are worth cultivating. The culture of them is in all respects the same as that of *Nymphæa*.

N. advena (stranger); hardy aquatic perennial, floating; flowers yellow, in July; North America; 1772. *N. Kalmiana* (Kalm's); hardy aquatic perennial, floating; flowers yellow, in July; Canada; 1807. *N. lutea* (yellow); hardy aquatic perennial, floating; flowers yellow, in June; England. *N. pumila* (dwarf); hardy aquatic perennial, floating; flowers yellow, in July; England. *N. sagittæfolia* (arrow-leaved); hardy aquatic perennial, floating; flowers yellow, in July; North America; 1824.

NYCTERINIA. [Scrophularineæ.] Pretty greenhouse plants, requiring to be grown in a sandy soil of peat and loam. Increased by cuttings or seeds. The perennials require an airy greenhouse, and care in watering. The annuals to be treated as half-hardy annuals.

N. lychnidea (lychnis-like); greenhouse evergreen sub-shrub; 1 foot; flowers white and purple, in May; Cape. *N. selaginoides* (selago-like); greenhouse annual; 9 inches; flowers white, with yellow eye, in summer; Cape; 1854.

NYMPHÆA. *Water-lily.* [Nymphæaceæ.] A family of beautiful water-plants, including some of the most desirable for cultivation in hardy aquariums. This genus includes several stove species, as well as the hardy ones; of which latter, nearly all have white flowers. The plants require to be planted in a layer of rich mud at the bottom of the water: and so that there is room enough for their floating foliage, they need little other attention. One of the best ways of fixing the rhizomes, or root-stocks, is to plant them in a common wicker basket filled with mud, the basket being dropped into the water where the plant is required. The tender kinds have to be planted in large pots or pans, which are sunk into cisterns of water; and, in order to secure the blooming of the plants, there ought to be provision for warming the water in the cisterns by some means They are increased by dividing the rhizomes. Both hardy and tender species are worth growing.

N. alba (white); hardy aquatic perennial, floating; flowers white, in June; England. *N. nitida* (shining); hardy aquatic perennial, floating; flowers white, in July; Siberia; 1809. *N. odorata* (sweet); hardy aquatic perennial, floating; flowers white, in July; North America; 1786. *N. pygmæa* (pygmy); half-hardy aquatic perennial, floating; flowers white, in July; China; 1805. *N. reniformis* (kidney-shaped); half-hardy aquatic perennial, floating; flowers white, in July; Carolina; 1823.

NYSSA. *Tupelo.* [Cornaceæ.] Hardy trees, with ornamental foliage, which turns a brilliant red in the autumn. Raised from seed, which should be sown where the plants are to stand, as they transplant with difficulty. Soil, moist loam.

N. multiflora (many-flowered); hardy tree; 20 feet; fruit purple, in autumn. *N. uniflora* (single-flowered) is an aquatic Southern species.

OAK. See QUERCUS.

OATS ANIMATED. See AVENA.

OBELISCARIA. [Compositæ.] Showy hardy perennials. They require the same treatment as Rudbeckia, to which they are allied.

O. columnaris (columnar); hardy perennial; 3 feet; flowers yellow, in August; North America; 1811. *O. Drummondii* (Drummond's); hardy perennial; 3 feet; flowers yellow and black, in July; North America; 1836. *O. pulcherrima* (prettiest); hardy perennial; 3 feet; flowers yellow and red, in August; Texas; 1835.

ŒNOTHERA. *Evening-primrose.* [Onagraceæ.] Showy hardy plants, mostly perennials and biennials, with a few annuals. The annuals require to be sown in May, where they are to flower, and to be thinned when they come up; or they may be sown in a patch, and planted out. Common garden soil. The biennial and perennial kinds should be sown in patches, and planted out when they are large enough, wherever they are to bloom. The latter grow best in peaty soil, and especially in situations where they are not subjected to drought. There are a large number of species. Most of the old-fashioned annual *Œnotheras* are now called *Godetia*.

Œ. biennis (biennial); hardy biennial; 4 feet; flowers yellow, in July; North America; 1629. *Œ. Drummondii* (Drummond's); half-hardy perennial; 1 foot; flowers yellow, in July; Texas; 1833. *Œ. Fraseri* (Fraser's); hardy perennial; 18

inches ; flowers yellow, in June ; North America ; 1811. *Œ. fruticosa* (shrubby) ; hardy perennial ; 3 feet ; flowers yellow, in August ; North America ; 1737. *Œ. Lamarckiana* (Lamarck's) ; hardy biennial ; 3 feet ; flowers bright-yellow, very large ; Texas ; 1860. *Œ. macrocarpa* (large-fruited) ; hardy perennial ; 6 inches ; flowers large yellow, in June ; North America ; 1811. *Œ. Missouriensis* (Missouri) ; hardy perennial ; 6 inches ; flowers large yellow, in June ; North America ; 1818. *Œ. odorata* (sweet) ; hardy biennial ; 2 feet ; flowers yellow, in June ; South America ; 1790. *Œ. pumila* (dwarf) ; hardy perennial ; 6 inches ; flowers yellow, in July ; North America ; 1757. *Œ. speciosa* (showy) ; half-hardy perennial ; 18 inches ; flowers white, in June ; North America ; 1821. *Œ. taraxacifolia* (dandelion-leaved) ; hardy perennial ; 9 inches ; flowers yellow, in June ; Peru ; 1822. *Œ. tetraptera* (four-winged) ; hardy annual ; 1 foot ; flowers white, in July ; Mexico ; 1796.

OLEASTER. See ELÆAGNUS.

OMPHALODES. [Boraginaceæ.] A genus containing two favorite plants, — the annual Venus's Navel-wort, and the early blooming dwarf *O. verna*, whose pretty little bright blue flowers are mistaken by persons not skilled in plants for the Forget-me-not, a very different thing. Both are of the easiest culture. The perennial will increase to any extent by division, and, when once planted, need not be disturbed for years ; for, within moderate limits, the larger the patch of such diminutive subjects, the better. It is very suitable for rock-work which is not too dry and exposed. The annual may be sown in the borders, towards the end of March, and again in May for a succession, and requires only good garden soil.

O. linifolia (Venus's Navel-wort) ; hardy annual ; 1 foot ; flowers white, in June ; Portugal ; 1748. *O. verna* (spring) ; hardy perennial ; 6 inches ; flowers blue, in April ; south of Europe ; 1633.

ONOBRYCHIS. *Saintfoin.* [Leguminosæ.] Hardy perennials. Soil, sandy loam. Increased by seeds. Some are pretty, but not of much importance.

ONONIS. *Restharrow.* [Leguminosæ.] A genus of hardy and half-hardy perennials and annuals. Some of the sub-shrubby species are suitable for large rock-work. Soil, sandy loam. Increased by seeds.

ONOSMA. [Boraginaceæ.] Perennial herbs, mostly hardy, and many of them pretty subjects for rock-work. The flowers are tubularly bell-shaped, and in all cases yellow or yellowish. They grow best on dry and rather sandy soil, such as exposed rockwork, being very liable to rot off in damp confined places; and the tenderer ones need protection from wet in winter. When seeds can be got, they make the best plants: they should be sown about May, either in pots for subsequent transplantation, or in the situations where they are to remain. If seeds cannot be had, they must be increased by cuttings of the young shoots, planted in sandy soil, and placed under a hand-glass.

O. echioides (echium-like); half-hardy perennial; 1 foot; flowers white, in April; south of Europe; 1683. *O. Gmelini* (Gmelin's); hardy perennial; 1 foot; flowers straw-colored, in June; Altai; 1829. *O. Orientale* (Eastern); half-hardy perennial; 6 inches; flowers yellow, in May; Levant; 1752. *O. polyphyllum* (many-leaved); hardy perennial; 1 foot; flowers pale-yellow, in July; Tauria; 1829. *O. rupestre* (rock); half-hardy perennial; 1 foot; flowers yellow, in May; Caucasus; 1819. *O. setosum* (bristly); hardy perennial; 1 foot; flowers yellow, in July; Russia; 1838. *O. stellulatum* (starred); hardy perennial; 6 inches; flowers yellow, in May; Croatia; 1819.

OPHELIA. [Gentianaceæ.] A pretty annual. Peat border. Seeds, to be sown in heat in April; the young plants planted out in May.

O. purpurascens (purplish); half-hardy annual; 9 inches; flowers purplish, in May; East Indies; 1836.

OPHIOPOGON. [Liliaceæ.] Hardy and half-hardy perennial. Sandy loam and peat. Division.

O. Japonicus (Japan); half-hardy perennial; 1 foot; flowers pale-purple, in June; Japan; 1784. *O. spicatus* (spiked); hardy perennial; 1 foot; flowers violet, in October; Nepaul; 1821.

These plants require protection in the Northern States.

ORIGANUM. *Marjoram.* [Lamiaceæ.] In this genus of hardy aromatic herbs are included two pretty greenhouse dwarf shrubs, which are excellent window plants. They increase by cuttings, and grow in sandy loam.

O. Dictamnus (Dittany of Crete); half-hardy sub-shrub; 1 foot; flowers purple, in little drooping heads like hops, in July; Candia; 1551. *O. Sipyleum* (Sipylian); half-hardy sub-shrub; 18 inches; flowers purple, in hop-like heads, in July; Levant; 1699.

ORNITHOGALUM. *Star of Bethlehem.* [Liliaceæ.] An extensive genus of bulbous plants, containing about a score of hardy species, and about twice that number of half-hardy ones. The flowers are star-like, and, in the majority of instances, white, often streaked inside or out with green. They grow readily in rich, light, loamy soil; the hardy ones planted out in the open borders or in beds, and the tender ones potted, and kept in a frame or on a shelf in a cool greenhouse. The taller species, with their long spikes of starry flowers, are very ornamental. They all increase by means of offsets, as is the case with other bulbs.

O. Arabicum (Arabian); half-hardy bulb; 18 inches; flowers white, in March; Egypt; 1629. *O. aureum* (golden); greenhouse bulb; 1 foot; flowers orange, in June; Cape; 1790. *O. comosum* (tufted); hardy bulb; 6 inches; flowers white, in July; Austria; 1596. *O. corymbosum* (corymbose); half-hardy bulb; 1 foot; flowers white, in April; Peru; 1823. *O. exscapum* (stemless); hardy bulb; 6 inches; flowers white, in May;

Italy; 1824. *O. lacteum* (milk-white); half-hardy bulb; 1 foot; flowers white, in June; Cape; 1796. *O. marginatum* (margined); hardy bulb; 9 inches; flowers greenish-white, in May; Asia; 1843. *O. montanum* (mountain); hardy bulb; 6 inches; flowers white, in May; Naples; 1824. *O. Narbonense* (Narbonne); hardy bulb; 18 inches; flowers white, in July; south of Europe; 1810. *O. niveum* (snowy); half-hardy bulb; 6 inches; flowers white, in May; Cape; 1774. *O. odoratum* (sweet); half-hardy bulb; 18 inches; flowers pale-yellow, in May; Cape; 1795. *O. pyramidale* (pyramidal); hardy bulb; 2 feet; flowers white, in June; Spain; 1752. *O. suaveolens* (fragrant); half-hardy bulb; 6 inches; flowers white, in June; Cape; 1826. *O. umbellatum* (umbelled); hardy bulb; 6 inches; flowers white, in May; England.

There are numerous other species deserving of cultivation.

OROBUS. *Bitter Vetch.* [Leguminosæ.] An extensive family of hardy perennials. Common light deep garden soil. Increased by division.

O. atropurpureus (dark-purple); hardy perennial; 1 foot; flowers deep-purple, in May; Algiers; 1826. *O. aurantius* (orange); hardy perennial; 18 inches; flowers yellow, in June; Iberia; 1818. *O. formosus* (showy); hardy perennial; 9 inches; flowers purple, in June; Caucasus; 1818. *O. vernus* (spring); hardy perennial; 1 foot; flowers purple, in May; Europe; 1629.

OSAGE ORANGE. See MACLURA.

ORNUS. *Flowering Ash.* [Oleaceæ.] Hardy deciduous trees, with white flowers. Common garden soil. Propagated by seeds.

O. Americana (American); 30 feet; flowers in May; North America; 1820. *O. Europæa* (European); 20 feet; flowers in May; Italy; 1730. *O. floribunda* (bundle-flowered); 30 feet; Nepaul; 1822. *O. rotundifolia* (round-leaved); 16 feet; flowers in May; Italy; 1697. *O. striata* (channelled); 30 feet; flowers in April; North America; 1818.

OXYDENDRUM. See ANDROMEDA.

OSTRYA. *Hop Hornbeam.* [Corylaceæ.] Hardy deciduous small trees, with fine foliage and ornamental fruit. Increased by seeds, and grafting on common Hornbeam. Rich deep moist soil.

O. Virginica (Virginian); 20 feet; flowers in May; North America; 1622. *O. vulgaris* (common); 20 feet; flowers in May; Italy; 1724.

OSWEGO TEA. *Monarda didyma.*

OXYTROPIS. [Leguminosæ.] A family of mostly hardy plants from Siberia, allied to Astragalus. Soil, sandy loam. Propagated by seeds sown where the plants are to remain, as they transplant badly. There are some forty species.

OXURA. [Compositæ.] A pretty showy chrysanthemum-like annual. Sow in the open border in May, and thin out the plants.

O. chrysanthemoides (chrysanthemum-like); hardy annual; 18 inches; flowers yellow and white, in July; California; 1834.

PÆONIA. [Ranunculaceæ.] Very showy plants, of easy culture in deep rich loam. Propagated by division, if herbaceous; if tree, or Moutan, by division, grafting, cuttings of the young shoots in spring, by layers and suckers, by layering the young shoots after ringing-round each bud so that each bud forms a plant. The shrubby species are sometimes called Moutan (which see). All the species are desirable, and few plants are more showy in the garden and shrubbery.

HARDY SHRUBS. — *P. Moutan* (Chinese-tree); 3 feet; flowers purple, in May; China; 1789. *P. albida-plena* (double-white); 2 feet; flowers white, in May; China. *P. Anneslei* (Annesley's); 3 feet; flowers pink, in May; China. *P. atropurpurea* (dark-purple-flowered); 4 feet; flowers purple, in May; China; 1846. *P. Banksii* (Banks's); 3 feet; flowers purple, in May; China; 1794. *P. carnea-plena* (double-flesh-colored); 2 feet; flowers in May; China. *P. globosa* (globular-flowered); 3 feet; flesh-color, flowers white and purple, in May; Shanghae; 1845. *P. lilacina* (lilac-colored); 3 feet; flowers lilac, in May; China; 1845. *P. Humei* (Hume's); 2 feet; flowers purple, in May; China; 1817. *P. papaveracea* (poppy-like); 3 feet; flowers white, in May; China; 1789. *P. parviflora* (small-flowered); 3 feet; flowers pale-rose, in May; Shanghae; 1845. *P. picta* (painted); 3 feet; flowers pale and deep rose-striped, in May; Canton; 1845. *P. Rawesii* (Rawes's); 2 feet; flowers pale-pink, in May; China; 1820. *P. rosea* (rosy); 3 feet; flowers pink, in May; China. *P. rosea-plena* (double-rose); 2 feet; flowers red, in May; China; 1804. *P. rosea-semi-plena* (semi-double rose);

2 feet; flowers red, in May; China; 1794. *P. salmonea* (salmon-colored); 3 feet; flowers pale-salmon, in May; China; 1846. *P. speciosa* (showy); 2 feet; flowers pink, in May; China; 1825. *P. Alexander II.* is a very large rich rosy-red variety; hybrid; 1860. *P. gloric Belgarum* is the largest Peony known; flowers very double, crimson; hybrid; 1857.

HARDY HERBACEOUS. — *P. albiflora* (white-flowered); 2 feet; flowers white, in May; Siberia; 1548. *P. albiflora candida* (white); 2 feet; flowers flesh-color, in May; Siberia. *P. albiflora festa* (pleasant); 2 feet; flowers white and pink, in June. *P. albiflora fragrans* (fragrant); 2 feet; flowers, red in May; China; 1805. *P. albiflora Humei* (Hume's double-crimson); 2 feet; flowers red, in May; China; 1808. *P. albiflora Pottsii* (Potts's); 3 feet; flowers crimson, in June; China; 1822. *P. albiflora Reevesii* (Reeves's double); 2 feet; flowers pink, in June; China; 1822. *P. albiflora rubescens* (ruddy); 2 feet; flowers pink, in May; Siberia. *P. albiflora Siberica* (Siberian); 2 feet; flowers white, in May; Siberia. *P. albiflora Tatarica* (Tartarian); 2 feet; flowers flesh-color, in May; Siberia. *P. albiflora uniflora* (single-flowered); 2 feet; flowers pink, in May; Siberia. *P. albiflora vestalis* (virgin); 2 feet; flowers white, in May; Siberia. *P. albiflora Whitleji* (Whitley's double-white); 2 feet; flowers blush, in May; China; 1808. *P. anomala* (anomalous); 18 inches; flowers crimson, in May; Siberia; 1788. *P. arietina* (ram); 2 feet; flowers purple; Levant. *P. arietina Andersonii* (Anderson's); flowers rose, in June. *P. arietina Oxoniensis* (Oxford); 2 feet; flowers pale-blush, in June. *P. Brownii* (Brown's); flowers red, in May; North America; 1826. *P. corallina* (coralline); 3 feet; flowers crimson, in May; England. *P. Corsica* (Corsican); flowers purple, in June; Corsica. *P. Cretica* (Cretan); 2 feet; flowers white, in May; Crete. *P. decora* (comely); 2 feet; flowers purple, in May; Turkey. *P. decora elatior* (taller); 2 feet; flowers purple, in May; Crimea. *P. decora Pallasii* (Pallas's); 2 feet; flowers purple, in May; Crimea. *P. humilis* (dwarf); 2 feet; flowers purple, in May; Spain; 1633. *P. hybrida* (hybrid); 2 feet; flowers red, in May; Siberia. *P. lobata* (lobed); 2 feet; flowers purple, in May;

Spain; 1821. *P. mollis* (soft); 18 inches; flowers purple, in May; Siberia. *P. officinalis* (shop); 3 feet; flowers red, in May; Europe; 1548. *P. officinalis albicans* (whitening); 3 feet; flowers white, in May. *P. officinalis anemoniflora* (anemone-flowered); 3 feet; flowers pink, in May; 1830. *P. officinalis Baxteri* (Baxter's); 3 feet; flowers crimson; Oxford. *P. officinalis blanda* (bland); 3 feet; flowers white, in May. *P. officinalis canescens* (hoary); 3 feet; flowers white, in May. *P. officinalis multipetala* (many-petaled); 3 feet; flowers crimson, in May. *P. officinalis rosea* (rosy); 3 feet; flowers red, in May. *P. officinalis rubra* (double-red); 3 feet; flowers red, in May. *P. officinalis variegata* (variegated-leaved); 3 feet; flowers crimson, in June. *P. paradoxa* (paradoxical); 2 feet; flowers purple, in May; Levant. *P. paradoxa compacta* (compact); 2 feet; flowers purple, in May. *P. paradoxa fimbriata* (double-fringed); 2 feet; flowers purple, in May. *P. paradoxa Grevillii* (Greville's); 2 feet; flowers purple, in May. *P. paradoxa peregrina* (straggling); 2 feet; flowers dark-purple, in May. *P. pubens* (downy); 2 feet; flowers red, in May. *P. Reevesiana* (Reeves's) 3 feet; flowers crimson, in May; China. *P. Russi* (Russ's); 2 feet; flowers crimson, in May; Sicily. *P. simpliciflora* (simple-flowered); flowers red, in May; Levant. *P. tenuifolia* (fine-leaved); 18 inches; flowers red, in May; Siberia; 1765. *P. tenuifolia flore-pleno* (double-flowered); 18 inches; flowers red, in May; Russia; 1831. *P. tenuifolia latifolia* (broad-leaved); 2 feet; flowers crimson, in June. *P. triternata* (thrice-three-leafleted); 3 feet; flowers purple, in May; Siberia; 1790. *P. villosa* (shaggy); 2 feet; flowers red, in May; south of Europe; 1816. *P. Witmanniana* (Witmann's); 2 feet; flowers greenish-yellow, in May; Abcharia; 1842.

For new varieties, which are constantly produced, consult the latest florist catalogues.

PALAFOXIA. [Compositæ.] Annuals and herbaceous perennials, thriving in sandy loam, and propagated by seeds and division. *P. linearis* is tender.

P. fastigiata (tapering); hardy perennial; flowers white, in

August; North America; 1823. *P. linearis* (narrow-leaved); tender perennial; flowers white, in June; Mexico; 1821. *P. Texana* (Texan); hardy annual; flowers brownish-red, in August; Texas; 1850.

PALMA CHRISTI. See RICINUS.

PANSY. See VIOLA.

PAPAVER. *Poppy.* [Papaveraceæ.] A genus of hardy plants, containing many weeds and some showy species: it comprises perennials, biennials, and annuals. Of the latter, the double-flowered varieties, sometimes known as Carnation and Picotee Poppies, are the most worthy of cultivation, and these are really gay as well as stately plants : besides which, if colors have any charm in a garden, it is almost impossible to enumerate the different tints that a pinch of good seed will produce. These annual kinds will overrun a garden if the pods of seed are not removed before ripening. For mixed or shrubbery borders, this may be no objection, as plants can be left where there is space for them, and the rest hoed up; but, in the more neatly kept parts of a garden, this scattering of the seed should be prevented, and a supply of plants raised by special sowing. The seeds may be sown in May, in patches where they are to grow, and thinned out to three or four strong plants in a patch ; or, if more convenient, they may be sown thinly in any open place out of the way, and, when large enough, planted in the borders and beds where they are wanted. Any plants which show flowers at all secondary in quality should be pulled up immediately, and none be left in the ground but very double and very pretty ones; the seed from these, or from the most beautiful of them, will give good varieties another year. The perennials want no culture, but to be planted in good garden soil, and left undisturbed: they increase by seeds or by division.

P. Alpinum (Alpine); hardy perennial; 9 inches; flowers white, in July; Austria; 1759. *P. amœnum* (lovely); hardy annual; 2 feet; flowers red and white, in June; India; 1830. *P. bracteatum* (bracted); hardy perennial; 3 feet; flowers scarlet, very showy, in May; Siberia; 1817. *P. croceum* (saffron); hardy perennial; 1 foot; flowers copper-color, in May; Altai; 1829. *P. nudicaule* (naked-stemmed); hardy perennial; 18 inches; flowers yellow, in July; Siberia; 1730. *P. Orientale* (Eastern); hardy perennial; 3 feet; flowers scarlet, very showy, in May; Armenia; 1714. *P. Rhœas* (common corn); hardy annual; 2 feet. The garden double-flowered varieties of this plant are very gay, of almost every color, red predominating, and variously variegated, and with the petals smooth-edged. *P. somniferum* (opium-bearing); hardy annual; 3 to 4 feet. Of this the double varieties only are desirable for gardens. They are of stately aspect, and very handsome; but differ from the last in being formed of a mass of small narrow petals or larger cut-edged ones. The colors are various, chiefly shades of red, purple, white, and blotched.

PAPER MULBERRY. See BROUSSONETIA.

PARNASSIA. [Hypericaceæ.] Pretty dwarf herbaceous perennials. Damp peaty soil. Propagated by division or by seeds.

P. asarifolia (asarum-leaved); hardy perennial; 6 inches; flowers white, in July; North America; 1812. *P. Caroliniana* (Carolina); hardy perennial; 9 inches; flowers white, in May; North America; 1802. *P. palustris* (marsh); hardy perennial; 9 inches; flowers white, in July; Britain; North America.

PASQUE-FLOWER. See ANEMONE.

PAULOWNIA. [Scrophularineæ.] A fine deciduous tree allied to Catalpa, scarcely hardy in New England, except in the most favored spots, in consequence of its producing very robust shoots, which seldom ripen; but doing well south of New York. Its large bunches of trumpet-shaped purplish flowers are very handsome. It should be planted in a dry soil, and in warm situations, where its vigorous shoots may be well ripened annually. Increased by layers, cuttings of the young shoots, and seeds.

P. imperialis (imperial); hardy tree; 25 feet; flowers purplish, in May; Japan; 1840.

PAVIA. [Sapindaceæ.] A small group of the Horse-chestnut family, consisting of handsome flowering trees of the smaller class. They grow in any deep lightish garden soil, and are usually increased by grafting on the common Horse-chestnut, or by layers.

P. discolor (two-colored); hardy shrub; 4 feet; flowers red and yellow, in June; North America; 1812. *P. macrostachya* (large-spiked); hardy shrub; 6 feet; flowers white, in July; North America; 1820. *P. rubra* (red); hardy shrub; 6 feet; flowers red, in June; North America; 1711. The varieties *humilis* and *humilis pendula*, both red-flowered, are desirable. These are selected on account of their small size.

PEA SWEET. See LATHYRUS.

PEACH. See PERSICA.

PEDICULARIS. *Lousewort.* [Scrophularineæ.] Hardy and half-hardy perennials, often very handsome, but not very easily grown. Damp peaty soil. Increased by seeds. Many species have been introduced. There are in all about thirty species, but the plants are not common in gardens.

PELARGONIUM. [Geraniaceæ.] A very large family of beautiful plants. The only ones however which call for our attention in connection with the flower-garden are the Scarlet Geraniums, so called, so popular for summer bedding. They require ordinary greenhouse treatment in the winter, or will survive in a warm, light cellar. The varieties are changing every year, and florists' catalogues will afford a fine collection of the various colors of red, pink, and white; and also fine variegated-leaved kinds. These kinds have sprung from *P. Bentinckianum, inquinans, zonale,* and others of the same character.

PENNISETUM. [Gramineæ.] A family of ornamental grasses, succeeding in any soil from spring-sown seeds.

P. villosum (hairy); hardy annual; apetalous; Brazil.

PENTHORUM. [Crassulaceæ.] Hardy succulent-leaved perennials. Common soil. Increased by division.

P. sedoides (sedum-like); hardy perennial; 1 foot; flowers yellow, in July; North America; 1768.

PENTSTEMON. [Scrophularineæ.] A large genus of hardy or half-hardy herbaceous perennials, sometimes sub-shrubby; among the most ornamental of summer-flowering plants. The best kinds for the flower-garden are the varieties of *P. Hartwegii*, often called *gentianoides*, which is sub-shrubby, propagates freely by cuttings, and blooms most profusely from August onwards till severe frost occurs. It should be wintered in cold frames, and planted out in spring. They may all be propagated by seeds or cuttings, less freely by division, according to their peculiar habits of growth; and require to be planted in a moderately rich light loamy soil to attain their full beauty, which is very considerable. Most of those marked half-hardy perennials which are not subshrubby, survive over winters, in favorable situations, and protected against excessive wet. It is, however, safer to shelter them in cold frames. They also survive better where there is a keen pure air.

P. atropurpureus (dark-purple); half-hardy sub-shrubby perennial; 2 feet; flowers deep rose-purple, in July; Mexico; 1827. *P. azureus* (azure); half-hardy perennial; 2 feet; flowers blue, in June; Mexico; 1848. *P. baccharifolius* (baccharis-leaved); half-hardy perennial, or perhaps biennial; 18 inches; flowers scarlet, in August; Texas; 1851. *P. barbatus* (bearded); hardy perennial; 3 feet; flowers light scarlet, in July; Mexico;

1794; often called *Chelone*. *P. campanulatus* (bell-flowered); half-hardy sub-shrubby perennial; 2 feet; flowers light rose-purple, in July; Mexico; 1794. *P. centranthifolius* (centranthus-leaved); hardy perennial; 3 feet; flowers deep scarlet, in July; California; 1834; often called *Chelone*. *P. cobæa* (cobœa-flowered); half-hardy perennial; 18 inches; flowers white and rose, in August; Texas; 1835. *P. crassifolius* (thick-leaved); half-hardy sub-shrubby perennial; 1 foot; flowers blue, in June; North America; *P. cyananthus* (blue); half-hardy perennial; 3 feet; flowers deep-blue, in July; Rocky Mountains; 1849. *P. diffusus* (diffuse); hardy perennial; 2 feet; flowers light-purple, in July; North America; 1826. *P. digitalis* (foxglove-like); hardy perennial; 2 feet; flowers whitish, in July; Arkansas; 1824. *P. Gordoni* (Gordon's); half-hardy perennial; 2 feet; flowers light-blue, in June; Rocky Mountains; 1845. *P. Hartwegii* (Hartweg's); half-hardy sub-shrubby perennial; 2 feet; flowers reddish-purple, in July; Mexico; 1825. Of this beautiful and useful plant, there are numerous garden varieties; the most distinct are: *albus*, creamy white; *coccineus*, scarlet; *diaphanus*, rosy; *McEweni*, rose; *Salteri*, white, bordered with rose; *Verplankii*, rose. *P. heterophyllum* (various-leaved); half-hardy sub-shrubby perennial; flowers rose-color, in July; California; 1834. *P. miniatus* (vermilion); half-hardy sub-shrubby perennial; 1 foot; flowers vermilion, in July; Mexico; 1846. *P. Murrayanum* (Murray's); half-hardy perennial; 3 feet; flowers scarlet, in August; Texas; 1835. *P. ovatus* (ovate); hardy perennial; 2½ feet; flowers deep-blue, in July; North America; 1826. *P. roseus* (rosy); half-hardy sub-shrubby perennial; 2 feet; flowers rose, in July; Mexico; 1825. *P. speciosus* (showy); half-hardy perennial; 3 feet; flowers light blue, in July; North America; 1827. *P. Wrightii* (Wright's); half-hardy perennial; 2 feet; flowers rich deep-rose, in June; Texas; 1851.

All the other species are worth growing where there is space for them.

PERILLA. [Lamiaceæ.] Half-hardy annuals, valuable

for their dark foliage. Light garden soil. Increased by seeds.

P. Nankinensis (Nankin); half-hardy annual; 18 inches; purple leaves; China; 1852.

P. ocymoides and *fruticosa* are not of much cultural value.

PERIPLOCA. [Asclepiadaceæ.] Hardy deciduous climbers, with glossy ornamental foliage. Loamy soil. Increased by layers and cuttings.

P. angustifolia (narrow-leaved); hardy twining shrub; 6 feet; flowers purplish, in July; south of Europe; 1800. *P. Græca* (Greek); hardy twining shrub; 12 feet; flowers purplish-brown, in July; Syria; 1597.

PERIWINKLE. See VINCA.

PERSICA. *Peach.* [Amygdalaceæ.] A well-known genus, containing some beautiful flowering shrubs. Good garden soil. Propagated by budding.

P. vulgaris (common); of this there are the following fine varieties,—*flore pleno* (double-flowered, white and pink); *foliis variegatis* (variegated-leaved); *pendula* (weeping); *sanguinea plena* (double red); *camilliaflora* (rich deep crimson double flowers, China, 1847); *rosaeflora* (deep rose double flowers. China, 1848).

PERSICARIA. See POLYGONUM.

PETASITES. [Compositæ.] Hardy herbaceous perennial, growing in common soil, and increased by division.

P. alba (white); hardy perennial; 9 inches; flowers white, in May; Europe; 1683.

PETUNIA. [Solanaceæ.] Showy, soft-stemmed, shrubby perennials, closely allied to Nierembergia. The garden Petunias have sprung from *P. nyctaginiflora* and *violacea;* the latter, in its original form, one of the richest of all plants for bedding out in the flower-garden, owing to its brilliant color. There are, however, few families in which cultivation has effected such a revolution as in this; for from the flimsy flowers of the old white, and the pointed blossoms of the old purple, have been produced flowers of circular outline, with thick corollas, and fluctuating beautiful colors. Petunias are propagated either by seed or cuttings. Seeds may be sown in March, on a hot-bed, and the plants treated as half-hardy annuals. Cuttings strike freely placed in a frame, with bottom heat: they should be planted in March and April, being obtained from old plants placed in heat, and from the tops of the earlier-planted cuttings, if a supply of young plants was not provided the previous autumn. The young plants require to be separately potted, hardened in a cold frame, and planted out in May, when the danger of frost is passed. A few plants should be kept in pots, rather stunted, for preservation through the winter in order to supply cuttings in spring; or young plants may be struck in August, and well hardened, and kept in the greenhouse on an airy shelf through the winter: such plants will, if vigorous and healthy, bloom earlier than spring cuttings. For this reason, a supply, more or less abundant, should always be struck at the end of the summer to keep over for planting out in spring.

P. nyctaginiflora (large-flowered); half-hardy perennial; 18 inches; flowers white, in June; La Plata; 1823. *P. violacea* (violaceous); half-hardy perennial; 18 inches; flowers rose-purple, in June; Buenos Ayres; 1831. This is sometimes called *P. Phœnicea.*

The names of the florists' varieties are arbitrary. Fine varieties may be selected from florists' catalogues. The double varieties are better fitted for the greenhouse than the garden.

PHACA. [Leguminosæ.] Hardy herbaceous perennials. Soil, sandy loam. Increased by seeds or division. The

GARDEN FLOWERS. 289

species are *Alpina, arenaria, astragalina, exaltata, frigida, lutea, Lapponica, oroboides, triangularis,* and many others.

PHACELIA. [Hydrophyllaceæ.] Pretty annuals, of the easiest culture in the open ground; the seeds being sown in May. There are some unimportant perennials.

P. congesta (crowded); hardy annual; 1 foot; flowers purple, in June; Texas; 1835. *P. fimbriata* (fringed); hardy annual; 1 foot; flowers white and lilac, in June; North America; 1840. *P. tanacetifolia* (tansy-leaved); hardy annual; 18 inches; flowers blue-lilac, in June; California; 1832. *P. vinifolia* vine-leaved); hardy annual; 18 inches; flowers light-blue, in September; Texas; 1834.

PHALANGIUM. [Liliaceæ.] Half-hardy herbaceous perennials, with pretty blossoms. Common soil. Increased by division.

P. Liliago (grass-leaved); half-hardy perennial; 1 foot; flowers white, in May; south of Europe; 1596.

PHALARIS. [Graminaceæ.] Hardy annuals. Common soil. Increased by seeds. *P. Canariensis* produces the canary seed. The other species are *P. appendiculata* and *commutata.*

PHARBITIS. *Gay-bine.* [Convolvulaceæ.] Annual and perennial twiners of graceful habit, with extremely gay flowers. Some of the species are tender; others may be treated as half-hardy annuals. The genus contains the well-known Convolvulus major, the plants commonly grown under that name including the varieties of *P. hispida, Nil, hederacea,* and perhaps some others. The colors of the Convolvulus major are varied: deep-purple, violet, light-blue, white, pale-rose, deep rose-crimson, and blue and white striped. This convolvulus should be sown in May, in patches, round a post or pillar, or at the foot of a stump of a tree, or where it can be provided with tall branchy stakes on which to twine, for the plant will grow ten feet high, and in season be covered with bloom; it is, however, characteristic of the plant to close its flowers during rains or in very cloudy weather, and at the approach of night. The varieties seed freely; but as the seeds soon shed after ripening, a good look-out must be kept for the pods. They may also be sown in pots in March, and kept in frames till May, and then planted out. They like a light rich soil. The other annual species require exactly the same management. A strong growing, somewhat shrubby species, *P. Learii*, is too handsome to be here omitted, though it requires a stove or warm greenhouse; it is a plant which grows and flowers well, provided it has room to extend its branches, and nourishment to support them. It likes a strong, rich, loamy compost.

P. barbata (bearded); hardy twining annual; 10 feet; flowers blue, in July; Virginia; 1729. *P. diversifolia* (various-leaved); greenhouse twining annual; 6 feet; flowers blue, in June; Mexico; 1836. *P. hederacea* (ivy-leaved); half-hardy twining annual; 10 feet; flowers deep-blue, in July; America; 1729. *P. hispida* (rough); half-hardy twining annual; 10 feet; flowers various, in June; South America; 1629. *P. Learii* (Lear's); stove or greenhouse shrub; 20 feet; flowers blue and purple, in July; Buenos Ayres; 1835. *P. Nil* (blue); half-hardy twining annual; 10 feet; flowers blue, in July; South America; 1597. *P. Purshii* (Morning-glory); hardy twining annual; 10 feet; flowers pale-blue, in July; Virginia; 1597.

PHASEOLUS. *Kidney-bean.* [Leguminosæ.] Twining plants, some annual and hardy, others requiring stove-heat. *P. multiflorus*, the well-known scarlet-runner bean, deserves notice as a flower-garden plant, from its showy appearance when in blossom. It is a plant well-adapted for covering summer-houses and temporary trellises: and is more or less ornamental from June to October. The seeds should be sown where the plants are required, in the month of May.

P. multiflorus (many-flowered); hardy climbing perennial; 10 feet; flowers scarlet or white, or white and scarlet, in July; South America; 1633.

PHEASANT'S-EYE. See ADONIS.

PHILADELPHUS. *Mock Orange, or Syringa.* [Philadelphaceæ.] Ornamental deciduous flowering shrubs. Confusion sometimes arises from the fact that the common name of this shrub, syringa, is the same word as the botanical name of the lilac-bush; and as both are shrubs, often introduced into gardens and shrubberies from their free-flowering qualities, the confusion is attended with inconvenience. The plants are widely different. The lilac *(Syringa vulgaris)*, as is well known, bears numerous small flowers in clusters, shaped something like an erect bunch of grapes. The Syringa, or Mock Orange *(Philadelphus)*, on the other hand, bears its flowers, which are large, and composed of distinct petals, either singly, or very few together; and they are called Mock Orange from the considerable resemblance between their blossoms and those of the orange-tree. Most of the species have a strong, but not very agreeable scent. Their leaves, moreover, have a taste similar to that of cucumbers. They are hardy shrubs, requiring no particular culture, but growing in ordinary garden soil, where it is not too damp; and are increased, either by means of layers, by cuttings, or by suckers. The flowers of all are white, with a bunch of yellow stamens in the centre. Nearly all are worth planting; but the following are the most distinct and handsome:—

P. coronarius (garland); hardy shrub; 6 feet; flowers white, in May; south of Europe; 1596. *P. floribundus* (many-flowered); hardy shrub; 8 feet; flowers white, in June; North America; 1815. *P. Gordonianus* (Gordon's); hardy shrub; 6 feet; flowers white, in July; North America; 1830. *P. inodorus* (scentless); hardy shrub; 6 feet; flowers white, in July;

North America; 1738. *P. latifolius* (broad-leaved); hardy shrub; 8 feet; flowers white, in June; North America; 1815. *P. speciosus* (showy); hardy shrub; 6 feet; flowers white, in June; North America; 1815.

PHILESIA. [Smilaceæ.] Beautiful hardy or half-hardy evergreen shrubs. Peat soil. Increased by cuttings. This plant will probably prove hardy.

P. buxifolia (box-leaved); half-hardy evergreen shrub; 2 feet; flowers large rose-crimson, in June; Antarctic America; 1850.

PHILLYREA. [Oleaceæ.] Desirable evergreen shrubs, valuable for their foliage and habit; the flowers being white and insignificant. Good garden soil. Propagated by layers or cuttings, under a hand-light. Not hardy at the North.

ORNAMENTAL EVERGREENS. — *P. angustifolia*, *P. lævis*, *P. latifolia*, *P. ligustrifolia*, *P. media*, *P. oleæfolia*.

PHLOMIS. [Lamiaceæ.] Hardy shrubs and herbaceous plants. Dry loamy soil. Increased by division, seeds, or, for the shrubby sorts, cuttings. Generally not hardy at the North.

P. Armeniaca (Armenian); half-hardy perennial; 1 foot; flowers yellow, in June; Armenia; 1834. *P. Cashmeriana* (Cashmere); hardy perennial; 2 feet; flowers lilac, in July; Cashmere; 1840. *P. fruticosa* (Jerusalem sage); hardy shrub; 3 feet; flowers yellow, in July; Spain; 1596. *P. herba-venti* (wind-herb); hardy perennial; 2 feet; flowers red, in August; south of Europe; 1596. *P. Samia* (Samos); hardy perennial; 3 feet; flowers purple, in June; Samos; 1714. *P. tuberosa* (tuberous); hardy perennial; 3 feet; flowers purple, in August; Siberia; 1759.

PHLOX. [Polemoniaceæ.] Beautiful hardy perennials, for the most part. The seedling varieties are numerous; some tall, others remarkably dwarf, and varying in color from clear white to pink, lilac, and purple, as well as striped.

They require arranging according to their heights, as well as according to their flowering season, when grown in collections; for some are early, others very late. Every year produces novelties; but many of the varieties are similar, consequently a few showy and strikingly different sorts should be selected, and these are very desirable in a flower-garden. In choosing Phloxes, those which are dwarf, and most abundant blooming, with individual flowers large and quite circular, should be selected. They grow well in any good light garden soil, if the situation is not too dry in summer, but thrive better in beds of peat soil. In sandy loam, enriched with equal parts leaf-mould, they also grow very luxuriantly. If in beds by themselves, and the plants are small, they require to be planted about a foot apart. They are propagated by parting the root, and may be raised from seed; the former perpetuates any approved variety, the latter gives us a chance of obtaining new ones. The established sorts are propagated by dividing the roots, or by cuttings of the flower-stems; and the plants should be allowed to remain two or three seasons, for they are the better for spreading out a little. New varieties are obtained from seed, which should be sown in May, and the young plants set out in rows in a nicely prepared bed. The next season, when they bloom, the best should be selected. The dwarf trailing species are fine for rock-work. *P. Drummondii*, an annual species, is a very beautiful plant, forming one of the most showy of flowering plants during summer. The colors vary a good deal, and there is no dependence on any seed bringing plants quite similar in color to the parent; but the general form of the plant, and its pretty and abundant blooming habit, are maintained. The seed should be sown in gentle heat in March or April; and, as soon as the plants are large enough to handle, they are to be pricked out an inch apart, in wide-mouthed pots, where, for economy of space, they may remain for three or four weeks, and may be kept in the greenhouse or in a frame. When they have grown so as almost to touch one another, they may be potted separately in pots three inches across, and placed under a garden light, where, if need be, they can be covered against frost. Here they may remain, with all the air that can be given in mild days, until their roots fill the pots, when they must be removed to five-inch pots, changing them without breaking the balls of earth. They may be replaced in the frame, unless the chances of frost have gone by, in which case the plants may be set out in the garden. They do well in the flower-garden if planted out in beds of rich light earth towards the end of May.

P. acuminata (pointed-leaved); half-hardy perennial; 4 feet; flowers pale-purple, in July; North America; 1812. *P. aristata* (awned); half-hardy perennial; 6 inches; flowers white, in April; Carolina; 1828. *P. stolonifera* (creeping); hardy perennial; 6 inches; flowers red and white, in May; North America; 1825. *P. divaricata* (early); hardy perennial; 1 foot; flowers pale-purple, in May; North America; 1746. *P. subulata* (awl-leaved); hardy perennial; 6 inches; flowers rose-color, in May; North America; 1786. *P. Drummondii* (Drummond's); half-hardy annual; 1 foot; flowers purple-rose, striped, or white, in July; Texas; 1835. *P. maculata* (spotted-stemmed); hardy perennial; 4 feet; flowers purple, in July; North America; 1740. *P. nivalis* (snowy); hardy perennial; 6 inches; flowers white, in April; North America; 1820. *P. omniflora* (all-flowering); hardy perennial; 1 foot; flowers white, in July; gardens. *P. paniculata* (panicled); hardy perennial; 1 foot; flowers various, in July; North America; 1732. *P. setacea* (bristly); hardy perennial; 6 inches; flowers flesh-color, in April; North America; 1786. *P. suaveolens* (sweet-scented); hardy perennial; 2 feet; flowers white, in July; North America; 1766.

Most of the species are handsome plants. The following are the best varieties: LIGHT.— *D'argent, Donaria, Ketelerii, Louis Mezard, Madame Aurelie Duriez, Madame de Brobeques, Madame Guldenschuh, Madame Marseau, Madame Sueur, Mrs. Standish, Roi Leopold, Speculum, Triomph de Twickel.* DARK.— *President Morel, Neptune, Madame Houllet, Madame Henricq, Madame Amazile Pothier, Henry Lierval, Evening Star, Dugueslin, Cromwell, Mille Prial.*

PHYGELIUS. [Scrophularineæ.] A very pretty bedding plant, flowering freely towards autumn in the border. Propagated by cuttings.

P. Capensis (Cape); greenhouse perennial; 1 foot; flowers red and orange, in September; Caffreland; 1854.

PHYLLODOCE. [Ericaceæ.] Pretty little shrubs, allied to Dabœcia, and Menziesia, and requiring the same treatment. Peat soil. Propagated by layers.

P. empetriformis (empetrum-like); hardy evergreen shrub; 6 inches; flowers pale red, in July; North America; 1810. *P. taxifolia* (yew-leaved); hardy evergreen shrub); 6 inches; flowers red, in July; North America, Europe, and Scotland.

PHYSALIS. *Winter Cherry.* [Solanaceæ.] A genus containing a half-hardy perennial, ornamental in autumn on account of its orange-colored berries. Common soil. Propagated by division.

P. Alkekengi (Alkekengi); half-hardy perennial; 1 foot; flowers white, in July; south of Europe; 1548.

PHYSIANTHUS. [Asclepidaceæ.] A greenhouse climber which, however, does finely planted out in summer in a rich warm border. Flowers, freely produced, white, with green and pink lining. The flowers have the curious property of catching the honey tubes of moths and butterflies, so that the insects cannot escape. Propagated by seeds and cuttings.

P. albicans (whitish); climber; 20 feet; flowers white, all summer; Buenos Ayres; 1830.

PHYSOSTEGIA. [Lamiaceæ.] Fine hardy perennials. They require the same treatment as Dracocephalum, and may be propagated in the same way, both being also increased, when requisite, by seeds sown in May or June, to produce blooming plants for the following year.

P. imbricata (imbricated); half-hardy perennial; 3 feet; flowers pale rose-purple, in July; Texas; 1833. *P. speciosa* (showy); hardy perennial; 4 feet; flowers rose-pink, in July; Siberia; 1822. *P. Virginiana* (Virginian); hardy perennial; 3 feet; flowers red or white, in July; North America; 1683.

PHYTEUMA. [Campanulaceæ.] Handsome hardy perennials, of easy culture in a dryish situation, and in good garden soil. There are about a score of species. They are, many of them, suitable for rock-work, and may be multiplied either by seeds or by division.

P. canescens (hoary); hardy perennial; 2 feet; flowers pale-purple, in July; Hungary; 1804. *P. comosum* (tufted); hardy biennial; 9 inches; flowers blue, in June; Austria; 1752. *P. orbiculare* (round); hardy perennial; 1 foot; flowers blue, in June; England. *P. Sibiricum* (Siberian); hardy perennial; 1 foot; flowers blue, in July; Siberia; 1817. *P. spicatum* (spiked); hardy perennial; 2 feet; flowers blue, in May; Europe; 1597.

PICEA. See ABIES.

PICOTEE. See DIANTHUS.

PHYTOLACCA. *Poke.* [Phytolaccaceæ.] A hardy tall-growing plant, ornamental in the shrubbery for its flowers and racemes of black berries. Rich deep soil. Increased by seed.

P. decandra (ten-stamened); hardy herbaceous perennial; 5 feet; flowers white and green, in August; North America; 1768.

There are many tender species.

GARDEN FLOWERS. 297

PILEWORT. See FICARIA.
PIMPERNEL. See ANAGALLIS.
PINGUICULA. [Lentibulaceæ.] Curious dwarf hardy perennials. Marsh, or boggy soil. Propagated by seeds or division.
PINK. See DIANTHUS.
PINUS. [Coniferæ.] Fine evergreen trees, generally hardy, and including some of our most valuable evergreens. They flourish in good light soil, and are easily propagated by seeds, or the rarer kinds by grafting.

P. Arabica (Arabian); Palestine. *P. Australis* (southern); 70 feet; Florida; 1730. *P. Austriaca* (Austrian; black); flowers in June; Austria; 1835. *P. Banksiana* (Banks's, scrub); 20 feet; flowers in May; North America; 1785. *P. Benthamiana* (Bentham's); 200 feet; California; 1847. *P. Brutia* (Calabrian); Calabria. *P. Bungeana* (Bunge's); north of China. *P. cembra* (cembra; Siberian); 25 feet; flowers in May; Siberia; 1746. *P. cembra pumila* (dwarf); Siberia. *P. Chilmalmana* (Chilmalm's); 46 feet; north of Mexico. *P. communis* (common). *P. communis rubra* (red); Scotland. *P. communis latifolia* (broad-leaved). *P. edulis* (eatable-seeded); North Mexico. *P. Ehrenbergii* (Ehrenberg's); 100 feet; Mexico. *P. excelsa* (tall); 100 feet; Nepaul; 1823. *P. Finlaysoniana* (Finlayson's); Cochin China. *P. flexilis* (pliant); New Mexico. *P. Fremontiana* (Fremont's); 20 feet; California; 1848. *P. Halepensis* (Aleppo); 40 feet; flowers in June; Levant; 1683. *P. Halepensis maritima* (maritime); 40 feet; flowers in May; south of Greece. *P. inops* (Jersey; poor); 30 feet; flowers in May; North America; 1739. *P. insignis* (remarkable); 60 feet; California; 1833. *P. insularis* (island); Philippines. *P. Koraiensis* (Corean); 10 feet; Corea. *P. Lambertiana* (Lambert's); 200 feet; North America; 1827. *P. Lambertiana brevifolia* (short-leaved). *P. laricio* (Corsican; larch); 80 feet; flowers in May; Corsica; 1814. *P. Llaveana* (La Llave's); 25 feet; Mexico; 1830. *P. macrocarpa* (large-coned); 120 feet; California. *P. Merkusii* (Merkus's); 100 feet; Sumatra. *P. mitis* (soft-leaved); 50 feet; flowers in May; North America; 1739. *P. monticola* (mountain-top); California; 1831. *P. Mugho* (Mugho); flowers in May; Austria. *P. Mugho humilis* (lowly). *P. Mugho obliqua* (twisted). *P. muricata* (prickly-coned); 40 feet; California; 1848. *P. osteosperma* (scaly-seeded); New Mexico. *P. Pallasiana* (Pallas's); 70 feet; flowers in May; Siberia; 1820. *P. parviflora* (small-flowered); Japan; 1846. *P. Persica* (Persian); south of Persia. *P. Peuce* (Peucean); Mountains of Rumelia. *P. pinaster* (cluster; pinaster); 60 feet; flowers in June; south of Europe; 1596. *P. pinaster Escarena* (Escaren's). *P. pinaster Lemoniana* (Sir C. Lemon's); 30 feet; flowers in May. *P. pinaster minor* (less-coned); 60 feet; flowers in May; France. *P. pinaster variegata* (variegated-leaved); flowers in May. *P. pinea* (stone-pine); 60 feet; flowers in June; south of Europe; 1548. *P. pinea Cretica* (Cretan); flowers in May; Crete. *P. pinea fragilis* (thin-shelled); 60 feet; flowers in May; south of Europe. *P. ponderosa* (weighty-wooded); 50 feet; North America; 1828. *P. pumilio* (dwarf); 20 feet; flowers in May; Europe. *P. pungens* (stinging); 40 feet; flowers in May; North America; 1804. *P. Pyrenaica* (Pyrenean); 50 feet; flowers in May; Pyrenees; 1834. *P. radiata* (radiated-scaled); 100 feet; California. *P. resinosa* (resinous); 80 feet; flowers in May; North America; 1756. *P. rigida* (stiff); 80 feet; flowers in May; North America; 1759. *P. rudis* (rude); Mexico. *P. Sabiniana* (Sabine's); 120 feet; flowers in March; California; 1832. *P. serotina* (late); 40 feet; flowers in May; North America; 1713. *P. strobiformis* (cone-shaped); 120 feet; Mexico. *P. strobus* (white pine; Weymonth); 200 feet; flowers in April; North America; 1705. *P. strobus alba* (white); 100 feet; flowers in May. *P. strobus brevifolia* (short-leaved); 100 feet; flowers in April. *P. sylvestris* (wood; Scotch); 80 feet; flowers in May; Scotland. *P. tæda* (frankincense); 80 feet; flowers in May; Florida; 1713. *P. tenuifolia* (slender-leaved); 80 feet; Guatimala. *P. tuberculata* (warted); 100 feet; California. *P. variabilis* (variable-two-and-three-leaved); 40 feet; flowers in May; North America; 1739.

Many of the above are not hardy, and there are some thirty other still more tender species.

PLATANTHERA. [Orchidaceæ.] A family of orchids, mostly hardy, formerly known as Orchis. Soil, peat, generally moist. All these plants are of difficult culture. The species are *P. obtusata, rotundifolia, orbiculata, Hookerii, bracteata, hyperborea, dilatata, flava, cristata, ciliaris, blephariglottis, leucophæa, lacera, psycodes, fimbriata,* and *peramœna ;* all natives of North America. The flowers are very handsome.

PLATANUS. *Plane-tree.* [Platanaceæ.] Hardy deciduous ornamental trees. Soil, deep loam. Propagated by seeds, cuttings, and layers.

P. Occidentalis (Western); 70 feet; North America; 1636. *P. aurea variegata* (golden-variegated-leaved); 70 feet; 1846. *P. integrifolia* (entire-leaved); 70 feet; 1845. *P. heterophylla* (various-leaved); America; 1842. *P. Orientalis* (Eastern); 50 feet; Levant; 1548. *P. acerifolia* (maple-leaved); 70 feet; Levant. *P. cuneata* (wedge-leaved); 20 feet; Levant; 1739. *P. Hispanica* (Spanish); 70 feet; Spain. *P. laciniata* (cut-leaved); 70 feet; 1845. *P. monstrosa* (monstrous); 70 feet; 1845.

The European species are somewhat tender.

PLATYCODON. [Campanulaceæ.] Hardy herbaceous perennials. Propagated by seeds and division in the spring, and by cuttings in the summer. Soil, sandy loam.

P. grandiflorum (large-flowered); hardy perennial; 1 foot; flowers blue, in June; Dahuria; 1782. Variety *alba*, from China, has white flowers; variety *alba plena* has semi-double flowers.

These plants are half-hardy in the Northern States.

PLATYSTEMON. [Papaveraceæ.] Pretty annuals, of prostrate habit. They like a cool situation, and a peaty soil, but will grow in any rich light earth. Sow about the middle of May.

P. Californicum (Californian); hardy annual; 1 foot; flowers sulphur-yellow, in June; California; 1823.

PLECTRANTHUS. See COLEUS.

PLATYSTIGMA. [Papaveraceæ.] Half-hardy perennials, allied to Platystemon. Light soil. Increased by seeds or division.

P. lineare (linear); half-hardy perennial; 1 foot; flowers yellow, in July; California; 1833.

PLECTRITES. [Valerinaceæ.] Hardy annuals, propagated from spring-sown seed in common soil; flowers white or rose. The species are *P. brachystemon* and *congesta*.

PLEUROGYNE. [Gentianaceæ.] A hardy annual, thriving in loamy peat, and easily grown from seed sown in May.

P. rotata (wheel-shaped); hardy annual; 9 inches; flowers blue, in August; Siberia; 1827.

PLUM. See PRUNUS.

PLUMBAGO. *Lead-wort.* [Plumbaginaceæ.] Pretty plants, with flowers somewhat like those of the Phlox. The majority are shrubs; some few are herbaceous, among which is *P. Larpentæ*, which is of dwarf, compact habit, and suitable for rock-work. *P. Capensis* is a desirable greenhouse shrub, which is most frequently grown too fast, and is, therefore, generally seen as a rambling plant. Soil, two-thirds loam, and one-third peat. The object should be to keep the plant dwarf and bushy: it is sure to grow tall enough after all the pains taken on it. Cuttings may be struck in sandy soil with or without bottom-heat, covering them with a bell-glass after inserting them. When rooted, pot them singly in three-inch pots, and, as soon as they fairly start into growth, take off the tops to encourage the lateral shoots: when they fill the small pots with the roots, remove them to larger ones. By continually checking any of the branches that ramble out of shape, the plant can be grown a very pretty object. It makes a fine bedding plant.

P. Capensis (Cape); greenhouse shrub; 4 feet; flowers pale blue, in June; Cape; 1818. *P. Larpentæ* (Lady Larpent's); half-hardy perennial; 1 foot; flowers deep-blue, in October; China; 1845.

PODOCARPUS. [Taxaceæ.] Half-hardy evergreen shrubs, or rather trees. Soil, loam. Propagated by cuttings of ripe shoots in sand, under glass.

PODOLEPIS. [Compositæ.] Pretty half-hardy annuals. The seeds may be sown in pots, or on a mild hot-bed in April, and planted out in sheltered situations in May for early blooming. A later crop may be had by sowing in the open ground in May. The plants must be well thinned. They grow a foot or upwards in height in rich light garden soil.

P. chrysantha (golden); half-hardy annual; 1 foot; flowers yellow, in July; New Holland; 1852. *P. gracilis* (slender); half-hardy annual; 18 inches; flowers rose or white, in July; New Holland; 1826.

PODOPHYLLUM. *Mandrake.* [Ranunculaceæ.] Hardy herbaceous perennial, with showy flowers, and yellow, scarcely edible fruit; thriving in deep moist loam, in the shade. Propagated by division. The plants are impatient of removal.

P. peltatum (shield); hardy perennial; 1 foot; flowers white, in May; North America; 1664. *P. Emodii* is a scarcely known California species.

PODOTHECA. [Compositæ.] Annuals of little horticultural importance, growing in the open border from seed sown in May.

POGOGYNE. [Lamiaceæ.] A hardy annual of easy culture. Common border soil. Propagated by seeds sown in May.

P. multiflora (many-flowered); hardy annual; 6 inches; flowers lilac, in August; California; 1836.

POLANISIA. [Capparidaceæ.] Hardy annuals, allied to Cleome. Seeds sown in a frame in April, and pricked out in the borders in May, will bloom in June.

P. Cheladonii (Cheladon's); hardy annual; 18 inches; flowers rose, in July; East Indies; 1792. *P. dodecandra* (twelve-anthered); hardy annual; 18 inches; flowers white, in July; East Indies; 1795. *P. graveolens* (strong-smelling); hardy annual; 18 inches; flowers yellowish-white; North America. *P. uniglandulosa* (one-glanded); hardy annual; 1 foot; flowers white and red, in July; Mexico; 1823. *P. viscosa* (clammy); hardy annual; 2 feet; flowers yellow, in summer; East Indies; 1730. Variety *icosandra* (twenty-anthered); 18 inches; flowers yellow, in July; Ceylon; 1730.

POLEMONIUM. *Greek Valerian.* [Polemoniaceæ.] Ornamental hardy perennials, of easy culture, growing readily in ordinary good garden soil, and increased by division of the plant, and, generally, very freely by seeds, which should be sown in June to produce flowering plants for the next year.

P. cæruleum (blue); hardy perennial; 2 feet; flowers blue or white, in June; Britain. There is a variety with variegated foliage. *P. gracile* (slender); hardy perennial; 1 foot; flowers blue, in June; Dahuria; 1818. *P. humile* (dwarf); hardy perennial; 1 foot; flowers blue, in July; North America; 1826. *P. Mexicanum* (Mexican); half-hardy perennial; 18 inches; flowers blue, in May; Mexico; 1817. *P. pulcherrimum* (prettiest); hardy perennial; 9 inches; flowers blue, in July; North America; 1827. *P. Sibiricum* (Siberian); hardy perennial; 2 feet; flowers white, in June; Siberia; 1800.

POLIANTHES. *Tuberose.* [Liliaceæ.] Greenhouse bulbs, annually imported from Italy. Soil, a rich sandy loam. Increased by offsets. When in growth, they are benefited by warmth at the root. For special culture, see "Flowers for the Parlor and Garden."

P. tuberosa (tuberous); greenhouse bulb; 3 feet; flowers white, single or double, in August; East Indies; 1629.

GARDEN FLOWERS. 303

POLYANTHUS. See PRIMULA.

POLYGALA. [Polygalaceæ.] A large family, of which the greenhouse species are chiefly important. *P. fastigiata, purpurea,* and *umbellata* are pretty, hardy annuals; and *P. alpestris, rubella,* and *paucifolia* are very showy perennials. All are of easy culture in garden soil.

POLYGONATUM. *Solomon's Seal.* [Liliaceæ.] Hardy herbaceous perennials. Common soil. Increased by division.

P. latifolium (broad-leaved); hardy perennial; 3 feet; flowers white, in May; Germany; 1802. *P. multiflorum* (many-flowered); hardy perennial; 2 feet; flowers white, in June; Britain. *P. vulgare* (common); hardy perennial; 2 feet; flowers white, in May; England. There is a variety *flore-pleno.*

POLYGONUM. *Persicaria.* [Polygonaceæ.] A large genus, not remarkable for floral attractions. There are, however, exceptions. *P. Orientale,* a common hardy annual, which is best self-sown, grows four or five feet high, much branched, with many gracefully nodding spikes of small red flowers, which become conspicuous from their aggregation. It requires no culture; but, if sown artificially, it may be done in May. *P. amphibium* is a beautiful hardy water-plant, with short floating stems, and rosy flower-spikes. *P. divaricatum* is a pretty hardy perennial, densely branched, forming a large mass, covered with feathery-looking bunches of creamy-white flowers. It is of the easiest culture in common soil, and increases by division. *P. vaccinifolium* and *Brunonis* are beautiful rock-plants: they increase by their self-rooting trailing branches, but are tender in the Northern States.

P. amphibium (amphibious); hardy aquatic perennial, floating; flowers rose, in July; England. *P. amplexicaule* (stem-clasping); hardy perennial; 2 feet; flowers pink, in July; India; 1837. *P. Brunonis* (Brown's); hardy evergreen perennial; 1 foot; flowers pink, in August; North India; 1845. *P divar-*

icatum (divaricate); hardy perennial; 3 feet; flowers white, in July; Siberia; 1759. *P. Orientale* (Eastern); hardy annual; 5 feet; flowers red, in July; East Indies; 1707. *P. vaccinifolium* (whortleberry-leaved); hardy evergreen trailing sub-shrub; flowers rose, in September; North India; 1845.

POMEGRANATE. See PUNICA.

PONTEDERIA. *Pickerel Weed.* [Pontederaceæ.] Showy aquatics, suitable for the borders of ponds. Flowers blue, in August. *P. angustifolia, cærulea, cordata,* and *lanceolata,* all natives of North America, are hardy perennials. Propagated by division.

POPLAR. See POPULUS.

POPPY. See PAPAVER.

POPULUS. *Poplar.* [Salicaceæ.] Hardy deciduous trees, some of which are valuable for shade and ornament. Propagated by seeds, layers, and cuttings. They succeed best in deep, moist, loamy soil.

P. alba (white Abele-tree); 40 feet; flowers in March; Britain. *P. angulata* (angular; Carolina); 80 feet; flowers in March; Carolina; 1738. *P. balsamifera* (balsamic); 70 feet; flowers in April; North America; 1792. *P. balsamifera foliis variegatis* (variegated-leaved); flowers in April. *P. balsamifera intermedia* (intermediate); flowers in April. *P. balsamifera latifolia* (broad-leaved); 40 feet; flowers in April. *P. balsamifera suaveolens* (sweet-scented); 70 feet; flowers in April; Russia; 1825. *P. balsamifera viminalis* (twiggy); 40 feet; flowers in April; Altai; 1826. *P. betulifolia* (birch-leaved; Black American); 40 feet; flowers in March; North America. *P. Canadensis* (Canadian); flowers in March; Canada. *P. candicans* (whitish-heart-leaved); 50 feet; flowers in March; North America; 1772. *P. canescens* (hoary); 40 feet; flowers in March; England. *P. canescens acerifolia* (maple-leaved). *P. canescens Ægyptiaca* (Egyptian); Egypt. *P. canescens Arembergica* (Aremberg); 1835. *P. canescens Belgica* (Belgian); south of Europe; 1835. *P. canescens hybrida* (hybrid); 40 feet; flowers in April; Caucasus; 1816. *P. canescens nivea* (snow-white). *P. canescens pendula* (drooping-branched). *P. fastigiata* (pyramidal; Lombardy); 70 feet; flowers in March; Italy; 1758. *P. fastigiata fœmina* (female); flowers in March; Italy; 1838. *P. Græca* (Greek; Athenian); 40 feet; flowers in March; Archipelago; 1779. *P. grandidentata* (large-toothed); 70 feet; flowers in March; North America; 1772. *P. grandidentata pendula* (drooping); 40 feet; flowers in March; North America; 1820. *P. heterophylla* (various-leaved); 70 feet; flowers in March; North America; 1765. *P. laurifolia* (laurel-leaved); flowers in April. *P. longifolia* (long-leaved); flowers in April; America; 1843. *P. monilifera* (necklace-bearing); 70 feet; flowers in May; Canada; 1772. *P. monilifera Lindleyana* (Lindley's waved-leaved); flowers in April; Canada; 1772. *P. monilifera variegata* (variegated-leaved); flowers in May. *P. nigra* (black); 30 feet; flowers in March; Britain. *P. nigra salicifolia* (willow-leaved); flowers in April; Floetbeck; 1834. *P. nigra viridis* (green-leaved); flowers in April; Britain. *P. pseudo balsamifera* (bastard-balsamic); flowers in April; America; 1843. *P. tremula* (trembling; aspen); 50 feet; flowers in March; Britain. *P. tremula lævigata* (smooth); 80 feet; flowers in March; North America; 1760. *P. tremula pendula* (drooping); flowers in April. *P. tremula supina* (lying-down); flowers in March; North America; 1824. *P. trepida* (trembling; American); 30 feet; North America; 1812. *P. tristis* (sad); flowers in April; North America; 1843.

PORTULACA. *Purslane.* [Portulacaceæ.] A genus of fine hardy annuals. They require a light rich soil, and a warm, sunny situation: when both soil and situation agree with them, they form very fine objects. Grown carefully in pots for the greenhouse, they are also very ornamental. The seeds should be sown in a hot-bed early in March, and the plants nursed on in frames, not too warm, being at first potted singly, and then shifted on as they may require until the beginning of June, when they may be either planted out, or shifted finally for blooming in pots. The new double varieties are very fine. Where these plants have once been grown, they sow themselves yearly.

P. Gilliesii (Gillies's); half-hardy perennial; 9 inches; flowers red and purple, in June; Mendoza; 1827. *P. grandiflora* (great-flowered); half-hardy annual or perennial; 9 inches; flowers yellow, or yellow and purple; Mendoza; 1827. *P. splendens* (splendid); half-hardy annual or perennial; 1 foot; flowers rose-purple, in May; Chili; 1839. *P. Thellusonii* (Thelluson's); half-hardy annual; 1 foot; flowers crimson or yellow, or reddish-purple, in June; Mendoza; 1839.

POTENTILLA. *Cinquefoil.* [Rosaceæ.] Hardy perennials, now becoming popular, and comprising some fine garden varieties, as well as very handsome species. They grow best in loamy soil, rich in vegetable matter, but not too full of dung. The roots should be taken up early in autumn, and parted; each crown or heart, with root attached, forming a plant: these may be either planted in a bed, to become established, or put out at once in the borders or the flowering-beds. A bed filled with the varieties of Potentilla has a very fine effect during the chief of the summer months. Seedlings should be raised from the best varieties, to obtain distinct kinds.

P. atrosanguinea (dark-blood); hardy perennial; 2 feet; flowers crimson, in June; Nepaul; 1822. *P. bicolor* (two-colored); hardy perennial; 2 feet; flowers yellow, margined red, in May; Nepaul; 1843. *P. formosa* (beautiful); hardy perennial; 2 feet; flowers rose, in June; Nepaul; 1822. *P. insignis* (showy); hardy perennial; 2 feet; flowers yellow, in May; Nepaul; 1840. *P. Thomasii* (Thomas's); hardy perennial; 2 feet; flowers yellow, in June; Italy; 1822.

FLORISTS' VARIETIES.—The following are good sorts: *Crimson* — Floral Beauty, fulgens, ignescens, King of Crimsons, McNabiana, Menziesii, Russelliana, Scarlet Gem. *Rose, with cream centre* — Hopwoodiana. *Scarlet, with yellow centre* — Plantii. *Yellow* — Argo, Julia, Primrose, Mulleri. *Yellow and bright red* — Sudbury Gem, Theodore. *Yellow and pink* — Garnieriana, Mackayana, Mayana.

Every year, however, produces new varieties, which supersede the old, though often no better.

PRICKLY POPPY. See ARGEMONE.

PRIMROSE. See PRIMULA.

PRIMULA. *Primrose.* [Primulaceæ.] Beautiful dwarf tufted growing herbaceous perennials, nearly all of which are hardy as respects cold. Of *P. vulgaris*, the common Primrose, there are double-flowered varieties of several colors. These grow best in a cool, moist, but well-drained situation, and prefer a soil of light loam intermixed with decayed tree-leaves. They are propagated by dividing the tufts into separate crowns with roots attached, which may be done in spring, and the young plants planted out in cool shady situations. By the following spring, they will become strong blooming plants. One variety of Primrose produces a bunch of flowers on the top of a common stalk; and this appears to be the origin of the garden plants known as Polyanthus. Most of the hardy species of Primula are extremely beautiful subjects in a pot-collection of Alpine plants, blooming in May. This class may be grown in pots or on rock-work, in peat and loam, and require chiefly to be kept cool and moist in summer, but in winter they must be kept rather dry as well as cool. Seeds of these may be sown about May, that the plants may acquire strength before winter.

Auricula (Primula Auricula). — The cultivated varieties of this species of Primula are commonly known as the Auricula. There is hardly a flower that presents such an appearance of artificial structure as the Auricula; the surface appears covered, like a butterfly's wing, with a powder, which the touch of the finger brings off, thereby spoiling the flower. A stage of Auriculas is a really beautiful sight. Some old books on the culture of this flower recommend the most nauseous composts for its growth. It is, however, absurd to pretend that any thing disagreeable is necessary for the purpose. Loam from rotted turfs, two-thirds, and decomposed dung fairly rotted into mould, one-third, will be found excellent compost for them to grow in; and if the loam be a little adhesive, which it ought not to be, some silver sand may be mixed with it. The pots in which they grow should be one-third filled with broken pots, to secure complete drainage; and, in potting the plants, the fibres of the roots should be spread out all round. The best way is to put the soil into the pot in the form of a cone, highest in the middle, and nearly as high as the edge of the pot; put the plant on this, with the fibres spread all round, and press it down on the soft light mould, so that the collar of the plant shall be just below the level of the edge of the pot; press the soil a little to the roots as the pot is filled, and water it. The Auricula may be grown to perfection in a common garden frame, with a glass to keep off heavy rains and hard frosts. It requires but little water all the winter. In February, the surface of the mould should be stirred a little, and thrown out, and the pots filled up again with a top-dressing of decomposed poultry-dung, sand, and cow-dung rotted into mould, equal parts; and from this time they may be regularly watered, have air on fine days, and be covered at nights and in frosty weather. In April, when in bloom, they must be shaded, or the sun would spoil the flowers.

Polyanthus (Primula vulgaris umbellata). — The Polyanthus is a well-known hardy perennial, blooming early in spring. Its flowers, variegated and richly colored, are elevated several together on the top of a common stalk. Of the same habit are the species, *P. elatior*, the oxlip, and *P. veris*, the cowslip, both of which, together with the common Primrose, are favorite subjects for planting in shrubberies, and in other shady parts of the flower-garden and pleasure-ground. These, with the Polyanthus, prefer a heavier loamy soil than that already recommended for double Primroses. They are propagated by division of the roots; and may also be raised from seeds. The seeds should be sown in March, in boxes of fine soil, put in a cool frame, and kept moist. The plants, as soon as they can be handled, may be pricked out an inch apart in other boxes, and when large enough, planted out in beds of the soil already mentioned. For varieties, it is best to consult the most recent florists' lists.

P. auricula (auricula); hardy perennial; 6 inches; flowers yellow, in April; Switzerland; 1596. This has sported into various colors. *P. cortusoides* (cortusa-like); hardy perennial; 1 foot; flowers rose, in June; Siberia; 1794. *P. elatior* (oxlip); hardy perennial; 1 foot; flowers yellow, in April; England. *P. farinosa* (mealy); hardy perennial; 6 inches; flowers rose, in June; England. *P. Helvetica* (Swiss); hardy perennial; 3 inches; flowers purple, in May; Switzerland. *P. minima* (least); hardy perennial; 6 inches; flowers purple, in April; south of Europe; 1819. *P. nivea* (snowy); hardy perennial; 3 inches; flowers white, in May; Siberia. *P. Palinuri* (Palinuri); hardy perennial; 6 inches; flowers yellow, in May; Naples; 1816. *P. Scotica* (Scotch); hardy perennial; 6 inches; flowers rose, in June; Scotland. *P. veris* (cowslip); hardy perennial; 6 inches; flowers yellow, in April; England. *P. villosa* (shaggy); hardy perennial; 3 inches; flowers purple, in May; Switzerland; 1768. *P. vulgaris* (Primrose); hardy perennial; 6 inches; flowers yellow, in March; England.

Most of these succeed better in the Northern States if protected in a frame in winter.

PRINCE'S FEATHER. See AMARANTHUS and POLYGONUM.
PRINUS. See ILEX.
PRIVET. See LIGUSTRUM.
PROVENCE ROSE. See ROSA.
PRUNELLA, or BRUNELLA. [Lamiaceæ.] Hardy herbaceous perennials. Common soil. Propagated by division. *P. grandiflora, Marryatti, ovata, vulgaris,* and varieties *elongata, flore plena, hispida, pinnatifida* and *rubra,* and *P. Webbiana,* are all useful border plants with purplish flowers. *P. ovata* is annual.

PRUNUS. *Plum.* [Drupaceæ.] Hardy deciduous tree, with showy flowers. Soil, dryish loam. Propagated by grafting or budding. The double-flowered and variegated-leaved varieties are very showy. *P. spinosa* is the Sloe-tree.

P. Japonica flore pleno is a fine hardy white flowering shrub, which, when in flower, contrasts beautifully with the flowering almond; China; 1846. *P. triloba* is a fine pink flowering species; China; 1847.

PSORALEA. [Leguminosæ.] Hardy herbaceous plants or greenhouse shrubs. For the former, good dryish sandy soil, and propagate by division or seeds; for the latter, peat and loam, and increase by cuttings in sand under glass.

PTELIA. *Hop-tree.* [Xanthoxylaceæ.] Hardy tree. Propagated by seed or layers. Common soil.

P. trifoliata (three-leaved); 12 feet; flowers green, in June; North America; 1704. *P. trifoliata variegata* (variegated-leaved); 12 feet; flowers green, in June; 1846.

PUCCOON. See SANGUINARIA.
PULMONARIA. *Lungwort.* [Boraginaceæ.] Hardy perennials. Common soil. Propagated by division.

P. angustifolia (narrow-leaved); hardy perennial; 9 inches; flowers violet, in May; Britain. *P. azurea* (light-blue); hardy perennial; 18 inches; flowers blue, in May; Poland; 1823. *P.*

Dahurica (Dahurian); hardy perennial; 1 foot; flowers blue, in May; Dahuria; 1812. *P. grandiflora* (large-flowered); hardy perennial; 1 foot; flowers pink, in May; France; 1819. *P. Sibirica* (Siberian); hardy perennial; 1 foot; flowers blue, in June; Siberia; 1801. *P. Virginica* (Virginian); hardy perennial; 18 inches; flowers blue, in May; North America; 1799.

PUNICA. *Pomegranate.* [Myrtaceæ.] Beautiful deciduous trees. Light rich soil. Propagated by cuttings, layers, or grafting. Should be wintered in a cellar.

P. granatum (common); half-hardy tree; 12 feet; flowers red or whitish, single or double, in July; south of Europe; 1548.

PURSLANE. See PORTULACA.

PYRETHRUM. *Feverfew.* [Compositæ.] A rather large genus, consisting mostly of hardy perennials, of the easiest culture; not very ornamental, with the exception of a double-flowered variety of *P. Parthenium*, which is showy, blooming in profusion throughout the summer and autumn. This variety is multiplied by cuttings, planted during summer under a hand-glass; the other hardy kinds by division. There are also some free-growing greenhouse shrubs, of little importance.

Chrysanthemum (*Pyrethrum sinense*). This popular plant is quite hardy; but as it blooms late in autumn, just at the season severe frost often occurs, it sometimes happens, that out-door plants which are one day in full beauty, and almost the only ornaments of the garden, are the next day blackened and cut up by the frost. For high culture, the plants require to be renewed every year by cuttings. They will spread in the ground and bloom for years; but if a dwarf plant is wanted, and the flowers are required in perfection, they must be renewed by cuttings. One plan, the object of which is to secure small dwarf plants in pots, is, in July, when the plants have grown two feet or more in height, to take off the tops three inches long, cut off the lower leaves, plant them in sandy soil, and cover with a hand-glass: they must be kept moist, and the pots set in a gentle hot-bed, and the glass wiped every morning. In a short time they will strike root; then pot them in five-inch pots, and grow them in the open air in a situation where they will have all sun. The soil in which they are potted should be loam and rotted dung, with a little silver sand. When the blooms are showing, they may be changed into larger pots, and removed into the house, where they will bloom in perfection. The plants having nearly expended their growth before the tops were taken off, the cuttings have not much more growth to develop, and therefore bloom in a dwarf state. There are other ways of growing this plant. The young suckers, or shoots from the root, may be taken off in February, placed in a gentle hot-bed till well rooted, and then potted singly in light soil, hardened off, and protected in a cold well-aired frame until May, when they may be set out of doors in an open place until the end of September. They must have two good shifts, and the tops may be twice or thrice pinched out, after two or three inches' growth, to produce bushy plants. In this way, large plants are formed, which become very ornamental. In all cases, the plants should have weak liquid manure or clarified soot-water, at every watering from the time the flower-buds show distinctly: nothing else is so effective in producing fine high-colored flowers.

There are two distinct classes of Chrysanthemums now cultivated: one tall-growing, with large flowers; the other dwarf, compact, with numerous smaller flowers. Both are highly ornamental; the latter class, called Pompones, being perhaps the most useful where only small greenhouses are available for blooming them. These naturally grow dwarf and bushy, and therefore do not require so much stopping as the others. They should not be topped oftener than once, but may be made to branch by good culture, and by spreading out the stems somewhat. They are also better propagated in spring than late in the summer. Chrysanthemums grow well against walls, and bloom magnificently if the season proves favorable. They are also almost unaffected by the smoke of cities and towns. For varieties consult florists' catalogues.

P. Parthenium flore-pleno (double-common); hardy perennial; 2 feet; flowers white, in July; England. *P. sinense* (Chrysanthemum); hardy sub-shrub; 3 feet; flowers various, in November; China; 1764.

There are many other species. Within the last few years, many fine hybrids have been obtained from *P. roseum*, which is itself a coarse, weedy flower. The following are fine enough to find place in any garden: *P. roseum album, Lysias, Mrs. Dix, Princess Alexandra, Purple Prince, Versailles, Defiance, Mr. Dix, Iveryana, striatum plenum, Nemesis, fulgens, Herman Stinger, floribunda plena, Wilhelm Kramper, Anne Holborn.*

PYRUS. See CYDONIA.

Q UAMOCLIT. *Cypress-vine.* [Convolvulaceæ.] Twining plants, the annual species of which should be raised in a hot-bed in April, and planted out in May. The seeds are very hard; and a very successful mode of making them germinate is to delay planting them till the warm days of June: choose a hot noon, plant the seed, and immediately water plentifully with boiling water. The plants will be above ground in thirty-six hours. The most common species are —

Q. coccinea (scarlet); half-hardy twining annual; 12 feet; flowers scarlet, in July; North America; 1818. *Q. vulgaris* (common); half-hardy twining annual; 8 feet; flowers crimson, in July; East Indies; 1629. There is a white-flowered variety.

Q. digitata, hederifolia, luteola, Phœnicea, serotina, and *triloba* are other annual species.

QUAKING-GRASS. See BRIZA.

QUELTIA. See NARCISSUS. The plants formerly called by this name are now known as Narcissus.

QUERCUS. *Oak.* [Amentaceæ.] Well-known valuable trees. There are some hundred species and varieties; but only a few are valuable for the garden, as, generally, they are too large-growing. The variegated and fastigate varieties are very desirable. As Oaks are found in all parts of the world, there are many tender species. The principal North American species are —

Q. Phellos (willow-leaved); 1723; and variety *humilis;* 1812.

Q. prinus (chestnut-leaved); 1730. *Q. bicolor* (white-swamp); 1811. *Q. montana* (rock-chestnut); 1800. *Q. castanea* (yellow-chestnut); 1816. *Q. prinoides* (dwarf-chestnut, chinquapin). *Q. nigra* (black); 1739. *Q. tinctoria* (dyer's); 1800 *Q. coccinea* (scarlet); 1691. *Q. ambigua* (gray); 1800. *Q. rubra* (red); 1739. *Q. macrocarpa* (overcup, white); 1800. *Q. alba* (white); 1724. *Q. virens* (live-oak); *Q. robur* (English oak).

Many of these are very ornamental street or lawn trees, growing to a great size, and attaining great age. In the autumn, the foliage of the scarlet oak is most conspicuous in woodland scenery, and continues uninjured by the frost later than that of most forest trees. The leaves of some of the oaks change in autumn to a rich yellow or brown; and in a plantation of different species we often see most exquisite contrasts of color. The foliage of many species clings to the branches until torn off by the winter's wind, or forced from the tree by the swelling buds in spring. Oaks are usually propagated from acorns, which should be gathered when ripe, kept in damp sand, or buried, during the winter, and sown in drills in spring. The young plants should be frequently transplanted, unless sown where they are to stand permanently, as the long tap-root renders the successful removal of a large tree very uncertain.

QUINCE. See CYDONIA.

RANUNCULUS. *Crow-foot*. [Ranunculaceæ.] A large genus, comprising many annual weeds and aquatics; but chiefly consisting of hardy herbaceous perennials, some of which are ornamental. It includes the common Crowfoot, the Buttercups of the meadow, as well as the florists' Ranunculus, which have sprung from *R. Asiaticus*. The cultivation of these beautiful flowers has puzzled florists a good deal. There is, however, one kind of compost in which they will thrive; and it is worth while to be at some pains to get it. It is obtained thus: Cut from a good loamy pasture the surface sod three inches thick; let these be piled on one another in ridges for a year, and then sliced down with a sharp spade so as to form a crumbly mass. Turn this over, and pick out all the wire-worms, grubs, and earwigs, and any other living pest you can discover. This done, let it be packed into a heap again, and remain another year, by which time all the herbage will have resolved itself into that kind of mould, which, if separate, we should call vegetable mould. At the end of the second year, let it be again turned, and examined in the same way to clear completely any remaining intruders. This soil, thus cleared of vermin, will grow the Ranunculus well. Composts of a stimulating and exciting character are used by some for the sake of getting the flowers a little larger; but there is always the risk of doing mischief: and those who have grown them on the stimulating plan have occasionally been visited by disease, and lost many of their tubers. In this loam, then, enriched as it is by vegetable mould, plant the roots in autumn, and protect the bed by a frame two inches below the surface; and press the earth close about them. When they come up, keep them clear of weeds; and, as they break the ground, loose about them, crumble it, and keep it pressed close round them. Water them freely in hot weather, and the instant they show the color of their blooms keep the sun off: they will very well repay the trouble. When the flowers are over, and the leaves are turning yellow, take up the tubers, and keep them out of ground till planting time. They may be raised from seeds in the same way as Anemones.

R. aconitifolius (aconite-leaved); hardy perennial; 1 foot; flowers white, in May; European Alps; 1596. *R. acris flore-pleno* (bachelor's buttons); hardy perennial; 2 feet; flowers yellow, in June; garden variety. *R. Alpestris* (Alpine); hardy perennial; 6 inches; flowers white, in July; Scotland. *R. amplexicaulis* (stem-clasping); hardy perennial; 1 foot; flowers white, in May; Pyrenees; 1633. *R. Asiaticus* (common garden); hardy perennial; 9 inches; flowers various, in June; Levant; 1596. The colors of the double garden varieties are very various. *R. chærophyllus* (chervil-leaved); hardy perennial; 1 foot; flowers yellow, in May; Portugal. *R. gramineus* (grassy); hardy perennial; 1 foot; flowers yellow, single or double, in May; Europe. *R. millefoliatus* (thousand-leaved); hardy perennial; 1 foot; flowers yellow, in May; Sicily; 1820. *R. platanifolius* (plane-leaved); hardy perennial; 3 feet; flowers white, single or double, in June; Alps; 1596. *R. rutæfolius* (rue-leaved); hardy perennial; 6 inches; flowers white, in June; Austria; 1759.

RAGGED ROBIN. See LYCHNIS FLOSCUCULI.

RESEDA. *Mignonette.* [Resedaceæ.] The botanical name of the mignonette is *Reseda odorata*. This universally admired annual is one of the most easily-grown of all plants; no matter when it is sown or where. Sow the seeds, and the plant, bloom, and seed soon reward us. It may be sown four times a year with advantage in pans, or pots, and may be planted out anywhere, three or four plants in a patch. It may be sown in pots, and be thinned; the plants taken out, being transplanted somewhere else. If in winter, the pots must be kept in the greenhouse, or in pits, or frames with glasses; if in summer, they may be in the open air. No plants will bear rougher treatment; none sooner show when they have been removed to better soil. Mignonette is nothing to look at except by means of a magnifying glass; it makes no show; but its scent, which has no superior among all the fragrant flowers of the garden, will always secure for it a place in the most *recherché* collections. Scatter the seed upon the borders; let the plants come up like weeds; they are acceptable anywhere — everywhere. It is so nearly hardy, that we have seen the old plants and young seedlings from the self-sown seed, standing side by side after a mild winter. Mignonette, although an annual, can be struck from cuttings, which in their turn do very well, and almost assimilate the plant to a perennial. They bloom more dwarf under these circumstances, but they are not the worse for that; and as to foliage, generally speaking, that is not much to look at after the plant begins to bloom, and does not improve the second year. Large quantities of mignonette are grown for the market; for which purpose it is generally sown in pots, half a dozen seeds sprinkled in each pot, and all of them submitted to the common garden frames with lights; the seeds are sown about September, and the plants have all the air that can be given all the winter. Of course, they keep growing, except in frosty weather; and in the spring months rapidly come forward. These plants show bloom very early, before they have grown much, and are in flower until others, sown in February and March, come in to succeed them. The Mignonette may be had in bloom all the year round by a succession of sowings. A sowing in July brings plants that flower from November till March ; a sowing the first week in September will carry on the blooming from March to July; and the spring-sown ones will do the rest. No frost must reach the pots in the winter-time, and the earth must be occasionally stirred upon the surface to let in the air.

R. odorata (scented mignonette) ; hardy annual ; 1 foot ; flowers greenish, all summer ; North Africa ; 1752.

There are many other species ; but they are of little value in the garden.

RESTHARROW. See ONONIS.

RHAMNUS. *Buckthorn.* [Rhamnaceæ.] The most important garden plant of this family is the well-known hedge plant *R. catharticus.* There are many other species.

RHEUM. *Rhubarb.* [Polygonaceæ.] Hardy perennials of coarse habit, but having a fine effect in rough borders, and in situations where bold-looking striking plants are desirable. Good garden soil. Increased by division or seeds.

RHODANTHE. [Compositæ.] A beautiful little half-hardy annual, whose flowers are like so many pink stars sprinkled all over the branches, and, when well grown, as delicate as the most elegant artificial flowers ; the petals are stiff and dry, and, if gathered when in good order, the flowers may be classed among those vulgarly called "everlasting." The soil adapted best for its healthy culture is a compost of loam, decomposed cow-dung, turfy peat, and sand ; two parts of the loam, and one of each of the rest, well incorporated, and passed through a coarse sieve. In a shallow pan of this compost, gently compressed by striking the pan on the table, and levelled even with the edge, the seeds should be sown in April, very thinly and evenly; with the hand spread flat, press the surface gently all over, and then, with a very fine sieve, shake enough compost over the seeds to cover them, and no more. The pan may be placed in a hot-bed, or in the stove. When the plants come up, let them be thinned a little, drawing out any weeds that may come up with them, and place them close to the glass. In a few days they will be large enough to prick out four or six in a three-inch pot; and, as soon as they have taken root, they may be put into the greenhouse, and allowed to grow until they nearly touch each other; but they must be kept near the light, and have air in very mild weather. When they are first pricked out, they must be shaded a day or two. They may next be planted singly in three-inch pots, and still kept near the glass. In these pots they may continue growing until the roots completely fill the space round the sides, when they may be transferred to five-inch pots, in which they may bloom. Continue to give them plenty of air, plenty of light, and moderate waterings. There are few annuals that compete with them for elegance of form, symmetry, and beauty of flower. The supernumerary pots of five or six plants each — that is, those not required for separate potting — should be set aside, and kept in the frames till the middle of May, when they may be turned out into the borders in the patches, without being disturbed. Being dwarf, they must be kept near the front. From those in the borders, seed may be expected; be careful to gather it as soon as the flowers lose their bright pink color; for, as the seed ripens, the petals get paler, and being a composite flower the seed is not within a pod, and would easily be lost. Pick off the flowers whole, and the seed easily rubs out. In warm situations and in light rich soils, the seeds for the out-door plants may be sown in May in the borders, and the patches then merely require thinning out.

R. Manglesii (Mangles's); half-hardy annual; 1 foot; flowers pink, in July; Swan River; 1832.

RHODOCHITON. [Scrophularineæ.] *R. volubile*, once called *Lophospermum Rhodochiton*, is a plant with much the habit and appearance of *Lophospermum*, but more slender; the blossoms have a saucer-shaped rosy calyx, and a deep purple, almost black corolla. The plant is increased by cuttings, which may be put in at any period between March and August, in sandy soil, and placed in a close shady place : mild heat assists their rooting. The young plants soon acquire strength, when placed in a moderate bulk of compost, which should consist of loam, peat, and leaf-mould in equal proportions, and used in rather a rough or lumpy condition. It is adapted for the open ground, and may be grown to a very pretty state; the branches being trained around several upright stakes forming a cylinder. In any case, the plants should be renewed annually. It requires the usual treatment of bedding out climbers.

R. volubile (twining); greenhouse climbing perennial; 12 feet; flowers rose and chocolate, in June; Mexico; 1833.

RHODODENDRON. *Rose-bay*. [Ericaceæ.] One of the most ornamental families of evergreen flowering shrubs, comprising great variety both of foliage and flower. Some of the wild species have superb flowers; but the seedlings raised in English gardens carry the splendor of this family greatly beyond that of any of the original species. *R. Catawbiense*, which has the best habit of all the American species, has been so improved from seed, that varieties may now be had of almost every color. The Indian and hardy species, too, have been so crossed, that the most superb varieties have been produced with the best qualities of several species combined. They must be seen in flower to be purchased with advantage. Peat soil is the most suitable for these shrubs ; but the hardy sorts will grow well planted either in fibry or heavy loams, which are improved by the addition of vegetable soil. They are propagated in a variety of ways. The common sorts increase plentifully from seeds, which are also resorted to (the flowers having been cross-fertilized), for the raising of new varieties. Sow the seeds in broad shallow pots, well drained, and filled with a mixture of two-thirds peat and one-third loam ; place them in a cold pit ; keep the soil moist, for it must not once dry after the seeds are in. When large enough, prick the young plants out at an inch apart, into other pots or pans, and, as they become larger, pot them singly ; or, if intended for the open air, plant them in peat-beds, giving them room from year to year by taking away alternate plants, and putting them elsewhere. They may continue in the beds till they flower. If there be any doubt of their hardiness, put hoops and mats over them ; but it is useless to raise tender ones, while there are so many fine hardy varieties. Approved sorts and rare species are propagated by layering, or by grafting on stocks of the common species, sometimes by cuttings.

R. arboreum (tree) ; half-hardy evergreen tree ; 20 feet ; flowers rose, in April ; Nepaul ; 1820. This species has given rise to many richly-colored hybrids. *R. Catawbiense* (Catawba) ; hardy evergreen shrub ; 4 feet ; flowers purple, in June ; North America ; 1809. The varieties of this afford all shades of colors, from purple and rose to pink and white. *R. ciliatum* (ciliate) ; half-hardy evergreen shrub ; 18 inches ; flowers purple or whitish ; Sikkim Himalaya ; 1850. *R. Dalhousiæ* (Lady Dalhousie's); half-hardy evergreen shrub ; 6 feet ; flowers white, in March ; Himalaya ; 1850. *R. formosum* (showy) ; greenhouse evergreen shrub ; 6 feet ; flowers white, in June ; India ; 1837. Called also *R. Gibsoni*. *R. hirsutum* (hairy) ; hardy evergreen shrub ; 2 feet ; flowers bright rose or white, in May ; Switzerland ; 1656. *R. Javanicum* (Javanese) ; greenhouse or stove evergreen shrub; 4 feet; flowers salmon or copper-color, in February; Java; 1847. *R. Ponticum* (Pontic); hardy evergreen shrub; 6 feet; flowers purple, in May; Gibraltar; 1763. This has sported into numerous varieties of various colors.

Almost all the species of Rhododendron are worth planting out doors, especially such of the Indian ones as ultimately prove hardy; the tenderer sorts being the best of all plants, along with Camellias, for cold conservatories. The following are fine varieties, hardy enough to withstand a New-England winter: *Archimedes, album elegans, album grandiflorum, atrosanguineum, Barclayanum, Blandyanum, Brayanum, Chancellor, Columbus, Delicatissimum, Duc de Brabant, Everestianum, giganteum, Leopardii, lucidum, Marc Antony, Nero, ornatum, Pardoleton, pictum, perspicuum, purpureum elegans* and *grandiflorum, roseum elegans, grandiflorum, pictum* and *superbum, Sherwoodianum, Victoria.*

RHUBARB. See RHEUM.

RHUS. *Sumach.* [Anacardiaceæ.] Hardy deciduous shrubs. Light loam. Increased by seeds, layers, or cuttings.

ORNAMENTAL SHRUBS. *R. copallina, R. Coriaria, R. Cotinus, R. typhina.*

RIBES. *Currant.* [Grossulariaceæ.] An extensive family of hardy shrubs, well suited for shrubberies. The very best, which grows freely in ordinary garden soil, is *R. sanguineum*, a deciduous plant, which about May is decorated with drooping bunches of scarlet blossoms. Of this there is a very handsome double-flowered variety, and another in which the blossoms are white. They are propagated without difficulty either by layers or by cuttings.

R. aureum præcox (early); hardy shrub; 4 feet; flowers yellow, in March; North America; 1812. *R. sanguineum* (bloody); hardy shrub; 4 feet; flowers red or white, single or double, in

May; North America; 1826. *R. speciosum* (showy); hardy shrub; 4 feet; flowers scarlet, in May; California; 1829.

Other species may be planted in extensive shrubberies.

RICINUS. *Palma Christi.* [Euphorbiaceæ.] For ordinary gardens, *R. communis*, or Castor-oil plant, is sufficient. It is one of those plants which, wherever there is room for them, should always find a place, for the sake of their fine expansive palmate foliage. The flowers are curious, but not showy. The seeds should be sown in a hot-bed in April, and the young plants potted singly, and grown in the frame for a few weeks, then transferred to the greenhouse or a cooler frame, and finally hardened off in a cold frame, ready for planting out by the end of May. The soil should be made rich for them; for, being grown on account of their foliage, it is desirable to encourage them, that the leaves may be fine and vigorous. The variety called *R. communis minor* is preferable, except where there is abundant space, when the variety *major* may be grown; the leaves of the latter are considerably the larger, though both are large. This plant, though a shrub or tree in its native climate, is destroyed here by our winter, and is therefore treated as a half-hardy annual.

R. communis (castor-oil plant); half-hardy shrub; 5 feet; flowers greenish-yellow, in July; East Indies; 1548.

This plant has latterly attracted much attention, and there are many very fine foliaged varieties which we may mention. *R. sanguineus, Borboniensis arboreus, Tunciensis, macrocarpus, spectabilis, albicans, leucocarpus, Africanus*, and *macrocarpus nanus*, afford every variety of white, green, and red foliage. The seed ripens as far North as Massachusetts in favorable seasons.

RICOTIA. [Cruciferæ.] A hardy annual, thriving in garden soil from seed sown in May.

R. lunaria (Moonwort); flowers blue, purple, in July; Egypt; 1757.

ROBINIA. [Leguminosæ.] Deciduous shrubs and trees, many of them of large size, as the False Acacia, or Locust-tree (*R. pseud-Acacia*), which, besides its elegant pinnate foliage, and drooping racemes of white sweet-scented flowers, furnishes a hard and durable timber. For the flower-garden and shrubbery, however, the species most appropriate is the Rose Acacia (*R. hispida*), for which the allied species, *R. macrophylla*, may be substituted in situations where there is space for its somewhat larger growth: both bear long drooping racemes of large rose-colored flowers. The Rose Acacias grow well in moderately good garden soil; but they require rather a sheltered situation, or their brittle branches are liable to be broken by the wind. They should be grown as standards.

R. pseud, acacia variety *Decaisneana*, is a charming hybrid, with rosy-pink flowers; 1862.

ROCKET. See HESPERIS.

ROMERIA. [Papaveraceæ.] Hardy annuals, allied to Glaucium. Common soil. Propagated by seeds sown in May.

The species are *R. hybrida, refracta,* and *vermiculata,* with purple, red, and violet flowers in June.

ROSA. *Rose.* [Rosaceæ.] The varieties, colors, and habit of the Rose are almost endless. They are grown either on their own roots, or budded on stocks — that is, stems — of the common Dog-rose. The Rose will grow well in any moderately-rich garden soil. In planting roses, cut all the ragged and damaged parts of the root clean with a sharp knife; if any part of the root is bruised, remove it; plant these the same depth that they have been growing before; prune out all the thin twigs or shoots from the head or bush; cut out all the branches which are in the way of others; cut back all the last year's wood to three eyes, and always make the cut sloping, and just above a bud. When they are growing, rub off the buds that are growing inward so as to crowd the head. It is a good plan to prune roses at two if not three seasons; for on the pruning the season of bloom depends. The early pruned ones grow as soon as the unpruned; the latter push the eyes towards the end, while the eyes next the stem do not push at all; by pruning off all the grown eyes, the ungrown ones have to begin their growth, when the pruned bushes have grown for a month, and thus later flowers are obtained. For the culture of this favorite flower, see Parkman's Treatise on the subject.

R. Banksiæ (Lady Banks's); half-hardy shrub; 20 feet; flowers white or yellow, in June; China; 1807. *R. bracteata* (Macartney's); hardy shrub; 3 feet; flowers white, in August; China; 1795. *R. centifolia* (cabbage); hardy shrub; 2 feet; flowers pink, in June; Caucasus; 1596. The parent of the garden varieties of Cabbage and Moss roses. *R. indica* (monthly); half-hardy shrub; 12 feet; flowers blush, all the year; China; 1789. From this have sprung the varieties of China and Tea-scented roses. *R. Lawrenceana* (Miss Lawrence's); half-hardy shrub; 1 foot; flowers blush, all the year; China; 1810: the parent of the Fairy roses. *R. rubiginosa* (eglantine); hardy shrub; 5 feet; flowers pink, in June; England. *R. semperflorens* (ever-blooming); hardy shrub; 6 feet; flowers deep crimson, all the year; China; 1789.

ROSE ACACIA. See ROBINIA.
ROSE BAY. See RHODODENDRON.
ROSE CAMPION. See LYCHNIS.
RUBUS. *Bramble.* [Rosaceæ.] Hardy trailing shrubs for the most part. Soil, rich loam. Propagated by cuttings and layers. A very extensive genus, which is generally well adapted for gardens.

R. fruticosus flore pleno (double); hardy deciduous trailing shrub; 10 feet; flowers light-red, in July; Britain.

RUDBECKIA. [Compositæ.] Showy hardy herbaceous perennials, from which the species of *Echinacea, Obeliscaria, Centrocarpha,* and *Dracopis* have been separated. Increased by seeds sown in May, to produce flowering-plants for the next year, or by dividing the old roots any time in autumn or spring, and planting the division with pieces of root attached. They grow readily in any good common soil.

R. laciniata (jagged-leaved); hardy perennial; 5 feet; flowers yellow, in July; North America; 1640. *R. lævigata* (smooth); hardy perennial; 3 feet; flowers yellow, in July; Carolina; 1812.

RUSCUS. *Butcher's Broom.* [Smilaceæ.] Evergreen undershrubs. Common soil. Propagated by suckers. These plants are not hardy in the Northern States.

CURIOUS EVERGREENS.—*R. aculeatus, R. hypoglossum, R. hypophyllum, R. racemosus.*

SABBATIA. [Gentianaceæ.] Hardy or half-hardy biennials and perennials. Soil, peat, kept moist. Increased by seeds or division.

S. angularis (angular); hardy biennial; 6 inches; flowers purple, in July; North America; 1826. *S. paniculata* (panicled); hardy perennial; 18 inches; flowers white, in May; North America; 1817. *S. stellaris* (starry); hardy biennial, dwarf; flowers rose, with a yellowish-green eye, in July; North America; 1827.

SAGE. See SALVIA.

SAGITTARIA. *Arrow-head.* [Alismaceæ.] Aquatic perennials, requiring various degrees of temperature. Rich, loamy soil. Increased by division. The plants require to be placed in water.

S. graminea (grassy); greenhouse aquatic perennial; 18 inches; flowers white, in July; Carolina; 1812. *S. latifolia* (broad-leaved); hardy aquatic perennial; 1 foot; flowers white, single, or double, in July; North America; 1818. *S. sagittifolia* (arrow-leaved); hardy aquatic perennial; 2 feet; flowers white, single, or double, in July; England. *S. sinensis* (Chinese); greenhouse aquatic perennial; 2 feet; flowers white, in October; China; 1812.

ST. JOHN'S WORT. See HYPERICUM.

SAINTFOIN. See ONOBRYCHIS.

SALISBURIA. *Maiden-hair Tree.* [Taxaceæ.] Hardy deciduous tree, ornamental on account of its habit and singular maiden-hair-like foliage. Soil, sandy loam. Propagated by layers or cuttings. *S. adiantifolia* is the only species, of which there is a fine variegated variety.

SALIX. *Willow.* [Saliceæ.] A large genus of deciduous shrubs and trees, a few of which are ornamental. Moist soil, rather loamy. Propagated by cuttings of the stouter shoots planted in spring.

ORNAMENTAL TREES. — *S. Babylonica,* and its varieties *crispa* and *Napoleona; S. cuprea pendula.*

There are some two hundred species and varieties.

SALPIGLOSSIS. [Solanaceæ.] Annuals or biennials, of a showy character, requiring the protection of a frame or greenhouse in winter; and except in very sheltered situations, where they may be planted out in summer, suited rather for pot-culture in doors than for the open air. They may be managed very much in the same way as the biennial species of *Schizanthus.* They require a light and rich compost. Probably they are all varieties of the same species. When well cultivated, they are showy plants.

S. atropurpurea (dark-purple); half-hardy biennial; 2 feet; flowers dark-purple, in June; Chili; 1827. *S. Barclayana* (Barclay's); half-hardy biennial; 2 feet; flowers brown and yellow, in June; gardens. *S. coccinea* (scarlet); half-hardy biennial; 2 feet; flowers scarlet or coppery, in June. *S. lutea* (yellow); half-hardy biennial; 2 feet; flowers yellow, in June. *S. picta* (painted); half-hardy biennial; 2 feet; flowers white and purple, in June; Chili; 1820. *S. straminea* (straw); half-hardy biennial; 2 feet; flowers yellowish, in June; Chili; 1824.

SALVIA. *Sage.* [Lamiaceæ.] There are two kinds of Salvia highly esteemed for the brilliance of their flowers, — *S. splendens,* scarlet, and *S. patens,* brilliant blue; but there are many more that have nearly equal claims, and scores that are merely weeds. Some of them are hardy, some half-hardy; some require a stove, some a greenhouse. Salvias grow freely in any moderately good soil, the best being a light loam with a third of rotted dung. The greenhouse kinds do well planted out in May, and potted again in September, and are better propagated annually by cuttings in July or August. The herbaceous sorts, or half-shrubby hardy perennials, do very well in the ordinary soil of the garden, and multiply by parting the roots, or by striking the young shoots. The raising from seed is very simple. The seed has to be sown in March, in wide-mouthed pots; the seedlings pricked out early, a few in a pot, to grow into strength, and planted out in May if they are hardy or half-hardy, or potted if they are tender. Even the tender ones may be planted out, so that they are potted early in September, and put into frames or greenhouses, or any other contrivance, to prevent the frost from injuring them. The stove varieties are not worth notice, and the others may all safely be treated like Geraniums, Verbenas, and other plants for bedding out. *S. patens* is a fleshy rooted plant, requiring to be kept dry in winter like a Dahlia root.

S. azurea (azure); hardy perennial; 5 feet; flowers blue, in August; North America; 1806. *S. chamædryoides* (germander-leaved); half-hardy shrub; 18 inches; flowers blue, in June; Mexico; 1795. *S. confertiflora* (crowded); stove shrub; 5 feet; flowers orange-red, in September; Brazil; 1838. *S. fulgens* (brilliant); greenhouse shrub; 5 feet; flowers scarlet, in July; Mexico; 1829. *S. gesneriflora* (gesneria-flowered); stove shrub; 3 feet; flowers scarlet, in winter; 1836. *S. glutinosa* (glutinous); hardy perennial; 3 feet; flowers yellow, in June; Germany; 1769. *S. Grahamii* (Graham's); half-hardy shrub; 4 feet; flowers purple or rose, in July; Mexico; 1829. *S. hians* (gaping); hardy perennial; 3 feet; flowers blue and white, in June; Cashmere; 1839. *S. Horminum* (Clary); hardy annual; 18 inches; flowers purple, in June; south of Europe; 1596. One variety is red-topped, another purple-topped.

S. leucantha (white-flowered); greenhouse shrub; 3 feet; flowers white, in July; Mexico; 1825. *S. patens* (spreading); half-hardy perennial; 2 feet; flowers blue or white, in July; Mexico; 1838. *S. pratensis* (meadow); hardy perennial; 3 feet; flowers purple, in May; England. *S. prunelloides* (prunella-like); half-hardy perennial; 6 inches; flowers blue, in June; Mexico; 1838. *S. pseudo-coccinea* (bastard); greenhouse sub-shrub; 3 feet; flowers scarlet, in July; South America; 1797. *S. Sclarea* (Clary); hardy biennial; 3 feet; flowers whitish and purple, in July; south of Europe; 1562. *S. splendens* (splendid); greenhouse shrub; 5 feet; flowers scarlet, in September; Mexico; 1822. *S. Tenorii* (Tenorie's); hardy perennial; 2 feet; flowers blue, in June; Italy; 1821.

SANDWORT. See ARENARIA.

SANGUINARIA. *Puccoon.* [Papaveraceæ.] Dwarf early-blooming hardy perennials. Soil, light loam. Increased by division. They are very ornamental and valuable on account of their early bloom.

S. Canadensis (Canadian); hardy perennial; 6 inches; flowers white, in May; North America.

The variety *grandiflora* has larger flowers. This plant has a tendency to produce extra petals, and promises well for a double variety.

SAMBUCUS. *Elder.* [Caprifoliaceæ.] Hardy shrubs, with white flowers and ornamental berries. Propagated by seeds or cuttings. Soil, deep rich damp loam. The variegated varieties are very desirable.

S. Canadensis (Canada); 6 feet; flowers in July; North America; 1761. *S. nigra* (black-fruited); 15 feet; flowers in June; Britain. *S. nigra foliis-argenteis* (white-variegated-leaved); 20 feet; flowers in June; Britain. *S. nigra foliis-luteis* (yellow-variegated-leaved); 20 feet; flowers in June; Britain. *S. nigra laciniata* (cut; parsley-leaved); 20 feet; flowers in June; Britain. *S. nigra laciniata aurea* (cut; yellow-striped); 20 feet; flowers in June; 1848. *S. nigra leucocarpa* (white-berried); 20

feet; flowers in June; Britain. *S. nigra monstrosa* (monstrous-striped-barked); 20 feet; flowers in June; Britain. *S. nigra pulverulenta* (powdered); 10 feet; flowers in June; Britain. *S. nigra rotundifolia* (roundish-leaved); 20 feet; flowers in June; Britain. *S. nigra virescens* (greenish); 20 feet; flowers in June; Britain. *S. pubens* (downy); 6 feet; flowers in North America; 1812. *S. racemosa* (racemed); 12 feet; flowers green and yellow, in May; south of Europe; 1566. *S. racemosa flavescens* (yellowish); 12 feet; flowers yellow and green, in May; south of Europe; 1596. *S. racemosa purpurea* (purple); 12 feet; flowers purple, in May; south of Europe; 1596.

SANGUISORBA. *Burnet.* [Rosaceæ.] Hardy herbaceous perennials of coarse habit, but elegant foliage. They grow readily in common soil, and are increased by division.

S. Alpina (Alpine); flowers yellow, in June; Altai; 1837. *S. Andersonii* (Anderson's); flowers pink, in July; Siberia. *S. Canadensis* (Canadian); 3 feet; flowers white, in August; Canada; 1633. *S. carnea* (flesh-colored); 4 feet; flowers red, in July; Siberia; 1823. *S. Mauritanica* (Mauritanian); 4 feet; flowers pink, in July; Algiers; 1810. *S. media* (middle); 4 feet; flowers flesh, in August; Canada; 1785. *S. neglecta* (neglected); 4 feet; flowers white, in July; Europe; 1800. *S. officinalis* (shop); 4 feet; flowers purple, in July; Britain. *S. officinalis auriculata* (eared); 4 feet; flowers pink, in July; Sicily. *S. præcox* (early-flowering); 3 feet; flowers pink, in May; Siberia; 1827. *S. tenuifolia* (fine-leaved); 4 feet; flowers pink, in July; Dahuria; 1820.

SANVITALIA. [Compositæ.] A procumbent half-hardy annual, requiring the ordinary treatment of half-hardy annuals. Sown in the border or in beds about the beginning of May, it will bloom about July. It is a suitable plant for the edges of beds.

S. procumbens (procumbent); hardy annual; 1 foot; flowers yellow, in June; Mexico; 1798.

SAPONARIA. *Soap-wort.* [Caryophyllaceæ.] Showy hardy plants, consisting of annuals and perennials. Among the latter is *S. officinalis flore pleno*, a vigorous growing subject of the easiest culture, which, as it propagates by fragments of its roots, is with difficulty extirpated where it has been once introduced, but does not spread very rapidly of itself. Another pretty species, forming indeed a beautiful object on rock-work during summer, but apt to suffer from damp in winter, and therefore requiring to be preserved at that season in a dry frame, is *S. ocymoides*, which spreads over the surface of the ground in patches of some size, covered with innumerable rose-colored stars, through the principal part of the summer season. This kind is best increased by seeds, when they are to be procured : these should be sown in May or June, and the young plants potted singly, using a compost of sandy loam, and keeping them sheltered from much wet and damp, in cool frames, through the first winter, when they may be planted out. When seeds are not to be had, cuttings must be planted in June or July, in sandy soil, under hand-lights, and these young plants wintered as before. A store of young plants should be so preserved annually. For a dwarf bed in a flower-garden, this species is well suited, on account of the mass in which its blossoms are produced : when so planted, the surface should be covered with stones, over which the branches of the *Saponaria* delight to spread. *S. calabrica* is a beautiful annual, of very much the same character in other respects.

S. cæspitosa (tufted) ; half-hardy perennial ; 6 inches ; flowers red, in July ; Pyrenees ; 1820. *S. ocymoides* (basil-like) ; half-hardy perennial ; 6 inches ; flowers rose, in June ; Europe ; 1768. *S. officinalis flore pleno* (officinal) ; hardy perennial ; 3 feet ; flowers pink, in July ; gardens. *S. prostrata* (prostrate) ; half-hardy perennial ; 6 inches ; flowers rose, in July ; Pyrenees ; 1824.

SARRACENIA. *Side-saddle Flower.* [Sarraceniæ.] Hardy

and half-hardy herbaceous perennials. Soil, sphagnum moss and fibry peat. *S. purpurea* is perfectly hardy, needing only a moist situation : the other species need greenhouse protection. Increased by division.

S. Drummondii, *S. flava*, *S. minor*, *S. purpurea*, *S. rubra*, *S. variolaris*, are all interesting plants, remarkable for the pitcher-like form of the leaves.

SAUSSUREA. [Compositæ] Hardy herbaceous perennials, with red or purple flowers, thriving in common garden soil, and propagated by division. There are about twenty species, natives of Siberia and the Caucasus.

SAXIFRAGA. *Saxifrage.* [Saxifragaceæ.] Hardy perennials, of close-tufted growth, mostly of small stature, and of simple beauty. All the species are admirably suited for rock-work, thriving when planted on raised banks among rough stones, which they soon cover with their matted branches. One species, *S. umbrosa*, is one of the most valuable of plants for town gardens : in fact, it thrives anywhere, — as well in the midst of smoke and shade as in the pure air. This grows a foot or more high, and has pink flowers prettily spotted, which are produced about May. The species flourish in any kind of light soil, and increase to any extent by division. They are sometimes planted as an edging to flower borders, and look very pretty, but require to be frequently replanted.

S. Cotyledon (pyramidal); hardy perennial ; 2 feet ; flowers white, in a pyramid, in June ; European Alps ; 1596. *S. crassifolia* (thick-leaved) ; hardy perennial ; 1 foot ; flowers pink, in April ; Siberia ; 1765. *S. granulata plena* (grain-rooted) ; hardy perennial ; 1 foot ; flowers white, in May ; gardens. *S. hypnoides* (moss-like) ; hardy perennial ; 6 inches ; flowers white, in May ; Scotland. *S. oppositifolia* (opposite-leaved) ; hardy perennial ; 3 inches ; flowers purple or white, in March ; Britain. *S. sarmentosa* (sarmentose) ; half-hardy perennial ; 2

feet; flowers white, spotted red, in June; China; 1815. *S. umbrosa;* hardy perennial; 18 inches; flowers flesh-colored, spotted, in April; Britain.

All the perennial kinds may be safely added to this small selection, which serves merely to indicate the variety comprised in the genus.

SCABIOSA. *Scabious.* [Dipsaceæ.] Hardy herbaceous perennials. Common soil. Increased by division. The species are *S. arvensis, Australis, Carpatica, dichotoma, dipsacifolia, pubescens, Salcedi,* and *stricta,* mostly white flowered.

SCARLET RUNNER. See PHASEOLUS.

SCHIVERECKIA. [Brassiceæ.] Hardy perennial rock-plants. Common soil. Increased by division.

SCHIZANTHUS. [Scrophularineæ.] Hardy annuals and greenhouse biennials. The plant is of branching, elegant, habit, and well covered with bloom; the flowers of an odd shape, with wings and lips of different colors. They are a very pretty tribe of plants, and for pot-culture, as well as the borders, are worthy of all gardens. Sown in the open borders, they bloom the more dwarf in proportion as the soil is poor; but the best way to raise them is on a hot-bed in March. The greenhouse biennial section is only suitable for pot-culture, and differs in requiring to be sown in July or August, and kept through the winter in small pots, on a dry, airy, greenhouse shelf. They bloom very late if sown in spring.

S. candidus (whitish); half-hardy annual; 2 feet; flowers whitish, in July; Coquimbo; 1840. *S. Grahami* (Graham's); half-hardy biennial; 2 feet; flowers lilac and yellow, in June; Chili; 1831. *S. Hookeri* (Hooker's); half-hardy biennial; 2 feet; flowers rose and yellow, in June; Chili; 1828. *S. pinnatus* (pinnate); half-hardy annual; 18 inches; flowers lilac and rose, in June; Chili; 1822. *S. retusus* (retuse); half-hardy biennial; 2 feet; flowers crimson and yellow, or white, in June;

Chili; 1831. *S. violaceus* (violet); half-hardy annual; 2 feet; flowers violet-purple, in July; gardens.

SCHIZONOTUS. [Rosaceæ.] A small genus of hardy shrubs, separated from Spiræa, and differing in having pinnate leaves. *S. tomentosus (Spiræa Lindleyana)* is a very desirable, hardy shrub, requiring the same mode of management as the shrubby species of Spiræa, and is propagated by cuttings and division.

S. tomentosa (downy); hardy shrub; 3 feet; flowers white, in May; India.

SCHIZOPETALON. [Brassiceæ.] *S. Walkeri* is a hardy annual, more curious than beautiful, but withal worth a place in any garden, not only for the singularity of its appearance, but also for the fragrance which it evolves towards evening. It is one of the cruciferous order, the flowers of which have four petals; but, in this case, these parts are curiously fringed: they are white on the face, dull-brown on the back. It should be sown in May, in moderately light soil, and will flower about July, successional sowings blooming on till September.

S. Walkeri (Walker's); hardy annual; 2 feet; flowers white and brown, in July; Chili; 1822.

SCHOUWIA. [Cruciferæ.] A hardy annual. Propagated by seed sown in light soil in May.

S. Arabica (Arabian); hardy annual; 9 inches; flowers purple, in July; Arabia; 1837.

SCILLA. *Squill.* [Liliaceæ.] A genus of bulbs, for the most part hardy, and ranking among the prettiest ornaments of the early spring. They are far too much neglected in gardens, though of the easiest culture, and very ornamental at a season when flowers are scarce. They grow very well in any moderately good garden soil, but have rather a preference for soil containing a considerable portion of peat-earth, or a free light loam; this is especially the case with several of the smaller kinds. They multiply rapidly by means of offsets, and their culture is very simple, for they merely require planting in the autumn (the bulbs being placed from two to four inches under ground, according to their size), and they may then remain year after year. Except for the sake of increase, the less they are disturbed the better. There are something like three dozen species recorded as being in cultivation, all of which are worth planting in a garden.

S. *amœna* (pleasing); hardy bulb; 3 inches; flowers blue, in May; Levant; 1596. S. *bifolia* (two-leaved); hardy bulb; 3 inches; flowers blue, in May; Europe and Asia Minor. S. *campanulata* (bell-flowered); hardy bulb; 1 foot; flowers blue, white, or pink, in May; Spain; 1683. S. *Italica* (Italian); hardy bulb; 9 inches; flowers blue, in May; Switzerland; 1605. S. *præcox* (early); hardy bulb; 3 inches; flowers deep-blue, in May; Siberia; 1790. S. *Sibirica* (Siberian); hardy bulb; 3 inches; flowers blue, in May; Siberia; 1795.

SCORPIURUS. [Leguminosæ.] Hardy annuals. Common soil. Increased by seeds.

SCROPHULARIA. [Scrophularineæ.] Hardy perennials. Common soil, rather damp. Propagated by divison.

SCUTELLARIA. *Skull-cap*. [Scrophularineæ.] A rather numerous family of dwarf herbaceous perennials, some of which are very ornamental. They are mostly hardy, showy, and worth growing in the mixed flower borders. They are not particular as to soil, and are readily increased by division, or, where the roots are indivisible, by planting as cuttings the young shoots produced from the crowns of the roots in spring. There is another class requiring greenhouse protection, at least in winter. These are increased by cuttings planted in sandy soil, and placed in a mild hot-bed; and the plants should be potted into rich soil of loam and leaf-mould, if grown in pots; but they may be planted out in a warm situation in the flower-garden by the beginning of June, to come into flower about August.

S. Alpina (Alpine); hardy perennial; 9 inches; flowers blue and white, in June; Hungary; 1752. *S. Columnæ* (heart-leaved); hardy perennial; 18 inches; flowers blue, in July; south of Europe; 1806. *S. scordifolia* (scordium-leaved); greenhouse perennial; 2 feet; flowers scarlet, in June; Mexico; 1841. S. *galericulata* (small-cupped); hardy perennial; 1 foot; flowers blue, in June; England. *S. grandiflora* (large-flowered); hardy perennial; 18 inches; flowers yellow and red, in July; Siberia; 1804. *S. Japonica* (Japanese); hardy perennial; 1 foot; flowers deep-blue, in June; Japan; 1838. *S. lupulina* (wolf); hardy perennial; 1 foot; flowers yellow and white, in July; Tartary; 1739. *S. macrantha* (large-flowered); hardy perennial; 1 foot; flowers purple, in July; China; 1844. *S. Ventenatii* (Ventenat's); greenhouse perennial; 2 feet; flowers scarlet, in July; St. Martha; 1844.

SCYPHANTHUS. [Loasaceæ.] A handsome twining plant, related to Loasa, and best treated as an annual. It may be grown in pots or trellises, or on the rafters of the greenhouse, or may be planted out for the summer in warm situations where the soil is light and dryish. In pots, it should be grown in a sandy mixture of loam and leaf-mould. The seeds should be sown in March, in a mild hot-bed, and nursed on till they are able to bear the temperature of the greenhouse, after which they may be planted out. They may also be sown in May in the borders.

S. elegans (elegant); half-hardy twining annual; 8 feet; flowers yellow, in July; Chili; 1824.

SEA LAVENDER. See STATICE.

SEDUM. *Stonecrop.* [Crassulaceæ.] A large family of succulents, comprising a great many kinds which are hardy herbs. They are well adapted for covering rock-work.

They are of the easiest culture, growing in almost any soil not retentive of moisture, but preferring that which is sandy. When established on rock-work, they grow almost without soil. A very handsome half-hardy kind, somewhat shrubby-habited, is *S. Sieboldii*, one of the prettiest of the species, having very glaucous leaves, and large heads of pink flowers; it forms a large tuft when grown in a large pot, and should have a light open soil. Increased by division.

S. acre (acrid); hardy perennial; 3 inches; flowers yellow, in June; England. *S. dasyphyllum* (thick-leaved); hardy perennial; 3 inches; flowers white, in June; England. *S. Kamtschaticum* (Kamtschatkan); hardy perennial; 6 inches; flowers yellow, in June; Kamtschatka. *S. rupestre* (rock); hardy perennial; 3 inches; flowers yellow, in June; England. *S. Sieboldii* (Siebold's); half-hardy perennial; 1 foot; flowers pink, in August; Japan; 1835. *S. Telephium* (Orpine); hardy perennial; 2 feet; flowers purple, in July; England. *S. villosum* (shaggy); hardy perennial; 3 inches; flowers pink, in June; England.

All the species of Sedum, and they are numerous, are desirable plants for rock-work.

SEMPERVIVUM. *House-leek.* [Crassulaceæ.] A family of succulents, related to Sedum, comprising many shrubby greenhouse species and a few hardy perennials. The hardy herbaceous kinds flourish in rather dry garden soil, and are increased by division. The best species are *S. arachnoideum, flagelliforme, globiferum, pumilum,* and *tectorum.*

SENECILLUS. [Compositæ.] Hardy herbaceous perennials, allied to Cineraria. Easily increased by seeds or division. Rich sandy loam.

S. glauca (sea-green); hardy perennial; 6 feet; flowers yellow, in August; Siberia; 1790.

S. purpurata, from Cape of Good Hope, with purple flowers, is not hardy in the Northern States.

SENECIO. *Groundsel.* [Compositæ.] An extensive genus of composite plants. The hardy herbaceous kinds are of little importance. *S. elegans* is an annual, requiring to be sown in the open border in the month of April, and again in June for a succession; the double-flowered varieties, which are very handsome, may be multiplied by cuttings, and treated as perennial sub-shrubs. The cuttings are struck in July or August. If for blooming in pots, they are shifted on like Cinerarias; but if for planting out in the flower-garden, where they make admirable beds, they may stand in the small pots till March, and then be removed into pots two sizes larger, in which they remain until they are planted out in the beginning of June, by which time they will be in flower. The young plants should be freely topped during autumn and winter, and the early spring, to make them bushy. The double white and the double purple are distinct, and very desirable kinds.

SERRATULA. [Compositæ.] A family of hardy herbaceous plants, generally purple-flowered, easily propagated by division, and growing in common garden soil.

SHEEP LAUREL. See KALMIA ANGUSTIFOLIA.

SHEPHERDIA. *Buffalo Berry.* [Eleagnaceæ.] Hardy deciduous shrubs or small trees, very ornamental when in fruit. The berry is eatable. Soil, deep sandy loam. Propagated by seeds. The plants are diœcious.

S. argentea (silvery); hardy tree; 16 feet; North America; 1820. *S. Canadensis* (Canadian); hardy tree; 10 feet; North America; 1759.

SIBERIAN PEA TREE. See CARAGANA.

SIEGESBECKIA. [Compositæ.] Hardy annuals, with yellow flowers, thriving in common garden soil. Sow in a hot-bed in April, and transplant to the border in May. *S. cordifolia, Iberica, Orientalis,* and *triangularis* are the species. *S. Iberica* has white flowers.

SIDESADDLE FLOWER. See SARRACENIA.

SIEVERSIA. [Rosaceæ.] Hardy perennials, with the habit and structure of Geum, and requiring similar treatment. They are mostly dwarf plants, and grow in light garden-soil, increase being effected by dividing the roots. Pretty plants for the border, or for rock-work.

S. montana (mountain); hardy perennial; 6 inches; flowers yellow, in May; Austria; 1597. *S. triflora* (three-flowered); hardy perennial; 9 inches; flowers yellow, in June; North America; 1826.

SILENE. *Catchfly.* [Caryophyllaceæ.] A genus of annual and perennial plants, bearing trusses of pink, red, pale-rose, and lilac blossoms, and lasting some weeks in bloom; The annuals may be sown thinly in the open border, where they are to remain. The perennial sorts grow in common soil, and are propagated by division.

S. Armeria (Lobel's); hardy annual; 18 inches; flowers pink or white, in July; England. *S. compacta* (compact); hardy annual; 18 inches; flowers pink, in July; Caucasus; 1823. *S. fimbriata* (fringed); hardy perennial; 2 feet; flowers white, in June; Caucasus; 1803. *S. maritima flore-pleno* (double-sea); hardy perennial; 6 inches; flowers white, in August; England. *S. pendula* (pendulous); hardy annual; 1 foot; flowers rose-pink or white, in May; Sicily; 1731. *S. regia* (royal); hardy perennial; 18 inches; flowers crimson, in June; North America; 1811. *S. Schafta* (Schaft's); hardy perennial; 6 inches; flowers deep-rose, in May; Russia; 1844.

There are more than a hundred other species.

SILVER FIR. See ABIES.

SKIMMIA. [Aurantiaceæ.] Evergreen shrubs, not hardy in the Northern States, bearing fragrant white flowers, and very ornamental in fruit. Good loamy soil. Propagated by cuttings, layers, or seeds.

S. Japonica (Japan); evergreen shrub; 3 feet; flowers white, in spring; China; 1852.

SKULL-CAP. See SCUTELLARIA.

SMILACINA. [Liliaceæ.] Hardy herbaceous plants. Light loamy soil. Propagated by division.

S. bifolia (two-leaved); 3 inches; flowers in May; north of Europe; 1596. *S. borealis* (northern); 1 foot; flowers yellow, in May; 1787. *S. Canadensis* (Canadian); 6 inches; flowers in June; 1812. *S. racemosa* (racemed); 1 foot; flowers pale-yellow, in May; 1640. *S. stellata* (starred); 6 inches; flowers in May; 1633. *S. trifolia* (three-leaved); 3 inches; flowers in June; 1812. *S. umbellata* (umbelled); 9 inches; flowers in May; 1778.

S. borealis, more properly *Clintonia borealis*, is a very pretty hardy evergreen, with yellowish flowers and beautiful blue berries.

SNAP-DRAGON. See ANTIRRHINUM.
SNEEZEWORT. See ACHILLEA PTARMICA.
SNOWBALL. See VIBURNUM OPULUS.
SNOWDROP. See GALANTHUS.
SNOWFLAKE. See LEUCOJUM.
SNOWY MESPILUS. See AMELANCHIER.
SOAPWORT. See SAPONARIA.

SOLANUM. *Nightshade.* [Solanaceæ.] This very extensive genus comprises plants greatly varied in their habit, and includes stove, greenhouse, and hardy kinds, annuals, perennials, and shrubs. Some of the species are valuable for the flower-garden; but they are generally rank-growing and weedy. *S. ovigerum* is the Egg-plant, which is often grown for ornament as well as use. All the species require a rich loamy soil, and are killed by the first frost. The greenhouse species comprise many valuable plants.

SOLDANELLA. [Primulaceæ.] A beautiful little group of minute perennial plants, and among the most interesting of the Alpine families, but seldom grown. They increase with facility by the process of dividing the roots. The compost for them should be sandy loam and peat, made very porous.

S. Alpina (Alpine); hardy perennial; 3 inches; flowers blue, in April; Switzerland; 1656. *S. minima* (least); hardy perennial; 3 inches; flowers blue, in April; Corinthian Alps; 1823. *S. montana* (mountain); hardy perennial; 3 inches; flowers blue, in April; Bohemia; 1816. *S. pusilla* (weak); hardy perennial; 3 inches; flowers violet-blue, in April; south of Europe; 1820.

SOLIDAGO. *Golden-rod.* [Compositæ.] Hardy herbaceous perennials, all producing yellow daisy-shaped blossoms, small individually, but, for the most part, produced so abundantly as to have a very conspicuous appearance: they mostly bloom in autumn, and some very late in the season. They are increased by dividing the roots, separating some of the young suckers, which are annually produced in abundance at the base of the plant. But few of the numerous kinds are required in one garden, as there is considerable sameness in their general aspect.

S. Canadensis (Canadian); hardy perennial; 2½ feet; flowers yellow, in September; North America; 1648. *S. humilis* (dwarf); hardy perennial; 1 foot; flowers yellow, in August; North America; 1811.

SOLOMON'S SEAL. See POLYGONATUM.

SOPHORA. [Leguminoseæ.] Herbaceous plants and hardy trees. Propagated by division, seeds, and cuttings. Rich loamy soil.

S. flavescens (yellowish); hardy perennial; 2 feet; flowers yellow, in June; Siberia; 1785. *S. galegoides* (galega-like); hardy perennial; 2 feet; flowers yellow, in June; Siberia; 1817. *S. Chinensis* (Chinese); hardy tree; 30 feet; flowers white, in August; China; 1763. S. *Japonica* (Japanese); hardy tree; 40 feet; flowers white, in August; Japan; 1763.

The weeping variety, and that with variegated leaves, are very desirable.

SORREL-TREE. See ANDROMEDA ARBOREA.

SOUTHERN-WOOD. See ARTEMISIA.

SPECULARIA. [Campanulaceæ.] A small family of hardy annuals, formerly comprised under Campanula. The common *S. speculum*, with purplish-lilac flowers, varies to white and rose-colored, and is distinct and pretty. The plants form a small spreading mass of about nine inches high, and may be had in bloom for the whole summer by successive sowing. The seeds may be sown — very thinly, for they are very small — in the open border, and should be very lightly covered. Six or eight plants are enough to form a patch.

S. speculum (Venus's looking-glass); hardy annual; 1 foot; flowers purplish-lilac or white, in May; south of Europe; 1596.

SPEEDWELL. See VERONICA.

SPHENOGYNE. [Compositæ.] A genus of composite plants, consisting of hardy annuals and greenhouse shrubs. The most useful is *S. speciosa*, a very pretty half-hardy annual, which may be had in succession through the summer by successive sowings. The plants grow well in rich light garden soil, and in favorable seasons are very ornamental.

S. speciosa (showy); half-hardy annual; 1 foot; flowers orange and black, in June; Cape; 1836.

SPÆROSTIGMA. [Onagraceæ.] Hardy biennials and annuals, of easy culture in the border, and propagated by seeds.

S. Chamissonis (Chamisso's); hardy annual; 1 foot; flowers yellow, in August; Russia; 1837. *S. hirtum* (hairy); hardy biennial; 6 inches; flowers yellow, in August; Russia; 1836. *S. minutiflorum* (small-flowered); hardy annual; 1 foot; flowers yellow, in August; Russia; 1837.

S. cheiranthifolium, a Chilian species, is not hardy.

SPERGULA. [Caryophyllaceæ.] Very pretty mossy plants, studded in June with white flowers. In England they are extensively used for lawns; but in this country our summer's sun dries them up. Stiff loamy soil. Propagated by division and seed.

S. pilifera (hairy); hardy perennial; 2 inches; flowers white, in June; Corsica.

SPIDERWORT. See TRADESCANTIA.

SPIGELIA. *Worm-grass.* [Gentianeæ.] *S. Marilandica* is a pretty hardy perennial herb, growing a foot high, and bearing tubular flowers, which are scarlet, tipped with green, and bear no inconsiderable resemblance to those of *Correa speciosa*. The plant prefers a cool and somewhat shady situation, where the soil is of a somewhat peaty character, — say half peat and half maiden loam. When in a thriving condition, it is a very pretty plant. It is propagated by division of the root.

S. Marilandica (Maryland); hardy perennial; 1 foot; flowers red and green, in July; North America; 1694.

SPINDLE-TREE. See EUONYMUS.

SPIRÆA. [Rosaceæ.] A very interesting tribe of hardy plants, some of them herbaceous perennials, others deciduous shrubs, handsome when in flower: nearly all bear white flowers in pyramidal spikes. The herbaceous kinds are beautiful in pots or in the borders; and the shrubs are pretty in plantations. The former are propagated by parting the plants and by cuttings; and the latter by layers, and by cuttings of the young wood. The herbaceous kinds spread a good deal, and may be divided easily. The shrubs are very useful in clumps, and can be pruned to any form. To propagate these, the branches should be layered in autumn. There are many species, of which those enumerated below are some of the best and most distinct.

S. ariæfolia (white-beam-leaved); hardy shrub; 6 feet; flowers whitish, in July; North America; 1827. *S. aruncus* (goat's-beard); hardy perennial; 3 feet; flowers white, in July; Siberia; 1633. *S. bella* (pretty); hardy shrub; 3 feet; flowers rose, in July; Nepaul; 1820. *S. callosa* (callous); hardy shrub; 3 feet; flowers deep-rose, in June; North China; 1852. *S. corymbosa* (croymbose); hardy shrub; 4 feet; flowers white, in July; Virginia; 1819. *S. Douglasii* (Douglas's); hardy shrub; 4 feet; flowers rose, in July; North America; 1814. *S. filipendula* (dropwort); hardy perennial; 2 feet; flowers white, single or double, in June; Britain. *S. hypericifolia* (hypericum-leaved); hardy shrub; 5 feet; flowers white, in May; North America; 1640. *S. lobata* (lobed); hardy perennial; 2 feet; flowers red, in July; North America; 1765. *S. opulifolia* (Guelder-rose-leaved); hardy shrub; 5 feet; flowers white, in June; North America; 1690. *S. palmata* (palmate); hardy perennial; 2 feet; flowers red, in July; China; 1823. *S. prunifolia* (plum-leaved); hardy shrub; 4 feet; flowers white, in March; China; 1844. The double-flowered variety, *flore-pleno*, is a beautiful shrub, with double white, button-like blossoms. *S. Reevesii* (Reeves's); hardy shrub; 4 feet; flowers white, in June; China; 1852. The double variety is the best. *S. ulmifolia* (elm-leaved); hardy shrub; 3 feet; flowers white, in June; Carniola; 1790.

SPREKELIA. [Amaryllidaceæ.] Beautiful stove or greenhouse bulbs. *S. formosissima*, the old *Amaryllis formosissimus*, is imported annually in large quantities, and does well bedded out and treated as a gladiolus. They may be grown as greenhouse bulbs, keeping them in the house on a very light shelf while the leaves are growing, and watering with weak manure-water while in full vigor; then ripening off, and keeping the bulbs quite dry in winter, until they show signs of flowering. Increased by offsets.

S. brevis (short-tubed); stove bulb; 1 foot; flowers green and red, in June; Bolivia; 1839. *S. formosissima* (Jacobæan lily); greenhouse bulb; 1 foot; flowers rich crimson-scarlet, in June; Guatemala; 1658. *S. glauca* (glaucous); greenhouse bulb; 1 foot; flowers scarlet, in May; Mexico; 1840.

SPRAGUEA. [Portulaceæ.] A very beautiful little plant, of recent introduction. Rich loamy soil. Propagated by seeds.

S. umbellata (umbelled); 9 inches; flowers white and purple; California; 1862.

SPRUCE FIR. See ABIES.

SQUILL. See SCILLA.

STACHYS. *Hedge-nettle.* [Lamiaceæ.] Herbaceous plants, hardy and tender, and annuals. Many of the greenhouse species are desirable. The annuals are worthless. Of the perennials, *S. Corsica, grandiflora, lanata, stricta,* and *setifera* are hardy. Light loamy soil. Increased by division.

STAFF-TREE. See CELASTRUS.

STAPHYLEA. *Bladder-nut.* [Staphyleaceæ.] Hardy deciduous shrubs, with showy foliage and white flowers. Light garden soil. Propagated by cuttings, layers, or by seeds, which vegetate slowly. The hardy species are —

S. pinnata (pinnate); hardy shrub; 6 feet; flowers white, in June; England. *S. trifoliata* (three-leaved); hardy shrub; 6 feet; flowers white, in May; North America; 1640.

STAR OF BETHLEHEM. See ORNITHOGALUM.

STARWORT. See ASTER.

STATICE. *Sea Lavender.* [Plumbaginaceæ.] Fine hardy or half-hardy perennials, growing vigorously in ordinary flower-borders, of good light loamy soil, where they throw up their widely-branching flower-stems with hundreds of small blooms, forming a complete feather of diminutive blossoms, for the most part white or blue. These perennials only require planting out, and, with watering in dry weather, they will increase in size, and flower season after season, until they may be taken up, and parted to multiply them. When the roots are taken up, they are divided so as to give at least one good heart to each piece of root; the roots being rather coarse. All the hardy kinds want the same treatment. The half-hardy kinds may be kept with the pro-protection of a frame, and are best grown in pots; or, at least, a store of plants should be kept in pots, if those in the borders are annually abandoned. Statices are now called Armeria.

S. bellidifolia (daisy-leaved); half-hardy perennial; 1 foot; flowers bluish-lilac, in June; Greece; 1810. *S. emarginata* (notched); half-hardy perennial; 2 feet; flowers bluish, in July; Gibraltar. *S. eximia* (choice); hardy perennial; 1 foot; flowers red, in July; Songaria; 1844. *S. Fortuni* (Fortune's); half-hardy perennials; 18 inches; flowers white and yellow, in July; China; 1845. *S. incana* (hoary); half-hardy perennial; 1 foot; flowers light-rose, in July; Levant; 1823. *S. Limonium* (common); hardy perennial; 18 inches; flowers blue, in July; England. *S. puberula* (downy); half-hardy perennial; 6 inches; flowers blue and cream, in June; Canaries; 1830.

All the Statices are worth growing.

STENACTIS. [Compositæ.] Hardy herbaceous perennials. Common soil. Increased by division.

S. speciosa (showy); hardy perennial; 2 feet; flowers purple, in July; California; 1831.

STERNBERGIA. [Amaryllidaceæ.] Hardy bulbs. Soil, sandy loam. Propagated by offsets.

S. colchiciflora (colchicum-flowered); hardy bulb; 6 inches; flowers yellow, in September; Hungary; 1816.

STIPA. *Feather-grass.* [Gramineæ.] Ornamental hardy perennial. Common soil. Increased by division.

S. pinnata (feathered); hardy perennial; 2 feet; flowers in July; Britain.

STOCK. See MATHIOLA.

STOKESIA. [Compositæ.] A fine half-hardy evergreen herb, requiring a little winter protection, but flowering finely in the border in summer. Good loamy soil. Propagated by seeds or division,

S. cyanea (azure); 2 feet; flowers blue, in August; Carolina; 1776.

STONECROP. See SEDUM.
STORK'S-BILL. See PELARGONIUM.
STRAWBERRY BLITE. See BLITUM.
STUARTIA. [Camellieæ.] A family of showy shrubs, very valuable for the garden. Soil, rich loam. Propagated by layers and cuttings. *S. pentagynia* is hardy as far North as Massachusetts, and is very conspicuous in August from its large white flowers with purple centre. *S. Virginica*, the other species, is not hardy.

STYRAX. *Storax.* [Styraceæ.] Hardy deciduous shrubs, with very pretty white flowers. Soil, rich sandy loam. Propagated by seeds, cuttings, and layers.

S. grandiflorum (large-flowered); 6 feet; July; North America; 1765. *S. lævigatum* (smooth); 4 feet; July; North America; 1765. *S. pulverulentum* (powdery); 4 feet; flowers in June; North America; 1794.

S. officinale, from the Levant, is half-hardy.

SULTAN. See CENTUREA.
SUMACH. See RHUS.
SUN-DEW. See DROSERA.
SUN-FLOWER. See HELIANTHUS.
SUN-ROSE. See HELIANTHEMUM.
SWALLOW-WORT. See ASCLEPIAS.
SWAN-DAISY. See BRACHYCOME.
SWEET ALYSSUM. See KONIGA.
SWEET-BRIER. See ROSA RUBIGINOSA.
SWEET GUM. See LIQUIDAMBER.
SWEET PEA. See LATHYRUS.
SWEET SCABIOUS. See ASTEROCEPHALUS.

SWEET SULTAN. See CENTAUREA MOSCHATA.
SWEET WILLIAM. See DIANTHUS BARBATUS.
SYMPHIANDRA. [Campanulaceæ.] Hardy perennial. Dry-ish sandy loam. Propagated by seeds or cuttings.

S. pendula (pendulous); hardy perennial; 1 foot; flowers white, in July; Caucasus; 1823.

SYMPHORIA. [Caprifoliaceæ.] Pretty deciduous shrubs, remarkable for the white berries which succeed their flowers, and remain through the winter. Common soil. Increased by suckers.

S. glomerata (clustered); hardy shrub; 4 feet; flowers whitish, in August; North America; 1730. A variegated variety is very ornamental. *S. racemosus* (racemed); hardy shrub; 5 feet; flowers pinkish, in August; North America; 1817.

SYMPHYTUM. *Comfrey.* [Boraginaceæ.] Coarse-growing, but in some instances showy hardy perennials. Common soil. Propagated by division or seeds.

S. asperrimum (rough); hardy perennial; 6 feet; flowers red and blue, in June; Caucasus; 1799. *S. Caucasicum* (Caucasian); hardy perennial; 4 feet; flowers azure, in June; Caucasus; 1820. *S. Orientale* (Eastern); hardy perennial; 3 feet; flowers white; Turkey; 1752. This spreads itself about, disappearing in one spot and re-appearing in others.

SYRINGA. *Lilac.* [Oleaceæ.] This family comprises the Lilac and its varieties. Well-known and favorite deciduous shrubs, of which there are several very distinct kinds: the common Lilac, *S. vulgaris*, gives white, red, and purple varieties; the Persian Lilac, *S. Persica*, has a white, as well as a cut-leaved, variety. There are some others, as *S. Josikæa*, and the Chinese, *S. Rothmagensis*. They chiefly differ in the size of the foliage and flower. All are hardy, and well deserving a place in all shrubberies. They are propagated by layers and suckers. All these species grow naturally in the form of bushy shrubs; but they are in every respect more desirable as standards. To make them grow as standards, the buds of the suckers with single stems are all rubbed off, but two or three placed at and near the top; and, as the top advances in height, the under branches are cut clean away, so that at no one time shall there be more than the few top branches. When the single stem, with its top three pair of branches, has reached the desired height, say six feet or less, the branches are allowed to remain on and grow; but the top is removed to prevent the tree growing higher, and the ends of the branches are also removed to encourage lateral shoots, which soon form a handsome head. In this form, the Lilac-tree may then be planted among evergreen shrubs, which will completely hide the stem, while it takes up scarcely any room.

S. Josikæa (Josika's); hardy shrub; 6 feet; flowers deep-lilac, in May; Germany; 1833. *S. Persica* (Persian); hardy shrub; 3 feet; flowers lilac, in May; Persia; 1640. *S. Rothomagensis* (Rouen); hardy shrub; 4 feet; flowers lilac, in May; China; 1795. *S. vulgaris* (common); hardy shrub; 6 feet; flowers lilac, purple, red, or white, in May; Persia and Hungary; 1597.

SYRINGA. See PHILADELPHUS.

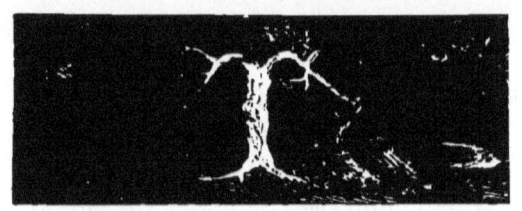

TAGETES. [Compositæ.] This genus contains the French and African marigolds, both well-known and showy annual flowers. The African is of a rich golden color, and very large. The French is of a rich brown, dark or light, but variously blotched or edged with bright golden yellow. In a large number of seedlings, scarcely two will give flowers alike, and indeed, on the same plant, it is difficult to find two in all respect identical. Both kinds are raised from seed; and, to get them early, they should be sown in heat about March. When they germinate, they must have plenty of air to prevent their becoming drawn up. Plant the French out towards the middle of May, about three in a patch, because the diversity of color assists by its contrasts in producing a good effect. This, however, does not apply to the African, which may be put out singly, because one plant makes show enough in a place. All single and semi-double ones ought to be pulled up and thrown away. Besides those sown in heat, others should be sown in the open ground to form a succession; for, although the first will keep blooming until the frost cuts them off, younger ones coming in are more compact plants. There is another annual kind which should find a place in all gardens, for its neat and elegant foliage, its rich orange flowers, and its compact and profusely flowering habit: it is *T. tenuifolia*, sold in seed-shops as *T. signata*. The flowers are small, compared even with the French Marigold, and they are single;

but, in soil not too rich, the plants form closely branched, compact bushes, and are literally covered with blossoms, which, in the mass, have a very charming effect. *T. lucida*, a pretty perennial, is propagated by division, and requires a greenhouse in winter, but is very effective as a bedding plant. *S. signata pumila* is a fine free-flowering dwarf variety.

T. erecta (African Marigold); hardy annual; 3 feet; flowers orange or yellow, in July; Mexico; 1596. *T. lucida* (shining); half-hardy perennial; 1 foot; flowers yellow, in July; South America; 1798. *T. patula* (French Marigold); hardy annual; 18 inches; flowers brown and gold, in July; Mexico; 1573. *T. tenuifolia* (fine-leaved); hardy annual; 2 feet; flowers orange-yellow, in July; Peru; 1797.

TALINUM. [Portulaceæ.] This genus contains some annuals, which, if raised in heat and bedded out in a sheltered place, are effective. Soil, sandy loam.

T. polyandrum (many-stemmed); flowers purple, in August; Australia; 1853. *T. purpuratum* (purple); flowers purple, in August; Mexico; 1826.

There are biennial and perennial species which are tender.

TAMARISK. See TAMARIX.

TAMARIX. *Tamarisk.* [Tamariscineæ.] Hardy shrubs, Common soil. Propagated by cuttings.

T. Gallica (French); hardy sub-evergreen shrub; 8 feet; flowers pink, in July; south of England. *T. Germanica* (German); hardy evergreen shrub; 8 feet; flowers pink, in July; Caucasus; 1682.

TARTARIAN HONEYSUCKLE. See LONICERA.

TAXODIUM. *Deciduous Cypress.* [Pinaceæ.] The most valuable species is *T. distichum*, which is hardy as far North as Massachusetts. It is a very graceful tree, with light sprays of feathery foliage, and succeeds in good loamy soil.

TAXUS. *Yew.* [Taxaceæ.] Fine evergreen shrubs or

trees. Deep loamy soil. Increased by cuttings in shady border, or by seeds. The Yew is hardy as far North as Massachusetts in sheltered situations, though liable to be browned by the winter's sun. The American Yew is perpectly hardy. The Irish Yew (*fastigiata*), is tender in the Northern States. The berries of the Yew are very beautiful.

T. baccata (common); berried; 20 feet; Britain. *T. baccata fastigiata* (tapering); 20 feet; Ireland; 1780. *T. baccata foliis variegatis* (variegated-leaved); 3 feet. *T. baccata fructuluteo* (yellow-berried); Ireland. *T. baccata procumbens* (lying-down); 8 feet; Europe. *T. baccata sparsifolia* (scattered-leaved). *T. baccata variegata* (variegated); 20 feet; Europe. *T. Canadensis* (Canadian); 20 feet; Canada; 1800.

TECOMA. [Bignoniaceæ.] A genus of elegant tubular-flowered plants, consisting of both evergreen and deciduous shrubs and climbers. *T. radicans* and its varieties are beautiful hardy deciduous climbers, very ornamental against a wall or a house: they grow well in good rich loam, and are propagated by layers. Also called Bignonia.

T. grandiflora (large-flowered); climbing shrub; 20 feet; flowers orange, in July; China; 1800. *T. radicans* (rooting); hardy climbing shrub; 30 feet; flowers orange, in July; North America; 1640.

TEESDALIA. [Cruciferæ.] A genus of annuals allied to Candytuft, and requiring the same treatment. The species are *T. iberis* and *lipidium*.

TELLIMA. [Saxifragaceæ.] Hardy perennials. Sandy loam and peat. Increased by division.

T. grandiflora (large-flowered); hardy perennial; 1 foot; flowers pink, in May; North America; 1826.

TETRAGONOLOBUS. [Leguminosæ.] Annuals and perennials, of which the former are most important. Propagated by seeds sown in May in common soil.

T. biflorus (two-flowered); hardy annual; 6 inches; flowers yellow, in July; Barbary; 1818. *T. purpureus* (purple); hardy annual; 1 foot; flowers dark-purple, in July; Sicily; 1769.

THALICTRUM. *Meadow-rue.* [Ranunculaceæ.] Hardy herbaceous perennials, worth growing in a mixed border for the sake of their pretty compound foliage, but having rather insignificant blossoms. They grow freely in common garden soil, and are increased by division of the plant.

T. aquilegifolium (columbine-leaved); hardy perennial; 3 feet; flowers purple, in May; Austria; 1731.

T. cornellum and *dioicum* are natives of our woods and meadows. *T. anemonoides*, or *Anemone thalictroides*, is a beautiful little spring-flowering plant: the double variety is very desirable. There are over sixty species.

THRIFT. See ARMERIA.
THROATWORT. See TRACHELIUM.
THORN-APPLE. See DATURA.

THUJA. *Arbor-vitæ.* [Coniferæ.] These are among the best of evergreen shrubs for the shrubbery, or as specimen plants on lawns. *T. Orientalis*, the Chinese Arbor-vitæ, is well known, and is admired for its close cone-shaped outline. *T. Occidentalis*, the American Arbor-vitæ, has the same habit, but is of looser growth. There is another elegant hardy species called *T. plicata*, not uncommon in gardens; and one much rarer, *T. pendula*, which has long slender drooping twigs, and is a most singular and very ornamental small tree. The commoner sorts grow well in any moderately favorable situation, preferring a somewhat moist but not marshy situation. They are best raised from seeds, sown in April, in a frame or covered bed. *T. pendula* should be kept dryer, and is increased by grafts or cuttings.

T. Occidentalis (Western); hardy evergreen shrub; 15 feet; flowers green, in May; North America; 1596. *T. Orientalis*

(Eastern); hardy evergreen shrub; 15 feet; flowers green, in May; China; 1752. *T. pendula* (drooping); hardy evergreen shrub; 10 feet; flowers green, in May; Tartary; 1828. *T. plicata* (plaited); hardy evergreen shrub; 10 feet; flowers green, in May; Nootka Sound; 1796.

THUIOPSIS. [Coniferæ.] A family of fine hardy evergreens, somewhat resembling the Arbor-vitæ, but with fine cut foliage. None are as yet very common. Propagated by cuttings. Common soil.

T. borealis (northern); hardy tree; 100 feet; Nootka Sound; 1855. *T. dolebrata* (silvery); hardy tree; 50 feet; Japan; 1850. Variety *variegata* has a yellow variegation; Japan; 1861. Variety *nana* seldom exceeds six feet in height; Japan; 1861. *T. Standishii* (Standish's); resembles the last, but has more slender and less silvery foliage; Japan; 1861.

THUNBERGIA. [Acanthaceæ.] Stove evergreen climbers. They thrive best in a mixture of turfy loam, peat, and rotted dung; but the best of them, *T. alata*, and its varieties, being very liable to attacks of the red spider, are best raised from seeds, and treated like tender annuals, only they require a trellis on which to train their branches. *T. alata aurantiaca* is the best, having deep orange blossoms, with a black centre; *T. alata alba*, with white flowers and a black centre, is also very pretty, and there are several others; the color of *T. alata* itself is buff-yellow, with a black centre. The varieties all bloom throughout the summer, and at that season are splendid objects in a greenhouse, if well managed: they may also be grown out-doors, and are very beautiful objects in the garden, preferring moist peat soil. All of the species, strike freely; and cuttings in sand, under a bell-glass, with a little bottom-heat, are rooted in a short time. The seeds may be sown in March, in wide-mouthed pots, and as soon as the plants are large enough, potted off in the smallest-sized pots, to be treated the same as cuttings; or planted in the borders in May.

T. alata (winged); stove-climbing perennials; 5 feet; flowers buff with black eye, in June; Africa; 1823. *T. alata alba* (white); stove climbing perennial; 5 feet; flowers white, with black eye, in June; Madagascar. *T. alata aurantiata* (orange); stove climbing perennial; 5 feet; flowers orange with black eye, in June; gardens.

THYMUS. *Thyme.* [Lamiaceæ.] Hardy evergreen perennials and sub-shrub. Soil, sandy loam. Propagated by divisions or cuttings. Many of them are beautiful rock-plants.

T. azureus (azure); hardy perennial; 6 inches; flowers purple, in June; south of Europe; 1830. *T. Corsicus* (Corsican); half-hardy perennial; 6 inches; flowers lilac, in June; Corsica; 1831. *T. lanuginosus* (woolly); hardy trailing perennial; flowers purple, in July; Britain.

TIARELLA. [Saxifragaceæ.] Hardy perennials. Common dryish soil. Increased by division.

T. cordifolia (heart-leaved); 6 inches; flowers white, in May; North America; 1731.

TIGRIDIA. *Tiger-flower.* [Iridaceæ.] One of the most showy and remarkable of flowers, but at the same time one of the most fugitive; the flowers last but a few hours, but there is a good succession of them produced. They are hardy bulbous-rooted plants, with the flowers large, singularly formed, like a cocked hat reversed, and beautifully spotted with a darker color upon a yellow or deep orange-colored ground. The two so-called species are very similar in all but having a darker or lighter ground color. The flowers last but the day they come out if the sun is pretty hot, which it generally is when they flower, in July. They do not grow more than twelve inches high, and should be planted in a mass, because there will then be a number of flowers open for some time; when planted singly, that is not the case, for there will be days when a plant will have none, and that, too, before it is out of bloom altogether. Plant them in May, three inches deep, and take them up in the autumn. Increased by offsets.

T. conchiflora (shell-flowered); half-hardy bulb; 1 foot; flowers yellow-spotted, in June; Mexico; 1823. *T. pavonia* (peacock); half-hardy bulb; 1 foot; flowers orange and red, in June; Mexico; 1796. *T. speciosa* is a hybrid between these two, with more of the nature of *T. pavonia*. T. Wheelerii is also a hybrid resembling *T. conchiflora*.

TILIA. *Lime* or *Linden*. [Tiliaceæ.] Well-known hardy ornamental trees. The American is the best. Propagated by seeds and layers. Soil, rich loam.

T. alba (white-wooded); 30 feet; flowers in July; Hungary; 1767. *T. Americana* (American); 30 feet; flowers in June; North America; 1752. *T. Americana heterophylla* (various-leaved); 30 feet; flowers in July; North America; 1811. *T. Americana laxiflora* (loose-flowered); 50 feet; flowers white in June; North America; 1820. *T. Americana pubescens* (downy); 20 feet; flowers in July; North America; 1726. *T. Americana pubescens leptophylla* (thin-leaved-downy); 20 feet; flowers yellow, in July; North America. *T. Europæa* (European, or common); 50 feet; flowers in July; Britain. *T. Europæa aurea* (golden-twigged); 50 feet; flowers in August; Britain. *T. Europæa dasystyla* (hairy-styled); 50 feet; flowers in July; Tauria. *T. Europæa laciniata* (cut-leaved); 50 feet; flowers in August; Britain. *T. Europæa microphylla* (small leaved); 50 feet; flowers in August; Britain. *T. Europæa pendula* (drooping); flowers in June; 1845. *T. Europæa platyphylla* (broad-leaved); 50 feet; flowers in August; Britain. *T. Europæa platyphylla aurea* (golden-broad-leaved); 20 feet; Britain. *T. Europæa rubra* (red-twigged); 50 feet; flowers in August; Britain. *T. Europæa variegata* (variegated-leaved); flowers in June; 1847. *T. Europæa vitifolia* (vine-leaved); flowers in June; 1846.

TOAD-FLAX. See LINARIA.

TOBACCO. See NICOTIANA.

TOLPIS. *Hawkweed.* [Compositæ.] A fine yellow-flowered annual, formerly called *Crepis barbata.* Sow in May in common soil. The flowers close in cloudy weather.

T. barbata (bearded); hardy annual; 2 feet; flowers yellow and purple, in July; 1620. The other species are *T. altissima, coronopifolia, grandiflora, umbellata,* and *virgata.*

TORREYA. [Taxaceæ.] Hardy evergreen trees. Deep loamy soil. Propagated by cuttings or seeds.

T. myristica (Californian nutmeg); hardy evergreen tree; 30 feet; California; 1851. *T. taxifolia* (yew-leaved); hardy evergreen shrub; 20 feet; Florida; 1840.

TOUCH-ME-NOT. See IMPATIENS.

TOURNEFORTIA. [Boragineæ.] *T. heliotropoides* is a heliotrope-like hardy or nearly hardy plant, not very showy, but a very free bloomer, and useful for small beds. It will grow in the open borders: a plant or two should be kept in a frame through the winter. It is increased either by seeds sown in May, or by cuttings; and is a low plant, flowering from May to August.

T. heliotropoides (heliotrope-like); half-hardy perennial; 1 foot; flowers lilac, in June; Buenos Ayres; 1829.

TRACHELIUM. *Throatwort.* [Campanulaceæ.] Half-hardy herbaceous perennials. Light loamy soil. Increased by seeds sown in spring in a gentle heat, and carefully grown while young.

T. cœruleum (blue); half-hardy perennial; 2 feet; flowers purple or white, in August; Italy; 1640.

TRADESCANTIA. *Spiderwort.* [Commelinaceæ.] The hardy perennial species of this genus are adapted for the common borders. They are readily increased by division, and only require to be planted in the common soil, and left undisturbed till they get too large, when they must be taken up and divided. The tender species are of less moment, except *T. discolor*, a curious stove species, and *T. iridescens*, a pretty dwarf free-blooming greenhouse herb.

T. subaspera (roughish); hardy perennial; 18 inches; flowers purple, in May; North America; 1812. *T. Virginica* (Virginian); hardy perennial; 18 inches; flowers blue, in June; North America; 1629.

This varies, with white, blue, red, crimson, and double-blue flowers.

TRAGOPOGON. [Compositæ.] A family of hardy biennials, thriving in common garden soil. Propagated by seeds. *T. floccosus, mutabilis*, and *roseus* are hardy border plants.

TRAGOPYRUM. [Polygonaceæ.] Hardy deciduous shrubs, propagated by layers, and growing best in moist, peaty soil.

T. buxifolium (box-leaved); 18 inches; flowers white, in July; Siberia; 1800. *T. lanceolatum* (spear-shaped); 2 feet; flowers pink, in July; Siberia; 1778.

TREE-PEONY. See MOUTAN.

TREFOIL. See TRIFOLIUM.

TRIENTALIS. [Primulaceæ.] A family of delicate little perennials, grown best in a shady situation in leaf-mould. Propagated by division.

T. Americana (American); 6 inches; flowers white, in June; North America; 1816. The European species *(T. Europæa)* much resembles this.

TRIFOLIUM. *Trefoil,* or *Clover.* [Leguminosæ.] Hardy herbs, many of which are annuals or biennials, and a large number perennials. They are not of much value as garden plants. *T. incarnatum*, with its scarlet flower-heads, is showy; and *T. uniflorum* is a very pretty minute perennial species, deserving a place among alpines. The annuals may be sown in April in the places where they are to flower. The perennials need only to be planted in ordinary soil.

T. incarnatum (flesh); hardy annual; 1 foot; flowers scarlet, in June; Italy; 1596. *T. lagopus* (hare's-foot); hardy annual; 18 inches; flowers red, in July; Spain; 1827. *T. megacephalum* (great-headed); hardy perennial; 1 foot; flowers pale-purple, in July; North America. *T. rubens* (red); hardy perennial; 2 feet; flowers deep-red, in July; south of Europe; 1633. *T. uniflorum* (one-flowered); hardy perennial; 3 inches; flowers red and white, in June; south of Europe; 1800.

TRILLIUM. [Trilliaceæ.] Curious small hardy herbaceous plants. The stem has three leaves, and the flowers three petals. They are tuberous-rooted perennials, and propagate but slowly by dividing the roots; but they may be raised from seed, which is inclosed in a berry. This may be sown in pans, and be raised in a frame, and pricked out, three or four in a pot, to grow; and lastly potted singly into sixty-sixed pots. All those curious in plants should grow them, though, like many other curious plants, they are greatly neglected. They flower very early in spring, and grow best in peat soil.

T. cernuum (drooping); hardy tuberous perennial; 1 foot; flowers white, in May; North America; 1758. *T. erectum* (erect); hardy tuberous perennial; 6 inches; flowers white, in May; North America; 1700. *T. grandiflorum* (large-flowered); hardy tuberous perennial; 6 inches; flowers white, in May; North America; 1799. *T. obovatum* (obovate); hardy tuberous perennial; 6 inches; flowers red, in May; North America; 1810. *T. sessile* (sessile); hardy tuberous perennial; 6 inches; flowers brownish-purple, in May; North America; 1759. *T. undulatum* (wavy); hardy tuberous perennial; 6 inches; flowers red, in May; North America; 1818.

TRITOMA. [Liliaceæ.] Beautiful half-hardy herbaceous plants, requiring a light dry soil, and warm or sheltered situation, in which they produce their upright spikes of drooping scarlet tubes, freely, in the autumnal months. They throw out suckers from their roots, by which they may be increased. They are sometimes called Kniphofia.

T. Burchellii (Burchell's); half-hardy perennial; 2 feet; flowers orange, in August; Cape; 1816. *T. pumila* (dwarf); hardy perennial; 1 foot; flowers orange, in September; Cape; 1774. *T. Rooperi* (Rooper's); hardy perennial; 3 feet; flowers orange-scarlet, in autumn; Natal; 1848. *T. Uvaria* (grape); hardy perennial; 2 feet; flowers orange, in August; Cape; 1707.

TROLLIUS. *Globe-flower.* [Ranunculaceæ.] Showy herbaceous perennials, quite hardy, growing in ordinary garden soil, and increased easily by parting the roots during the dormant season.

T. Asiaticus (Asiatic); hardy perennial; 1 foot; flowers deep-yellow, in May; Siberia; 1759. *T. Europæus* (European); hardy perennial; 1 foot; flowers yellow, in May; Britain.

There are many other species.

TROPÆOLUM. *Indian Cress.* [Tropæolaceæ.] Soft-stemmed climbing herbs, part of which are annual, and others perennial, having tuberous roots. *T. majus*, the common Nasturtium, as it is called erroneously, and its varieties, may be sown in the open ground in May, where it is to bloom through the summer, and requires neither care nor attention. These are beautiful plants everywhere — in rich ground, covering the surface with foliage and flowers, or climbing up stakes, and hiding unsightly fences or other objects, or potted and placed on the window-sill, where the burning heat and limited food arrests their vegetation, but adds profusion to the blossoms, and intensity to their colors. *T. minus* is smaller, but equally effective in its way. The double orange-colored variety of *T. majus* is a greenhouse plant, as is also the double scarlet Nasturtium, which is the double-flowered variety of *T. minus*. These are increased by cuttings, and preserved, like other half-hardy things, in the greenhouse during winter for planting out in summer, where they thrive in hot, dry situations. *T. peregrinum* is the canary-bird flower, and thrives well in the border in summer, producing its yellow, curiously-shaped flowers profusely.

T. Tom Thumb is a fine variety of *T. majus*, forming a clump; flowers bright-yellow; hybrid; 1859. There are many others of this type.

HARDY ANNUALS. — *T. majus* (greater); 6 feet; flowers orange-yellow, in July; Peru; 1686. *T. majus atrosanguineum* (dark-red); 3 feet; flowers dark-red, in August; Peru. *T. minus* (smaller); 1 foot; flowers orange and yellow, in August; Peru; 1596. *T. peregrinum* (canary-bird flower); 6 feet; flowers yellow, in September; New Grenada; 1810.

TRUMPET-FLOWER. See BIGNONIA and TECOMA.

TUBEROSE. See POLIANTHES.

TULIPA. *Tulip.* [Liliaceæ.] Hardy and very showy bulbs. The variegated Tulips of the gardens are the progeny of *T. Gesneriana*. The bulbs are planted in October or November, and bloom in May. They grow in nothing so well as in plain, good, sandy loam, taken from a pasture with the turf rotted in it; and it is the custom to dig out the bed from two to three feet deep, that this soil may be placed therein. They are planted six inches apart, the bed being four feet wide, and containing seven flowers across. The tallest flowers, which are known well to the fanciers, are planted in the centre row; those a little shorter, in the rows next to the middle; and the shortest, outside: so that the tulip-bed when in flower looks like a bank of bloom. The small offsets are planted in separate beds, until they grow large enough to plant in the principal beds. They are raised from seed to produce new varieties, and they multiply by offsets. The seeds may be sown in pans or wide-mouthed pots, in the early spring or the autumn, and placed in a garden frame. They will come up, and about June turn yellow, and die down, but little bulbs will have formed: some take them up and replant them; but, if they are not too thick, they may be left until the next year. It will be five or six years before they bloom. The Van Thol Tulip, a pretty early sort, is the *T. suaveolens:* this blooms naturally in April, and is very well adapted for forcing even much earlier than this. Few of the other species are cultivated except as curiosities.

T. Gesneriana (Gesner's); hardy bulb; 2 feet; flowers red or striped, in May; Levant; 1577. The florists' varieties are of a garden origin. *T. oculis solis* (sun's-eye); hardy bulb; 1 foot; flowers red, with dark eye, in April; Italy; 1816. *T. præcox* (early); hardy bulb; 9 inches; flowers scarlet and yellow, in April; Italy; 1825. *T. suaveolens* (Van Thol); hardy bulb; 6 inches; flowers scarlet and gold, in April; south of Europe; 1603. *T. Turcica* (Florentine); hardy bulb; 9 inches; flowers yellow, in April; south of Europe.

There are some twenty other species.

TULIP-TREE. See LIRIODENDRON.

TUSSILAGO. *Colt's-foot.* [Compositæ.] A genus of hardy or half-hardy plants, doing best in rich loamy soil. Propagated easily by division. The species are *T. alba, Alpina, discolor, farfara, fragrans, frigida, lævigata, nivea, palmata,* and *sagittata.*

ULEX. *Furze.* [Leguminosæ.] This well-known, gay-flowering plant is not hardy in the Northern States. It grows in any soil, and is propagated by seed.

U. Europæa (common); evergreen shrub; 4 feet; flowers yellow, in May; Britain. The double-flowered variety, *U. Europæa flore-pleno*, is the most beautiful. *U. nana* (dwarf); evergreen trailing shrub; 18 inches; flowers yellow, in August; England.

ULMUS. *Elm.* [Ulmaceæ.] Hardy deciduous timber-trees. Soil, deep, dry, sandy loam. The common sorts are propagated by seeds, layers, or grafts; the varieties by grafting.

U. alata (winged); 30 feet; North America; 1820. *U. alba* (white; Hungarian); 30 feet; Hungary; 1824. *U. Americana* (white; American); 40 feet; North America. *U. Americana alba* (white branched); 40 feet; North America. *U. Americana foliis-variegatis* (variegated-leaved). *U. Americana incisa* (cut-leaved); North America. *U. Americana pendula* (drooping); North America; 1820. *U. Americana rubra* (red-branched); 40 feet; North America; 1824. *U. campestris* (English field); 80 feet; Britain. *U. campestris acutifolia* (acute-leaved); 80 feet; Britain. *U. campestris alba* (white); 80 feet; Britain. *U. campestris betulæfolia* (birch-leaved); Britain. *U. campestris Chincnsis* (Chinese); China. *U. campestris foliis-aureis* (leaves golden-variegated); Britain. *U. campestris foliis-variegatis* (leaves variegated with white); Britain. *U. campestris latifolia* (broad-leaved); 80 feet; Britain. *U. campestris nana* (dwarf);

2 feet; Britain. *U. campestris parvifolia* (small-leaved); 20 feet; Siberia; 1822. *U. campestris stricta* (upright); 80 feet; Britain. *U. campestris viminalis* (twiggy); 30 feet; Britain. *U. fulva* (slippery); 60 feet; North America. *U. glabra* (smooth); 60 feet; Britain. *U. glabra latifolia* (broad-leaved); Britain. *U. major* (greater); 40 feet; Britain. *U. montana* (mountain; Scotch or Wych); 40 feet; Britain. *U. montana fastigiata* (pyramidal; Exeter); Exeter; 1826. *U. montana nigra* (black); 40 feet; Ireland. *U. montana pendula* (drooping); Britain. *U. montana rugosa* (rough-leaved); 40 feet; Britain. *U. montana vulgaris* (common); 40 feet; Britain. *U. suberosa* (cork-barked); 40 feet; Britain. *U. suberosa alba* (white-barked); Britain. *U. suberosa angustifolia* (narrow-leaved); Hertford. *U. suberosa erecta* (upright); 80 feet; Britain. *U. suberosa foliis-variegatis* (variegated-leaved); 80 feet; Britain. *U. suberosa latifolia* (broad-leaved); Hertford. *U. suberosa vulgaris* (common); 80 feet; Holland.

UROSPERMUM. *Sheep's-beard.* [Compositæ.] A hardy perennial, with showy yellow flowers. Soil, common loam. Propagated by seed.

U. Dalechampi; hardy perennial; 2 feet; flowers yellow, in July; south of Europe.

UVULARIA. [Melanthaceæ.] Neat, dwarf, hardy, herbaceous perennials. They grow with ordinary attention in the common soil of gardens, preferring a cool situation, without stagnant moisture, and are propagated by division.

U. grandiflora (large-flowered); hardy perennial; 1 foot; flowers yellow, in May; North America; 1802. *U. perfoliata* (perfoliate); hardy perennial; 9 inches; flowers yellow, in May; North America; 1810. *U. sessilifolia* (sessile-leaved); hardy perennial; 6 inches; flowers cream-colored, in May; North America; 1790.

VACCINIUM. *Whortleberry.* [Vaccinaceæ.] Hardy, deciduous, or sometimes evergreen shrubs, mostly ornamental. Soil, sandy loam or peat. Propagated by suckers or layers. There are many species in cultivation. Some of the East-Indian species are very beautiful, but are not hardy. The hardy species are not very showy, but are useful in a shrubbery.

VALERIANA. *Valerian.* [Valerianaceæ.] Hardy perennials, some of which are pretty, but not remarkably ornamental. They may all be grown in the open border, in ordinary garden soil. They increase readily by division of the plants.

V. Celtica (Celtic); hardy perennial; 1 foot; flowers white, in June; Switzerland; 1748. *V. dioica* (diæcious); hardy perennial; 1 foot; flowers flesh-color, in May; England. *V. montana* (mountain); hardy perennial; 1 foot; flowers light-red, in June; Switzerland; 1748. *V. Phu* (Phu); hardy perennial; 3 feet; flowers white, in June; Germany; 1597. *V. Pyrenaica* (Pyrenean); hardy perennial; 3 feet; flowers pink, in June; Scotland. *V. tuberosa* (tuberous); hardy perennial; 18 inches; flowers pale red, in June; south of Europe; 1629.

VALERIANELLA. *Lamb's Lettuce.* [Valerianaceæ.] Hardy annuals, mostly weedy or salad plants. *V. congesta* is pretty. Common soil. Increased by seeds.

V. congesta (crowded); hardy annual; 1 foot; flowers red, in July; Columbia; 1826.

VENEDIUM. [Compositæ.] A genus containing some

half-hardy showy annuals. Light, rich soil. Propagated by seeds, which should be sown in May where they are to bloom.

V. calendulaceum (marigold-like); half-hardy annual; 1 foot; flowers yellow, in August; Cape of Good Hope; 1852.

VENUS LOOKING-GLASS. See SPECULARIA.

VENUS NAVELWORT. See OMPHALODES.

VERATRUM. [Melanthaceæ.] Hardy herbaceous plants of tall coarse habit, but with fine ornamental foliage, and having a very distinct habit and appearance, and therefore desirable in large mixed borders. They increase by division, and grow in ordinary garden-soil.

V. album (white); hardy perennial; 3 feet; flowers greenish, in July; Europe; 1548. *V. nigrum* (black); hardy perennial; 3 feet; flowers dark-chocolate, in July; Siberia; 1596. *V. viride* (green); hardy perennial; 5 feet; flowers greenish, in June; North America; 1742.

VERBASCUM. *Mullein.* [Scrophularineæ.] Hardy perennials, strikingly effective in large borders, or towards the margins of shrubberies. They are easily-grown plants, thriving in any garden soil, and only need to be sown where they are to bloom, each patch being thinned away, leaving only the strongest. The seeds should be sown about June in one year, to produce flowering plants for the next season. They are mostly biennials, and young plants should therefore be raised from seeds annually. The perennials are increased both by seeds and division.

V. alopecurus (fox-tail); hardy perennial; 3 feet; flowers yellow, in July; France; 1820. *V. Austriacum* (Austrian); hardy perennial; 5 feet; flowers yellow, in July; Austria; 1818. *V. blattaria* (moth); hardy biennial; 4 feet; flowers yellow, in July; England. *V. formosum* (handsome); hardy biennial; 2 feet; flowers yellow, in July; Russia; 1818. *V. grandiflorum* (large-flowered); hardy biennial; 4 feet; flowers yellow, in July; Europe; 1820. *V. Phœniceum* (purple); hardy perennial; 3 feet;

flowers purple, in June; south of Europe; 1796. *V. spectabile* (showy); hardy biennial; 2 feet; flowers yellow and purple, in July; Tauria; 1820. *V. thapsus* (shepherd's club); hardy biennial; 6 feet; flowers yellow, in July; England. *V. triste* (dark); hardy perennial; 2 feet; flowers yellow and red, in July; south of Europe; 1688.

There are about fifty other species.

VERBENA. *Vervain.* [Verbenaceæ.] Beautiful flower-garden plants, consisting for the most part of perennial species, requiring protection during winter. The race of half-hardy Verbenas has given rise to those fine seminal varieties, which are now, during summer, to be seen decorating every garden. *V. Melindres* or *chamædrifolia* was one of the first favorites; but, like most of the other species, it has been lost amid the more beautiful sorts that have sprung up under the florists' care. It is the creeping habit, however, and abundant bloom of *V. Melindres*, which has given much of their value to the florists' seedlings; their size and the more erect habit and fragrance observable in recent varieties having been derived from *V. teucrioides*. The Verbena strikes freely under a bell-glass in light sandy soil, and very quickly in a mild hot-bed; and it grows freely in any rich light soil. New varieties are raised from seeds. The seeds should be sown in pans, and placed in a greenhouse or frame, the young seedlings planted out in beds six inches apart, until it is seen what flowers they produce, when such as are worthy may be propagated. In gardens, those which approach nearest to the admirable habit of *V. Melindres* — which creeps along the ground, spreading and rooting at every joint, until it covers a bed like a carpet, and throws up its umbels or trusses of flowers all over its allotted space — should be selected.

V. Melindres (Melindres); half-hardy perennial; 1 foot; flowers scarlet, in June; Buenos Ayres; 1827. *V. multifida* (many-cleft); half-hardy perennial; 6 inches; flowers purple, lilac, or white, in July; Chili; 1839. *V. pulchella* (neat); half-hardy trailing perennial; flowers purple or white; Buenos Ayres; 1827. *V. radicans* (rooting); half-hardy trailing perennial; 6 inches; flowers pink, in July; Chili; 1832. *V. sulphurea* (sulphur); half-hardy perennial; 1 foot; flowers pale-yellow, in July; Chili; 1832. *V. teucrioides* (teucrium-like); half-hardy perennial; 2 feet; flowers whitish, in July; Monte Video; 1837. *V. Tweediana* (Tweedie's); half-hardy perennial; 18 inches; flowers rose-crimson, in June; Brazil; 1834. *V. venosa* (veiny); half-hardy perennial; 2 feet; flowers rose-purple, in May; Buenos Ayres; 1830.

For fine varieties, consult florists' catalogues. The following can, however, be recommended. WHITE — *Mrs. Holford, Snowflake, Anne.* WHITE, DARK CENTRE — *Fairest of the Fair, Viscountess Emlyn, Earl of Shaftsbury.* PEACH — *Great Eastern, Salmon, Ida.* REDDISH SCARLET — *Gen. Simpson.* SCARLET — *Defiance, Phenomenon, Foxhunter, Lord Raglan.* CRIMSON — *Admiral Dundas, Jean Bart, Geant des Batailles.* PURPLE — *Ariosto, Purple King, Azucena, Zampa.* BLUE — *Garibaldi.*

VERBENA LEMON. See ALOYSIA.

VERONICA. *Speedwell.* [Scrophularineæ.] A very large genus, consisting almost entirely of hardy perennials. About a score are insignificant annuals; half a dozen are sub-aquatics; some half-dozen are shrubs requiring greenhouse protection; and the rest are hardy perennials, most of the larger-growing of which are adapted for the mixed borders, and are really showy with their long narrow close spikes of flowers, usually blue. These latter may be said to require no culture; they grow with the greatest facility in garden soil of of any description, increase extensively by partition of the roots, and live through all the inclemencies of winter and the droughts of summer without suffering material detriment.

V. Caucasica (Caucasian); hardy perennial; 6 inches; flowers blush, in July; Caucasus; 1816. *V. crassifolia* (thick-leaved); hardy perennial; 2½ feet; flowers blue, in July; Europe; 1822. *V. elegans* (elegant); hardy perennial; 2 feet; flowers pink, in June; south of France; 1822. *V. formosa* (handsome); half-hardy evergreen shrub; 3 feet; flowers white, in April; Van Diemen's Land; 1835. *V. glabra* (smooth); hardy perennial; 4 feet; flowers blue or white, in July; south of Europe; 1804. *V. grandis* (grand); hardy perennial; 18 inches; flowers white, in August; Siberia; 1826. *V. hybrida* (hybrid); hardy perennial; 1 foot; flowers blue, in July; England. *V. incana* (hoary); hardy perennial; 2 feet; flowers blue, in July; Russia; 1759. *V. incisa* (cut-leaved); hardy perennial; 2 feet; flowers blue, in July; Siberia; 1739. *V. longifolia* (long-leaved); hardy perennial; 3 feet; flowers blue, white, or flesh-colored, in August; south of Europe; 1731. *V. paniculata* (panicled); hardy perennial; 2 feet; flowers blue, in June; Russia; 1797. *V. salicifolia* (willow-leaved); half-hardy evergreen shrub; 3 feet; flowers lilac, in September; New Zealand; 1843. *V. speciosa* (showy); half-hardy evergreen shrub; 3 feet; flowers purple or rose, in July; New Zealand; 1835. *V. Virginica* (Virginian); hardy perennial; 5 feet; flowers white or flesh-colored, in July; Virginia; 1714.

VERVAIN. See VERBENA.

VESICARIA. [Brassiceæ.] Hardy annuals or perennials. Common soil. Multiplied by seeds, division, or cuttings, according to habit. *V. utriculata* is a beautiful rock plant.

V. grandiflora (large-flowered); hardy annual; 1 foot; flowers yellow, in July; Texas; 1835. *V. utriculata* (bladder); hardy perennial; 1 foot; flowers sulphur-yellow, in May; Levant; 1730.

VETCH. See VICIA.

VIBURNUM. [Caprifoliaceæ.] A genus consisting for the most part of hardy shrubs. The Guelder-rose, *V. Opulus*, is very familiar in shrubberies: the bloom is white, in bunches that form complete balls, and, being abundant, is very effective. This is generally propagated from suckers, which come up, like those of the Lilac, very freely. There is a great variety of species, but few are so handsome as the Guelder-rose. *V. macrocephalum* and *plicatum* are, however, fine showy shrubs. Rich loamy soil. Increased by layers, cuttings, or suckers.

V. macrocephalum (large-headed); hardy shrub; 10 feet; flowers white, in May; China; 1845. *V. Opulus* (Guelder-rose); hardy shrub; 8 feet; flowers white, in May; Britain. *V. plicatum* (plaited); hardy shrub; 10 feet; flowers white, in May; China; 1845.

Many of our native species, such as *V. prunifolium, Lentago, dentatum,* and *lantanoides,* are very handsome shrubs.

VICIA. *Vetch.* [Leguminosæ.] Hardy annuals or perennials. Common soil. Propagated by seeds or division.

VINCA. *Periwinkle.* [Apocynaceæ.] Pretty, hardy, shrubby plants, always dwarf and evergreen, generally of trailing habit, and well adapted for covering the surface of the ground in shady situations where little else will live. They are increased by separating the rooted trailing shoots. Common soil. *V. rosea,* and its variety *alba,* and *ocellata,* are properly stove shrubs, but do finely as bedding plants in rich soil, in a warm exposure: they may be raised from seed in a hot-bed or from cuttings. They should not be planted out until all danger of cold weather is over. Natives of East Indies.

V. herbacea (herbaceous); hardy evergreen trailing perennial; 6 inches; flowers purple, in June; Hungary; 1816. *V. major* (greater); hardy evergreen trailing shrub; 18 inches; flowers blue, in July; England. *V. minor* (lesser); hardy evergreen trailing shrub; 1 foot; flowers blue, in May; England.

There is a variety with variegated leaves.

VIOLA. *Violet.* [Violaceæ.] A large genus of pretty

herbaceous plants, almost all of which are hardy. The first to be mentioned is the Sweet Violet, *V. odorata*, of which the common wild forms should be planted in abundance in every shrubbery for the sake of their sweet blossoms. For general cultivation, the varieties known as the Neapolitan, the Russian, and the Tree-violet, are the best. The Russian is quite hardy, and requires only to be planted in rich soil, which must be renewed, in part at least, annually. The others need higher culture. To grow the Neapolitan a bed of rich light soil must be made up; and about the beginning of May, the old plants must be divided into two, three, or more, according to their size. These young plants are put out, and carefully watered, when necessary, through the summer; and are either allowed to bloom in these beds, some protection being afforded them to keep off heavy rains and frost, or they are taken up about the end of September, potted, and the pots kept in a cold dry frame during winter, with such other protection as the season renders necessary. They may be forced in frames by the application of gentle heat: and by this means, it is no unusual thing, with the luxurious, to have violets all the winter. The Tree-violet is a double-flowered, dark variety, which, if kept trained to a single stem, acquires the appearance of a miniature tree. This requires to be grown as a hardy plant in frames; the soil being turfy loam, decomposed cow-dung, and leaf-mould in equal parts. To secure the tree-like habit, the crown of vigorous young plants must be encouraged to push upwards by the removal of all lateral growth; otherwise this variety spreads out its runners just like other violets. There are several other varieties of the Sweet Violet; but these are the best. The whole genus, with one or two tender exceptions, are worth cultivating as hardy perennials. They grow very freely in good garden soil, preferring loam moderately rich. Increased by division. Those which grow with stems, like the Heartsease, or Pansy, should be frequently renewed from cuttings, which should, moreover, be, as far as possible, the young shoots from the root, in preference to the tips of the older shoots.

Pansy (Viola tricolor). — The numerous varieties of this popular flower, frequently called Heartsease, originated from the common three-colored Violet. Like the varieties of the Pink, these require to be constantly renewed by striking cuttings; for, as may have been observed by many who have grown them, the blooms come smaller and out of character as the plants get larger and older. It is true, there are more flowers on the plants when they enlarge; but there is a great alteration for the worse in their colors and forms. The ground in which they thrive most is good rich loam. They should be grown in beds six inches apart every way. The side-shoots make the best plants. They should be stripped off when they are two inches long; and may be put into the ground half their length, and covered with a hand-glass: if the place be shady, so much the less trouble, but, if not, the hand-glass must be covered so as to keep off the hot sun; the cuttings must be kept well watered till rooted. To have the Heartsease in perfection, there should be a constant supply of cuttings; and when they are struck, which will be seen by their beginning to grow, they should be very carefully lifted, so as to break none of their fibres, and planted out wherever they are to bloom, whether it be in the borders or in beds. After they are planted out, they should be well watered. When the plants get large, cut them down close; and all the shoots that come will make excellent cuttings. The Pansies, which are of all sorts of colors, should be had in bloom all the year, except in winter, a succession of young plants being raised for this purpose.

V. Altaica (Altaic); hardy perennial; 6 inches; flowers purple, in May; Siberia; 1808. *V. blanda* (charming); hardy perennial; 6 inches; flowers white, in May; North America; 1803. *V. calcarata* (spurred); hardy perennial; 6 inches; flowers bluish, in May; Switzerland; 1752. *V. grandiflora* (large-flowered); hardy perennial; 6 inches; flowers yellow, in June; Switzerland. *V. lutea* (yellow); hardy perennial; 6 inches; flowers yellow, in June; England. *V. ochroleuca* (yellowish); hardy perennial; 6 inches; flowers straw-colored, in June; North America; 1800. *V. odorata* (common); hardy perennial; 6 inches; flowers blue or white, in May; England. *V. Palmaensis* (Palmer); half-hardy perennial; 1 foot; flowers purple-lilac, in May; south of Europe; 1836. *V. palmata* (broad-leaved); hardy perennial; 6 inches; flowers blue, in May; North America; 1752. *V. parnassiæfolia* (parnassia-leaved); hardy perennial; 6 inches; flowers yellow, in winter and spring; Patagonia; 1850. *V. pedata* (pedate); hardy perennial; 6 inches; flowers blue, in May; North America; 1759. *V. Rothomagensis* (Rouen); hardy perennial; 6 inches; flowers blue, in July; France; 1783. *V. stricta* (upright); hardy perennial; 1 foot; flowers pale-blue, in May; Europe; 1822. *V. tricolor* (three-colored); hardy perennial; 6 inches; flowers various, all summer; Britain.

There are many other species.

VIPER'S BUGLOSS. See ECHIUM.

VIRGILIA. [Leguminosæ.] A fine hardy tree, producing long racemes of locust-like flowers, and very ornamental in flower and leaf. Deep rich soil. Propagated by seeds and layers.

V. lutea (yellow); hardy tree; 30 feet; flowers white, in June; North America.

VIRGINIAN CREEPER. See AMPELOPSIS.
VIRGINIAN STOCK. See MALCOLMIA.
VIRGIN'S BOWER. See CLEMATIS.
VISCARIA. [Caryophyllaceæ.] A small genus, allied to

Lychnis, containing some neat small-growing perennials, as *V. vulgaris, neglecta, Alpina,* and *Helvetica,* forming pretty rock-plants. These perennials are increased by carefully dividing the dense tufts of branches which they form, retaining a share of roots to each slip if possible, and treating the divisions rather as cuttings than as plants, by keeping them in a close frame until they begin to grow. These like a very open soil, containing pounded bricks or old mortar, or any substance of similar texture. The genus also contains two very showy hardy annuals, *V. Cœli-rosa* and *oculata.* These may be sown in the open borders with other hardy annuals in May.

V. Alpina (Alpine); hardy perennial; 6 inches; flowers pink, in May; Scotland. *V. Cœli-rosa* (Rose of Heaven); hardy annual; 18 inches; flowers rose, light eye, in June; Levant; 1713. *V. Helvetica* (Swiss); hardy perennial; 3 inches; flowers red, in June; Switzerland; 1814. *V. neglecta* (neglected); hardy perennial; 9 inches; flowers white, in May; England. *V. oculata* (dark-eyed); hardy annual; 18 inches; flowers rose, dark eye, in June; Algiers; 1843. *V. Suecica* (Swedish); hardy perennial; 6 inches; flowers pink, in June; Sweden; 1824. *V. vulgaris* (common); hardy perennial; 1 foot; flowers pink, in May; England.

WAHLENBERGIA. [Campanulaceæ.] Hardy or half-hardy perennials and annuals. The latter should be sown in heat in March, and potted or planted out to flower; the former increase by division or seeds. Soil, sandy loam.

WALL-CRESS. See ARABIS.
WALLFLOWER. See CHEIRANTHUS.
WALNUT. See JUGLANS.
WATER-LILY. See NYMPHÆA.
WATER-PLANTAIN. See ALISMA.
WATER-REED. See ARUNDO.

WEIGELA. [Caprifoliaceæ.] Very handsome hardy deciduous shrubs. They are free-growing, striking readily from cuttings or from layers, and grow vigorously in good garden soil. The blossoms, at first white, but changing to rose-pink, are produced, generally in great profusion, in spring.

W. amabilis (lovely); hardy shrub; 3 feet; flowers pink, in May; Japan; 1852. *W. rosea* (rosy); hardy shrub; 3 feet; flowers pink, in May; China; 1844. *W. Middendorffiana;* hardy shrub; flowers white, shading to pale-yellow, spotted with carmine; south of Russia; 1856.

There are other species, and a variety with variegated foliage.

WASHINGTONIA. [Coniferæ.] A magnificent hardy evergreen tree. Soil, loam. Increased by seeds. This tree will survive as far north as Massachusetts.

W. gigantea (gigantic); hardy evergreen tree; 200 feet; flowers deep purple, in July; California; 1844.

WHITLAVIA. [Hydrophyllaceæ.] Hardy annuals, of ornamental character. Rich light soil. Increased by seeds.

W. grandiflora (large-flowered); hardy annual; 2 feet; flowers deep purple, in July; California; 1853.

WHITLOW-GRASS. See DRABA.
WHORTLE-BERRY. See VACCINUM.
WILLOW. See SALIX.
WINDFLOWER. See ANEMONE.
WINTER ACONITE. See ERANTHIS.
WINTER CHERRY. See PHYSALIS.

WISTARIA. [Leguminosæ.] Hardy, vigorous-growing deciduous climbers. *W. sinensis*, formerly named *Glycine sinensis*, is a perfectly hardy, climbing shrub bearing long racemes of purplish-lilac flowers before the foliage is produced. Young plants, when newly planted, are often of slow growth; but as soon as they get established they grow very rapidly. The flowers are, however, produced on spurs of the old wood. It is propagated by layers, which root freely if pegged under ground any time during autumn.

W. frutescens; hardy climbing shrub; 20 feet; flowers deep purple, in summer; North America; 1724. *W. sinensis* (Chinese); hardy climbing shrub; 25 feet; flowers lilac or white, in May; China; 1818; the white variety in 1846.

WITCH HAZEL. See HAMAMELIS.
WOLFSBANE. See ACONITUM.
WOODBINE. See AMPELOPSIS and CAPRIFOLIUM.

WULFENIA. [Scrophularineæ.] Hardy herbaceous plants, requiring a dry soil. Propagated by seeds and division.

W. Amherstianæ (Amherst's); hardy perennial; 6 inches; flowers lilac, in July; Chinese Tartary; 1846. *W. Carinthiaca* (Corinthian); hardy perennial; 1 foot; flowers blue, in July; Carinthia; 1817.

WYTCH ELM. See ULMUS MONTANUS.

XANTHIUM. *Small Burdock.* [Compositæ.] A genus of weedy plants of easy culture. The flowers are inconspicuous, but the foliage may be effective in masses. The species are *X. strumarium, Orientale, spinosum*, and *echinatum*. Easily propagated by seeds.

XANTHORHIZA. *Yellow-root.* [Ranunculaceæ.] A hardy shrub, increasing rapidly by suckers. Soil, sandy loam, rather moist. The dark-purple flowers are very pretty in early spring, and the foliage is delicate and pretty.

X. apiifolia (parsley-leaved); hardy shrub; 3 feet; flowers purple, in May; North America; 1766.

XANTHOXYLUM. [Xanthoxylaceæ.] A hardy tree, growing in any garden soil, and very easily propagated by seeds or root-cuttings.

X. fraxineum (ash-like); hardy tree; 15 feet; flowers white, in April; North America; 1759.

There are other species, mostly tender.

XERANTHEMUM. [Compositæ.] Hardy annuals of the composite kind, now almost expelled from gardens by the gayer annuals from California and elsewhere. They must not be confounded with the showy yellow and white Everlasting flowers (as they are called), which have been, and indeed now are, sometimes named Xeranthemum. They are among the most easily cultivated of annuals, requiring only to be sown about May in the open border, and thinned out for flowering. A succession may be sown a month later than the first sowing, if it is required.

X. annuum (annual); hardy annual; 3 feet; flowers purple or white, in July; south of Europe; 1570.

XEROPHYLLUM. [Melanthaceæ.] A genus of pretty but rare half-hardy plants, with spikes of white flowers resembling Helonias. The foliage appears withered, whence the name. Good garden soil. Propagated by seeds.

X. setifolium (bristle-leaved); half-hardy perennial; flowers white, in June; North America; 1823. This plant is also known as *X. asphodeloides* and *X. tenax*.

XYLOSTEON. A subdivision of the Honeysuckle family (Caprifoliaceæ), including some of the shrubby Honeysuckles. See LONICERA.

XYRIS. *Yellow-eyed Grass.* [Xyridaceæ.] A genus of very pretty yellow flowers, of which one species is very common in open sandy or peat bogs. If cultivated in a mass, the flower would be effective. Soil, peaty sand. Propagated by seed.

X. bulbosa (bulbous); hardy perennial; 6 inches; flowers yellow, all summer; North America. *X. Caroliniana* (Carolinian); hardy perennial; 18 inches; flowers yellow, in August; North America. *X. fimbriata* is a Southern species.

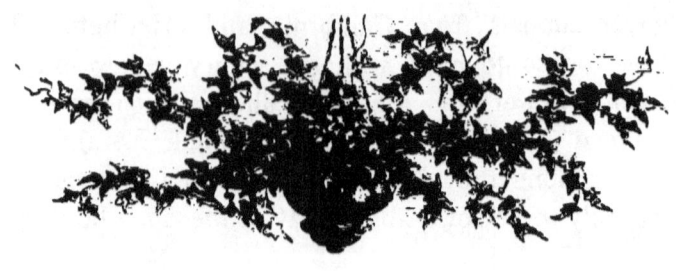

Y. gloriosa (glorious); evergreen shrub; 4 feet; flowers greenish white, in July; America; 1596. *Y. recurva* (recurved); half-hardy evergreen shrub; 3 feet; flowers greenish-white, in August; Georgia; 1794. *Y. superba* (superb); half-hardy evergreen shrub; 10 feet; flowers white, in August; history unknown.

The only species perfectly hardy in New England is *Y. filamentosa*, though the others occasionally survive. There is no better plant for massing. The most effective manner of growing this plant is to set about a dozen strong plants in a large circular bed in a lawn, the soil being deep and well manured. The plants will display wonderful vigor of growth, and will often send up flower-spikes eight feet high, covered with hundreds of blossoms. These spikes of bloom are very effective by moonlight, and there is a foolish belief that the plant only blooms about the time of the full moon. The foliage should be protected by a slight covering of evergreen boughs from the winter's sun. Seedlings vary much in foliage.

ZAUSCHNERIA. [Onagraceæ.] A pretty plant for bedding, though its blooming season is often shortened by the frost. It forms a dense bushy mass, covered with scarlet fuchsia or honeysuckle-like erect flowers. Garden soil. Propagated by cuttings and division. It requires greenhouse protection in winter in the Northern States.

Z. Californica (Californian); half-hardy perennial; 18 inches; flowers scarlet, in August; California; 1847.

ZENOBIA. See ANDROMEDA.

ZINNIA. [Compositæ.] A genus of Mexican annuals, bearing flowers of many different colors, seedling varieties having become numerous. The most ornamental species is *Z. elegans*, which grows best in peaty soil, and in a cool situation. The plant may be termed coarse, and is better-looking in moderate than in rich soil. The seed may be sown in the open ground, or in heat, according to the time it is desired to be in flower. When large enough, it may be planted out at once into beds a foot apart, or in the border three in a patch. When seed has been saved from a single plant, and none other has been near, the plants have come pretty constant to the parent; but, generally speaking, in the seed that is purchased we obtain all the colors from scarlet to light-pink and to dark-crimson, and all the shades from dark-chocolate to light-purple and lilac. It is a difficult matter to produce, year after year, anything like constancy in annuals; for the only way is to destroy all others that can cross the seed, or to isolate those for seeding, so that nothing can reach them. Muslin bags have been tried with some effect; but it must be done very early. The double varieties are brilliant ornaments of the garden, and come true from seed. They were introduced from India in 1858.

Z. elegans (elegant); half-hardy annual; 18 inches; flowers various, in July; Mexico; 1829. *Z. multiflora* (many-flowered); hardy annual; 2 feet; flowers dull-red, in August; Mexico; 1770.

ZYGADENUS. [Melanthaceæ.] A family of herbaceous perennials, allied to Veratrum, natives of North America. Soil, moist peaty loam. Propagated by division. Flowers greenish-white. *Z. glaucus, leimanthoides*, and *glaberrimus* are among the species.

www.ingramcontent.com/pod-product-compliance
Lightning Source LLC
Chambersburg PA
CBHW030344230426
43664CB00007BB/530